Clare Debenham is a tutor in the Department of Politics, University of Manchester.

'This account of birth control and feminism is the result of many years' work. It is packed with fascinating details that will intrigue and inform readers familiar with the birth control campaigners as well as those discovering them for the first time.'

> Sheila Rowbotham, socialist feminist historian and the author of *Dreamers of a New Day: The Women Who Invented the Twentieth Century*

'Was birth control a feminist issue? For anyone who reads this book, the conclusion will be a resounding yes…Debenham provides a useful history of the birth control movement from the opening of the first clinic in 1921, to 1973 when the NHS finally provided family planning services. *Birth Control and the Rights of Women* is at its best when it uses direct testimony from activists and from the women Debenham interviewed.'

> Carmel Quinlan, *Times Literary Supplement*

'This is a highly readable book. As Mrs Cooke lamented in 1923, what was the good of the franchise to women if she could not call her body her own?'

> June Purvis, Emeritus Professor of Women's and Gender History, University of Portsmouth.

Birth Control and the Rights of Women

Post-Suffrage Feminism in the Early Twentieth Century

Clare Debenham

I.B. TAURIS
LONDON · NEW YORK

New paperback edition published in 2018 by
I.B.Tauris & Co. Ltd
London • New York
www.ibtauris.com

First published in hardback in 2014 by I.B.Tauris & Co. Ltd

Copyright © 2014 Clare Debenham

The right of Clare Debenham to be identified as the author of this work has been asserted by the author in accordance with the Copyright, Designs and Patents Act 1988.

All rights reserved. Except for brief quotations in a review, this book, or any part thereof, may not be reproduced, stored in or introduced into a retrieval system, or transmitted, in any form or by any means, electronic, mechanical, photocopying, recording or otherwise, without the prior written permission of the publisher.

References to websites were correct at the time of writing.

ISBN: 978 1 78831 284 4
eISBN: 978 1 78672 999 6
ePDF: 978 0 85772 533 2

A full CIP record for this book is available from the British Library
A full CIP record is available from the Library of Congress

Library of Congress Catalog Card Number: available

Typeset by OKS Prepress Services, Chennai, India

Contents

Acknowledgements		vii
Abbreviations		ix
1	Rediscovering the Post-suffrage Birth Control Campaign	1
2	The Emergence of the Birth Control Movement	17
3	Birth Control – a Feminist Issue?	34
4	Anatomy of the Birth Control Clinics	56
5	Challenging the Opposition	89
6	Shifting Ideologies: Birth Controllers, Feminists, the Malthusian League and Eugenics Society	109
7	Working the Political Parties	131
8	The End of the Campaign?	154
	Appendix: Collective Biography of Birth Control Activists	171
	Notes	227
	Bibliography	253
	Index	285

'What does it avail a woman that she has the franchise if she cannot call her body her own, and is at the mercy of her husband's desires and wishes.'

Mrs M.B. Cooke, *Woman's Leader*, 4 May 1923

Acknowledgements

I would like to thank my doctorate Supervisors at the University of Manchester, Professor Kevin Morgan and Dr Jill Lovecy in the Department of Politics, for their endless patience and ability to inspire with their enthusiasm. They have opened up new avenues of intellectual challenge for me to explore. I am grateful to my Examiners, Professor Pat Thane and Karen Clarke, who provided thoughtful comments on this thesis.

Over the course of this research many academics have been incredibly generous with their time. These include Sheila Rowbotham (University of Manchester), Martin Pugh, Richard Cleminson (University of Leeds), Karen Hunt (Keele University), Alan Kidd and Melanie Tebbutt (Manchester Metropolitan University), and Joyce Goodman, Andrea Jacobs and Stephanie Spencer (University of Winchester).

In my research I visited many archives. Archives comprise much more than a collection of documents and archivists went out of their way to share their knowledge with me. Amongst those who were especially helpful were Audrey Canning of Glasgow Caledonian University; Lesley A. Hall of the Wellcome Library; Karen Kukil of Sophia Smith Collection, USA; Father David Lannon, Salford Diocesan Archives; Sue Slack of Cambridgeshire City Libraries College; Darren Treadwell of the Labour History Archive; Mervyn Wilson of the Co-operative College; and the late Ruth Frow of the Working Class Movement Library.

I am grateful to Tomasz Hoskins, my editor at I.B.Tauris, for all his encouragement.

Central to this thesis, I have been privileged to interview some courageous birth control pioneers who included Mrs Elsie Plant, Sister Beatrice Sandys, Mrs Florence Travis and Aunt Polly. I would also like to acknowledge the generous assistance given to me by the relatives of the birth control pioneers including those of Marie Stopes, Charis Frankenburg, Mary Stocks, Fenella Paton and Dilys Dean.

Lastly, I would like to thank my husband Ron Marsden, my sons Ian and Richard and my business partner, the late Christine Carr, for their unfailing interest and encouragement. Without their belief in its value, this research would never have come to fruition. I hope my granddaughter Emily Marsden, now aged thirteen, will in time come to recognise the struggles fought for her own and subsequent generations.

Abbreviations

FPA	Family Planning Association
MSMC	Manchester and Salford Mothers' Clinic
MSWCA	Manchester and Salford Women Citizens Association
NBCC	National Birth Control Council
NBCA	National Birth Control Association
NCW	National Council of Women
NKWWC	North Kensington Women's Welfare Centre
NUSEC	National Union of Societies for Equal Citizenship
NUTG	National Union of Townswomen's Guilds
NUWSS	National Union of Women's Suffrage Societies
SCBCRP	Society for Constructive Birth Control and Racial Progress
SJC	Standing Joint Committee of Industrial Women's Organisations
SPBCC	Society for the Provision of Birth Control Clinics
WCA	Women Citizens Association
WCG	Women's Co-operative Guild
WBCG	Workers' Birth Control Group
WI	National Federation of Women's Institutes
WLL	Women's Labour League
WSPU	Women's Social and Political Union

1 Rediscovering the Post-suffrage Birth Control Campaign

My research has taken place over thirty years and encompasses the birth of my children, my doctorate and lecturing at two universities. However, the issue of birth control and the rights of women seems to me to be as relevant now as when I first started looking at the subject. This research poses questions on an overlooked subject and some of the findings are controversial. I hope this will serve as a stimulus for further research as new material on the subject is now emerging, particularly at the grassroots level. This chapter sets the birth control campaign in the context of women's rights and addresses the questions of why feminism in the inter-war period has been overlooked and why such an important campaign has been largely ignored by academics and political activists.

A partial explanation for the omission to study birth control and women's rights may be found in the more recent history of the women's movement and its definition of waves of feminism. On 27 and 28 February and 1 March 1970 women's groups from around the country met at the first National Women's Liberation Conference at Ruskin College, Oxford, to discuss the challenges facing women and the liberation movement and to work out a series of demands. Later in 1970 the newly formed Women's National Co-ordinating Committee announced the resulting four basic demands, which included free contraception and abortion on demand. The movement's demands were printed on banners and on a petition handed to the Prime Minister on 6 March 1971 when four thousand people marched through London on the movement's first International Women's Day march. The women's movement of the 1970s believed in the importance of 'our bodies, ourselves' and marched to the mantra, 'Every child a wanted child.'[1]

These late twentieth-century feminists explored their own history. They searched for antecedents and located them in the dramatic marches and gesture politics of the suffragette movement which had mounted a campaign to obtain the right to vote on equal terms to men. In 1893 the National Union of Women's Suffrage Societies was formed by Millicent Fawcett and this concentrated on traditional forms of protest such as leafleting, public meetings and lobbying public figures. However in 1903 Emmeline Pankhurst formed a militant organisation, the Women's Social and Political Union. Militant members chained themselves to railings, set fire to post boxes and slashed paintings. Emily Wilding Davidson died after she threw herself at the King's horse in the Derby on 5 June 1913 and suffragettes had their health damaged by force feeding under what came to be known as the Cat and Mouse Act. There were large demonstrations meeting the prisoners on release from Holloway Prison and spectacularly orchestrated processions of WSPU members dressed in long white dresses with WSPU sashes.

Eventually the suffragettes gained their objectives, but how far violent tactics contributed to this is debatable. After the end of World War One, when the suffragettes had suspended operation, the Representation of the People Act 1918 was passed enfranchising women over thirty who met property qualifications. This gave 8.4 million women the right to vote in parliamentary elections. In another ten years the Representation of the People's Act 1928 extended the franchise to women aged over twenty-one on equal terms to men.

Justifiably, the struggle for the suffrage has attracted meticulous academic attention and scholarly research. These range from postgraduate courses on gender studies to GCSE courses such as those offered by Edexel examining board which also included women's suffrage. The house of Mrs Pankhurst in Manchester has been saved from demolition and there is material on the suffrage movement in the National Archives as well as other leading archives. There have recently been critical accounts of the suffrage movement of which the following are a brief selection. The direction of the suffrage movement has been analysed.[2] There have been edited books which include articles on significant activists such as Emmeline Pankhurst and Dora Montefiore.[3] Interesting biographies of leading suffragists have been meticulously researched as well as accounts of young members who have been given a voice.[4] There have been insightful discussions of class as well as examinations of regional influences.[5]

However, there has been a popular belief amongst academics that after the suffrage was achieved feminists drifted away from political activity.

William O'Neil, writing in 1969 was scathing in his assessment of the lack of feminist activity in Britain and the United States during the inter-war years, contending that it lacked any sense of direction and intellectual purpose.[6] He argued that the suffrage movement had provided feminism with a false sense of unity and after the gaining of the franchise it collapsed. Interestingly O'Neil commented that 'satisfactory explanations for the collapse of feminism are not easily come by.' Arguably this was because there was no collapse of feminism. He was not alone in his dismissal of inter-war feminism for Susan Kingsley Kent categorically declared that feminism, as a distinct political and social movement, ceased to exist as early as the 1920s.[7]

Yet later assessments show this scenario of the disappearance of the women's movement to be an oversimplification. In 1984 the academic Dale Spender painted a hypothetical picture of the reactions of suffrage activists such as Mrs Cooke after the vote was won:

> They packed up the hammers and picked up the stones, bundled up the banners and badges, supposedly sold or stored the printing presses and posters, disbanded their organisations, said fond farewells to friends – and returned tired, but contented, to the confines of domesticity. Or did they?[8]

Spender correctly argued that this picture was pure fiction and having acquired a taste for political activism many women carried on campaigning whether it be in the peace movement, housing reform or reproductive rights issues.[9] Cheryl Law perceptively commented that using the yardstick of the exceptional militant suffrage activity to judge subsequent women's achievements has inevitably led to distortions thereby 'consigning women to another fifty years of obscurity'.[10]

Increasingly there is a recognition of the importance of feminist activity in the inter-war years. Wendy Sarvassy argued that many women did not retire from public life after the suffrage campaign but instead put their energies into legislative welfare reforms.[11] Cheryl Law also maintained the continuity of feminism as evidenced in post-suffrage activity. She examined the means by which the women pursued political power and how they created organisational networks to campaign against existing inequalities.[12] Indeed Gaynor Williams examined women's political activity in Liverpool and found that there existed a varied and vibrant women's movement in the inter-war years.[13] The 2011 Conference in the University of Sheffield aptly titled 'After the Suffrage. What happened after the vote was won,' pointed to the richness and diversity of feminist activity after women could vote. The gaining of the suffrage gave women added confidence to enter public life and campaign for feminist issues. As Mary Stott, *Guardian* journalist and political activist, famously asserted to Dale Spender, 'There's always been a woman's movement this century.'[14]

Examining the results of her collective biographical study, Johanna Alberti concluded that women who were active suffragists in 1918 continued to be involved in feminist campaigns right up to 1928.[15] Significantly, four of her subjects were also actively involved with the birth control movement: Mary Stocks, Eleanor Rathbone, Reverend Maude Royden and Eva Hubback.

There are many definitions of feminism but the Society for the Provision of Birth Control Clinics (SPBCC) can be seen as a feminist organisation in the terms of distinguished sociologist Olive Banks. She emphasised the importance of collective action when she termed feminist 'any group that has tried to change the position of women, or the ideas about women.'[16] Her approach is important because she referred to the dynamics of groups and social change rather than to an individual woman's dissatisfaction with her position in society. Investigating what it meant to be a member of feminist groups in Britain in the 1920s and the 1930s is a central concern. Olive Banks explained, in *Faces of Feminism*, how feminists, particularly those from the left, were drawn to the birth control campaign. Importantly, she described birth control as a social movement and made particular reference to Mary Stocks' achievements. Similar definitions of feminism to that of Olive Banks have been employed by Johanna Alberti, Cheryl Law and Anne Logan all of whom stressed the importance of societal change in making a positive development in women's lives.[17] Many feminists had experience of working in local government even before they had been given the right to vote in national elections. From 1907 women ratepayers could be elected to borough and county councils. This was extended in 1919 to all adult women and my Collective Biography shows a number of activists elected to local councils. Yet serving on local councils was not dramatic work. Many women birth control activists had experience of this apparently mundane service. Patricia Hollis perceptively wrote that 'it takes nerves and strength to smash windows and endure hunger strikes as the suffragettes did; it also takes considerable courage to impose yourself on a board where your presence is deeply resented, and to offer your services of a most personally demanding kind, year in and year out.'[18]

We can see the importance of grassroots activism and locality in women's politics. My Collective Biography details the women who were prominent in local government and were birth control activists. Women councillors often felt more comfortable campaigning at the local level, where they could retain their community links, than at the national level. Eleanor Rathbone had been the first woman to be elected to Liverpool City Council. Her political opportunity resulted from the Qualification of Women Act 1907 when she successfully stood as an Independent councillor in a 1909 by-election. Ruth Dalton, Labour Party MP and birth control supporter, allegedly turned down an opportunity to extend her parliamentary career to return to her elected seat on the London County Council: 'There we do things. Here it all seems to be all talk.'[19] Edith How-Martyn, although she failed to be elected an MP, was elected Middlesex County Council's first woman member and Elizabeth Cadbury, though not successful in standing as an MP, served as a Liberal councillor in Birmingham. Eva Hartree, a Cambridge councillor, was elected Mayor and this was no doubt why she was selected as Chairman of the Cambridge Mothers' Clinic. There were a number of local politicians who were able to use their positions to further the birth control cause. Mary Barbour (Glasgow Mothers' Clinic) was the first Labour woman to be elected to Glasgow town council in 1927 and was the Corporation's first woman Baillee. In towns such as Manchester women took advantage of 1918 legislation which advised that at least two women should serve on the Maternity and Child Welfare Committee. This was seen as offering women positive opportunities for influencing an area in which they had special knowledge. As will later be seen, Shena Simon by her alliance with other local councillors was able to influence Manchester Council policy on municipal birth control clinics.

How then are we to account for the lack of coverage of the political activities of the birth control pioneers? In 1974 historian Sheila Rowbotham published her influential book, *Hidden from History*, where she questioned why certain aspects of the women's struggle had not been recognised.[20] This book searches for answers as to why the battle for the suffrage has been given popular and academic attention, but the struggle for reproductive rights has largely been ignored. More recently Sheila, in her later book *Dreamers of a New Day*, discussed the activists of the early twentieth-century feminists who have been partially forgotten 'because they were not were engaged in heroic acts or glitzed with glamour. But societies are recreated in more ways that meet the eye. The mundane, the intimate, the individual moment of anger, the sense of association: all contribute to the fabric of daily life.' She rediscovered their idealism and included the birth control activists as 'dreamers'.[21]

In the 1970s feminists looked for a heritage. To acknowledge their inheritance women from the Women's Liberation Movement termed themselves second-wave feminists, the first wave being that of the suffrage movement. Yet the metaphor of waves is misleading as it implies that the early feminist movement had ebbed away until it was rediscovered by activists in the 1970s. Indeed the metaphor of the wave has been criticised by political scientists in other contexts as being misleading.[22] If an aquatic metaphor is to be used then that of the slow progress of a river is more helpful as this implies continuity. Birth control was essentially a feminist campaign.

There was a connection between the gaining of the vote and the campaign for birth control rights. It was no coincidence that the two campaigns involved political opportunities which led to mobilisation of their supporters. Christine Bolt compared the early twentieth-century women's movements in the United States and Britain in terms of social movements and examined the extent of 'spillover' (cross fertilisation of ideas) between social movements.[23] There was a cross fertilisation of ideas between the suffrage movement and the birth control movement who believed expectations had been raised. Significantly Mrs Cooke stated in the quotation which is the keynote of this book that the winning of the suffrage in itself was not enough to bring freedom. As Pat Thane later argued, though the vote was valuable in the long term and set women free, it did not immediately change the lives of working-class women battling against poverty.[24] She controversially made a case for birth control, as opposed to the suffrage as having an immediate impact on the lives of working-class women. Indeed over forty years ago Richard Titmuss recognised the importance of birth control as an important factor in contributing to gains in women's health and female emancipation.[25]

However, while the drama of the mass mobilisation of the suffrage campaign has captured the popular and academic imagination, the birth control movement has not been extensively publicised or researched by later generations, with the exception of flashes of interest in the flamboyant Marie Stopes.[26] The historian Brian Harrison made the telling point that historians, like journalists, often appreciated the dramatic and outrageous.[27] Linda Ward, in her doctoral study of the 1920s birth control campaign, remarked in her Preface that despite its significance the subject had largely been ignored and undocumented. In the ensuing decades this situation has largely gone unchanged.[28]

Admittedly the birth control campaign has not been completely ignored. The historian Kate Fisher, in her comprehensive study of birth control in inter-war Britain, did mention the SPBCC and individual clinics but afforded them far less attention than Marie Stopes clinics.[29] She has researched studies examining sexual behaviour in Britain in the inter-war years, some of which have focused on particular geographical areas. However, academic perspective and methodology led her to be sceptical about the spread of birth control advice amongst 1920s women.

The main objective of the SPBCC was the provision of municipal birth control clinics which would be free and easily accessible to working-class mothers. The Society believed this was too important to be left to the voluntary sector. Birth control was important in providing self-determination for women in the way that the rubber sheath, which could easily be purchased in chemists, provided self-determination for men. There is compelling evidence that the SPBCC regarded birth control as involving more fundamental issues than the use of mechanical medical devices. The SPBCC saw birth control as giving women freedom to control their bodies and was not regarded as a palliative welfare reform. Therefore mothers were encouraged by the clinics to control their own fertility rather than relying on husbands.

The SPBCC was a feminist organisation, founded by women for the good of other women. It was also an altruistic organisation. Most SPBCC members did not gain any direct benefit from the organisation, and indeed invested time and money. Although they had access to private medicine they supported the SPBCC because they believed the control of fertility to be a basic right for all women.

Although the birth control movement can be analysed in terms of social history or medical history, it is here being framed in terms of social movement theory. David Snow had a specific interpretation of the concept of framing: 'The conscious strategic efforts by groups of people to fashion shared understandings of the world and of themselves that legitimate and motivate collective action.' The framing process is rooted in the symbolic interactionist understanding which claims that meanings are not automatic but are socially constructed through an interpretative process. David Snow draws an analogy to picture frames which make a coherent whole of what is in the frame and defines what is irrelevant or 'out of frame'.[30] It is therefore important to understand how women focused on the injustice of differential access to birth control.

Social movement theory invites comparison of the birth control movement with other social movements such as the Chartists in nineteenth-century Britain, the Suffragettes or the Civil Rights Movement in the USA. This fits in with the approach of Linda Gordon and Jimmy Elaine Wilkinson Meyer who also consciously treated the American birth control activities as a social movement.[31]

Social movements possess a sense of grievance and, unlike structured political parties, are characteristically loose, amorphous organisations. Certainly the birth control activists felt a sense of grievance that women should be denied control over their bodies and that this freedom was available to rich women. Social movements often do not have formal membership. British sociologist Colin Barker also pointed out the central importance of coalitions. 'Movements are complex assemblages, networks of groups and individuals with different histories, powers, social ties (including ties to existing power set-ups), pre-existing patterns of organisation, cultural assumptions and traditions.'[32] Thus when we speak of the birth control movement we have to be aware that there were significant differences between members in terms of politics and tactics. This diverse group was drawn together in a common purpose: it included Kensington titled women, those living in Glasgow inner city, Labour Party supporters, Conservatives, eugenicists and humanists.

Significantly the birth control activists regarded themselves as being part of a social movement. It is evident that Mary Stocks, co-founder of the Manchester and Salford Mothers' Clinic (MSMC), regarded her membership of the SPBCC as not involving isolated, random acts but rather being part of a coherent social movement. 'What fun it was being in an unpopular movement, which we knew was going to win.'[33] Mary Stocks recognised participation in the birth control campaign was dangerous but identified a common purpose as a sustaining and unifying factor. This sense of belonging to a movement and having fun was reflected in other post-suffrage organisations including the Townswomen's Guild.[34]

It is important to consider whether the group is an insider or an outsider group. The sociologist Howard Becker's work in *Outsiders* has been drawn upon by social movement theorists who made the point that those actors who regarded themselves as excluded were motivated to challenge the existing order.[35] Indeed social movements can be regarded as a collective response to a group's experience of subordination. However, sometimes outsiders may be more educated and more middle class than the insiders operating within the political system. In the case of the birth controllers the situation was fluid. Although there were working-class activists such as Mary Barbour, a number of the women such as Charis Frankenburg enjoyed a wealthy lifestyle and Lady Muriel Willoughby was extremely well connected. Yet their political activities were still restricted in the 1920s.

As the birth controllers were politically in a weak position they needed to form alliances to challenge the established dominant political agendas. It was necessary to attract allies with resources, either power or material resources.[36] If groups did not have the political resources themselves it was important for them to frame their demands so they would resonate with groups that did hold power or material resources. Thus we can see the attempts of the SPBCC to attract the support of women's organisations, sympathetic political organisations such as the Women's Co-operative Guild and even the Eugenics Society.

Mobilising structures are seen by political scientists as having particular importance in the beginning of the life of a social movement. They reject the traditional concept of social movements suddenly appearing out of anger and frustration in favour of tracing a social movement's gradual emergence out of pre-existing networks and groups. They stress the importance of the mobilisation of the full range of informal institutions including families, networks of friends, prayer groups and caucuses as well as the more formal institutions of political parties.[37]

Timing is important in explaining social change and the ability to seize political opportunities.[38] Initiating events, such as in the suffragette movement or Civil Rights Movement when Rosa Parks refused to give up her seat on a bus in the segregated Southern USA, are seen as having important consequences. The dismissal of Nurse Daniels will be shown to be significant for the growth of the birth control movement. Policy entrepreneurs such as Eleanor Rathbone, from outside government, introduced new ideas into public policy arena.

The members of the SPBCC regarded themselves as being equals and deliberately endeavoured to lessen differences between them. Class differences were often minimised by the members themselves. Dora Russell of the Workers' Birth Control Group (WBCG) in her draft copy of *The Tamarisk Tree* stressed the inclusiveness of the executive committee of the WBCG and played down class divisions, 'We were of all sorts, intellectuals, middle and working-class.'[39] This statement was an exaggeration as the small WBCG committee contained the daughter-in-law of an Earl and the daughter of a Lord. In spite of her aristocratic connections Dora Russell identified herself as an ordinary member of the Labour Party in contrast to the four women who sat on the National Executive Committee (NEC).

The organisation of many social movements is non-hierarchical. The SPBCC demonstrated an aspiration to inclusiveness which clearly demarcated it from Stopesian autocracy. While there were disagreements over policy, particularly between SPBCC clinic doctors and lay members, they generally appear to have been amicably resolved and there were no recorded instances of sudden resignations. As Alberto Melucci commented on the organisation of social movements, 'Leadership is not concentrated but diffuse, it is limited to specific aims, and different people can assume leadership roles, depending on the function to be fulfilled.'[40]

The emphasis of the SPBCC was on the importance of grassroots membership. Indeed Mary Stott the *Manchester Guardian* suffragist and journalist called the second chapter of her autobiography 'Grassroots' as it covered the formation of the National Union of Townswomen's Guilds (NUTG).[41] She stressed that decisions in these women's organisations tended to be made collectively and contrasted this with the Pankhursts' autocratic organisation of the Women's Social and Political Union (WSPU). 'If you joined the WSPU you accepted the rule of the Pankhursts or you were replaced.'[42] From a similar perspective Pamela Graves repeatedly referred to Labour women creating an effective grassroots socialist movement which aimed at improving the welfare of working-class women and their families. She pointed out that the birth control campaign was endorsed by local Labour Party women members rather than the national leadership.[43]

It was in their local communities that most people, particularly women, practised their politics. Local studies are now being regarded as valid enterprises in their own right rather than as an 'add on' to national studies.[44] A number of recent studies have shown the importance of locality, and the significance of local context is one of the key questions this thesis seeks to explore. Elizabeth Crawford's detailed research on the growth of suffrage in thirteen regions of Britain has shown how local forces interacted.[45] Krista Cowman in her discussion of the political influences on Merseyside on the development of women's political organisations from 1890 to 1920 made the pertinent point that 'local studies move interpretations of political activity from the decisions and alliances of a small number of national leaders to an investigation of how these affected the actions, priorities and affiliations large numbers of individual members.'[46] The importance of locality can also be seen in her national study of paid organisers of the WSPU.

Similarly, June Hannam and Karen Hunt have pointed to the importance of not regarding the birth control campaign in solely metropolitan terms but recognising the importance of the local context.[47] Hunt stressed the importance of the local political culture in shaping grassroots experiences of Labour women. She concluded that what it meant to be a woman member of the Labour Party differed from place to place. Even a geographical and administrative area such as London cannot be regarded as uniform. For example, Lara Marks' study of maternity practices in London covering the 1920s demonstrated that there were marked differences between the boroughs in birth control provision.[48] The local political cultures and party alignments, ethnicity and religion, gender employment patterns can influence the birth control struggle. Comparative studies of Glasgow/Liverpool and Salford/Manchester have pointed out that even where class structure and religion were apparently similar, the interplay of extraneous factors made policy decisions concerning birth control clinics very different.[49]

This research has drawn on a wide variety of literary and oral sources ranging from official reports to diaries, to a selection of interviews both with myself and other academics.

The autobiographies of the leading protagonists of the birth control movement show how later respectability can frame memories of events. Mary Stocks and Charis Frankenburg described the formation of the MSMC in their autobiographies which were written over forty years after the events. The middle-aged respectable Mary was a very different person from the impetuous young woman of the earlier era. Similarly Charis, when she wrote her autobiography, had become a Freeman of the City of Salford with added responsibility. A further difficulty for the researcher is that the events surrounding the founding of the MSMC and SPBCC formed only a small part of the activists' eventful lives.[50]

Given the lack of immediacy in their autobiographies it is fortunate that many of the birth controllers, particularly Marie Stopes, were inveterate letter writers. These letters had the advantage of having been written immediately after the events and were not intended for publication. Particularly illuminating is the series of letters Mary Stocks wrote to Marie Stopes concerning the general progress of the Manchester and Salford clinic.⁵¹ There is also a series of letters in 1931 that Mary Stocks wrote to a supportive Mrs Margaret Pyke, then Secretary of the Birth Control Trust, concerning Manchester City Council's apparent lack of progress. Again there is the view that the letters are constructions of reality and can never just be a record of events.⁵²

The narratives of the minute books from the various women's political organisations provide a rich source of data as well as providing a useful counterweight to memory. Hannah Mitchell, who served as an Independent Labour Party (ILP) councillor in Manchester, scathingly wrote in her autobiography that 'I believe in complete equality, and was not prepared to be a camp follower, or a member of what seemed to be a permanent Social Committee, or official cake maker to the Labour Party.'⁵³ Indeed the minute books of women from the three main party political organisations show a commonality of cause: recruiting members, selling copies of the relevant magazines, fund-raising and decisions on teas. However, these minutes showed that the women also discussed important topics such as birth control and family endowment as well as their branches' relationship to the national party.

A growing form of dissemination of birth control knowledge in the 1920s was the publication of articles and books on birth control, of which Marie Stopes was the most popular exponent. Private birth control libraries lent books out to friends. Marie naturally had an extensive library which besides being available for her personal use was lent in her clinics. Marie scrawled extensively on books with which she disagreed. Lella Secor Florence's book on the Birmingham birth control clinic had 'Rubbish' scrawled over it by Marie Stopes.⁵⁴ Linda Ward in her doctoral thesis on birth control regretted that much birth control literature has been lost owing to its transient nature.⁵⁵ However, a survey of internet booksellers shows that a surprising amount of ephemera on birth control has survived.

The local press has provided valuable contemporary coverage of the SPBCC clinics, particularly their openings and details of visiting speakers. Members of the SPBCC proved proactive and skilful at using the media. Mary Stocks wrote to Marie Stopes describing the MSMC public meeting and her coup in attracting a well-known academic, 'Carr Saunders, we have to impress *The Manchester Guardian*.'⁵⁶ The members of the SPBCC also learned to use the correspondence columns of the local papers. Thus the *East London Advertiser* published a spirited correspondence about the opening of the new birth control clinic in its Letters columns from June 1926 to September 1926.[57] How much coverage the clinics obtained depended on the independence of the editorial policy. The *Stockport Express* reported Marie Stopes' birth control meetings in that town in 1923.[58] However, the Oxford Family Welfare Association complained that the *Oxford Times* had, because of outside pressure, discontinued its advertisement which it had run in preceding weeks and this had resulted in a loss of patients.[59] At the other extreme was the female journalist of the 'Woman's Outlook' in the *Eccles and Patricroft Journal* who was allowed considerable editorial freedom and was supportive of the pioneering birth control clinic in Salford.[60]

The SPBCC tried to disseminate its ideas through writing articles for sympathetic journals. The *Woman's Leader*, the publication of the National Union of Societies for Equal Citizenship (NUSEC), which was edited by Mary Stocks, showed the development of NUSEC's ideas on birth control. *Birth Control News*, founded by Marie Stopes, naturally gave full coverage of any event at which she spoke but also provided useful accounts of general birth control meetings and conferences which were ignored by national and local papers. *Birth Control News* first broke the news of the permissive Memorandum 153/MCW which had deliberately not been publicly circulated.[61] Catholic papers such as the *Catholic Federalist* were scathing in their attacks on birth control and were countered in the above publications, particularly in *Birth Control News*.[62]

Birth control was an issue for which there was no political consensus. The ILP paper, *The New Leader*, under Henry Brailsford was sympathetic to the birth control cause and published articles and letters in support. *Labour Woman* under the editorship of Dr Marion Phillips was ambiguous concerning birth control as was the party. After initial enthusiasm the Women's Co-operative Guild (WCG)'s *Woman's Outlook* stopped covering the issue, but local WCG magazines such as the *Manchester and Salford Co-operative Herald* continued to report enthusiastically the activities of the MSMC. An almost complete set of *Woman's Outlook* is in the Co-operative Society Archives in Manchester. Although *Labour Woman* did not continue to feature the birth control debate, *Liberal Women's News* was supportive of the SPBCC and gave detailed coverage of the birth control campaign in its magazine.[63]

Oral sources tell the historian less about events, though these are important, than about how they are experienced and remembered. When I started this research in 1970, oral history was just coming to be recognised though it was obvious that it was able to give those previously unheard a voice. This research confirms Luisa Passerini's analysis of her oral history interviews concerning women's birth control experiences in 1920s Italy, 'No one's story is wrong, but we need more than the story itself to understand what it means.'[64] One of the main advantages of the oral history approach is to provide emotional understanding of the way the birth control campaign affected the participants. Birth control pioneers such as Mrs Elsie Plant and Sister Beatrice Sandy were able to provide dramatic accounts. Close relatives of the leading SPBCC birth control pioneers have given interviews describing their emotions. These include the son and daughter-in-law of Marie Stopes, the daughter of Mary Stocks and the daughter of Charis Frankenburg.

I have deliberately not included in this book the studio photos or portraits of the women featured in this book. These staged photographs of participants with their period costumes do not convey the spirit of the women. The technology shows women passively frozen in time. Instead I have relied on their words to paint a picture.

An important feature of this book is the creation of a Collective Biography of the founders of the original birth control clinics. The women are not of peripheral importance and their endeavours lie at the centre of the birth control movements. Some of the women are already high profile such as Eleanor Rathbone and Ellen Wilkinson but others are barely remembered. These include Elsie Plant who arranged for Marie Stopes to lecture in Stockport, Alice Onions who braved fierce opposition to found the Wolverhampton clinic and Miss Hilda Shufflebotham who risked her professional career to provide obstetric advice in Birmingham. Each of the clinic founders showed moral courage in fighting for an unfashionable cause.

The networks and political affiliations have been traced of over a hundred of the founding members of each clinic affiliated to the SPBCC founded in the 1920s. Every clinic provided a detailed list of committee members and consulting doctors, so it was possible to trace affiliations to other voluntary bodies or political organisations through contemporary newspapers and magazines such as the WCG's *Women's Outlook*. The local archives of each of the early SPBCC clinics have been consulted, as well as relevant archives in London and abroad. However, this study is by no means definitive, and it is hoped that readers will go on to carry out their own research into the birth control pioneers.

Johanna Alberti adopted a biographical approach to explore the lives of fourteen women who had been suffragists and who had been politically active between 1914 and 1928. I agree with her argument that the study of women's lives and relationships helps an understanding of the choices that they made. The concept of 'webs of friendship', as developed by Liz Stanley is relevant to this research. She believed that feminist organisations, often operating in a hostile political environment are more richly complex than at first believed and that they cannot be understood without an in-depth analysis of the networks and friendships in the organisations.[65]

To adapt the 1970s feminist slogan, 'The personal is the political,' the personal life of the protagonists did have an influence on their actions. This would apply to well-known activists such as Marie Stopes as well as little known activists such as Evelyn Fuller of the Walworth Road clinic or Marion Phillips, the Labour Party politician.

This book traces the development of the birth control movement as it searched for allies within the women's movement and mainstream political parties. The study shows how the pioneers found the resources to face religious and medical opposition. The social background of the founders and the mothers is examined as the birth control movement has been criticised for being dominated by middle-class women and failing to reach working-class mothers. Birth control pioneers had to make difficult choices, and their motivation is discussed for embracing eugenic ideas. The divisions between head office strategy and the campaigning activities of grassroots members are explored. Finally the Family Planning Association's success is explained when Mrs Barbara Castle at last made birth control provision part of the National Health Service.

2   The Emergence of the Birth Control Movement

Sheila Rowbotham is one of the social commentators to describe how, after the end of the First World War, there was a challenge to the old order in cultural values.[1]

It important to examine the motives behind changing fertility, and in this the concept of modernisation is crucial. The birth control movement framed its scientific methods as being in tune with the age. Marie Stopes, in her scientific career, was certainly a modern woman and indeed she wrote an article for a popular paper extolling a low birth rate as being desirable for 'the modern woman'.[2] Significantly this cutting was archived in Dora Russell's papers. Middle-class women, such as novelist Vera Brittain regarded birth control as the modern way and believed this attitude was reaching working-class women who were demanding change. In Salford, Evelyn Glencross' working-class mother affirmed that she had been content with childbearing but she wanted a different life for her daughters.[3] Eleanor Rathbone MP wanted women to obtain scientific information about birth control from clinics rather than from 'the quack round the corner or some ignorant old woman'.[4]

The political landscape had changed after the First World War. Besides the granting of the suffrage, there were new party political alignments and increased state intervention in health matters with the creation of a dedicated health ministry. Superficially it appeared that there were new opportunities for women to participate in political activity. The electorate was enlarged in 1918 with women over thirty now qualifying to vote in national elections by holding, or their husband holding, land or premises valued over £5.00. This meant that rented property could be used as a qualification as well as property which was owned by the woman. Subsequently all adult women over the age of twenty-one were granted the vote in 1928.

Political parties in the 1920s were in a state of flux which presented challenges to birth controllers. None of the short-lived administrations provided coherent, consistent leadership and none found an effective solution to the country's underlying social and economic problems. While the Conservatives continued to remain a significant force in administrations after 1922, being a dominant element in coalitions, the balance of power between the other political parties changed. The most significant domestic political shift of the inter-war period was the decline of the Liberal Party and its replacement by the Labour Party as the progressive party in British politics. In 1929 the Labour government, headed by Ramsay MacDonald, had 291 MPs elected. However, party lines were still comparatively fluid with Josiah Wedgwood, Alfred Mond, Ernest Simon and Oswald Mosley, amongst those MPs with a concern for birth control who changed party allegiance.

None of the main parties became a vehicle for feminist politics, although at first Labour appeared to be the more sympathetic. There were still progressives after the First World War such as the Socialist Henry Brailsford who was a birth control supporter.[5] However, Robert Skidelsky argued that part of the Labour Party's success was due to the fact that the leadership distanced themselves from radical policies.[6] Indeed Labour, which had been sympathetic to women's suffrage demands, turned down an opportunity to extend the vote.

Many politically aware women came to realise that the legal change in the granting of the suffrage was not a universal panacea, and that it was not until women had control over their reproduction that freedom could be maintained. As has already been noted, Mrs Cooke wrote to NUSEC (successor to NUWSS) *Woman's Leader* explaining that the franchise alone could not free mothers. Another former suffragist, Maude Royden, a single woman and editor of the NUWSS magazine, was shocked to discover that many working women did really believe that, having promised to obey their husband, their bodies ceased to be their own. Maude Royden, eventually a Free Church minister, came to support the birth control cause. She was a suffragist who had worked with Eleanor Rathbone politically, as well as being a social worker with her in Liverpool.

The career of Marie Carmichael Stopes exemplified the new frontiers in career and life choices that were available to women in the twentieth century. Marie was one of the most brilliant scientists of her generation, gaining a first class honours degree from the University of London, her DPhil from the University of Munich and a London DSc, making her one of the youngest holders of this degree in the country. Her specialism was paleobotany, the study of plant fossils, and she was appointed as the first woman science lecturer at the University of Manchester.

Although superficially paleobotany had little in common with twentieth-century birth control practices, Marie gained from her academic experiences. She could communicate with her students and with predominantly working-class audiences such as the Ancoats Brotherhood. She successfully worked in a predominately male environment. She came to recognise the value of publicity and cultivating personal relationships. Marie was excellent at analysing scientific problems and working out how established rules could be circumvented.

In 1911 she married the Canadian botanist Reginald Ruggles Gates, but after four years she wished to end the relationship. Divorce was lengthy and costly but Marie's research showed that she could have the marriage annulled if it had not been consummated. Controversially, she obtained a medical certificate which was presented by her solicitor and stated she was still virgo intacta. Although it was unlikely given her scientific background, Marie claimed she had not realised her marriage was unusual and she only learned the truth because she had consulted material held at the British Museum. On 8 May 1916 the case came to court and her marriage was annulled. Many women would have been traumatised by having their sex life discussed in public but Marie seemed to thrive on her celebrity status. Her friend Mary Stocks recalled how in the early 1920s Marie fascinated a whole restaurant by her account of married life. 'My dear would you believe it! After three years of married life I was still a virgin!'[7]

Marie distilled her research from the British Library into her most influential book which was titled without a hint of irony, *Married Love*. The rationale for her books was that 'in my own marriage I paid such a terrible price for ignorance that I feel knowledge gained at such a cost should be placed at the service of humanity.' *Married Love* was written while Marie was technically still a virgin, but this did not inhibit her pronouncements which stressed the woman's right to sexual pleasure.

Marie Stopes acknowledged her debt to Edward Carpenter and Havelock Ellis who discussed sexual matters in their work. She argued that instinct was not enough, as evidenced by her disastrous first marriage and that the husband needed to woo his wife for both to obtain sexual pleasure through orgasm.[8] However, the reason her books were so popular was that they were accessible and written in an almost poetic style. Just three examples of her style are: 'the body of the loved one's simple sweetly coloured flesh,'[9] 'every night there should be tender companionship and whispered intimacies,'[10] 'the man must tenderly woo her before each act of coitus.'[11] This was too overblown for some intellectuals but nevertheless her literary style meant her books could comfortably be read by women without being regarded as pornographic.

Her work, in the feminist tradition, asserted the right of the woman to sexual pleasure and to control of her body. The wife should be able to enjoy sexual relations without feeling depraved. Marie stressed that women were not sexless but that there were differences in sexual response between women and men, citing the moon-month rhythm of women. 'When is it that the normal healthy woman feels desire or any up-welling of her sex-tides?'[12] Marie urged couples to carry out their own research as well as acknowledging the need for further academic research. After chapter eight on 'Abstinence' the next chapter discussed 'Children'.[13] She quoted a number of case studies and advised delay before starting a family and this section showed that she was already interested in the topic of birth control. Marie asserted that many couples suffered from too many pregnancies and, while condemning abortion, recommended medical methods of controlling pregnancies by shutting out sperm.

Married Love caused a sensation when it was published and by 1923 it had sold over three hundred and ninety six thousand copies and reached its fourteenth edition. It appealed to the middle and upper classes. The diplomat Harold Nicolson approvingly wrote to his wife Vita Sackville West, the writer, that he had just purchased *Married Love* and she must read it.[14] Indeed the social historian Ross McKibbin in his Preface to

Married Love described it as a 'book whose moment had come'.[15] Although Richard Soloway found it 'cloyingly romantic' he correctly explained its success by putting it in the context of the post-World War One society where the old mores had been challenged and middle-class women in particular wanted more sexual as well as political independence.[16]

Marie Stopes' work has been criticised as being only accessible to the middle classes but the evidence does not support this. Marie developed a conscious strategy of reaching out to a working-class audience. For instance, while working as a lecturer at the University of Manchester, her field research into coal balls in the North West had already brought her into prolonged contact with mining communities and she continued to have a good relationship with them. She wrote articles in popular papers such as *John Bull* and in 1919 *A Letter to Working Mothers* was produced at only 1/6d. Robert Roberts in his autobiography *The Classic Slum* set in pre-war Salford described how her birth control message made an impact on local working-class consciousness through these cheap papers.[17] Similarly Mrs Richardson, Marie's secretary, later reported how she had to reply to hundreds of letters after the *John Bull* articles appeared.[18]

The influence of Marie Stopes was all pervasive in working-class as well as middle-class culture, young and middle aged. Her name even percolated into to the school playground rhymes in 1924, possibly via the music halls:

> Jeannie, Jeannie, full of hopes
> Read a book by Marie Stopes.
> But to judge from her condition,
> She must have read the wrong edition.[19]

Another child who found the works of Marie Stopes particularly interesting was the future politician Shirley Williams. She entitled her autobiography *Climbing the Bookshelves* and the object of this enterprise was to reach the works of Marie Stopes which were on top shelves and had been purchased by her mother the feminist Vera Brittain and her father the academic George Catlin.

Historians such as Pamela Graves have confidently asserted that few working-class couples could have afforded *Married Love* and so its message was lost on them.[20] These claims ignored Marie's flair for publicity. It was through her widespread coverage in the newspapers that

Elsie Plant, living in Cheshire, related how she heard about Marie and made contact. Later Elsie purchased her own copy of *Married Love*.[21]

The popularity of *Married Love* cut across sex and class and religion. It was even read out loud in the Catholic town of Liverpool. Bessie Braddock's biographer described how working-class Bessie Braddock, the future Labour MP, strode the street 'in the mental company of Dr Marie Stopes'. Bessie read publicly from the book while most women were not even sure it should be read privately. Bessie began to hold street corner meetings on what she called scientific birth control.[22]

The themes raised in *Married Love* were elaborated by Marie as she maintained the phenomenal rate of writing one book a year. In particular two books were relevant to her campaign of birth control. *Radiant Motherhood*, 1920, was intended for the readers of *Married Love*. It started from the romantic premise that every lover desired a child which will be conceived in beauty. However, a later chapter draws on her experience in Manchester and is starkly titled 'the cost of coffins'. Here she starkly asserted that there were more coffins bought by poor working class women for their dead babies than by middle-class women. Marie said she was fighting on their behalf to give them knowledge which would end this tragedy. In 1924 *Contraception: Its Theory, History and Practice* stated in the introduction that it was intended for the medical profession but this was a token disclaimer as it was obviously aimed at the intelligent lay person. The book contained explicit diagrams and Stopes provided detailed descriptions of the contraceptive devices available including her Pro-Race cervical 'cap'.

Marie met Humphrey Verdon Roe when she was searching for a backer for the publication of *Married Love*. His views supporting birth control were well known in progressive circles and Dr Binnie Dunlop, secretary of the Malthusian League, had put him in touch with Marie. She needed £100.00 to finance the publication by Fifield of *Married Love* which was quickly repaid. After a courtship when Humphrey was on active service in France they were married in 1918. Humphrey was a Manchester businessman who had jointly founded the famous aircraft firm, AVRO. He had become convinced of the advantages of birth control. He saw the distress of his workforce caused by having more children than they could support, and therefore offered to generously endow a birth control unit at St Mary's Maternity Hospital in Manchester.[23] He proposed to give £1,000 a year for five years and £12,000 on his death (he was about to fight in the First World War). However, though supported by local figures such as Councillor Margaret Ashton, his endowment was refused, presumably because it was too politically sensitive.

Humphrey also accompanied and supported Marie on her speaking tours and spoke at the Queen's Hall Meeting in 1921. Marie attracted large audiences whenever she spoke. She had started off her birth control campaign in 1921 ambitiously filling Queen's Hall, London with a rally of over two thousand people including the great and the good, politicians and celebrities. She was also prepared to travel to the provinces to spread the message, even when pregnant. Elsie Plant estimated that two thousand people heard Marie speak at the Armoury in Stockport, a meeting she helped to organise in November 1923.[24] Some of these were politically committed, as the meeting was organised through the Socialist Church, but the vast majority of her audience were just curious.

Elsie remembered Marie's determination to speak at the meeting. Her husband did not want his wife to over-tire herself as she was pregnant. However, Marie was advertised in the local press to speak on 'The ideals of birth control, both personal and national' and did not want to disappoint her audience. She strongly argued that birth control information should be given at all municipal ante-natal and child welfare centres across the country. Elsie was critical of Marie's talk, which she regarded as simply a résumé of the main points of *Married Love*, but it was generally agreed that the meeting was a resounding success. Marie kept in touch with Elsie after the meeting but Elsie told me that Marie 'wasn't a team player as she was so aggressive. She had her own ideas as to what was best.' Other people came to share Elsie's perceptive assessment.[25]

Birth control was not just an academic exercise for Marie Stopes who turned it into a practical crusade. With her husband she founded her own organisation, the Society for Constructive Birth Control and Racial Progress (SCBCRP), which was based in London. As sociologist Laurie Taylor reflected, 'Marie Stopes was an idealist who had quite fortuitously been handed the means for realizing her ideals.'[26] Often when founding a new social movement, members look to a charismatic leader of an existing one, but Marie's personality alienated the other birth controller pioneers.

The SCBCRP with Marie as President was autocratically run, and Marie brooked no opposition, for instance to the use of her recommended high domed cervical cap or to her use of medical doctors. The women's leader Eleanor Rathbone of NUSEC was even less enamored with Marie Stopes: 'There is Dr Marie Stopes, as hard to silence as a mosquito shrilling out her message.'[27] Marie imperiously declared to Dr Evelyn Fisher of the SPBCC 'I'm not the Cabin Boy in this movement. I'm the Admiral.'[28] The SPBCC, unlike the SCBCRP, consisted of a federation of autonomous clinics, each with its own governing body.

In 1921, three years after the granting of the partial suffrage for women, two events took place which were barely noticed at the time but which were later recognised to be highly significant. On 17 March at ten in the morning there was a huddle of apprehensive women waiting outside a converted shop at 61 Marlborough Street which was in a poor district in London's overcrowded East End. Although the shop door opened, none of the frightened women ventured inside. At last the Receptionist, Mrs Richardson, came out to them and reassuringly led each of them through to the shop, taking their hands for confidence.[29] The shop was the first birth control clinic in Britain and it had been courageously started by Marie Stopes and her husband Humphrey Roe. Those early patients had no doubt heard horrifying scare stories of wombs being removed and compulsory sterilisation. However, as a result of personal recommendation, attendance at the clinic gradually grew.

Aware of Marie Stopes' innovation, another group of birth controllers opened a clinic on 9 November 1921 at 153a East Street, Walworth, behind the Elephant and Castle public house, situated in a poor part of London. The building was non-descript with a discreet side entrance. Like the Marlborough Street clinic, attendance was poor with only two women coming in November and eight in January 1922. However, attendance increased and the clinic eventually became the flagship clinic of the SPBCC. At first it offered advice on infant welfare but it became obvious that the demand was for birth control information and this service was dropped. Volunteers had to face abuse by being called whores and pelted with eggs. The clinic was defaced with graffiti and had its windows smashed.

In 1921 women were going to these clinics to be fitted with a new, more reliable method of birth control. This was not available in state clinics or hospitals. In Marie Stopes' clinics they were fitted with a small cervical cap, and in the SPBCC clinics they were fitted with a larger appliance called the Dutch cap. These were both manufactured out of rubber and women had to practice inserting them in their vagina as well as using spermicidal jelly. These women did not want to rely on their husbands' use of condoms. Men could buy condoms from chemists in large towns or through mail order. However, besides being widely regarded as unaesthetic, condoms were regarded as unreliable. Male contraceptive devices did not give women the control over their bodies that Mrs Cooke had advocated in 1923.

Birth controllers, by demonstrating that their voluntary clinics were successful, wanted to force the government to provide municipal birth control clinics which would be free and easily accessible to working-class mothers. They campaigned for working-class mothers to be given the same opportunities for birth control as middle class women who could pay to consult private physicians. The SPBCC believed birth control was too important to be left to the voluntary sector, but was prepared to provide clinics as a temporary measure until state provision was achieved. Many medical men and government officials were initially sceptical that working-class mothers would have the persistence to regularly attend the clinics and carry out cumbersome medical procedures in cramped surroundings.

The SPBCC was founded in 1924, although as has been seen, some clinics had existed previously. Unlike the SCBCRP, which was initially London-based, the federated clinics of the SPBCC in the 1920s were widely distributed geographically in England and Scotland, though not Wales. These included Aberdeen (November 1926), Birmingham (April 1927), Cambridge (August 1925), East London (June 1926), Glasgow (September 1926), Liverpool (July 1926), Manchester and Salford (1926), North Kensington (November 1924), Newcastle-upon-Tyne (January 1929), Oxford (November 1926), Walworth Road London (1921) and Wolverhampton (May 1925). Marie Stopes knew many of the founders of the SPBCC clinics which were opened by local volunteers, particularly those in Liverpool, Manchester and Salford, and Aberdeen.

The busiest SPBCC clinic was Walworth Road, London. Its annual reports showed that Walworth Road in the first eight years of existence saw 20,929 patients. It is rare that we have information about paid lay members of the clinics but the exception is Evelyn Fuller of Walworth Women's Welfare Centre. Evelyn trained as a teacher and was appointed Superintendant of Walworth Women's Welfare Centre when it was taken over by the SPBCC from the Malthusian League. She remained Secretary from 1923–36 and under her leadership the clinic gradually expanded and provided a model for other SPBCC clinics. She was also Secretary of the SPBCC. Evelyn was hardworking and evidently well liked by the working-class mothers. She was described by Mrs Player, one of the volunteers, as being sympathetic and tactful in her treatment of patients. She was also liked and admired by many clinic workers with whom she was in contact although she preferred working on her own rather than in a committee.

In 1926 Evelyn wrote an illustrated booklet for those volunteers considering starting a birth control clinic. She included a diagram of the Walworth Road layout. This was a practical booklet covering the choice of accommodation, sanitary arrangements and hours of opening. She pointed out these must fit in with school hours and there must be toys for young children. Evelyn also provided a list of recommended equipment as well as an example of a case card. She placed great emphasis on the lay workers being sympathetic as many of their patients were shy and nervous.

Evelyn travelled to Zurich in 1931 and delivered a paper on the SPBCC to an international symposium on contraception. Although her delivery was hesitant, her paper was well received because it arose out of her experience at Walworth Road. She stressed that the most important thing was to gain the confidence of the patient, and to treat them not as so many cases but as individual human beings to whom a knowledge of birth control is a matter of vital and urgent importance.

She continued her work efficiently and conscientiously until 1936 when she suffered a breakdown from overwork, was dismissed and eventually committed suicide revealing a colourful past life. Mrs Lawther, founding member of the East London SPBCC clinic indignantly accused the Executive Committee of discharging Evelyn in a heartless manner because of her illness and leaving her destitute. She and others resigned from the SPBCC East London clinic in protest at Evelyn's treatment.

The provincial clinics also attracted large patient numbers. Charis Frankenburg, co-founder of the MSMC, calculated that in their first eight years their clinic had seen over three thousand two hundred new patients, some travelling to Salford from as far away as Sheffield over twenty miles away.[30] The distinguished gynaecologist Sir John Peel calculated that by the end of 1927, nine SPBCC birth control clinics had collectively seen 23,000 new patients and 17,000 return patients. Whereas the research of Kate Fisher showed that many of her interviewees were indifferent to birth control clinics, nevertheless women did attend the clinics in significant numbers.

Mary Stocks and Charis Frankenburg founded the MSMC. Initially it was Charis who wrote to Marie Stopes asking if she could put her in touch with anyone locally who was interested in the birth control issue. Marie gave her the name of Mary Stocks who she recognised as being an old school friend from St Paul's Girls School. Although Mary had not enjoyed St Paul's, the two women had much in common. Unusually at that time both women had been to university, Charis to Somerville Oxford and Mary to London School of Economics. Mary and Charis supported women's suffrage and continued to belong to women's organisations. They married into comfortable lives, Charis to an industrialist and Mary to a university lecturer. They were happy to have small families, Charis had four children and Mary had three. In their autobiographies they wrote how they could afford to employ nannies and household staff which allowed them to pursue outside interests. They possessed a sense of public duty and were both magistrates, Mary in 1930 and Charis in 1938. There were also significant political differences. Mary was a committed Fabian Socialist while Charis was an active Conservative who was conscious of being in a minority in the birth control movement. Mary Stocks was one of the few people to have a lasting friendship with Marie Stopes right up to her death.

Mary was the MSMC's first Chairman and Charis Secretary. Charis was unusual in that she had training as a midwife. She wanted to serve in France as a nurse in the First World War and so in 1915 she enrolled on a midwifery course at Clapham Maternity hospital. The course could be taken in three months, but she decided to take the longer more in-depth course of six months. She used a legacy from her godmother to pay for her course. Amongst her fellow students was the feminist Maude Royden (later Rev) who she rated outstanding as a nurse. Maude was later to work with Eleanor Rathbone in Liverpool. Charis became a Certified Midwife with the Clapham Maternity Hospital Midwife Certificate of Honour. Charis arrived at Chalons-sur-Marne Maternity Hospital in France on 4 October 1915. Her French language skills were good, she had a sound nurse's training but nevertheless the work was hard. She wrote that 'I felt like a marionette on the verge of hysteria.'[31]

Mary and Charis raised funds for the MSMC, appointed staff organised publicity to attract working-class mothers. Mary devoted a great deal of time to working at the clinic, so much so that Eleanor Rathbone was afraid she would neglect her campaign for family allowances. Mary was a committee member of the SPBCC and its successor the NBCC. She was also close friend of Ernest and Shena Simon from Manchester who also became involved with birth control campaign.

It was not easy to start these birth control clinics and there were failures. Manchester and Salford SPBCC tried to run a clinic for miners' wives in Cannock Chase, but after two years this failed because of lack of funds. A former miner attempted to found a clinic in Abertillery in 1925 with advice from Marie Stopes but, because of vehement opposition from the local Free Churches, the clinic closed.[32] Women were too frightened to attend. After the successful meeting in Stockport in 1923, Marie Stopes urged Elsie Plant to start a birth control clinic, but this never materialised because of lack of political support. The birth controllers faced violent opposition.[33]

The early birth control clinics were founded in heavily populated urban areas because it was comparatively easy to reach working-class mothers. However, Marie recognised the needs of rural mothers and to her credit tried to reach out to them. As well as maintaining her London clinic, in 1928 she enterprisingly purchased two horse-drawn caravans, to carry out birth control work in areas including Wales. These travelling clinics were run by nurses who found the conditions cramped and difficult. This experiment ended when one caravan was set on fire and a local Catholic woman was convicted of arson.[34] Marie was later to found birth control clinics in Scotland and Northern Ireland.

The popularity of Marie Stopes' books and her talks meant birth control could be discussed privately by partners and in the public domain by political parties and women's organisations. Formerly birth control had been widely condemned as having connotations with prostitution and not something that respectable women and men would use. Indeed in the 1970s I interviewed two married women who were living in the mill-town of Glossop, Derbyshire and were young women in the 1920s. 'There was this man who came selling things in the back room of the pub on Fridays. But we wouldn't have wanted our husbands to have bought anything like that.'[35] This was in spite of the fact that birth control, unlike abortion, was perfectly legal and condoms could be bought from chemists in large towns.

Caroline Walker convincingly argued that Marie Stopes made discussion of birth control almost respectable.[36] Former suffragist Maude Royden who was a single woman and a Free Church minister was able to raise the issue as was Eleanor Rathbone, also a single woman, and leader of NUSEC. However, in the 1930s unmarried Ellen Wilkinson, then part of the Labour establishment, demurred at publicly discussing birth control.

The birth control controversy that was to erupt in 1922 involved the Ministry of Health, a department which was created in 1919 to direct the medical and public health functions of central government. It was a significant development for central government to intervene in the nation's health care. The department was concerned with maternal mortality but distanced itself from birth control. In 1922 there were rumblings of discontent from both sides of the birth control debate. The Catholic Women's League, alarmed at the publicity of Marie Stopes, protested to the Liberal Minister of Health. Sir Alfred Mond received them sympathetically and ruled that municipal maternity and child welfare centres were not to issue birth control information but to refer women to private doctors or hospitals. But there was no mass reaction when the consequences of the Mond ruling were gradually realised.[37] Edith How-Martyn and Mary Breed were later to point out the contradictions in the Mond ruling. 'Married working-class women (unless they are themselves "employed persons") are not within the scope of the National Health Insurance Act. They have no panel doctor and frequently cannot afford a private doctor. Hospitals are too busy with their present tasks to undertake the duty.'[38]

It appears that the initiating event in the birth control campaign was not the political Mond ruling, but the dismissal of Nurse E. Daniels in December 1922. It is always easier to identify with a human face rather than an abstract principle. Nurse Daniels was a health visitor employed by Edmonton District Council and informed mothers attending the council-run maternity centre that they could obtain birth control information from a nearby Marie Stopes' clinic. She had previously been warned about her conduct by the Medical Officer of Health but nevertheless persisted in her actions which resulted in her dismissal. Her dismissal provided a national as well as a local focus. There were five hundred names on the petition in her support presented by the local Unemployed Women's Committee, a packed Protest Meeting organised by the New Generation League and an unsuccessful intervention in the House of Commons by her local Labour MP for Edmonton, Mr F.A. Broad.[39] However, her dismissal was upheld by the Ministry of Health.

It is important to recognise that Nurse Daniels' action, like that of civil rights activist Rosa Parks who refused to yield her bus seat to a white person, was not random or accidental but self-conscious and calculated. Nurse Daniels was already a member of the New Generation League and was determined, with the backing of the League, to publicly challenge the ruling that local authorities could not provide birth control information. Nurse Daniels was portrayed as a martyr to the cause. Significantly, one prominent person who did not give Nurse Daniels support was Marie Stopes herself. Marie Stopes held that Daniels had ignored the orders of a doctor and so broken her professional code, yet Marie Stopes was usually dismissive of the rules of the medical profession.[40] It might also be that Marie was reluctant to have media attention diverted from her organisation.

After her dismissal Nurse Daniels continued to campaign for birth control. She sent her business card to the American birth control campaigner Margaret Sanger which recorded that Nurse Daniels had travelled to Holland to obtain further training, presumably at Dr Aletta Jacobs' pioneering birth control clinic which had opened in 1882. Nurse Daniels eventually established her independent clinic in Brighton, Sussex.[41]

Hans Kreisi argued that there is rarely one clear initiating event in social movements, a 'Rosa Parks moment'.[42] However, it is generally agreed that Nurse Daniels' actions started an important sequence of events. Pamela Graves stated that there needed to be a small spark to light the enthusiasm for a birth control campaign and this was provided by Nurse Daniels.[43] Gillian Scott also believed that Nurse Daniels' actions became a focus for a left-wing campaign to broaden working-class access to birth control.[44] Similar positive evaluations of the importance of Nurse Daniels' actions in the history of birth control are made by both Peter Fryer and Audrey Leathard.[45]

On 9 May 1924 a deputation of eighteen people, representing the main birth control groups, met with John Wheatley, who was then Labour Minister of Health. The deputation was introduced by F.A. Broad who was MP for Edmonton who had taken up the case of Nurse Daniels in his constituency. The deputation included Dorothy Jewson MP, H.G. Wells, Stella Browne, Dora Russell and Dr Frances Huxley. A wide variety of interested parties were represented by Jenny Baker and Humphrey Verdon Roe (SCBCRP and representing his wife Marie Stopes), Mrs Gilbert Murray (SPBCC) plus a representative from the Labour Party Women's Section and *New Generation*. They demanded that 'welfare centres shall be permitted to allow their doctors to give birth control information to such mothers as may desire it.'[46]

Not surprisingly John Wheatley, a Catholic, reiterated the government's position by issuing Circular 517 on 24 June 1924 in which he wrote: 'It is not the function of an ante-natal centre to give advice on birth control, and exceptional cases where the avoidance of pregnancy seems desirable on medical grounds should be referred for particular advice to a private practitioner or hospital.'

Birth Control News of June 1924 reported John Wheatley's subtle distinction between allowing access to knowledge and distributing knowledge – this distinction was not sustainable in practice. Those who had previously wished to work within the system realised it was not going to accommodate their demands. Dora Russell famously wrote in her autobiography *The Tamarisk Tree* that 'Mr Wheatley had stirred up a hornet's nest: all through 1924 we buzzed and stung.'[47] Dora Russell had already joined the highly publicised campaign to support Rose Witcop and Guy Aldred when they were prosecuted in 1923 under the law for obscene publications for reprinting Margaret Sanger's *Family Limitation*.[48]

The birth control issue became increasingly politicised in the 1920s. By 1923 the issue was debated by the Women's Co-operative Guild and a supportive resolution passed. It was raised at the Labour Party Women's Conferences in 1925, 1926, 1927 and 1928 and there was overwhelming support for the issue. It was also raised at the 1926 Labour Party Annual conference in Blackpool. Liberal women also pressed for birth control provision in their magazine and at their conferences. Individual Conservative women, such as Charis Frankenburg, also tried to raise the issue within their party.

The consequences of John Wheatley's ruling included the formation of the WBCG and the SPBCC in 1924. At the close of the 1924 Conference of Labour Women, a large number of women stayed behind to form the WBCG. The Labour MP Dorothy Jewson was appointed President and the Vice-Presidents included the MPs Ernest Thurtle and F.A. Broad. The Committee included SPBCC members Mrs Ella Gordon, Wolverhampton and Mrs Lowther, Durham.[49] Lesley Hoggart in her detailed analysis described how the WBCG acted as a pressure group within the Labour Party to try to change the party's policy on birth control.[50] The WBCG regarded its prime aim as mounting a systematic political campaign so that the state would provide information for working-class women. Dora Russell was one of the leading members in this group. Lesley Hoggart felt that the WBCG accepted that motherhood would be the norm for most of these women but wanted to increase their control over reproduction. The WBCG saw itself as complementing rather than being in competition with the SPBCC. SPBCC was less overtly political and worked directly with working-class mothers on practical issues. The SPBCC, after John Wheatley's ruling, realised that the government was not going to change policy, and committed itself to increased direct action by opening more clinics.

The dismissal of Nurse Daniels had parliamentary repercussions. NUSEC relied on the help of sympathetic, usually male backbenchers, to introduce private members' bills. These included the Conservative Major Hills and Labour Ernest Thurtle MP. These tactics were in contrast to the confrontational style of Marie Stopes. There were not clear-cut divisions between parties on the birth control issue, as was revealed when Labour MP Ernest Thurtle of the WBCG unsuccessfully attempted to introduce a private member's bill on birth control in 1926. This Bill challenged the ruling which stopped maternity and child welfare authorities from giving contraceptive advice to women who needed it for health reasons. However, in April 1926, in the House of Lords, a similar birth control measure to that of Ernest Thurtle was introduced by the Liberal Lord Buckmaster, Vice-President of the Malthusian League.[51]

Lord Buckmaster, Lord Chancellor in Asquith's wartime Cabinet, used a mixture of philanthropic and Darwinian arguments and argued that, 'the question is whether the knowledge which is being withheld from the poor and which is possessed and practiced by the rich should not be free.' The motion was approved by 55 votes to 44, the vote going against government policy. Therefore, the British House of Lords was the first legislative body in the world to pass such a resolution on birth control, though this did not commit the government to a course of action. Mary Stocks, a Fabian, attended the debate as she personally knew many of those taking part, such as Lord Balfour of Burleigh, and wrote that it was one of the most significant parliamentary debates she had ever witnessed.[52] Lord Balfour addressed the public meeting for the launch of the MSMC. However, the SPBCC came to realise the lack of authority that Buckmaster's Bill possessed as it was not binding on government.

The birth control campaign had taken practical action in founding clinics from 1921 onwards. However, the birth control campaigners realised after the government's response to the dismissal of Nurse Daniels that they could not rely on it to provide funding for more clinics. Although there was no effective action from Parliament, the birth control issue was gaining momentum within the feminist organisations and was being placed on the political agenda by the grassroots members of the main political parties.

3 Birth Control – a Feminist Issue?

This chapter examines the strength of feminism in the inter-war years and the choices feminist organisations had to make about their political direction. The birth control activists were able to draw on their new-found political experience at local and national level but they had to convince feminist organisations, which were much more powerful than previously thought, that birth control was a feminist issue.

One of the most influential feminists was Eleanor Rathbone, both as a theorist and as a tactician. In 1893 she went up to Somerville College, Oxford University and took a degree in Philosophy. However, she did not pursue an academic career but returned to Liverpool to become involved in women's suffrage and social work activities. In 1897 she became parliamentary secretary to the Liverpool Suffrage Society and in 1919 she took over from Millicent Fawcett as president of the post-suffrage organisation the NUSEC. Eleanor regarded the winning of the franchise not as an end in itself but as an opportunity to create a new world for women. She was one of the first women to take advantage of new political opportunities in local and national government and was the first woman to be elected to Liverpool City Council in 1909. In 1929, the first election in which all women over twenty-one could vote, Eleanor was returned as an Independent MP representing the Combined English Universities which comprised the universities of Liverpool, Birmingham, Bristol, Durham, Leeds, Manchester, Reading and Sheffield.

Eleanor became involved with social issues through her father's business interests. He was a concerned constituency MP. Her work brought her into contact with the Victoria Women's Settlement in Liverpool where she met Elizabeth Macadam, a Scottish social worker, who became her lifelong companion. They first co-operated on a scheme to enable social workers to be trained at the Liverpool School of Social Studies. Elizabeth's practical support for Eleanor has always been recognised but undoubtedly Elizabeth's background in the Social Sciences also influenced Eleanor. Elizabeth was an intellectual soul-mate.

Eleanor Rathbone, an intensely private person, is often regarded as a one-dimensional intellectual. Yet, there was another side to her. One of their few surviving letters shows Eleanor's depth of feeling for Elizabeth. 'Oh, my dear, my dear. If you knew how much your life, your cares, your future, your happiness meant to me at bottom, you would not think me the self-absorbed creature I seem.'[1] These feelings can be seen in terms of romantic friendships which were 'loving, nurturing relationships between women who deliberately remain sexually and emotionally independent of men, but which do not necessarily involve physical sexuality'.[2] Eleanor also had a close circle of friends including Eva Hubback and Mary Stocks. She also appeared to be at ease with small children. Ann Patterson, Mary Stocks' daughter told me that on visits as a child to Eleanor she remembers Eleanor being especially kind to her and always being an ample source of sweets. She sensed that Elizabeth Macadam was much more aloof with her.[3]

Eleanor Rathbone was at the forefront of the debate about feminism which in turn determined the priorities of NUSEC. It is certainly true to talk of 'feminisms' rather than feminism and in the first part of the twentieth century there were two opposing master frames of feminism: the belief that a woman should be equal to a man and that a woman is different from a man. Although in the 1920s the debate was keenly contested, both Olive Banks and Brian Harrison, taking a wider perspective, believed that equality and new feminism stemmed from a single historical process.[4] There were undoubtedly common intellectual roots, but we must also examine the campaign from the perspective of contemporaries. The differences in philosophy and tactics were so keenly felt that they split organisations and severed friendships. The contested claims of equality feminism and new feminism, drawing on different cultural traditions, can be followed in the NUSEC paper *Woman's*

Leader, and *Milestones*, a collection of NUSEC Presidential Addresses. The owner of *Time and Tide*, Lady Rhondda, although an equal rights feminist, was keen to maintain her paper's impartiality and published contributions from both sides of the debate. Indeed she controversially held that not all suffragists were feminists:

> There are two groups – feminists and reformers. The latter are not in the least feminist, do not care tuppence for equality for itself, and if they are interested in it at all it is for a means for an end. Therefore these women reformers wanted the vote because they felt it would help their reforms – prison reform, infant welfare reform etc.[5]

The equal-rights feminists were influenced by the ideas of the Enlightenment and the writings of Mary Wollstonecraft and John Stuart Mill. These writers placed emphasis on the importance of a person as a human being, whatever their sex, and demanded those rights that men held. Roy Porter believed that it was Wollstonecraft's general ideas on the worth of women and their education that made her an inspiration for equal rights feminists rather than any specifics on political activism. The suffragist Millicent Fawcett had written an Introduction to the centenary edition of Wollstonecraft's *A Vindication of the Rights of Women* first published in 1792, so bestowing on her work the equal rights feminism imprimatur. Valerie Bryson argued that although John Stuart Mill was not the first politician to put the case for women to have the vote, he was the first to make a serious attempt to achieve his by attempting to introduce an Amendment to the 1867 Reform Bill which sought to enfranchise women on the same terms as men.[6] John Stuart Mill was also an influential political philosopher whose *Subjection of Women* was published in 1869, in which he attacked the prevailing 'separate spheres' ideology and argued for increased women's educational opportunities. 'What is wanted for women is equal rights, equal admission to all social privileges; not a position apart, a sort of sentimental priesthood.'[7]

John Stuart Mill and Mary Wollstonecraft were two of the writers who influenced the equal rights feminists' campaign for equal employment opportunities, equal access to education at all levels and an end to the double standard of sexual morality. The novelist Rebecca West scathingly puts the case for equal pay for men and women teachers in a wider societal context. 'The real reason why women teachers are paid less highly than men who are performing the same work is the desire felt by the mass of men that women in general should be subjected to every possible disadvantage.'[8]

The equal rights philosophy was particularly relevant to the suffragettes in their struggle for the vote. At first the NUSEC was over-optimistic about the consequences for women of gaining the partial suffrage, but then it ambitiously proceeded in 1919 to campaign for other reforms such as economic, legislative and social changes which would secure a real equality of liberties, status and opportunities between women and men. The first of its six campaigning points was the demand for equal pay for equal work. It reiterated the demand for an equal franchise, called for women to be elected to Parliament to carry forward an equal rights programme and demanded women be admitted to the legal profession. There was also a demand for equality in the private sphere, for divorce law reform, pensions for widows and equal rights in guardianship. Lady Rhondda subsequently founded her own equal rights feminist organisation, 'The Six Point Group'. Equal rights feminists were distrustful of the new feminists who, they claimed, emphasised gender differences to the detriment of freedom of opportunities for women.[9] They regarded new feminism as a conservative political philosophy which advocated the importance of women staying at home to fulfil their traditional roles as wives and mothers.

The divisions over equality feminism versus new feminism cut across generations. The young middle-class novelist Winifred Holtby declared provocatively, 'Personally I am a feminist and an Old Feminist because I dislike everything that New Feminism implies.' She wished to be able to pursue her career as a novelist without the distractions of fighting injustices.[10]

However, new feminists were also dissatisfied with women's place in society and by the mid-1920s new feminist thought, with its emphasis on women being 'different but equal', came to dominate the NUSEC. New feminists were asking fundamental questions about the position of women in the family. NUSEC member Mary Stocks, editor of their magazine the *Woman's Leader*, was also concerned to broaden out the traditional concerns of the movement from 'The narrowly equalitarian type of feminism which confines its ambition to the attainment of liberties and opportunities already enjoyed by men.'[11] Olive Banks believed that it was Eleanor Rathbone's contention that the majority of women were destined to be mothers, and it was with their needs as mothers that NUSEC should be concerned.[12] In the inter-war years and beyond, the state of motherhood was not regarded as conservative or reactionary but part of the natural order.[13] Eleanor Rathbone was not alone in attacking society's uncaring attitude towards mothers as 'a monstrous injustice and criminal folly'.[14] This had been exemplified by the treatment of mothers in the First World War. Thus Maude Royden complained that a woman who bore children and ran a household was treated as 'an arrested man and a perpetual minor, but a woman who could clip tickets on a tram car was recognised as a "superwoman" – in other words, a man'.[15]

Eleanor Rathbone was irritated by the perceived selfishness of some privileged so-called feminists. She claimed that these women rested on their achievements once they got all they wanted for themselves. These achievements included the suffrage, the right to stand for Parliament and the opportunity to enter learned professions.[16] She dubbed these women the 'me too' feminists. Eleanor claimed that her vision of an ideal society was radical and that changes in women's lives had to be more far reaching than those advocated by equal rights feminists which she regarded as being too narrow:

> The women's movement comprises a large number of reforms, all of which are 'feminism', but only some of them 'equality'. The equality reforms are necessary and immensely important. They consist in breaking away the fetters and restrictions which prevent them from developing their capacities and doing their best work. But this aim of enabling women to be and do their best work will not have been accomplished even when every sex barrier has fallen.[17]

For Eleanor Rathbone the achievement of narrow equality on its own was not enough, and in her 1925 Presidential Address she succeeded in persuading NUSEC to adopt new feminist policies including family endowment (later known as family allowances) and birth control. Her 1925 Presidential Address was entitled 'The Old and the New Feminism'. This welcomed the increasing influence of new feminist ideas:

At last we can stop looking at our problems through men's eyes and discussing them in men's phraseology. We can demand what we want for women, not because it is what men have got, but because it is what women need to fulfill the potentialities of their natures, and to adjust to the circumstances of their own lives.[18]

However, the veteran suffragist Millicent Fawcett, amongst other committee members, regarded this as a step towards practical socialism. The equal rights campaigners also believed that by extending NUSEC's activities the organisation was diluting its energies for equal rights campaigns.

Eleanor Rathbone's influence enabled the new feminists to concentrate their efforts on two issues: birth control and endowment of motherhood. She had fundamentally disagreed with the remark made at the 1926 Labour Party Annual Conference that 'Information as to artificial methods of birth control has nothing to do with feminism.'[19] Mary Stocks had framed the birth control campaign as being rooted in a woman's right to self-determination and, like Eleanor Rathbone, as a way of achieving the emancipation of motherhood.[20] Mary provocatively asked in *Woman's Leader*, 'can (she) be forced to bear her husband a child every year through all the best years of her life?' Her question framed the problem and also suggested intended action.[21]

By 1927 the debate still raged in NUSEC and the issue which ultimately divided the equal rights feminists from the new feminists was that of protective legislation. Susan Pedersen, Rathbone's biographer, believes it was a tactical mistake by Eleanor Rathbone to pursue the issue, but arguably the issue was forced upon her.[22] There was general agreement that long working hours, heavy lifting, and dangerous manufacturing processes, such as leaded paint, were unsuitable for women, but there was disagreement about methods of protection. The equality feminists had already resented women being dismissively grouped with minors in the Women, Young Persons and Children's Act of 1920. They mistrusted protective legislation which they perceived as being used by employers to restrict women's entry into certain types of employment rather than to protect them from dangerous manufacturing practices. The equal rights feminists pressed for these dangerous processes to be banned for both sexes and argued that legislation for the protection of the workers should be based, not upon sex, but upon the nature of the occupation.

Eleanor Rathbone sensibly accepted this principle of protective legislation but urged NUSEC to take into account the opinion of the workers themselves, the likelihood of success and the interests of the community. She correctly held that this was an important issue for women who belonged to socialist organisations and who had campaigned for this protective legislation. Her amendment was passed by the narrow majority of 81 votes to 80 but thereupon eleven of the twenty-four members of the Executive resigned from NUSEC feeling that the principle on which the suffrage struggle had been undertaken had been undermined. One of those to leave was Edith Bethune-Baker of the Cambridge SPBCC who features in my Collective Biography.

The evidence does not support Jane Lewis' claim that weak feminism had little impact on the birth control campaign in the inter-war years.[23] Although she acknowledged the contribution of individual feminists such as Mary Stocks, Jane Lewis argued that NUSEC was never in the forefront of the campaign for birth control. She repeatedly stated that NUSEC was content to follow the lead of the SCBCRP and the National Birth Control Association (NBCA). However a reading of NUSEC's literature and Eleanor Rathbone's statements, challenges this argument. Mary Stocks framed the birth control campaign as being rooted in a woman's right to self-determination and, like Eleanor Rathbone, regarded it as a way of leading to the emancipation of motherhood. 'Birth Control being a subject now widely discussed, and one which very specially affects women, as well as the general welfare of the community, the NUSEC resolves to promote the study of this question, and recommend such study to its Societies.'[24]

Eleanor Rathbone admitted that a narrow view of feminist issues might not include family endowment, birth control and housing but she felt they were questions which women needed to address if they were to shape their own destinies. Throughout the 1920s both Eleanor Rathbone and Mary Stocks campaigned on the issue of birth control as an issue of concern to NUSEC and which added to NUSEC's manifesto. For the new feminists, the birth control issue was not just about the mechanics of contraception but was elevated to a matter of principle of a woman's freedom of choice.[25] Mary Stocks repeated in 1927 that, 'large sections of women demanded with formidable insistence the right of self-determination in the matter of maternity, with full access to knowledge of birth control methods as they consider it necessary for its achievement.'[26] Mary Stocks set out the position of NUSEC on birth control in the pamphlet, *Family Limitation and Women's Organisations*, 'the feminist today is asking for something more than identity of treatment in a world designed for men to reflect their own experiences and fulfill their own needs. She is asking for a proportionate share in the ordering of that world.'[27]

This argument was amplified the following year in a *Woman's Leader* editorial, 'Is birth control a feminist reform?' where the editor argued that mothers' lives were considered expendable and their work was undervalued by society.[28] The occupation of motherhood was not considered in the same light as coal-mining which, though dangerous, at least had some safety regulations. The author concluded, 'that is why we regard the provision of expert and disinterested birth control advice, as in one aspect, *a feminist reform*' (original italics).

Eleanor Rathbone described how people viewed the relationship between family allowances and birth control and explained, 'I regarded the two subjects as the positive and negative of voluntary parenthood.' In *The Case for Family Endowment* she justified how people came to support both causes: 'They have their roots in the same fertile sub-soil of disaffection: disaffection with the intolerable conditions under which millions of mothers today live out their strenuous lives and perform their difficult task: dissatisfaction with society's complacent condonation of the wastage of their invaluable product, human life.'[29] Eleanor Rathbone admitted that a narrow view of feminist issues might not include family endowment and birth control but she felt they were questions which women needed to address if they were to shape their own destinies.[30]

Eleanor Rathbone regarded motherhood not as a brief biological event, nor as a service provided for one man, but as a contribution to society as a whole which would absorb women for most of their adult lives.[31] She questioned the view that keeping a family was a praiseworthy leisure, part-time occupation for the male sex. Historian Martin Pugh saw in Eleanor Rathbone 'a bold and realistic attempt to work with social change and, in effect, to accept that most women aspired to marriage and motherhood.'[32]

Eleanor Rathbone's contribution to the birth control movement has been barely acknowledged, even in Susan Pedersen's detailed biography. This is perhaps because Mary Stocks, her first biographer and close friend, gave prominence to Eleanor Rathbone's other campaigns and omitted that of birth control. Yet Eleanor contributed to the changed intellectual climate which made the birth control campaign possible. She gave generously to the clinics and discussed birth control at public meetings such as in Poplar and bravely chaired the public meeting to inaugurate the SPBCC clinic in Salford. Eleanor Rathbone appreciated the difficulty in the diffusion of birth control ideas and spoke of working-class mothers 'passing the torch from hand to hand'. She was outspoken in her support for birth control and stated at a national public meeting in 1926 which included the National Union of Teachers, the Standing Joint Committee of Industrial Women's Organisations and the Women's National Liberal Federation. 'Whatever may be our opinion this is a matter on which the individual has a right to decide for herself, and that the poorest woman should not be debarred by her poverty from getting the information which is open to well-to-do women.'[33]

From the perspective of the twenty-first century we can now recognise that essentially the objectives of equal rights and new feminists were similar. Certainly in the debate over protective legislation, equal rights feminist and new feminists criticised one another for positions they did not hold. Winifred Holtby, proclaimed herself as an equality feminist, but was nevertheless sympathetic to issues central to new feminism such as birth control and abortion. The portrayal of maternal death in her finest work *South Riding* exposed society's hypocrisy. In a sensitively written cameo, Holtby described the dilemma of Annie Holly, married to a building labourer, barely able to cope with her six children, but who was not able to deny her husband sexual relations. She found she was pregnant again in spite of being advised against further pregnancy by her doctor. 'I've taken stuff to stop it and half killed myself but it's no good.'[34] Yet there was no hope and no reprieve as Annie met a lingering death. In her history, *Women in a Changing Civilisation* Winifred Holtby stressed the important contributions of the birth control movement, specifically naming Marie Stopes, Margaret Sanger and Councillor Margaret Ashton from Manchester.[35] Her close friend, the novelist Vera Brittain, supported Marie and birth control clinics and Brittain's criticism of the Papal Encyclical was reproduced in *Birth Control News*.[36]

Just as equal rights feminists recognised the importance of the birth control campaign, so many new feminists also campaigned on equality issues. Martin Pugh was one of a number of commentators who have highlighted the contribution of new feminists to equality issues.[37] Maude Royden, as well as espousing new feminist principles, fought for women to be ordained priests in the Church of England.[38] Mrs Emmanuel of Birmingham NCW and SPBCC successfully campaigned to have the marriage bar against the employment of married women doctors lifted.[39] New feminists, such as Councillor Shena Simon and Mary Stocks, campaigned on issues such as the removal of the marriage bar for female teachers in Manchester. They argued that since the end of the First World War this bar did not apply to female doctors. When in 1944 Mary Stocks sat on the wartime McNair Committee on the training and supply of teachers, she influenced the committee's recommendation that if a married woman has the time and inclination to teach, the deciding factor should be her professional competence.[40] Mary Stocks was very clear about women's right to undertake paid work outside the home, 'I say that it is for the woman to decide whether or not it is desirable for her to work outside the home, and not for any public authority, which chooses to enquire into her relations with her husband, the economic circumstances of her relatives, her prospects of child bearing, as the case may be.'[41]

In practice, women found it difficult to make a choice between equality feminism and new feminism. Alison Oram, in her study of inter-war women teachers, believed the distinction between equality and new feminists to be unhelpful. She examined their attitude towards feminist politics and significantly concluded that women teachers could identify with ideas of femininity and difference in their work, at the same time as campaigning for equal pay and the ending of the marriage bar.[42] Although they came from different intellectual traditions there was far more that united than divided them.

Jane Lewis remarked worthy goals were not hard for feminists to find and these causes were often more diverse than the single issue suffrage campaign.[43] Feminists took advantage of the new political opportunities of the 1920s to join in campaigns which particularly involved women as wives and mothers: anti-poverty, housing and maternal mortality. Women's groups tried to alleviate the worst excesses of unemployment, which often resulted in the ill health of mothers who sacrificed themselves. In Salford, where the MSMC was founded, it was reported by the Medical Officer of Health in 1925 that there were 8,881 registered as unemployed. At the end of the MSMC's First Annual Report in 1926 case studies were given and carefully framed to show the need of working-class mothers. The MSMC tried to assist miners' wives in Cannock Chase by starting an outreach birth control clinic where one hundred and sixty-four women were treated, often accompanied by hungry children.[44] Committee members drew attention to the chronic deprivation of working-class mothers even in supposedly affluent areas such as London and Cambridge. The Oxford clinic doctor, Dr Isabelle Little described her experiences in the early days of the clinic in Jericho when 'apprehensive women who were poor with large families' came in desperation to the clinic.[45] Similarly the founders of the Birmingham SPBCC clinic declared they had started the Centre 'with the definite object of striking a blow at poverty, overcrowding, disease and dirt'.[46]

Feminists were also concerned with the issue of maternal mortality, believed to be affected by an inadequate diet and sub-standard housing. Maternal mortality rates remained static and in some years slightly increased, even though infant mortality was being reduced.[47] Irvine Loudon's statistical research showed maternal mortality remained high until 1935. Sylvia Pankhurst, the suffragette and revolutionary socialist, highlighted in her book the loss of life to maternal death. She quoted the Manchester Medical Officer of Health, Dr Veitch Clark, as stating that although childbirth was not a disease it ranked first amongst the killing diseases in mothers of childbearing age.[48]

Anna Davin linked the campaign for the protection of motherhood to imperialist doctrines valuing women as providers of the race.[49] However, concern at maternal deaths came from all sections of society. Their rhetoric did not just define a woman's value to the nation in terms of her child bearing but in terms of individual tragedies and their effect on families. In 1926 Dr Richmond, Medical Officer of Health for Stockport, was concerned that the rate of death in childbirth had remained consistently high for the last twenty years – in 1924 alone there were twelve maternal deaths.[50]

This failure to lower maternal mortality rates in the inter-war years was a concern to successive governments. As Jane Lewis pointed out, maternal mortality was second only to tuberculosis as the major cause of death amongst married women between 1911 and 1930. Moreover, between 1923 and 1936 the rate actually rose. She argued that if statistics for maternal morbidity had been presented, the situation of working-class mothers would have been shown to be even worse.[51]

Dame Janet Campbell, a government medical officer who chaired a number of government enquiries into maternal health, appreciated the importance of maternal mortality. She produced two major reports: *Maternal Mortality* in 1924 and the significantly titled *Protection of Motherhood* in 1927. She believed that, 'the unexpected loss of life is a tragedy to the family. It is not infrequently associated with the death of the infant for whom the maternal life has been sacrificed, and it is often followed by the impaired health and nutrition of the remaining children.'[52]

Although Janet Campbell found one in every two hundred and fifty mothers died in childbirth, which was in line with other studies, significantly she did not publicly endorse birth control as a way of lessening maternal mortality. She specifically maintained that it was not the function of maternity centres to provide birth control information.

It was birth control campaigners within the Labour Party, rather than Janet Campbell, who made the causal link between uncontrolled fertility and maternal deaths. In her famous outburst at the 1926 Labour Party Conference, Dora Russell argued the case for birth control, and made a comparison of rates of maternal mortality with the 'death rates of men's most dangerous trades'.[53] She deliberately shocked her audience by declaring that it was four times as dangerous for a woman to bear a child as for a man to work in a mine which was men's most dangerous occupation. In Liverpool, Labour Councillor Bessie Braddock (later MP) challenged local political and religious orthodoxy in 1937 by publicly stating that in the previous year eighty-seven women had died in child-birth in Liverpool and that probably three-quarters of them would have been alive if they could have had access to birth control measures to avoid pregnancy.[54]

The Manchester Maternal Mortality Committee was just one of a number of voluntary committees throughout the country looking at the problem in the local context and having close connections to the birth control movement. Naturally, former midwife Charis Frankenburg of the MSMC played a prominent role in this Committee, being able to contribute expert knowledge. Judith Emanuel in her thesis on maternal politics in Manchester in the inter-war years, argued that there was a broad consensus on the Committee and pointed out how Charis Frankenburg's professional knowledge had been drawn on by the Committee in its investigation of the death immediately after childbirth of Molly Taylor, a young Jewish mother.[55] It had cross-party membership in the 1920s under the Chairmanship of the redoubtable Alderman Nellie Beer, and achieved consensus. Charis Frankenburg and Nellie Beer were Conservatives, but in the 1920s there were several Labour members. Nellie Beer later remarked that 'although we were of different political parties, we were never at loggerheads.'[56] Mary Stocks believed that in Manchester, unemployment added to 'the tribulations of mothers under the perpetual strain of unwanted pregnancies and frequent miscarriages. Indeed the poor health of working mothers was beginning to be a reproach to our existing, or rather non-existing, medical services.'[57] The Manchester Maternal Mortality Committee only met once a quarter and, according to Judith Emanuel's research, those who wanted to play a more active role attended the MSMC. Charis Frankenburg explained her interest in birth control as arising from her experiences on the Manchester Maternal Mortality Committee and this might have been so for other maternal mortality activists who joined the birth control campaign.[58]

Eleanor Rathbone, as President of NUSEC, was the most prominent suffragist to support birth control, but the Executive Committee of the SPBCC contained a number of women who were known to have been involved with the suffrage movement. Mary Stocks, one of the founders of the MSMC had supported the suffrage movement as a schoolgirl when she marched with the NUWSS, chalked messages on pavements, distributed their literature and served on its Executive Committee.[59] The suffrage leader Mrs Fawcett was god-mother to her first child. Mary later remarked on the continuity of the suffrage and birth control campaigns:

> When I had occasion to visit a number of localities all over Britain in the service of other causes such as family allowances, birth control – it was observable that many of the women who were playing an active and intelligent part in local affairs were the same women who had once played an active part in the suffrage agitation. Such, in addition to the vote, has been its gift to posterity.[60]

There was continuity between the birth control clinic's committee members and commitment to earlier suffrage activity. Charis Frankenburg, the co-founder of the MCMC, accompanied her mother to hear the Pankhursts speak and, while still a student at Oxford, organised a debate on women's suffrage. Her daughter, Ursula Kennedy, remembered her mother maintaining strong feminist principles throughout her life. Mary Stocks recognised that women accustomed to fighting for one cause may transfer their commitment to another campaign if they perceived it to be similar. Thus the co-founders of the MSMC successfully asked the well-known actor Sybil Thorndike to serve on the MSMC Advisory Council. She had previously been involved with the WSPU when she was appearing at the Horniman Theatre, Manchester, 'I took the Chair at a Suffragette meeting yesterday, I never felt such a fool, but after a bit I got quite worked up about women's wrongs.'[61]

Not surprisingly, as the Collective Biography at the back of this book shows, there were many members of the Executive Committees who had been committed suffragists. These included Edith Bethune-Baker of Cambridge, Elizabeth Cadbury of Birmingham, Eva Hartree of Cambridge, Edith How-Martyn of Walworth Road, Constance Masefield of Oxford, Lillian Mott of Liverpool and Helen Pease of Cambridge. Other leading suffragists who supported birth control included Mrs Pethick Lawrence who made donations to the North Kensington Women's Welfare Centre.

It would be simplistic to claim that all suffragists supported the birth control movement which had previously been regarded with distaste as a diversion from the suffrage. Indeed Miss Quinn, a staunch Catholic, who had been imprisoned for her suffrage activities and so revered, was bitterly opposed to birth control. Miss Quinn, a representative of the Tailor and Garment Workers Union, consistently spoke against birth control at Labour Party Women's Conferences such as the one in 1928. However, the opposition of Miss Quinn was an exception and if individual members of the suffrage movement were concerned with the birth control issue, it was usually, like Ellen Wilkinson MP, to support it.[62]

After the Parliamentary Qualification of Women Act the SPBCC did have some allies in the House of Commons. My Collective Biography shows that a number of women who were members of the SPBCC stood for Parliament. As has been seen the most influential of the SPBCC's MPs was Eleanor Rathbone who represented the Combined English Universities from 1928 to 1946. In 1929 three supporters of the SPBCC were elected as MPs. Ruth Dalton who served on Walworth Road and North Kensington Mothers' Clinics was returned as Labour MP for Bishop Auckland though she chose to serve only briefly. Cynthia Mosley, a member of Wolverhampton Mothers' Clinic was elected as Labour MP for Stoke-on-Trent. In 1931 Leah Manning who worked on Cambridge Mothers' Clinic was elected Labour MP for East Islington and the local SPBCC wrote asking her to promote the birth control cause in Parliament. Given that in 1929 there were only fourteen women MPs, the number of candidates with SPBCC links was significant. However, these women were often marginalised as MPs, serving only short terms of office.

Political lessons were learned from the suffrage campaign but the days of gesture politics had passed. Thane argued that this was because the women's organisations were now political insiders, rather than outsiders. NUSEC recognised the importance of taking early action and identifying key decision makers. They briefed the officials and committees who advised the Minister and were able to provide welcome expertise on technical matters. Thus Nancy Astor MP was provided with briefing notes from Eva Hubback, NUSEC's parliamentary secretary, as well as providing research material for civil servants. Eva Hubback also perfected the technique of well-timed 'Letters to the Editor'. She used this strategy for both the end of the suffrage campaign and the SPBCC campaign. These actions were termed by Rathbone as 'backstage wire pulling' and though NUSEC did not gain public recognition, even amongst its own supporters, this strategy was effective tactically.

The feminists had learned how to move from confrontation to negotiation. As Eleanor Rathbone stated in her First Presidential Address of 1920, 'It requires courage to brave misrepresentation, odium and imprisonment, but it requires an equal and perhaps rarer courage to plant seeds that will require a generation to grow to maturity and spend a lifetime in fostering them.'[63] They were able to compromise in order to achieve their aims and use much more low-key tactics. Eleanor declared that:

> There are reformers whose idea of taking a citadel is to march round it blowing trumpets, and when that fails, to batter it with rams, if necessary with their own heads. We sometimes used the battering ram, but if the wall proved too strong for us we withdrew a little and investigated every other method of overcoming that wall, by climbing over it, or tunnelling under it, or perhaps labouring to dislodge a stone at a time, so that just a few invaders could creep through. And we acquired by experience a certain flair which told us when a charge of dynamite would come in useful and when it was better to rely on the methods of a skilled engineer.[64]

The SPBCC realised they could not achieve a change in birth control policy on their own. They looked to other outsider groups, particularly women's organisations to create broader alliances. In the 1920s there was a complex network of women's organisations but in practice there was not a wide choice of allies available to the SPBCC. For example Caitriona Beaumont in her detailed study of non-feminist societies in the interwar years points out that the YWCA, the NUTG and the WI did not discuss birth control as it was felt to be too contentious and would offend some of their members' religious beliefs.[65]

Within both the WI and the NUTG, which was a development of NUSEC, there were individuals in influential positions who supported the birth control campaign but were unable to place it on the political agenda of these powerful women's organisations. Martin Pugh's evaluation of the WI is correct in that the organisation managed to successfully maintain a balance between feminism and citizenship, femininity and domesticity.[66] It is significant that Lady Trudie Denman, the much respected first Chairman of the WI, did not consider it judicious to raise the issue of birth control with the WI even though she personally supported Walworth Women's Welfare

Centre, became Chairman of the National Birth Control Council (the forerunner of the Family Planning Association) and committed thousands of pounds of her own money to the birth control cause.[67] Martin Pugh referred to Denman as creating a fragile bridge for birth control. This assessment is questionable as Lady Denman was successful precisely because she rigidly compartmentalised her private beliefs and her national role.[68] Similarly, although Mary Stocks was a Vice-President of the NUTG, that body did not endorse birth control in the inter-war years.[69] Stocks never attempted to make birth control part of NUTG policy.

However, the birth controllers were able to form political alliances with two influential national women's organisations: the National Council of Women (NCW) and the Women's Citizens Association (WCA). The leaders of these two organisations, unlike other women's organisations, were prepared to recommend action on birth control to their members. J. Howes in her study of women's organisations, argued that these played an important part in focusing on local issues which were important to the lives of ordinary women.[70] Although Howes judged the social composition of these organisations as being primarily middle class, she regarded the results of their political and social campaigning as being to improve the lives of women as a whole. Both the NCW and WCA had branches in towns such as Salford where the SPBCC held birth control clinics.

The NCW had evolved out of the National Union of Women Workers which in the 1880s linked a wide range of charitable and religious organisations. Its aims included removing discrimination against women, encouraging the participation of women in public life and acting as a co-ordinating body.[71] At the height of its popularity it had expanded to 1,450 societies. Although by the mid-1920s the NCW had decreased in the size of its members, it was still influential. A commitment to birth control was regarded by the NCW to be in line with its policy of action 'to improve the quality of life for all, and in particular the status of women'.[72]

Many of the birth control pioneers were members of the NCW and two prominent members became Presidents: Elizabeth Cadbury from Birmingham from 1905 to 1907 and Eva Hartree from Cambridge from 1935 to 1937. In Manchester Charis Frankenburg, Mary Stocks and Shena Simon were all members of the NCW as well as the MSMC. Ethel Emanuel, in a long period of office was Secretary, Treasurer and President of the Birmingham NCW as well as serving on the NEC. She was Chairman of the SPBCC Birmingham Women's Welfare Centre for nearly twenty years from 1932 to 1951.[73] The Birmingham Women's Welfare Centre affiliated to the NCW in 1929.

Birth control featured prominently in the NCW's discussions in the 1920s as well as subjects such as women police, temperance, the peace process and maternal morbidity. As early as 1923 the Southend branch passed a resolution urging that birth control advice be given to married women at ante-natal clinics. In 1924 the first objections to this birth control policy predictably came from the Catholic Women's League.[74] In 1926 Miss Hertz reported that the Manchester branch was holding a meeting on birth control with speakers from both sides. Later in the year the Executive Committee was asked to comment on the successful birth control bill introduced by Lord Buckmaster in the House of Lords. They declined to take any action on this until it had been before the General Representative Council. In 1929 a motion on birth control was selected by ballot to be one of the resolutions to be placed before their Annual Meeting to be held in 15, 16, 17 October in Manchester. Mary Stocks, representing NUSEC, moved that the conference:

> calls upon the Ministry of Health and upon Local Authorities to allow information with respect of methods of Birth Control to be given by medical officers at Maternity and Child Welfare Clinics in receipt of government grants in cases in which either a married mother asks for such information, or which, in the opinion of the medical officer, the health of the patients renders it desirable.[75]

Mary Stocks believed that the debate was not whether there was to be birth control advice, as this was already available to middle-class mothers, but whether all women should have the opportunity of obtaining scientific advice from doctors who knew them personally. She condemned the commercialisation of birth control advice which was expensive and often untrustworthy. Mary claimed that poor mothers were ignorant, desperate and frightfully shy.[76] The resolution was seconded by Mrs

Lillian Mott of the SPBCC clinic in Liverpool. Mary Stocks' speech was praised by the *Woman's Leader* which, given her links to the paper, would have been expected, 'This (resolution) was moved by Mrs Stocks in a speech so brilliant and so perfectly fitted for the occasion that the general opinion expressed by delegates that it was the best speech on the subject they had ever heard.' Her speech was also complimented by various other sympathetic women's organisations such as the Manchester and Salford Women Citizens Association which reported that it was 'a brilliant and comprehensive speech, which received prolonged applause'.[77]

The resolution was passed by a large majority without amendment, only the members of religious women's organisations voting against it. Significantly these included Anglican as well as Catholic bodies. The Catholic Women's League, St Joan's Social and Political Alliance, The Mothers' Union, Girls' Friendly Society (GB) and the Girls' Friendly Society (Scotland) stated that they wished to dissociate themselves from the resolution. However, they did not withdraw from the NCW.[78] Linda Ward considered that little action was taken on birth control by the NCW but this writer contends that their actions both nationally and locally had considerable influence.[79] The NCW continued to support the birth control clinics, as individual members and as a national organisation. The NCW joined with SPBCC and NUSEC in organising an influential national conference on birth control in 1930 which was aimed at sympathetic local authorities.

The other key ally of the SPBCC from amongst the women's organisations was the Women's Citizen's Association (WCA) whose aim was to provide political education and mobilise women to take advantage of their new suffrage opportunities. Joanne Smith in her doctoral thesis convincingly argued that the WCA was a feminist organisation.[80] Eleanor Rathbone had pioneered the WCA in Liverpool in 1914 and by 1918 branches had been formed throughout the country. Consequently, women members of the WCAs were able to engage in the political process and address problems faced by women, and were able to make demands for political and economic progress. WCAs could draw on support from organisations established in the pre-war women's movement. Although nationally the WCA's leadership did not take a strong line on birth control, it did support local action by its members.

It was important for the birth controllers, politically weak on their own, to network. There was overlapping membership of NUSEC, WCA and the NCW at both national and local levels. Members of the SPBCC were elected to leadership positions in the NCW and WCA. For example Mary Stocks served on the Executive Committee of NUSEC, was a member of the NCW, was heavily involved with the MSWCA was a founding member of the MSMC and was a Fabian. Charis Frankenburg, also a founder member of the MSMC, was a member of the WCA, a member of the NCW and a staunch Conservative. These women certainly used these informal networks to their advantage. Key members of the MSMC were elected to the Executive Committee of the MSWCA including Mary Stocks, Charis Frankenburg and Shena Simon. Charis was joint Honorary Secretary of Salford WCA, and vice-chairman of the Salford WCA 1933 to 1945. It was probably through their membership of Salford WCA that Charis Frankenburg knew Mrs Annie Eccleshall who owned a pastry shop in Greengate and bravely let out the top rooms for the MSMC's birth control clinic.[81]

The Manchester situation illustrates how local women's organisations successfully networked on the SPBCC initiative. The MSWCA was influential in the area with its membership peaking at three thousand members during the year 1933 to 1934. MSWCA had a number of unique features, for instance producing a monthly magazine, the *Woman Citizen* in which it profiled women standing for public office. Shena Simon was the chief 'originator' of the MSWCA and Joyce Goodman recognised that Shena's charisma, tenacity, grasp of detail and personal circumstances made her a powerful political force.[82] Talks on their local birth control clinics were of particular interest to the MSWCA members. Mary Stocks wrote that 'The women's organisations heard us gladly. They were the people who knew at first hand or second hand the stresses and strains of uncontrolled pregnancies.'[83] The MSWCA magazine recorded that Stocks in 1927 spoke to a number of branches of the MSWCA, such as Chorlton-cum-Hardy a suburb of Manchester, on birth control. These talks to members about the MSMC raised the profile of the clinic and encouraged attendance. Emily Glencross, a working-class woman from Salford, related how her mother had heard Charis speak on the MSMC at a MSWCA meeting and decided to take action with regard to her daughter's birth control needs.[84] This advocacy coalition, made up of people from different local parties, was successful in establishing a municipal, as opposed to the voluntary, birth control clinic in Manchester. In Manchester the leading birth control campaigners on the council were Councillor Shena Simon (then Liberal) and Councillor Annie Lee (Labour). As late as 1927 the council had resisted birth control provision in their clinics but by 1929 Councillor Annie Lee who was the Labour councillor for Gorton and an avowed feminist asked:

> if he (Alderman Jackson) did not think the committee (Public Health Committee) ought to give instruction in birth control in connection with their clinics. Alderman Jackson said...he thought it would be extremely unwise to associate the mere idea of birth control with the infant welfare centres and clinics.[85]

After his negative answer, systematic lobbying of Manchester councillors was carried out by Annie Lee and Shena Simon. They were able to operate as well-placed insiders within the council while at the same time drawing on support from outsider women's groups.

By 1930 the minutes of the council's Maternity and Child Welfare Sub-Committee reported that they had received resolutions on the matter from the NCW, MSWCA and Manchester organisations such as the Rusholme Women's Co-operative Guild, Gorton Labour Party and Manchester Branches Association for Co-operative Guild Representation on Public Bodies.[86] Mary Stocks had given talks to many of these organisations and successfully urged them to write to the Manchester City Council about the provision of birth control information at their municipal clinics.

The debate over the endorsement of birth control must be seen in the context of the wider feminist debates in the 1920s. These were not merely theoretical debates, but passionately held guides for practical action. The fact that these debates were held at all showed that feminism rather than being dormant was awake and well. Although the differences between the followers of equality feminism and new feminism can be exaggerated, it is significant that those women who occupied leadership positions in NUSEC were committed new feminists. As a consequence

Eleanor Rathbone declared that birth control was not a peripheral issue to NUSEC but was central to new feminism. Individual members of the SPBCC were active as MPs and councillors but they were still on the periphery of political life. In spite of the risk of offending members two women's organisations, NUSEC and NCW supported the birth control campaign as well as individual members from WCA. This was in contrast to the strategy of Marie Stopes who found it difficult to make enduring alliances.

4   Anatomy of the Birth Control Clinics

The previous chapters have looked at national debates, but this chapter examines issues of locality in the formation of the local birth control clinics. Social movement theorists have emphasised the importance of mobilising structures, both formal and informal, through which groups seek to organise and they have looked at the ties that bind members into a social movement.[1] Resources and networks are shown to be particularly significant. This chapter therefore addresses six related questions. Firstly, to what extent did the foundation of the SPBCC clinics exclusively involve the mobilisation of upper- and middle-class women? Secondly, how effective were the women of the SPBCC in mobilising human and financial resources? Thirdly, what were the gender roles in making birth control decisions? Fourthly, how were statistics and case studies framed by the SPBCC to attract popular support? Finally and perhaps most importantly, to what extent was there trust between the middle-class women workers and the working-class mothers who were patients?

This research, by drawing on contemporary documentation from SPBCC clinics and interviews with birth control users, adopts a different perspective to earlier studies which often criticised the clinics for being ineffectual and failing to reach those most in need. Angus McLaren, in his history of contraception, claimed that the few clinics which were founded in the 1920s had difficulty in attracting working-class women 'who were intimidated if not repelled by the male, medical, middle class atmosphere'.[2] Kate Fisher's doctoral study of birth control led her to draw similar conclusions, asserting that 'clinics struggled to convince many potential patients to accept their particular principles but did not make them more attractive to the working class communities they targeted.'[3] Drawing on the results of her interviews in Oxford and South Wales, she agreed with McLaren that there was a disjunction between the middle-class birth controllers' scientific aspirations and the approach of working-class people.[4]

This chapter investigates whether SPBCC activists were drawn from a narrow social milieu or whether they came from a broader social spectrum. To gain a more detailed picture, this research therefore draws on archive material giving details of over one hundred SPBCC members, whose particulars are contained in my Collective Biography. Recent research has shown the diversity of women's social backgrounds in political activity in the early twentieth century. The suffrage movement, although predominantly middle class, contained a significant proportion of working-class members.[5] As Anne Logan argued in her appraisal of women's entry as magistrates, 'It would not be entirely safe to assume that the early twentieth-century women's movement was completely middle-class or that working-class women entirely lacked feminist sympathies or a willingness to serve.'[6] Krista Cowman also found that the backgrounds of the WSPU organisers were extremely diverse.[7]

Undoubtedly, there were rich and well connected women who were founder committee members of the SPBCC clinics. Lady Muriel Willoughby of the Walworth Women's Centre was described by R.E. Dowse and John Peel as being one of a number of high-profile aristocratic women to serve on its committees.[8] Other upper-class SPBCC members included the Hon. Mrs Dighton Pollock who was a founder committee member of North Kensington Women's Welfare Centre (NKWWC). She was the daughter of Lord Buckmaster who introduced the successful Bill on birth control clinics in the House of Lords in 1926. There were also wealthy women such as Mrs Elizabeth Cadbury of the Birmingham clinic who was a member of the famous Quaker family, and Eileen Laski, of the MSMC who was the sister of entrepreneur Simon Marks of the drapers shops Marks and Spencer.[9] Ann Patterson, daughter of Mary Stocks, recalled how even as a child she was aware of the difference in the wealthy lifestyle when she visited Charis Frankenburg at her spacious home in Upton Prior in Cheshire.[10]

The accepted convention in the inter-war years was that middle-class women were supported by their husbands and did not undertake paid full-time employment after marriage. Mrs Constance Masefield, of the Cambridge clinic, the wife of the poet laureate John Masefield, was unusual in that she founded her own private school. However, the majority of committee members of the SPBCC, though comfortably off, were not from the aristocracy or the conspicuously wealthy, but fulfilled the role of wives of professionals such as doctors or teachers. Mary Stocks, the Chairman of the MSMC was married to John Stocks, subsequently Vice-Chancellor of the University of Liverpool, and six other SPBCC committee members were married to either university lecturers or leading educationalists. Mrs Lella Secor Florence, an Executive Committee member of the Cambridge Women's Welfare Centre and later Birmingham Women's Welfare Centre, was married to Professor Sargent Florence. Mrs Ruth Dalton and Mrs Helen Pease, Cambridge were also married to university lecturers. Mrs Lillian Mott, Liverpool, was the wife of Charles Mott, the Director of Education for Liverpool, and Mrs Gilson, Birmingham, was married to a head teacher of a leading boys' school. Mary Stocks regarded herself as a dowdy social worker and was amused by the Catholic press's description of the birth controllers as 'idle women who visit matinees and sit with cigarette between their painted lips.'[11] A further four committee members from local clinics were married to doctors.[12]

The opening up of higher education to women meant that there was an increasing number of highly educated Executive Committee members: fifteen of the Executive Committee members profiled had gone up to university and obtained degrees. Five women SPBCC members attended Cambridge University and three studied at Oxford University, including Eleanor Rathbone and Constance Masefield.[13] Charis Frankenburg also attended Somerville College, Oxford where she met detective writer Dorothy L. Sayers and the novelist Winifred Holtby. The novelist Vera Brittain recalled Charis Frankenburg being a student with her at Somerville in the period immediately before the First World War and described her as potentially interesting in *Testament of Youth*.[14] Those attending provincial universities included Edith Bethune-Baker who graduated from the University of Birmingham and Edith How-Martyn who attended Aberystwyth University. Ruth Dalton and Mary Stocks attended the London School of Economics and Mary

Stocks was awarded a first class honours degree. Mary contrasted the equality she experienced at the LSE pre-1914 with Oxford where she felt the women were there on sufferance.[15] Women students could attend lectures, sit the examinations but not receive degrees and it was not till 1920 that women became full members of Oxford University.

Apart from Constance Masefield's teaching career and Mary Stocks' lectures in Economic History at Oxford and later for the Workers' Educational Association, none of the Executive Committee members appeared to have developed their academic careers. Lillian Mott of the Liverpool clinic was a gifted mathematician who was urged by her husband to continue her academic career after graduating but refused to take that opportunity.[16] However, it could be argued that women like Eleanor Rathbone drew on their academic training in the pursuit of their research interests.

Women who had obtained medical qualifications, unlike teachers, continued to practice as doctors even after marriage. The consultant Miss Hilda Shufflebotham of Birmingham practiced as a doctor after her marriage to fellow lecturer Professor Lloyd. As my Collective Biography of fifteen SPBCC clinic doctors shows there were growing numbers of female doctors qualified to give birth control advice at SPBCC clinics.

A number of SPBCC committee members, while not being in paid employment, did devote themselves to public service. A year after women over thirty were granted the vote, the Sex Disqualification (Removal Act) was passed in 1919 which allowed women to serve as magistrates. Anne Logan identified a number of former suffragists who became magistrates.[17] The SPBCC Executive Committee members who served as magistrates included: Mary Barbour (Glasgow), Edith Bethune-Baker (Cambridge), Lady Brooks (Birmingham), Elizabeth Cadbury (Birmingham), Charis Frankenburg (Manchester and Salford), Eva Hartree (Cambridge), Helen Pease (Cambridge), Eleanor Rathbone (Liverpool) and Mary Stocks (Manchester and Salford).[18] Mary Stocks was appointed to the Magistrates Bench in 1930 and her daughter remembered how the experience of hearing from women charged with abortion strengthened Mary Stocks' determination to campaign for birth control.[19]

Social movement theorists have also appreciated the value of the collectivist approach and that of webs of friendship. Douglas McAdam, when discussing the motivation of those joining a campaign, also stressed the importance of links to others already involved.[20] Krista Cowman emphasised the intense camaraderie of the WSPU organisers that arose out of the circumstances in which they worked.[21] Thus statements that individual birth control pioneers set up birth control clinics on their own is misleading as it ignores the support of friendship and family networks.

One important example of the friendship web was that which centred on Marie Stopes. She was significant, not just because of her role in founding the SCBCRP, but also because she served as a resource for the SPBCC. After Charis Frankenburg's request to Marie Stopes for a local contact in the Autumn of 1925, it was Marie who put her in touch with Mary Stocks.[22] Mary Stocks carried out a regular correspondence with Marie Stopes during 1926.[23] Marie Stopes travelled extensively. In 1923 she visited Stockport and spoke to an audience of thousands in the Armoury.[24] She addressed medical students in Liverpool in 1925 and as an indirect result the Liverpool Mothers' Welfare Clinic was founded. Marie also gave advice to Fenella Paton about the running of her birth control clinic in Aberdeen and visited her home.[25]

These overlapping friendship networks were a characteristic of women's organisation, in the 1920s and were a valuable resource. Mary Stocks, a leading member of the SPBCC, was also a committee member of NUSEC and a close friend of Eleanor Rathbone, its President. Susan Pedersen, Eleanor Rathbone's biographer, felt she regarded Mary Stocks almost as a daughter so it was appropriate that Stocks wrote Eleanor's first biography.[26] Eleanor Rathbone financially supported the SPBCC clinics in Manchester and Liverpool as well as developing NUSEC's policy on birth control. Both Charis Frankenburg and Mary Stocks were members of the MSWCA and NCW. Charis Frankenburg was an active member of the Conservative Party and knew Mrs Annie Ecclesall, the MSMC's first landlady in Greengate Salford, both from her membership of that party and from their membership of the MSWCA. Charis would also have known Alderman Nellie Beer of the Manchester Mortality Committee from their membership of the local Conservative Party.

Family networks were also important at the start of newly formed SPBCC clinics. In Aberdeen, Fenella Paton involved her mother and half a dozen friends in the setting up of the Women's Welfare Centre.[27] Fenella Paton quickly found it was easier to work with a small circle of friends rather than through the local authority bureaucracy. In Salford, Charis Frankenburg also involved her mother-in-law, Frances Ann Frankenburg, and husband Sydney. However, family ties as well as providing resources could sometimes be inhibiting. Charis Frankenburg's political and social connections enabled her to locate suitable premises for the clinic a few doors away from her husband's family rubber garment factory. Members of Charis' extended family were appalled by the publicity surrounding Charis' actions and the public opprobrium it bought. One cousin made a heartfelt comment in an interview with me; 'They supported what she was doing but my parents just wished she had opened her clinic anywhere but Greengate.'[28]

The evidence of annual reports and biographies confirms the commitment of these upper- and middle-class women to their clinics. The contemporary American researcher Caroline Hadleigh Robinson's research led her to conclude that 'Englishwomen of leisure apparently take their duties much more seriously than women of other nations, and these "honorary" superintendents are quite apt to be at the clinic most of their time, really attending to the details of administration' such as ordering supplies and completing case-cards.'[29] Freda Lightfoot described the time-consuming administration of her fictitious clinic based on the MSMC where case cards were meticulously completed with the patients' details and appointments arranged and checked.[30]

The contribution of middle-class women to the birth control movement is recognised partly because they were avid letter writers and, like Mary Stocks, published autobiographies. In contrast, there are few accounts of the role of working-class women in the SPBCC, either written or oral. This lack of records has contributed to the role of working-class women in the SPBCC having been overlooked. It would, of course, have been difficult for many working-class mothers, lacking domestic help, to take a leading role in SPBCC and other women's organisations. Charis Frankenburg later admitted that she had the resources to devote to the birth control campaign because she had a nurse for the youngest, the elder boy was at boarding school and she had staff to run the house.³¹ However, though a minority, it is clear that working-class women did play a significant, if under-acknowledged, role in the SPBCC.

Many working-class women active in the SPBCC appeared to have been motivated to found SPBCC clinics through their political activism whether ILP, Labour Party or the Communist Party. As will be seen in a later chapter the party political leadership may have had difficulties endorsing the birth control campaign but their grassroots membership enthusiastically made their own decisions. As has been seen in the previous chapter, one of the most committed birth controllers, who organised Marie Stopes' meeting in Stockport, was Elsie Plant who lived seven miles from Manchester. She had been a suffragette and believed, like the SPBCC members profiled in the previous chapter that, 'a person should be a person in her own right.'³² Elsie had married William Plant, a hat block maker, and they were both enthusiastic members of the Labour Church which they organised. They traced Marie Stopes through publicity in the national press and it was under the auspices of the Labour Church that they invited her to speak.³³ In spite of failing to found a clinic in Stockport before the Second World War, Elsie Plant persevered and was later involved in the successful foundation of a Family Planning Clinic.³⁴

Possibly the most powerful working-class activist was Mary Barbour, the founder Chairman of the Women's Welfare and Advisory Clinic in Govan, Glasgow. Her father was a carpet weaver and she became a thread twister and then a carpet printer. In 1895 she married David Barbour, who was an engineer in the shipyards. They settled in Govan. She became a member of Kinning Park Co-operative Guild and the ILP. In 1915 she organised tenants' committees to resist the wartime rental increases and evictions. These successful rent strikes culminated in one of the largest demonstrations in Glasgow, and thousands of women, nicknamed 'Mrs Barbour's Army' by political activist Willie Gallacher, together with shipyard and engineering workers, massed at the sheriff's courts in the town centre.

In 1920 Mary Barbour stood for election to Glasgow Council and was the first Labour woman councillor to be elected. She had a special interest in issues that affected women in their everyday lives such as housing conditions, municipal laundries and children's playgrounds. She regarded socialist and feminist campaigns being interconnected, 'When we obtain even these few ideals, we shall have won the emancipation of working class housewives. Up to now women have been drudges and slaves of a wicked economic system.'[35] She was later appointed the first woman Baillie on Glasgow Corporation. Her interest in contraception stemmed from a birth control campaign with miners in Lanarkshire and in 1925 she was the driving force behind the formation of the Glasgow SPBCC clinic. Barbour maintained her involvement with the clinic even after leaving Glasgow Council.

My Collective Biography shows how working-class women also had a significant input in the SPBCC clinics in Wolverhampton and Newcastle-upon-Tyne. In Wolverhampton Mrs Alice Onions was influenced by her father, a boot repairer and shop owner, who held strong socialist beliefs. He was a prominent member of the ILP hosting, amongst others, Ramsay MacDonald. She was a founder member in 1925 of the Wolverhampton Women's Welfare Clinic.[36] In Newcastle-upon-Tyne two wives of influential miners' leaders, related by marriage, Mrs Lottie Lawther and Mrs Steve Lawther, were instrumental in opening the Newcastle-upon-Tyne Women's Welfare Centre.[37] They were both members of Blaydon District Labour Party.[38] Mrs Steve Lawther lived in a tenement but accommodated visitors such as Dora Russell and Mrs Claire Tamplin who had come to Newcastle to assist in the local birth control campaign.

In Manchester at the MSMC, one of the Receptionists, Mrs Bessie Wild, was a member of the Women's Co-operative Guild and a Communist Party member.[39] She discussed the clinic with fellow Party member Mrs Elsie Booth.[40] Elsie herself used pessaries bought from a chemist in London Road in the centre of Manchester, but when she realised that a neighbour of hers needed birth control advice she took her to the MSMC. 'I took a woman and she had eight bloody kids and she was full of TB.' This was hardly the measured middle-class language of Mary Stocks and Charis Frankenburg as heard in their taped interviews held in the National Sound Archive.

However, even more important than the contribution of individual working-class women, was the active support of the WCG. The WCG had an important role in founding clinics but, as will be discussed later, there was tension, not between middle-class and working-class women, but between WCG grassroots members and their leaders. The backing of the WCG members as well as providing practical support also had symbolic importance as it meant the SPBCC could not be easily dismissed as a purely middle-class organisation. The Guild attracted 'respectable working class' women whose families had grown up, and who had more freedom with time and money.[41] The WCG aided the SPBCC by taking collections, providing voluntary work for the clinic, and generally publicising its work amongst the members. Mary Williams, who attended the MSMC clinic in the 1920s, recalled that there was little publicity about the MSMC but she learned about its work from the WCG and subsequently visited the clinic.[42] The enthusiasm of the WCG for birth control was evident in other SPBCC clinics. Alice Onions of Wolverhampton was a member of the WCG. In Glasgow Mary Barbour gained her political experience through membership of the Kinning Park Co-operative Guild which was the first Guild to be established in Scotland. When the Liverpool Mothers' Clinic was being started the committee members discussed how best to involve the WCG. It was decided to approach two members of the WCG who were already known to the committee.[43]

The WCG played a particularly important role in founding and supporting the MSMC. Mrs Hescott (Secretary of the Manchester branch of the WCG) was a founder member of the MSMC and continued to serve on the Executive Committee when her term of office at the WCG expired.[44] Its Second Annual Report names as committee members Mrs Ball (who had taken over from Mrs Hescott as Secretary of the Manchester branch WCG) and Mrs Norburn (Secretary of the Downing Street branch of the WCG).[45] Downing Street WCG, was of one of the longest established guilds in Manchester and as such was extremely influential. Mrs Ball, Mrs Hescott and Mrs Norburn were still serving on the MSMC Executive Committee from 1928 to 1929. The 1930 photograph published in the *Manchester and Salford Co-operative Herald* of Mrs Norburn with her fellow committee members of the Downing Street WCG showed a group of self-assured, smartly dressed women.[46]

There was a marked gender division amongst the founders of the SPBCC clinics, with eight of the first ten SPBCC clinics being started by women with men playing a supporting role such as providing finance or chauffeuring duties. The East London clinic in Stepney was the exception. This was started on the initiative of Captain Gerald Leigh, Lord Ivor Spencer Churchill and Councillor Lawder, a coalition of Conservative and Labour interests. However, Councillor Mrs Lawder repeatedly wrote to her local paper putting forward the view that overburdened women had a right to control the size of their families and took an active role in the SPBCC.[47] In the Oxford SPBCC clinic, although Dr Collier took the lead in calling a meeting in 1926, he was supported by his wife and the six members of the committee were all female. In Abertillery, the miners' representative David Duggar, tried to found a clinic in his local hospital, but arguably one of the factors in its early failure may have been the lack of involvement of key local women's organisations.[48]

The committees enthusiastically mobilised material resources for the clinics. Mary Stott, an early member of the Townswomen's Guild and a journalist with the *Manchester Guardian*, referred to a myth that women could not work together.[49] Yet the SPBCC women had to be able to co-operate because in effect they were running a small business. Apart from Constance Masefield, none of the women had that work experience but, as has been seen, many had gained experience of organisation from the suffrage movement. The financial survival of the SPBCC clinics was by no means guaranteed as was illustrated by the forced closure for financial reasons of the Cannock Chase clinic for miners' wives.[50]

Though the majority of committee members were women they welcomed male assistance in practical matters as financial security was a priority. According to Charis Frankenburg's autobiography, her husband Sydney made generous donations to the MSMC.[51] However, in 1926 the largest single donation to the MSMC of £120.00 came from a Mr S.A. Boulton.[52] Within four months of its inaugural meeting the MSMC's Executive Committee had raised £193.00 and at the end of the first financial year donations and subscriptions had totalled £534.12.6d.[53] This meant, amongst other things, wages and rent could be paid, supplies could be ordered, and if necessary medical treatment be provided free of charge. Significantly, a single male benefactor played a critical role in establishing two clinics. Sir John Sumner generously supported both South Kensington and Birmingham clinics. The *1927–1928 Annual Report of the Birmingham Women's Welfare Centre* stated that the Centre received regular donations from the Women's Co-operative Guilds in the surrounding area.[54] Though their average donations were five shillings as compared to Sir John Sumner's £90.00, this still showed widespread commitment by the guilds at a period when their funds were stretched.[55]

The committee of the MSMC did all in its power to keep charges to a minimum while allowing women to retain their self-respect. 'There is no fee for any visit except the first when a fee of 1/- is charged and appliances advised by the doctor are supplied at cost price – in cases of destitution all charges are remitted.'[56] Emily Glencross reported that as her husband was unemployed, she was given appliances free at the MSMC.[57]

The women recognised the importance of locality for their patients. The clinic had to be in a familiar location with which working-class mothers would feel at ease. Evelyn Fuller advised that clinics should be on a ground floor, located in a heavily populated area and with good transport. The Liverpool Mothers' Welfare Clinic placed an advertisement for premises in the local paper, 'Wanted: small flat or unfurnished rooms for Birth Control Centre: preferably ground floor. Convenient for trams; central.'[58] The committee's confidential minutes showed that they were looking for premises 'near slums but not in them'.[59] The Walworth Road clinic occupied shop premises on a corner site as did North Kensington.[60] The annual reports showed that the Oxford clinic was located in the working-class area of Jericho. In Aberdeen the clinic was situated in the stone terraces of Gerrard Street in the centre of the town, and in Glasgow the Women's Welfare and Advisory Committee had acquired three rooms in a shop situated in Govan Old Road.[61] Muriel Bradshaw, a Birmingham clinic doctor, made the point that the first clinics there were often held in rooms in privately rented houses and that her clinic was initially situated in a private house in Castle Street which was a narrow lane off High Street.[62]

The arrangements in the early clinics were so informal that the division between patients and volunteers was blurred. In Wolverhampton the clinic was situated in a railwayman's house and Alice Onions sterilised equipment over an open fire.[63] Shop premises were a popular choice of venue and were utilised in Salford, Glasgow, Newcastle-upon-Tyne and Walworth Road, London. SPBCC members had to persuade reluctant landlords to allow them to rent rooms for a controversial purpose. As has already been noted in this chapter, the MSMC's premises were obtained through Charis Frankenburg's contact with the sympathetic pie shop owner who was a member of the same women's organisation. Mary Stocks praised the suitability of accommodation for the MSMC clinic. 'Our premises were in one respect fortunately situated; for they were on an upper floor approached through a shop which sold meat pies. This meant that shy clients were not readily identifiable from the street as visitors to the clinic – they might equally be regarded as pie purchasers.'[64]

Semi-hidden entrances, as in the narrow lane in Birmingham, were an important factor for clients facing religious opposition and condemnation from relatives or friends. It was therefore the middle-class committee members who had to cross into unfamiliar territories which could be frightening. Dr Olive Gimson, the doctor at the MSMC, prudently employed her dogs to guard the car in Salford. Dilys Dean paid tribute to the academic wives who made the difficult journey on their bicycles in all weathers to the unfamiliar territory of the MSMC clinic.[65]

Marie Stopes' clinic on Holloway Road was also in a converted shop.[66] The internal space was female centred. Marie argued that the interior of clinics should be as a sanctuary to place mothers at their ease. She took care with the decoration of the clinic's rooms, with cherubic prints, dark oak furniture and potted plants. The decor reflected the taste of a middle-class home and a sympathetic journalist described the clinic's interior in positively lyrical terms, 'On the old Jacobean table a huge jar of pink and white roses with up-climbing branches of tender green.'[67] The members of the MSMC were less elaborate in their decor but arranged for the rooms to be decorated prior to the opening. The Executive Committee explained that 'when the patient comes, she goes into a waiting room which is as cheerful as we can make it, where we have toys for the small children and facilities for the mother to wash her hands.'[68] A cartoon which accompanied Mary Stock's article portrayed the enthusiasm of the early birth control pioneers as they prepared their clinics for patients.[69]

Having mobilised human resources in setting up the clinics, it was important to win the trust of their client group, working-class mothers. Thus a central issue is how far birth control decisions were gendered and what effect this had on attendance at the clinics. One of Kate Fisher's major research concerns was with birth control practices in the 1920s and 1930s and how the size of families was negotiated by the husband and wife.[70] She believed that, because birth campaigners between the wars had concentrated on the role of women, the role of men had been ignored. Kate Fisher wished to correct this view and present a more complex picture. Indeed she argued that male networks concerning birth control information were more extensive than that of their wives. She concluded that in the first half of the twentieth century 'it was primarily husbands, not wives who took responsibilities for birth control strategies.'[71] Kate Fisher argued that women were reluctant to take an active role in birth control strategy as they did not want to be regarded as sexual beings. They preferred to be regarded as ignorant and chaste. They also disliked, according to Kate Fisher's research, using female appliance methods. She found that men's contraceptive knowledge was seen by both sexes as being more extensive than their wives who were content not to be seen to have sexual knowledge.[72]

Kate Fisher's conclusions concerning the role of husbands are different from those of this study, which sees mothers taking the initiative in birth control matters. Although her samples were larger than this research, contacts were obtained from local authority day centres rather than by self-referral. Crucially she interviewed husband and wife together, and found little knowledge of the SPBCC clinics. Though there was a SPBCC clinic in Oxford, given the members in her sample, it was unlikely that any of her interviewees would have attended it. In contrast the interviews for this study were with women, who all had had experience of using birth control in the inter-war years, and who were interviewed on their own.[73] Certainly two women interviewed for this research preferred their husbands to take the initiative in contraception, but they were the exceptions.

This research shows that women did not have access to the kind of male work-place networks as identified by Kate Fisher, but they did have access to other networks. Lella Secor Florence was an exception when she wrote of her Cambridge clinic that medical referrals were more important to them than discussions with neighbours: 'It has not been my experience, as it seems to have been at other clinics, that women discuss birth control with their neighbours and send them to the Clinic after they have been themselves.'[74] Working-class mothers had access to female friends and family networks. 'The elder woman brings her daughter "so she shall be spared what I had to go through."'[75] This was the case when Evelyn Glencross' mother insisted on arranging birth control provision for her daughter and daughters-in-law at the MSMC and similarly Mrs M's friend took her daughter to the Walworth Road clinic. This use of female networks accords with the findings of Melanie Tebbutt who highlighted the function of gossip in the transmission of information and the importance of the role of the older woman.[76]

It was the women in this study who took the initiative to visit their SPBCC clinics. They went on their own, though husbands were supportive and in Mrs M's case her husband even minded the children. The space inside the clinics was cramped, so there was often physically no room for husbands. The Liverpool clinic asked wives whether their husbands had been told of their visit but, knowing the required answer, they unsurprisingly replied that their husbands knew and approved. Dr Phoebe Bigland reported that there were only a few cases when the husband had not been informed and this was because he was violent or an alcoholic.[77] In Liverpool husbands gave their wives money for contraception when they could afford it and encouraged their attendance at the SPBCC.[78] Certainly male methods of birth control such as withdrawal (cheap) or the use of the sheath (easy to use) still remained common.

The SPBCC recognised the importance of face-to-face communication. Mrs Claire Tamplin, from the North Kensington Mothers' Clinic was released from her role as administrator to be 'an outside organiser' and make contact with local working-class mothers. She later travelled to Newcastle-upon-Tyne to help found a birth control clinic there.[79] The SPBCC organised a range of meetings to attract different audiences. Open-air meetings took place in London which attracted interested passers-by, but made their speakers easy targets. The Hon. Mrs Gilbert Murray of the Walworth clinic regularly addressed open-air meetings at which rotten apples were thrown at her, but she did succeed in attracting at least one working-class woman, a mother of fourteen children.[80] Ella Gordon spoke in local schools to publicise the Wolverhampton Mothers' Clinic and this is where she recruited Alice Onions.[81] There were public meetings in town halls such as at Salford which was reported in the *Manchester Guardian* and aimed at attracting middle-class supporters.[82] As has already been discussed in Chapter Two, the Executive Committees spoke to sympathetic women's groups such as WCG and WCA about their work.

The SPBCC members, while recognising the importance of word of mouth in reaching working-class mothers, also tried a variety of other forms of communication. Local papers were an obvious source of contact. As has already been noted, the *East London Advertiser* carried a series of letters concerning the newly opened clinic.[83] Mary Stocks remembered writing carefully phrased letters to local papers and arranged for journalists from the *Manchester Guardian* to cover events such as the public meeting in Salford Town Hall.[84] Lady Balfour had an article published in the *Kensington News*.[85] The Oxford Mothers' Clinic placed what they considered, to be a discreet advertisement on the front page of the *Oxford Times* but this was withdrawn by the paper after only a few weeks and then only reluctantly reinstated.[86] In contrast, the sympathetic Women's Editor of the *Eccles and Patricroft Journal* praised the establishment of the MSMC describing the organisers as a 'dedicated group of women'.[87]

The SPBCC had their leaflets printed and distributed them to houses in streets immediately adjacent to the clinics. Sister Beatrice Sandys, in her interview with me, recalled collecting some spare leaflets and passing them on to her mothers.[88] Enterprisingly, the North Kensington Mother's Clinic not only had leaflets printed but negotiated to have posters placed in London Underground stations.[89]

The SPBCC wanted to replace fatalistic attitudes over family size with their modern belief that women could take positive steps to regulate their fertility. Novelist Naomi Mitchison regarded this as a dilemma for middle-class women as well as those from the working class.[90] The North Kensington clinic identified the confusion of mothers who 'still rely on muddling through in the belief she may not get pregnant or attempt an abortion when pregnancy is an established fact'.[91] Attitudes changed slowly, as is illustrated by a Mass Observation Survey of a thousand London mothers aged twenty to forty-five which was carried out in 1945. This contained the following coding for responses to a question on birth control methods: 'decide in advance; work it out as you go along; leave it to chance; depends.'[92] The last two choices, admittedly made in chaotic wartime London, proved surprisingly popular. Therefore it was not true, as J. Ferch optimistically claimed in 1932, 'that the demand for knowledge comes from the women themselves, who having a certain degree of freedom…are no longer willing to take it for granted that they are here merely to breed children.'[93] Indeed Kate Fisher rightly pointed out that the new female methods were often distrusted.[94] None of the SPBCC clinics such as North Kensington, Manchester and Salford Mothers' Clinic or Newcastle-upon-Tyne reported a rush of women to the initial sessions and all of them had to break down the initial resistance of women who had to be persuaded to abandon methods that had been used for generations.

The SPBCC opposed abstinence as a means of birth control even though it was advocated by many of the churches and some of the medical profession. It was practiced by many working-class couples but although it was cheap it was not regarded as efficient and not in the sole control of the wives. Dr Letitia Fairfield, a former suffragette, who was at first sympathetic to the birth control cause believed that abstinence led to 'a mutilated, tortured life'.[95] The dangers of abstinence were framed by the SPBCC on health grounds as well as impracticality. A typical case was presented by the Cambridge Women's Welfare Association, 'He had become quick tempered and unreasonable; the wife was depressed and miserable, and had doubts whether she would be able to live with her husband.'[96]

The American eugenicist Norman Himes in a contemporary study of clients attending the SPBCC clinics found that coitus interruptus was their most popular method of birth control, followed by the sheath and abortion.[97] Fisher's research, covering this period, also found that the most widespread male method of birth control was coitus interruptus. However, this thesis questions Fisher's bold assertion that wives maintained a conscious ignorance of contraceptive practices and preferred to let husbands take responsibility for birth control. 'Many women left it to their husbands to decide the details of contraceptive acts and avoided discussion of the issue.'[98]

This study emphasises the proactive role of wives, and coitus interruptus could often be seen as a joint decision. Certainly some women were aware of female appliance methods but still preferred coitus interruptus because it was cheap and did not require elaborate preparations. Mrs Elsie Plant, who became a friend of Marie Stopes after organising her birth control talk in Stockport in 1923, confessed in her interview that she had never tried Marie's rubber check pessary as it was clumsy and inhibiting. Instead her husband carried on successfully practicing coitus interruptus. 'I should have been hauled over the coals if Marie had known!'[99] Lella Secor Florence expressed the view of the SPBCC when she condemned coitus interruptus as being unreliable and regretted that couples retained this method in spite of unwanted pregnancies.[100]

The SPBCC also criticised the use of male appliance methods. The popular belief was that condoms were sabotaged, but the SPBCC more accurately believed they were unreliable because the cheaper condoms were made out of poor materials.[101] However, a more fundamental objection by the SPBCC was that this method, although cheap and comparatively easy to use, again left fertility in control of the man. Condoms were disliked by men for being uncomfortable and by women as they had connotations of prostitution. Aunt Polly, then aged seventy-nine, described the attitudes in Glossop of the 1930s to me: 'Well, there was this man who came selling Durex to the men in the pub on Fridays. But we wouldn't like our husbands to use anything like that.'[102] Aunt Polly left school at eleven, worked as a weaver, was twice married and had ten children. However, for many couples condoms were rejected not because of aesthetic considerations but for reasons of cost. For instance, when Mrs Florence Travis's husband was in work as a docker they bought pessaries and condoms, but when he was out of work she could not afford them and turned to abortifacients.[103]

Newcastle Women's Welfare Clinic, in promoting their birth control measures in 1931, reported that 'many of local women are at the mercy of quack remedies, always unreliable, often harmful'.[104] Indeed abortion was regarded as a legitimate birth control strategy by many working-class mothers. Recent studies by Barbara Brookes and Emma Jones identified the different inter-subjective definitions of abortion by working-class mothers, the birth controllers and the medical profession.[105] These differences were recognised by both Marie Stopes and the SPBCC clinic workers:

> Various interesting conclusions have emerged from this year's work. The popular confusion between abortion and contraception has been demonstrated by the number of pregnant women who visited the Clinic in such cases in the belief that they can obtain there the relief which they are accustomed to regard as the orthodox means of family limitation.[106]

Charis Frankenburg, the former midwife, was aware of local methods used to bring on a period, such as jumping repeatedly from the eighth step of stairs. Mary Stocks' daughter, Hon. Ann Patterson, described how her mother was aware of the misery of abortion, especially after she became a magistrate.[107] This was also the experience at Walworth Road where their clients, according to N.E. and V. Himes, often confused birth control with abortion.[108] Both Marie Stopes and the SPBCC clinics were approached by women wanting abortions who appeared to have blurred the distinction between contraception and abortion. They believed that abortion was not illegal if it was carried out in the early months of pregnancy 'prior to quickening' and before the mother began to feel foetal movements at sixteen weeks.[109] Similarly it was generally believed that self-administered abortion was permissible but not paid abortion. Aunt Polly, who had dismissed condoms as not respectable, freely described the methods used in her neighbourhood in the inter-war years for terminating a pregnancy: 'Women used to try all sorts of things to bring on a period. They would jump off slop stones in the kitchen or jump down stairs or else they would dose themselves with Sennapods. Some would swear by Nurse Brightmore's tablets at 25/-. Sometimes nothing worked....'[110]

The workers in the Walworth Women's Welfare Centre reported widespread use of drugs to bring on a period 'usually with injury to themselves as individuals and as mothers'. Many went to the chemist and obtained a medicine which resulted in them having a perpetual period.[111] They did not regard these as abortions as the shared understanding was that abortions were only carried out by professional abortionists who extorted money.

In one sense abortion, though dangerous, could be seen as a feminist strategy as it gave women control. Barbara Brookes explained the continuing popularity of abortion by arguing that women felt it gave them more self-determination than relying on their husband's skill with coitus interruptus.[112] The mother was thus able to take decisions about family size and the spacing of children. Barbara Brookes argued that working-class women possessed a common culture, and solutions to problems were shared in a neighbourhood network of support.[113] Patricia Knight also regarded abortion as having a central place in female subculture, seeing men as being excluded when women turned to female friends and relatives.[114] However, later studies showed men often played a supportive role in obtaining abortions.[115]

The SPBCC could have framed their arguments in terms of the illegality of abortion practices but instead concentrated, like the British Medical Association, on the health implications. Charis Frankenburg of the MSMC was convinced that sepsis from back-street abortions was one reason that government statistics showed that the rate of maternal mortality remained static in the inter-war years instead of falling like the levels of infant mortality. Birth control pioneer Elsie Plant was also aware of the widespread use of abortion in Stockport: 'People lost their lives. It was a terrible cruel world for women.'[116] However, the rate of maternal death from abortions was not high given that the number of abortions per year was estimated by the British Medical Association as being between 110,000 to 150,000 with half of these being illegal.[117] Taken in this context, the number of maternal deaths from illegal abortions which were mostly caused by sepsis, were proportionately small. Women must have calculated that it was a risk to health worth taking.

The SPBCC clinics framed their methods as being modern and scientific. The importance of their scientific approach was eloquently expressed by the Birmingham Women's Welfare Centre:

> We would stress the fact that instead of persons experimenting in the dark on their own account, or relying on ignorant gossip (abortion not being the least frequent result of such lack of proper information), the Clinic can put the sum of human knowledge on the subject into the woman's hands in a straightforward manner, under medical supervision, and at low cost.[118]

The clinics emphasised to working-class mothers the advantages to their health of rejecting debilitating birth control remedies. The female staff at the SPBCC clinics promoted female-centred birth control methods. However, there were contradictions in this insistence on this approach. The method most generally advised by the SPBCC clinics was the spring-rimmed vaginal diaphragm, in conjunction with spermicidal jelly and douching. Ironically the women who attended the SPBCC clinic often had experienced several difficult pregnancies resulting in tears to the cervix and so arguably this was the least suitable method for them. Yet Dr Gimson at the MSMC recommended the dutch cap for female contraception twice as many times as Dr Bigland at the Liverpool Mothers' Clinic.[119] It was likely that the MSMC doctor decided that just as women would not be in control during coitus interruptus, neither would they be in control if they had to rely on the husband's use of condoms. One mother quoted by the Birmingham clinic said, 'My husband is a good chap really but he's often drunk and I wouldn't trust him to see we didn't have any more babies.'[120] Not every SPBCC member agreed with the practices of clinics such as the MSMC. Lella Secor Florence who worked at the Cambridge clinic felt their methods were impractical for women in overcrowded housing, being time consuming, fiddly and requiring privacy.[121] Edith How-Martyn convincingly argued that from the point of view of the patient, a less reliable method which she could readily use was better than a more reliable which she could only use with difficulty.[122] At her clinic in Walworth Road, women were offered the option of the sheath with a spermicidal jelly and she believed, because of the difficulties experienced by the women, that this combination was the most reliable method.

The SPBCC clinics, as well as attracting their target client group of working-class mothers, also endeavoured to obtain the sympathetic support of both governmental and voluntary agencies. Therefore it was important to understand how the statistics and case studies were framed by the SPBCC. The American researcher Caroline Hadleigh Robinson obtained data from seventy American and European birth control clinics in a survey and analysed occupation, family size and maternal health. Although she acknowledged that the clinics were used by a cross section of the population, it was their use by working-class women which was deemed important from her eugenic perspective.[123] Caroline Robinson's data in Table 1 shows that by far the busiest SPBCC was the 'flagship clinic' of Walworth Road which had on average 127 new applicants a month. In the first eight years of existence 20,929 patients had been seen.

Clinic	Founded	New Patients per Year	Cumulative Total
Walworth Road	1921	3881	20929
North Kensington	1924	372	1813
Wolverhampton	1925	193	1187
East London	1926	468	1549
Cambridge	1925	138	627
Manchester & Salford	1926	261	1173
Glasgow	1926	187	706
Oxford	1926	38	158
Birmingham	1927	607	1379
Aberdeen	1926	142	365
Liverpool	1926	101	234

Table 1: Applicants at SPBCC clinics, 1921–9, Robinson (1930), p.11.

One of the most influential investigators was the American Norman Himes. He was quite open about the intention of his research: 'I propose to show by a study of the occupational distribution of the husbands of patients attending the clinic, and by a survey of wage incomes, that the clinics are reaching to a modest degree, the wives of the unskilled and semi-skilled workers.'[124] He and his wife Vera visited all the SPBCC clinics in 1928 and their visits were reported in the minutes of clinics such as Liverpool and Manchester.[125] In addition Vera Himes carried out home visits on behalf of the Walworth Road clinic. As Norman Himes was a eugenicist, *Eugenics Review* was a fitting publication for his findings. However, Norman Himes argued that the spread of ideas was far greater than represented by the numbers attending SPBCC clinics. He believed that 'it seems clear that the English clinics, all of which have been founded since 1921, have been influential in disseminating contraceptive advice to the lower classes.'[126] Nevertheless, just as Kate

Fisher may have underestimated the spread of birth control advice, so Norman Himes may have been over optimistic in his assessment of the dissemination of birth control knowledge.

Contemporary opponents of birth control argued that the working-class mothers would not persist in methods which required prolonged commitment. Therefore it was important for the SPBCC to prove their methods could be successfully utilised by working-class mothers. Mary Stocks believed that the SPBCC was reaching their target group and were encouraging patients to form an ongoing relationship with the clinic, 'We are convinced that the great mass of the women we are helping are overworked married mothers.'[127] Norman Himes' statistics showed that the wives of unskilled workers were represented at the nine SPBCC clinics in a greater proportion than in the general population (34% compared to 13%), and so concluded that these clinics were successfully reaching the working classes. Table 2 shows the regional variations in occupations, with the dockers' wives attending the Liverpool clinic while in the Glasgow clinic there were miners' wives. Ninety per cent of the SPBCC's patients were working-class mothers, with around 40–50 per cent being the wives of unskilled or semi-skilled workers. The SPBCC records show that in North Kensington the wives of street hawkers, window-washers and car-cleaners attended, as well as transport workers from the nearby bus depot.

Location	Skilled	Unskilled	Semi-skilled
North Kensington	37.9	32.8*	
Manchester	32.6	11.1	31.0
Wolverhampton	12.6	5.6	77.9
Cambridge	32.0	17.0	25.2
Liverpool	46.8	16.2	19.6
Birmingham	24.2	13.9	40.0
Glasgow	34.6	18.0	24.6
Aberdeen	38.5	7.3	20.2

Table 2: **Summary of occupational status of husbands at birth control clinics** – data collected in 1927. N.E. Himes, 'British birth control clinics' (1931) *A Guide to Birth Control Literature*. *Unskilled and semi-skilled occupations were combined for North Kensington.

Although the majority of clients at the SPBCC clinic were working-class mothers, Norman Himes had found there was also a significant attendance from the business and professional classes.[128] Attendance at the clinics predictably reflected the social composition of the locality: Cambridge clients included the wives of university professors, a dentist's wife and the wife of a Primitive Methodist minister; Liverpool's clients included the wife of a master mariner and the wife of a manager of an ironmonger; North Kensington included the wives of officers from the armed services and MSMC had the wife of a teacher. However, the attendance of the middle-class mothers at the clinics is completely omitted in the annual reports of the SPBCC clinics and their presence ignored. Presumably this would detract from the clinic's emphasis on successfully attracting working-class mothers.

The occupational class distribution presented by the clinics and used by Caroline Robinson and Norman Himes is not completely accurate as there were practical difficulties in classifying occupations by researchers who were unfamiliar with manual work practices. Often the wives were not able to describe their husband's occupation and were not informed of the amount of his earnings.[129] Unfortunately it was rare for any systematic details to be given about the occupation of the wife before her marriage or any work on marriage even though at the time of the Depression her wages might be crucial to the household's economy. An exception to this was Dr V. Russell's, *Evidence to the Inter-Departmental Committee on Abortion* which included detailed data on her female Manchester patients.[130] Occasionally the clinic did record the wife's occupation in their case studies but this was never carried out as a routine. 'Mrs H. Aged 44. thirteen children, twelve living. Before marriage she had worked in a brickyard, carrying bricks.'[131] These details were provided as an explanation for the woman's continuing good health in spite of her high number of pregnancies.

The SPBCC countered claims of immorality by framing their reports to show that the women who attended the clinic did so out of a sense of responsibility to limit or space their families and were not prostitutes as critics claimed. Norman Himes showed in his Table 3 that the typical mother who attended the clinics was already in her thirties and her husband was two years older. The majority of the mothers had been married for over eight years and wanted birth control advice because they did not wish put the strain of unplanned pregnancies on their marriages.

Location of Clinic	Years Married	Ages	
	Arithmetic Mean	Wife Mean	Husband Mean
North Kensington	8.7	31.3	33.9
Manchester	8.8	31.0	33.5
Wolverhampton	8.2	30.8	no data
Cambridge	9.7	32.2	34.9
Liverpool	9.8	31.8	34.8
Glasgow	9.5	31.3	34.6
Aberdeen	10.0	31.1	33.4

Table 3: Extract from social data on 3,296 cases on British birth control clinics. N.E. Himes. 'British birth control clinics', *Eugenics Review* (1928, p.159).

The opponents of birth control had claimed that family limitation was a sign of degeneration because women were trying to avoid the inconvenience of child bearing. The researchers showed that most of the women who were coming to the clinic for birth control advice already had large families. Norman Himes showed, in Table 4, that mothers wished to limit their families after two children. However, there were mothers who had ten, eleven, twelve, thirteen, fourteen pregnancies. As family size increased there were a high proportion of miscarriages and still births. Thus the eighteen women who had eleven pregnancies had one hundred and thirty living children but seventy-two unsuccessful pregnancies. It was these statistics that especially concerned the birth controllers, as frequent childbearing could lead to high levels of maternal mortality.

Although Dame Janet Campbell in her studies of maternal mortality had identified eight pregnancies as being the danger number in maternal mortality, the research from the North Kensington SPBCC clinic showed that the damage to a mothers' health could occur much earlier depending on poverty and overcrowding.

Number of Pregnancies	Women	Pregnancies	Living Children	Losses
None	43	0	0	0
One	151	151	147	10
Two	187	374	337	41
Three	173	519	436	85
Four	130	520	398	128
Five	91	455	360	100
Six	72	432	334	100
Seven	36	252	171	83
Eight	31	248	196	53
Nine	29	261	188	75
Ten	18	180	129	52
Eleven	18	198	130	72
Twelve	11	132	79	54
Thirteen	7	91	64	27
Fourteen	3	42	36	6

Table 4: Analysis of results according to number of pregnancies reported in the first 1,000 cases of North Kensington clinics. Total pregnancies, living children and losses. N.E. and V. Himes, *Hospital Social Service* (1929) p.591.

Officially the SPBCC policy was not to give contraceptive advice to childless couples. Dr Phoebe Bigland of Liverpool would not give contraceptive advice to a mother unless she had at least three children, even though the policy of the Executive Committee was to provide birth control advice to all married women who requested it.[132] Dr Olive Gimson, of the MSMC took a more liberal attitude and recognised the value of the clinic's services during the long industrial depression. Evelyn Glencross' husband, a labourer, was out of work and so she explained to Dr Gimson that they then did not feel they could financially support a family. 'The doctor was more than satisfied and said there would be no charge for the articles.'[133]

The SPBCC researchers were also framing cases and statistics to argue against the government's view that it was theoretically possible to separate out health reasons for seeking out birth control advice (deemed just acceptable) from economic reasons (considered selfish and unacceptable). This was why the SPBCC clinics included selected case studies at the end of their annual reports showing the link between economic circumstances and medical conditions. Even amongst those whose husbands were in employment, their incomes were not high. The MSMC surmised that, 'A great majority are the wives of men earning £2.00 and £3.00 a week. Some are the wives of unemployed or invalided men.'[134] In their next report they reiterated the case for economic motives as 'though the cases of urgent medical necessity are frequent, an increasing number of women are actuated by a prudential motive.'[135] The MSMC Committee argued that with the onset of the Depression there was an increase in male unemployment and the level of benefit was not adequate to support a large family. One consequence was the wife often had to have a part-time job, such as taking in washing, in order to keep the family, which added to her exhaustion, and in addition they felt that the housing conditions for poor families were often cramped and sub-standard. 'Members of the Committee firmly believed that mothers were being responsible by attending the MSMC. A profound sense of parental responsibility for the well-being of their existing children actuates their desire to incur no further pregnancies because of inadequate housing or wages.'[136]

The eugenicist Caroline Robinson's analysis of data relating to clinic attendance also led her to find that 'economic reasons predominate, with health next, and spacing of children comes third but infrequently.'[137] Having listened to the mothers' histories as they presented themselves at the clinic, the MSMC opposed the government's policy, which stated that working-class mothers should only be eligible for birth control advice on health grounds. They felt this was unrealistic as in practice it was impossible to separate health needs from economic requirements. Economic hardship was shown to lead to the mothers' ill health, both physical and mental. Lella Secor Florence referred to the misery, the suffering, the bitterness of unwilling women coerced into producing unwanted children.[138]

Below is a selection of cases drawn from the annual reports of three SPBCC clinics throughout the country in the 1920s which were carefully framed to show that it was difficult to separate health reasons from economic motivation for birth control. The quotations are extensive to give a flavour of the reports. The frankness of mothers is revealing:

Birmingham Women's Welfare Association, Mrs G. aged 35, has had 6 children, the last being twins. She then had 2 deliberate miscarriages in succession, and feeling very ill, came to us for advice. She returned in 7 months time to say she was very pleased with the advice received and that it was proving satisfactory. She gets 45s a week from her husband.[139]

Birmingham Women's Welfare Association, Mrs N. Seven living children, lost twins at 8 months, and had several miscarriages – one deliberately. Her own doctor forbade more children, but would give no advice when asked beyond: 'Keep your eyes open; there are plenty of ways.' She was on the verge of getting a separation, and was going back to her mother. She returned after one year, saying that she had had the happiest year of her life. She did not hate her husband now that the fear of pregnancy was removed.[140]

Cambridge Women's Welfare Association, Mrs X. 'I have five children. I have had two miscarriages and a baby that died. My little girl has St Vitus Dance, There is always a baby in the house. I am sure I do not want any more. There is always a doctor here.'[141]

North Kensington Women's Welfare Association, Mrs E. aged 29. Pregnancies 7; all are living, the eldest is nearly 10. Husband, a bus conductor gives the wife nearly £3.00 per week. She came after six months saying how pleased she was. She and her husband had said they could now *enjoy* the children.[142]

The examples chosen by the Executive Committee were framed to elicit sympathy and show how women were undeserving victims of circumstances. For instance Glencross' case card could hypothetically have read, 'Mrs-, aged 24, healthy, no children, husband out of work', but this would not have conveyed the required message. Instead the case histories show that some of the mothers had up to thirteen pregnancies and were so desperate that they admitted trying abortion. It was reported that their husbands were often sick with TB or syphilis and children often died at birth or infancy.[143] The SPBCC clinic framed these case studies as an endorsement of their methods.

How far there was a shared understanding between those that ran the clinics and the mothers who attended them is not clear. Certainly there have been many examples of middle-class women feeling they could improve the lives of working-class women while not appreciating the constraints of low income and sub-standard housing. These philanthropic enterprises included lady sanitary inspectors who visited working-class women in their homes and provided advice.[144] Anne Logan summed up the dilemma of one twentieth-century Poor Law worker as 'Lady Bountiful or Community activist?' Certainly middle-class 'do gooders' with little in common with working-class women were resented by them as judgemental and patronising.[145] Kate Fisher in her study of inter-war birth control clinics in Oxford and Wales argued that clinics frequently failed to appreciate the disjunction in attitudes between the women who ran the clinics and the situation of the working-class mothers who came for help. 'They struggled to convince many potential patients to accept their particular principles but did not attempt to tailor their clinics to make them more attractive to the working-class communities they targeted.'[146] Similarly Caroline Walker pointed out the tensions that arose in some of the Marie Stopes' clinics between the nursing staff and their working-class patients. She believed that this could be attributed to frustration on the part of the professionals who believed unswervingly in the efficacy of their clinic's birth control appliances.[147]

Working-class women were often frightened of hospitals but, as Dr Helena Wright of the North Kensington SPBCC clinic explained, 'They came to us because we were all women. Women doctors, women nurses, women running the clinic.'[148] Sceptics claimed that working-class mothers would have difficulty in committing to the discipline of regular appointments and elaborate contraceptive regimes. However, many women did become loyal clients at their local clinic.[149] There was usually a high degree of empathy between privileged middle-class clinic workers and overworked working-class mothers on low incomes and with little outside support. Admittedly this was not always the case. The following account by Flora Blumberg of her follow-up visits on behalf of the MSMC stands out precisely because her value judgements were exceptional:

> Just as surely as we knocked on a door and saw a half-tin of Nestles milk on the table, together with a half-eaten loaf, and butter or margarine in its original paper, and several layers of dirty dishes, just as surely would the patient produce her pessary from a drawer in the sideboard, and explain how she had failed. So a spotless doorstep would be found a success – a clean painstaking woman who had taken the trouble to follow carefully the instructions given her and had succeeded in her object.[150]

Flora Blumberg was so convinced that the SPBCC's methods could not have failed that she placed the onus for failure on the mothers' shortcomings. Even she conceded the difficulties for working-class mothers and later in the same report explained that, 'We realised the methods might be difficult to teach to uneducated women and difficult to practice under cramped conditions.'[151]

Clients at the SPBCC clinics were able to relax in a way that was not possible in other health care situations. Perceptively Mr Chapple, Senior Gynaecologist at Guy's Hospital, stated that often women did not consider themselves sufficiently ill to go to a general hospital because they knew there would be a long wait, no real privacy and a difficulty in continuity of treatment.[152] Lara Marks recounted in her study of East London that at the London Hospital women had to wait hours to be seen and then their appointment time averaged only thirty seconds. It was the aim of the SPBCC to give their mothers the attention that private patients were accorded over their birth control needs.[153]

Kate Fisher stressed that the voluntary clinics were concerned with far wider issues than birth control and pointed out their work in identifying other gynaecological conditions and cancers.[154] The SPBCC adopted a holistic approach and addressed mental as well as physical concerns. Members of the SPBCC such as Frankenburg recognised the importance of allowing the mothers time for themselves which in many cases must have been a rare luxury. Marie Stopes in her book, *Contraception* wrote that explaining the mechanics of contraception was not enough as the mothers 'needed deep personal understanding and help'.[155] Similarly Charis Frankenburg described the situation at their clinic in Salford. 'Our mothers feel they have been talked to by somebody who understands their problems. We do not hurry them. They talk a long time, and it generally takes a long time to diagnose the particulars.'[156] Charis described how mothers came in to the MSMC in floods of tears to which the volunteer's response was, 'Tell me about it.'[157] Lella Florence wrote of her Cambridge clinic, 'Every woman was encouraged to talk about herself and her experiences as long as she felt inclined.'[158] Again, in North Kensington it was emphasised that the clinic's policy was to allow the mother 'as much time and skill and patience as if they were private patients'.[159] Liverpool Mothers' Clinic began to give out cups of tea on Wednesday afternoons as the Committee realised this 'gave great comfort' and allowed an opportunity for informal conversations.[160]

A common theme of the clinics' accounts was how apprehensive women were, particularly on their first visit. When Marie Stopes opened her first birth control clinic in 1921 none of the women queuing outside would enter until she instructed the Receptionist to go out and lead each one by the hand inside the clinic.[161] The North Kensington SPBCC clinic reported that initially very few mothers attended the clinic as they were shy and nervous.[162] Evelyn Fuller of Walworth Road SPBCC emphasised that as many of the women were shy at their first visit, there must be an atmosphere of privacy and friendliness.[163] Mary Stocks later explained at the NCW's Conference in 1929 that 'no one realised how shy, ignorant and desperate the average married woman without means could be.'[164] Not only did the policy of being sympathetic enable the mother to relax, it meant that the contraceptive cap could be fitted more accurately, and the doctor could detect any other underlying illnesses.

Class differences appeared to be lessened inside the clinics. The most striking example of this is the case of Mary Williams who attended the MSMC. Mary Williams recognised Charis Frankenburg from her days working at Charis' husband's family factory in Greengate, Salford where she did hand sewing and buttonholing on rubberised garments. Although Mary was only a young girl and this was her first job, she joined a union and went on strike because of bad wages and poor conditions. The local rumour was that Charis was only involved with birth control because her husband was a rubber manufacturer. In spite of this Mary admired Charis. Mary repeatedly praised Charis when interviewed by Manchester Studies, describing her as being 'an exceptionally good woman'.[165] She remembered Charis and Mary Stocks 'pottering about with the jellies'. Neither of these two energetic women could be described as 'potterers' but sorting out stores would have provided an ideal opportunity to talk with their patients. As Charis' daughter, Ursula Kennedy, commented in her interview with me, 'Mother would talk to anyone.'[166]

There were other examples of the clients relating well to staff at the clinics. Evelyn Glencross admired the women helpers at the MSMC, and the wife of a waterside labourer, paid tribute to the helpfulness of the staff at the Walworth clinic.[167] Mrs Barrett, a lay worker at the Liverpool clinic, was described as having 'the lovely art of friendliness by which the patient however nervous was soothed and reassured before she came to the doctor for further questioning and examination.'[168] In the smaller clinics personal relationships were particularly important as stressed by Alice Onions, a working-class mother herself in Wolverhampton. Significantly, Alice Onions qualified after the Second World War, with fellow Wolverhampton Mothers' Clinic member Winifred Strange, as a marriage guidance counsellor.[169]

An important factor in the clinics' successes was that the nurses and lay workers were mothers themselves. The volunteers were not regarded as distant authority figures and this enabled meaningful relationships to be formed. Nor was there any evidence of the eugenic arguments which Anna Davin so succinctly summarised. 'If the survival of infants was in question it must be the fault of the mothers and if the nation needed future healthy citizens…, then the mothers must improve.'[170] The SPBCC volunteer workers started from a completely different perspective as they stressed they shared a common bond of motherhood with their working-class patients. The volunteers were deliberately selected for their ability to relate to working-class mothers. North Kensington Executive Committee members felt it was appropriate that in the first five years of the clinic's existence many of their committee had babies of their own and the three main committee members of the MSMC were all young mothers with twelve children between them.[171] Charis Frankenburg deliberately took her young baby to the clinic as a visual aid in the same way that she used the physical presence of the working-class mothers at the inaugural public meeting. 'My own baby used to accompany me to distant meetings so as not to miss her six o'clock feed.'[172] Charis wanted to underline the point that she was not anti-babies but wanted the family to be well spaced.

The sharing of the common experience of motherhood provided a common bond. As Alison Jagger pointed out, the role of emotions has been traditionally ignored by political scientists and contrasted unfavourably with rational judgements, thoughts and observations. She regarded the study of emotion and empathy as being particularly valuable in the study of women's reality, and of other subordinate groups.[173] The clinics consciously used the bond of motherhood to achieve success. While not denying the importance of class, the clinic workers were able to forge relationships across those barriers.

In this context, the emotion of motherhood has been given a different interpretation from the ideology of motherhood described by Anna Davin in her ground-breaking article on 'Imperialism and motherhood'.[174] Initially the ideology of Motherhood was also the attitude of the Eugenics Society as discussed by her, but the emotion of Motherhood as understood by the SPBCC provided a common emotional bond between workers and patients and was seen in terms of individual fulfilment. Rather than forcing motherhood on reluctant women it was understood that the clinics were there for the opposite purpose – to help working-class women limit their families.

The SPBCC committee members appreciated that they needed the active support of working-class mothers. Indeed, NKWWC stated that 'old patients are the best propagandists'.[175] Thus the skilful politician Charis Frankenburg wanted the working-class mothers, probably members of the WCG, prominently seated at the public meeting to launch the MSMC. 'We shall also see that those who are most concerned, the working class mothers, are strongly represented on the platform.'[176] Her philosophy was that the clinics were not being run to provide an agreeable leisure occupation for middle-class women and so the needs of the working-class mothers must be central.

This chapter argues that there was a greater social mix in the SPBCC clinics than has been recognised. There were a number of women from privileged background who became involved with the SPBCC. At a time when it was unusual for women to enter higher education, the Collective Biography shows that a high proportion had entered university. Also SPBCC members had also taken advantage of changes in legislation to become magistrates, local councillors and to stand as MPs.

There were significant friendship networks amongst the founders of clinics, particularly centring round Marie Stopes, Mary Stocks and Charis Frankenburg, though an analysis of the social background of founders of the SPBCC shows wide variation in social class. However, the SPBCC clinics were not just founded by upper- and middle-class women, as there was also a significant input by working-class women, such as Mary Barbour, Glasgow, and Alice Onions, Wolverhampton, who were committed socialists. As has been seen, the contribution of the

Women's Co-operative Guild was highly valued not just in Salford but also in Birmingham and Glasgow.

Working-class mothers had their own networks of family and friends and used these to access SPBCC clinics. The organisers were keen to place the clinics in areas where working-class women would feel anonymous to neighbours and comfortable in the clinics. Unlike Fisher's respondents these working-class wives took the initiative in locating and attending the SPBCC clinics although husbands may have given financial or moral support

The SPBCC kept detailed records of those attending the clinics not only for medical reasons, but to frame evidence to government for the need for municipal birth control clinics. The SPBCC annual reports drew on these statistics and case studies and these were carefully framed to counter the hostile arguments against birth control as encouraging promiscuity.

This study argues that there appeared to have been sympathy between the lay workers and the working-class mothers. Kate Fisher believes that staff of the clinics often did not realise the complexity of their clients' attitudes to birth control but a number of SPBCC nurses and lay workers were of working-class origins.[177] Moreover, the lay workers saw their role as being far more than providing birth control advice – they saw themselves as giving the working-class mothers space to express themselves. The volunteers were specifically selected for their ability to relate to the mothers and an important factor was that they were all mothers themselves. Indeed the lines between volunteer and patient were often blurred.

5   Challenging the Opposition

SPBCC member Mary Stocks, identified the two main centres of hostility to the SPBCC clinics as the churches and the medical profession. She maintained that it was cursed by the Roman Catholic Church, distrusted by the Church of England and ignored by the medical profession.[1] The birth controllers who mounted a spirited opposition to these groups included Mary Stocks, Charis Frankenburg and Dr Helena Wright. This chapter analyses the inter-relationship of these two major social institutions with the birth control movement at both local and national levels. There were a range of tactics available to the SPBCC and they selected those that they considered to be most appropriate to win over the opposition.

At the turn of the twentieth century both the Catholic and Anglican churches proclaimed the importance of marriage whose prime purpose was procreation. These institutions argued that sanctity of life was paramount and this took place at the moment of conception. Therefore they maintained that for man to interfere with the process of conception was to go against God's law. Just as the medical opposition was reluctant to even discuss birth control, as by implication it involved sexual relations, so many churchmen also found the topic distasteful. Yet these attitudes were not to go unchallenged, for instance as early as 1924 Mrs E.F. Wise was reported in the *Manchester Guardian* as declaring that 'the churches had no right to tell the helpless women in the slums that it was the will of God that they should bear a child every year.'[2]

The flamboyant tactics of Marie Stopes were in contrast with the restrained approach of the SPBCC. Marie Stopes employed dramatic actions reminiscent of the gesture politics of the suffrage movement. She intended to shock the Catholic Church when she informed the national press that she had chained one of her books to the font in the Catholic Westminster Cathedral.[3] In contrast, instead of confrontation the SPBCC employed conciliatory arguments that were carefully framed to appeal to sympathetic members of the Anglican Church and the medical profession. The arguments that the SPBCC employed included those of feminism, modernism and scientific advances.

Marie's actions attracted publicity. She also entered into protracted battles with the Catholic Church. In particular there was the libel case against the Catholic Dr Halliday Sutherland who accused Marie of experimenting on the poor. Dr Sutherland went on to quote Professor Anne McIlroy, professor of Obstetrics and Gynaecology at the Royal Free Hospital, who condemned Marie's methods as the most harmful available. Her lawyers urged her not to sue as the book had only sold eight hundred copies but Marie would not be deterred.[4] The case started in February 1923, lasted two years, went through three courts and incurred her with heavy costs. Although Marie lost the case it was reported in most major newspapers, and so gave her free publicity. The case was later analysed by Muriel Box in *The Trial of Marie Stopes*.[5] In 1923, to vindicate her methods, Marie presented herself at the hospital disguised as a work-grimed charwoman (cleaner) and was indeed fitted with a vaginal rubber cap by Professor McIlroy.

In her magazine *Birth Control News* there was rarely an issue which did not carry a prominent attack on the Catholic Church. In 1930 Pope Pius XI issued an encyclical on Christian marriage (*Casti Conubii*) which regarded birth control as a mortal sin and the ruin of former civilisations.[6] Marie Stopes reproduced the encyclical in its entirety in *Birth Control News*, highlighting the section condemning 'any use whatsoever of matrimony exercised in such a way that the act is deliberately frustrated in its natural power to generate life'.[7] The *Catholic Herald* regarded birth control as one of the three most important issues of the day for Catholics, alongside Catholic schools and the threat of socialism.[8]

It was not just the Catholic hierarchy who abhorred Marie Stopes and her principles. She was an anathema to many ordinary Catholics and in 1929 one of her birth control caravans was burnt out by a Catholic woman in Bradford who admitted its destruction.

CHALLENGING THE OPPOSITION

Whereas the Catholic hierarchy maintained its opposition to birth control the Anglican Church was more pragmatic and altered its position from an absolutist one in line with the Catholic Church to one which was more sympathetic to the principles of the SPBCC. In 1908 the Lambeth Conference of Anglican bishops had declared that the purpose of marriage was solely for procreation and that, 'deliberately tampering with nascent life is repugnant to Christian morality'.[9] However, in the next ten years attitudes gradually changed. One of the key birth control policy entrepreneurs was Lord Dawson of Penn who presented reasoned arguments for birth control. It was not just what he said, but the importance of the position he occupied. Lord Dawson was both a respected church man and an eminent member of the medical profession, being the personal physician to King George V. Lord Dawson publicly criticised the findings of the 1920 Lambeth Conference by appealing to the Church to reappraise the birth control question 'in the light of modern knowledge and the needs of a new world'.[10]

Lord Dawson sensationally argued that the love advocated by the Lambeth Conference was 'an invertebrate, joyless thing, not worth having'.[11] He criticised the bishops for encouraging abstinence which was often ineffective and led to a joyless marriage. He contended that the desire to limit families was undertaken from honourable motives. 'Baby after baby every year or eighteen months exhausts a woman's strength.'[12] Just as analgesia in childbirth was initially viewed as unnatural so, he argued, would attitudes to birth control change in the modern world. As well as receiving widespread press coverage his influential speech was subsequently published under the title 'Love, Marriage, Birth Control'. He later framed birth control as a scientific advance rather than 'a double dose of original sin'.[13] Nearly fifty years later the eminent consultant gynaecologist Sir John Peel described Dawson's 1921 speech as one of the most important events in the twentieth-century history of birth control.[14]

It is important to note that there were, in this period, significant informal contacts between the birth controllers and leaders of the Anglican Church. Mary Stocks of the MSMC wrote that she was, in 1926, 'fortunate in finding [William Temple] installed as Bishop of Manchester on our arrival in that City. Apart from him our contacts with the Church were slight.'[15] William Temple already had a close relationship with the Stocks' family as he had been at school with John Stocks. Mary Stocks in her autobiography described their regular contact. William Temple, an Anglo-Catholic, was highly influential in the Anglican Church, becoming Archbishop of York in 1929 and Archbishop of Canterbury in 1942. Flann Campbell pointed out there was a significant shift in Anglican opinion on birth control in the 1920s, and William Temple was in sympathy with the liberal view of social concerns.[16] It is inconceivable that Mary Stocks did not use regular informal family meetings with him to press the case for birth control.

The bishops attending the 1930 Lambeth Conference had further contact with the SPBCC and its supporters. A letter from Mrs Hubback of NUSEC to the Archbishop of Canterbury (Mary Stocks was then Chair of NUSEC) urged the bishops to take note of the growth of public opinion in favour of birth control and in particular the report of the conference of public health authorities on the provision of birth control information. The Archbishop of Canterbury replied that the bishops had already individually received copies of the report.[17] Dr Helena Wright of the SPBCC North Kensington clinic then addressed over three hundred bishops at Church Hall, Westminster on behalf of the National Birth Rate Commission (SPBCC's successor).[18] She framed her arguments in a non-emotional way by explaining her clinic's work. Her talk was illustrated by case studies of overworked mothers.

In 1930 there was considerable satisfaction in SPBCC when a compromise resolution on 'marriage and sex' at the Lambeth Conference was passed by 193 votes to 67, altering the position of the 1920 Conference. Although the Anglican bishops still stated that the preferred form of family limitation was abstinence, it was now agreed that birth control was permissible in certain circumstances: 'in those cases where there is such a clearly felt moral obligation to limit or avoid parenthood, and where there is a morally sound reason for avoiding complete abstinence... other methods may be used, provided this is done in the light of Christian principles.'[19]

Birth control was therefore left to individual judgement. The Birmingham SPBCC clinic formally welcomed the Anglican Church's change of attitude.[20]

The position of the Mothers' Union demonstrated just how far the Anglican Church had moved its position on birth control. In 1919 the Mothers' Union Central Council passed a strong resolution opposing 'the selfish limitation of the family and adopting the absolutist position that all artificial checks were against the law and nature of God'.[21] As has been seen, the Mothers' Union, along with the Catholic women's organisations, refused to endorse the birth control resolution of the National Council of Women in 1929. The Mothers' Union leadership continued to adhere to its condemnation of birth control even after the 1930 Lambeth Conference. This caused Archbishop William Temple to write to Mrs Boustead, President of the Mothers' Union and advise her that 'The Mothers' Union must face the fact that the majority of Bishops did declare that the use of contraceptives by married persons is in certain circumstances right, at least in the sense "not wrong".'He went on to give the Mothers' Union the option of continuing to uphold their stance on total prohibition but warned, 'The Mothers' Union needs to recognise that some of its members hold the use of contraceptives to be legitimate and yet the Mothers' Union makes their loyalty suspect.'[22] The Mothers' Union did change its position under pressure from the Archbishop so that decisions on family limitation became a private matter.

The Collective Biography shows that there were individual members of the Mothers' Union who were prepared to make a public commitment to birth control clinics. Mrs Claire Tamplin remained a prominent member of the Mothers' Union as well as being a founder member of the North Kensington Women's Welfare Centre, and also helped found the SPBCC clinic in Newcastle-upon-Tyne in 1929. The minutes of the Liverpool Mothers' Welfare Clinic show that Mrs Albert David, wife of the Anglican Bishop of Liverpool, served on its council but she had to maintain a low profile for fear of compromising her husband.[23] Yet by 1932 the Bishop of Liverpool was reported as saying, 'Parents have not only the right but the duty to space the births of their children.'[24] Former suffragette Mrs Bethune-Baker was a founder member of the Cambridge SPBCC clinic and was also the wife of the Professor of Divinity at Lady Margaret's College, University of Cambridge. Presumably she did not believe her position on birth control compromised her husband.

Like the general population, there were divisions in the Jewish community on the issue of birth control. The orthodox view was that every Jew should marry and have children unless medically unfit and therefore those Jewish women who supported birth control were criticised.

'Young Jewish women are degenerating. They are beginning to sacrifice at the shrine of the god of social obligation the health and well-being of generations yet unborn.'[25] Linda Gordon Kuzmack found in her research that 'Anglo-Jewish feminist activities paralleled those of their English peers in nearly all aspects of life.'[26] She observed that many progressive-minded Jews could be found in the suffragist middle-class suburbs of Edwardian London and Manchester. The involvement with the birth control movement was often likely to come from those who administered the elaborate system of Jewish Charities. Charis Frankenburg's daughter believed her mother regarded her involvement in the MSMC clinic and the SPBCC's birth control campaign as being part of the strong Jewish tradition of caring for the community, and therefore in keeping with her family's religious beliefs.[27] Charis persuaded her mother-in-law to become an MSMC committee member. Again in Newcastle-upon-Tyne it was an outsider, a Jewish businessman, who provided the clinic with its first premises in a fish shop when they had been refused elsewhere. He also carried out propaganda work for them and encouraged women to attend the clinic.[28]

Linda Kuzmack referred to the 'bond of sisterhood' forged by the interaction of Jewish women with their Christian peers, and in which Jewish women helped to shape the policies, methods and tactics of the organisations to which they belonged.[29] Nationally and locally there was a number of distinguished Jewish women who played an important role in advancing the case of birth control. Eva Hubback was a committee member of NUSEC and sat on the Executive Committee of the National Birth Control Council. Flora Blumberg in 1931 travelled to Geneva to present a paper at an international conference organised by the American birth control pioneer Margaret Sanger, and eventually succeeded Mary Stocks as Chair of the MSMC. Her Jewish identity was important to her, and throughout her life she maintained strong links with Jewish organisations, serving as President of the Lodge of B-nai Brith, the international Jewish organisation for women.[30] Another important

Jewish member of the birth control movement was Eileen Laski. She was the sister of Simon Marks, of the famous Marks and Spencer department stores, and joined another influential Manchester Jewish family when she married Norman Laski in 1926. On the break-up of her marriage, she moved to London, serving on the executive committee of the SPBCC. She organised fund-raising events for the SPBCC with the future Labour MP Dr Edith Summerskill.[31]

The importance of Jewish women to local birth control campaigns such as in Stepney, was described by Lara Marks in her detailed study of East London maternity practices.[32] She noted the prominent role in Stepney of the Jewish councillor, Councillor Miriam Moses who in 1927 called for the establishment of a municipal birth control clinic. The eventual decision by Stepney Council in 1931 to establish a municipal birth control clinic echoed the political situation that existed in Salford.[33] In Stepney the Irish Catholic councillors opposed the resolution for birth control clinics, but the Jewish councillors, of all political parties, supported this motion. Ethnic-religious identity therefore remained an important factor in shaping the politics behind the provision of maternal and infant welfare facilities into the 1930s.[34]

Medical opposition and religious opposition to the SPBCC often overlapped, for instance Catholic doctors such as Dr Halliday Sutherland were particularly vocal in their opposition to birth control. There was also medico-religious opposition from women doctors, for instance Dr Mary Scharlieb, a practising Catholic, considered birth control a pernicious evil as it prevented the natural consequences of marriage.[35] Dr Mary Scharlieb and Dr McIlroy, who was involved in the libel trial of Marie Stopes, were amongst the most high-profile critics of birth control. Dr Letitia Fairfield converted to Catholicism and then completely changed from being pro-birth control to being anti-birth control.

The medical profession in the inter-war years gave the appearance of being generally uncomfortable with birth control, which many doctors believed to be untested and unsafe. The profession's leaders held that if birth control was to be undertaken it should be under its sole control and not provided by voluntary clinics run by lay people. In 1923 there was a special edition of *The Practitioner* devoted to the issue of birth control, and, whereas the medical profession was divided about the desirability of birth control, they were united in condemnation of decisions resting with non-medical personnel.³⁶ Dr Eric Prichard believed 'knowledge of contraceptive methods are in the wrong hands' and Sir Maurice Abbott Anderson thought 'the use of contraceptives are at the present time unsavoury and harmful and should only be used in the hands of the medical profession.' The emphasis was on 'control by the medical profession'. As Dr Florence Barrett wrote in her critical view of birth control, 'If it is *necessary* to prevent conception, doctors can give full instruction on methods which are safe.'³⁷

A contemporary eugenicist, Norman Himes, claimed that the spread of birth control knowledge had been 'by diffusion downwards from the medical profession'.³⁸ However, the evidence from the SPBCC clinics does not support this assertion and Charis Frankenburg correctly judged that doctors were usually ignorant of birth control methods, indifferent or hostile. Although there were instances of birth control clinics founded by doctors, these were exceptions. The Oxford Mothers' Family Welfare Clinic was founded as a result of a meeting called in April 1926 at his house by Dr William Collier, the Senior Physician in Oxford. He was able to interest forty-two people in this project, many of them medical contacts, and subsequently Dr Isabelle Little was employed at the clinic.³⁹ However, the records of the other SPBCC clinics showed it was lay workers who took the initiative and raised funds to found clinics.

There was occasionally friction between the lay members of the Executive Committees and the doctors. This legitimising procedure was constructed so that laymen would remain laymen. The medical paradigm included the definition of reproduction as a specialist subject in which only doctors were experts. Birth control was medicalised. However, lay members held power because it was they who appointed the doctors and paid their wages. There was conflict because doctors maintained that their professional training meant they should not be subservient to lay members. In Liverpool there was conflict between Dr Phoebe Bigland, who judged that patients should have at least three children, and the Executive who were far more flexible on this issue.

In relation to birth control, the most influential members of the medical profession were undoubtedly the Chief Medical Officers of Health, as they had the power to set the birth control agenda in their locality. The SPBCC paid special attention to converting these decision-makers by convincing them that their birth control methods were scientific and modern. One of the earliest and most articulate supporters of birth control clinics was Dr Killick Millard, the Medical Officer of Health for Leicester who persuaded his council to make provision for birth control advice at municipal clinics.[40] Dr Letitia Fairfield initially wrote to the Archbishop of Canterbury supporting Dr Killick Millard and condemning the Mothers' Union's view of the selfishness of family limitation. Letitia drew on her eighteen years work with the poor in Edinburgh, Dublin, Manchester and London to make a case against the idealised view of a large happy family. 'Big families mean dirt, vermin of the person, poor physical standard, semi-starvation, neglected ailments, overcrowding, and a generally low standard of child-welfare.'[41] In Manchester the newly appointed Medical Officer of Health, Dr Veitch Clark, was regarded as a moderniser sympathetic to the idea of birth control clinics and he worked closely with the MSMC to found the first municipal birth control clinics in the country at Crumpsall and Withington.

These progressive Medical Officers of Health were in a minority. Dr Newsholme, the Chief Medical Officer of Health for Birmingham, was bitterly opposed to birth control clinics and wrote to Dame Janet Campbell at the Ministry of Health in 1928 that he was convinced that birth control appeared to be an aggravator rather than a cure of grave social evils.[42] The Birmingham Maternity and Child Welfare Committee declared, under his influence, that concentration on teaching the value of self-restraint would be likely to achieve a greater degree of good than the activities of municipal birth control clinics.[43] These views were shared in other areas such as Aberdeen where there was vociferous opposition to birth control from the local medical establishment led by a Professor M'Kerron.[44]

This disapproving attitude percolated down from the doctors to the nursing profession. Sister Beatrice Sandys worked as a midwife at Hope Hospital in the 1930s where she knew the members of the MSMC Clinic Executive Committee and explained to me that they used to push leaflets through the door at night. However, the senior medical staff at the hospital were bitterly opposed to the clinic and the Matron instructed her staff, 'If you see any of these leaflets, burn them.' Beatrice disobeyed Matron's instructions, risking dismissal by collecting the leaflets and giving them to her patients. She then encouraged her mothers to visit the clinic at dusk through the back alleys:

> *The mothers wanted to know, didn't they, how to stop it, so I told them. I knew there was a Clinic. I told them where to go.*
>
> Was that brave of you?
>
> *No. Not really. I stayed with Matron in the District Nurses Home. I doubt if she would ever get to know because I wouldn't be telling her.* (laughs)[45]

In 1922 Nurse E.S. Daniels had been dismissed from her post with Edmonton District Council for doing far less.

Each SPBCC clinic succeeded in having a doctor attending every session and my Collective Biography profiles fifteen doctors who were connected to individual clinics. My research highlighted the difficulties of birth control clinics in obtaining the services of women doctors. The North Kensington Clinic Committee discussed this matter and decided to advertise in the *Lancet* which resulted in six applications.[46] Female doctors, in a minority at medical school, faced hostility in the profession. Those who had qualified at the turn of the century were often suspicious of contraceptive practices. Dr Letitia Fairfield had claimed that of the hundreds of medical practitioners, mostly women, with whom she had discussed birth control, she had only found three that were opposed. Nevertheless, her view is not borne out by contemporary literature which exhibited the general distaste of doctors for the subject.

My Collective Biography shows that SPBCC women doctors were exceptionally committed, though politically diverse. Women doctors fully recognised that involvement with the birth control movement was not a good career move. Dr Cornelia Winter of Wolverhampton Welfare Centre declared that she had risked her practice and career when she took up her position at the Centre.[47] There appears to have been no clear-cut distinction between those doctors who sat on the SPBCC's advisory Executive Committees and those who actually treated patients. The following examples illustrate the hostility the birth control doctors experienced and the varied backgrounds from which they were drawn. Feminism seems to have been important to all three.

In Birmingham the highly respected gynaecologist Miss Hilda Shufflebotham was a founding member of Birmingham Women's Welfare Association. As a consultant, she had the most to lose professionally by being involved with the birth control campaign. However, she took the risk of openly seeing complex cases at her consulting rooms at Birmingham Maternity and Women's Hospital. She was committed to the rights of female doctors and her illustrious career contained many instances of her pioneering work for women patients and women in her profession. She was one of the first woman consultants at Birmingham Maternity and Women's Hospital, the first woman professor in Birmingham Medical School, the first woman president of the Royal College of Obstetricians and Gynaecologists (RCOG), the first woman president of any of the four Royal Colleges. Eventually she was honoured as Dame Hilda Rose and her portrait is hung in the RCOG. Throughout her life and in her will she supported the Medical Women's Federation.

Dr Phoebe Bigland, the founding doctor of the Mothers' Welfare Centre in Liverpool, was also a member of the Medical Women's Federation and attended a committee meeting in November 1921. In 1922 she sat on its committee to examine the effects of birth control on 'imperial health and national welfare'. She had heard an inspirational speech by Marie Stopes in Liverpool. However, when appointed as clinic doctor in 1926 she did not visit Marie's Society for Constructive Birth Control and Racial Progress, but instead underwent her training at Walworth Road with the SPBCC. Her successor in Liverpool, Dr Macaulay, described Phoebe as an alarming personality who was very thin and tremendously energetic and spoke in a high rather nasal voice. Phoebe had pronounced views on abortion, prostitution and the number of children a mother should bear which were more rigid than the committee members. Phoebe carried on working at the clinic even when terminally ill, and so Dr Macaulay believed Phoebe possessed tremendous intellectual and physical courage.[48]

Dr Mabel May, on the Committee of the MSMC, personally saw patients at the Salford clinic. Her motivation appeared to have been political as well as humanitarian. She had served in the First World War with a unit sponsored by the NUWSS and during the inter-war years was an active member of the local Labour Party. She was selected by Declan

McHugh as being one of the two hundred most active Manchester Labour members in the inter-war years. Mabel was a member of Rusholme District Labour Party and gave talks on birth control to the local Labour parties and Women's Co-operative Guilds. According to the *Manchester and Salford Co-operative Herald*, she told Hulme WCG in December 1926, 'Even if she was not a Socialist the environment with which she came into contact in the course of her professional duties would have made her so.'[49]

The women doctors were certainly not motivated by the need for a financial reward but rather by an evangelical desire to spread the birth control message. Dilys Dean reported that in the early years of the MSMC Dr Gimson generously waived her salary in order to give the voluntary clinic more resources.[50] Dr Isabelle Little of the Oxford clinic also waived her fee in the clinic's first year. Dr Hilda Macirone of Birmingham, as well as treating patients, made a donation to help its foundation. After the negative experiences with Dr Haire at Walworth Road, the doctors were all female and the clinics gave this female presence due prominence in their publicity. Thus the Wolverhampton Women's Welfare Centre had in bold typeface in the centre of its handbill, 'Lady Doctor Attends'.[51]

By 1927 the SPBCC clinics were sufficiently developed to hold annual doctors' conferences at which were representatives from Walworth, East London, Birmingham, Cambridge, Manchester, Oxford, Rotherham and Wolverhampton. These contacts served the additional function of providing support for the SPBCC doctors in a hostile medical environment.[52] Thus Fenella Paton, founder of the SPBCC Aberdeen clinic, initially rejected affiliation to the Society for Constructive Birth Control and Racial Progress when it was offered by Marie Stopes, explaining that her clinic was affiliated to the NSPBCC (formerly SPBCC) 'because my doctor trained at Walworth; they gave me a grant to start with and we have always found their methods very satisfactory. We have been working in this way for the last eight years and I really have no wish to change.' Fenella went on to state that the other birth control clinics in Scotland, used the same methods and therefore they were able to exchange information.[53]

Dr Phoebe Bigland had maintained that the hardest part of an up-hill battle to spread birth control methods was to engage in a dialogue with her own medical profession. Dr Olive Gimson of the MSMC stated that 'she was prepared to share with any members of the medical profession who may be interested, such technical experience she has gained' and in 1930 the MSMC Committee identified the promotion of 'instruction to medical practitioners' as being one of its main functions.[54] Given the absence of contraceptive training as part of the general curriculum of medical schools it was significant that the SPBCC realised the importance of the professional training it could provide for fellow doctors and medical students. Medical students were smuggled in after dark to clinics such as MSMC, North Kensington and Walworth.[55] Annual reports record that doctors and nurses from the MSMC, Aberdeen, Glasgow and Liverpool visited Walworth Road for instruction.

This research indicates the appointment of doctors to clinics may have been as much for the benefit of the SPBCC and its need to win medical allies as for the benefit of working-class mothers. The SPBCC policy clearly differentiated itself from Marie Stopes who distrusted doctors and only employed nurses in her SCBCRP clinics. Marie only referred problematic patients to Dr Jane Hawthorne and even this relationship deteriorated.

Many working-class women were suspicious of doctors and were reluctant to consult them, not just on the grounds of cost. They related well to the SPBCC nurses who were often local women and mothers. For instance the SPBCC acknowledged the important role of the nurses in their annual reports and Nurse Rae, of the SPBCC clinic in Aberdeen was later described as 'motherly and understanding'.[56] Marie Stopes praised Nurse Jones at the miners' wives hospital clinic founded at Abertillery as being pleasing and sympathetic, though typically she critically added that the nurse should acquire a more definite polish and finish in her work and appearance.[57] Nurses received specialist training. Nurse Daniels (late health visitor Edmonton Council) announced in the leaflet promoting her private birth control clinic, that she had studied in Holland where she received specialist instruction.[58] The SCBCRP nurses appeared perfectly competent, working independently of doctors in Marie Stopes' clinics and in her two birth control caravans.

So why did the SPBCC restrict their nurses to an educational rather than a diagnostic role? Charis Frankenburg of the MSMC was also a qualified midwife, and must have known that her nurses were competent. However, her training would have also alerted her to the necessity for strict medical etiquette. Thus if the SPBCC were framing their arguments for the medical profession, they also needed to gain their trust. This could be done by differentiating themselves from SCBCRP and having doctors as an integral part of their organisation. The differences in the approach of the two organisations is illustrated by the medical profession's dismissal of Marie Stopes' illustrious scientific background. Dr Helena Wright had met Marie Stopes before working abroad for several years. On her return she sceptically revisited her, to 'see what an expert in fossil biology, was doing with an enterprise which was by its nature medical'.[59] Helena Wright preferred the approach of the SPBCC clinic in North Kensington where she could maintain her professional autonomy and so she joined the SPBCC clinic.[60]

The fact that the SPBCC did not alienate the medical profession meant that the local clinics had referrals from them. Gradually the SPBCC clinics achieved their aims and began to gain the trust of the medical profession. Rightly the SPBCC clinics were proud of the good relationships they were forging with the medical profession. In 1927 the Cambridge clinic reported that fifteen doctors had referred patients, seven more than the previous year. The other clinics, such as MSMC and Liverpool, were increasingly gaining referrals of working-class mothers from doctors.

The investigation of birth control methods was intended to impress the medical profession by providing convincing scientific arguments. The SPBCC formed a Birth Control Investigation Committee in October 1926 to promote the medical research on, and co-ordinate the experiences of, different clinics. The committee was chaired by the high status Professor Sir Humphrey Rolleston (President of the Royal College of Physicians) and consisted of one group of academics and another of lay workers.[61] A further contribution to the development of best practice was an international symposium held in Zurich in 1930, to which representatives from the SPBCC, Walworth Road and the MSMC contributed.[62]

Whereas technical studies evaluating the manufacture of condoms or the dimensions of the cervical cap were useful and objective, the SPBCC clinics' statistical procedures on evaluating success of their methods were less objective. Although the clinics welcomed independent researchers, the latter were basically reliant on the clinic's own data. Several clinics such as those run by Marie Stopes conducted their own follow-up studies and used dubious statistical measures of 'success' such as the non-return of patients. The MSMC, not to be outdone, claimed that in their first 1,212 cases they had had only eight 'failures', but one of their criteria for success was that the mothers had not returned to the clinic complaining of difficulties or become pregnant.[63] Lella Secor Florence of the Birmingham clinic was more sceptical, 'We drew gradually to the views that either our Clinic was unique and our patients were more stupid or careless than others, or that all workers in the birth control movement had allowed themselves to be deceived by a general impression of success derived from letters and visits from grateful patients.'[64]

There were important regional variations on how religious and medical influences affected the development of the SPBCC. The interplay of forces affecting the progress of local birth control movements in 1923–6 is analysed in four different localities. These are Stockport, Glasgow, Salford and Liverpool. The SPBCC used established political tactics such as letters to local newspapers, informal contacts and public meetings but the opposition, particularly the Catholics, used violence to protect its interests.

There was a strong Labour Party presence in the four areas studied which included socialist Sunday schools, Clarion cycling clubs and active socialist social and cultural programmes. Throughout the 1920s in Salford there were Labour victories with Ben Tillett, Joe Tooley and A.W. Haycock all being returned as MPs.[65] In Glasgow there was also a move by the electorate to Labour from Liberal with John Wheatley amongst the ten Labour MPs being returned in the 1922 general election. In 1925 Arnold Townsend won the Stockport constituency for Labour in a by-election. The SPBCC tried to convert the Labour leadership to their cause by pointing out the dire housing conditions.

In these towns, living conditions gave cause for concern and local Medical Officers of Health gave cautious backing to the birth control pioneers on humanitarian grounds. In 1926 the Government Commissioner wrote that in Glasgow, 'everywhere we noticed an almost total lack of sanitation, conveniences being few and for the most part out of repair and in some cases leaking down the stairs and even into the houses.'[66] In Stockport, Medical Officer of Health, Dr Richmond also drew attention to the unsatisfactory condition of the town's housing stock which mostly consisted of 'two up and two down' with outside privies which had not been converted into mains drainage, and damp cellar dwellings still in use. He then noted that there was serious overcrowding with 'two or three families huddled in one cottage.'[67] Dr Richmond was concerned that the rate of death in childbirth had remained consistently high for the last twenty years – in 1924 it was twelve maternal deaths. In Salford, Lancashire the Medical Officer of Health in 1930 expressed the view that living conditions in his town were amongst the worst in the country with the exception of West and East Ham.[68]

The influence of the local Catholic Church was a particularly important factor in Stockport, where birth controllers presented reasoned arguments but were threatened with violence. In 1923 under the auspices of the Labour Church, former suffragette Elsie Plant invited Marie Stopes to speak on birth control in Stockport. Marie Stopes had an enthusiastic audience of thousands in the Armoury and she encouraged Elsie and her husband to start a birth control clinic. However, the Catholic Young Men's Guild threatened physical reprisals and extra stewards had to be employed. Elsie Plant recalled that 'we had a "black mark" against us. The Chairman of the Labour Party was against us saying we had lost them votes.'[69] The local Labour Party successfully blocked the move for a clinic, fearing to lose the Catholic Labour vote, and it was not until after the Second World War that a voluntary clinic was eventually established.

In Glasgow the birth controllers met similar opposition but had more resources. Joan Smith argued that the strong Liberal tradition restrained Protestant/Catholic sectarianism and enhanced the growth of municipal socialism.[70] Glasgow ILP had a strong tradition of supporting women's rights such as the suffrage campaign, and doubtless this contributed to Labour's support there of the birth control clinic which was founded in 1926. The personal popularity of Labour councillor and rent strike activist Mary Barbour was influential in ensuring support for the SPBCC clinic. As an insider, a member of the council, she was well placed to argue the SPBCC's case.

In Salford there was similar conflict. The MSMC was regarded by the Catholic establishment as mounting a direct challenge to its authority and it became a contentious issue in 1926. It was understandable that Dr Henshaw, who was only enthroned as Bishop on 21 December 1925, should view the MSMC as a threat.[71] Certainly the principles of Bishop Henshaw and his motto 'incrementum det Deus' (may God give the increase) were diametrically opposed to that of the birth controllers whose clinic was directly opposite the Cathedral. In 1926 Bishop Henshaw was quick to use the Catholic press to denounce the existence of the MSMC and their methods in emotional, inflammatory language, 'Horrible things, strange filthy things… The powers of evil have refined their methods and unsavoury subjects are clothed with scientific names… one of these centres has been opened up not far from the Cathedral.'[72] The following month Bishop Henshaw was quoted using equally colourful language about the clinic's methods, 'Birth Control, an abomination in Catholic eyes is infinitely worse than the unnatural vices of Sodom and Gomorrah. Filthy knowledge is not less filthy because it is imparted in a "clinic", or "centre".'[73]

The national and local Catholic papers also launched vitriolic attacks on the birth controllers in Salford. The previous year Tom Burns had written to the *Salford Reporter* on behalf of the Catholic Federation condemning proposals to provide advice on birth control in state-funded institutions. 'We believe the majority of our fellow citizens, and especially the women of the poorer classes in whose name and upon whose behalf the proposers profess to speak, regard the whole business with repugnance and disgust.'[74]

It is clear that the Catholic press was trying to make the activities of the MSMC a class issue, contrasting the middle-class backgrounds of the MSMC's Executive Committee with the working-class backgrounds of the Salford mothers. The committee members were portrayed as social parasites. Charis Frankenburg was a particular focus for the Catholic press's opprobrium. The *Catholic Herald* repeatedly used anti-Semitic and xenophobic language when referring to her, 'It is passing strange that this lady of "German Jew" name should be exhibiting so much solicitude for the working class.'[75]

In contrast to the MSMC's reasoned arguments, Bishop Henshaw came close to incitement to violence when he declaimed from his pulpit in 1926 that 'I hope the time is not far off when the people of Greengate chase it from their streets.'[76] The Executive members of the MSMC were genuinely worried for their own safety and concerned for the security of the clinic. Ann Patterson, Mary Stocks' daughter, remembered listening at the dinner table to her mother expressing concern that some Catholics might use physical violence.[77]

Unlike the Stockport situation, members of the MSMC Executive Committee in Salford had the advantage of having influential allies whom they lobbied for support. An indignant Mary Stocks wrote to her friend Nancy, Lady Astor, protesting about the Bishop's activities. Lady Astor was a Conservative MP and at that time one of the few women members of parliament. Mary Stocks called upon Lady Astor to help if the Salford situation should deteriorate and wrote to Astor complaining that Bishop Henshaw was inciting his poorly educated and impoverished flock to violence:

> He episcopises over a large congested slum population here and so far as I can make out he wishes them to remain congested in order that he may exercise a more complete sway over their minds and morals...
>
> Recently he has been urging his flock to hound us with hue and cry from the district. They won't do it of course (as a matter of fact they greatly prefer us to the Bishop) but nevertheless the suggestion is a direct incitement to violence.[78]

In the event, Nancy Astor's help proved to be unnecessary, and subsequently Mary was joyfully able to inform her that, 'As a matter of fact it is great fun being at war with a Bishop. I only wish it were a Cardinal. Doubtless it will be soon. And then there remains the Pope!'[79]

In fact, it was Charis Frankenburg's actions that served to restrain Bishop Henshaw because, through her influential father-in-law and her husband, she had useful contacts. Charis recalled in her autobiography that after their representations, the Chief Constable of Salford sent for the Bishop's Secretary and Charis Frankenburg believed that as a consequence of their conversation, Bishop Henshaw's utterances became less inflammatory.[80] However, he continued to mount a sustained attack against birth control throughout his term of office. As late as 1937 he wrote in his Lenten Pastoral Newsletter that 'They might with justice call our time the Era of Universal Birth Prevention and attribute to it the disasters which will most surely follow the continuance of this social and moral evil.'[81]

Bishop Henshaw's denunciation of the MSMC had unintended consequences. Instead of leaving the MSMC to languish in obscurity his public condemnation helped draw his congregation's attention to its work. Although the MSMC's letters to the newspapers had not been published, partly because of the 1926 General Strike, the Protest Meeting organised by the Catholic Church attracted widespread coverage. Ironically, this gave the MSMC publicity it had previously lacked:

> We had circulated a manifesto among our friends and other people likely to be interested, but although we had deliberately refrained from propaganda, it was provided for us by the protest meeting. The most usual answer to the routine question put to patients 'How did you hear of the Clinic?' was 'through the protest meeting.'[82]

No doubt the majority of Catholics were reluctant to use mechanical birth control but a significant minority were prepared to try the new methods and visit the clinic. Condemnation by the Catholic Church often acted as a spur. The Birmingham clinic also reported that the opposition in public meetings had actually advertised their services in a way they could not afford.[83] Thus Stephen Fielding's assertion in his doctoral thesis that Catholic mothers were less likely to use appliance methods of birth control than non-Catholics is true, but nevertheless underestimates the impact of the SPBCC clinic in raising the subject.[84]

Birth control became an issue in the Salford municipal election of 1926. The local Labour Party had made gains in 1925, particularly at the expense of the Liberal Party. However, in 1926 Labour lost Trinity ward which contained two Catholic churches and had a high percentage of Catholic voters. One explanation of Labour's loss is that it was a protest vote against the MSMC clinic. John Henry in his detailed political local study of inter-war Salford correctly argued that overall there was little evidence that the clinic lost the Labour Party significant votes as other

Catholic wards continued to vote Labour.[85] The co-founders of the MSMC had sufficient political resources to withstand Catholic opposition.[86]

In Liverpool the SPBCC kept a low profile but there were similar emotive arguments by the opposition. Joan Smith identified the importance of Tory sympathies and Irish nationalism which resulted in employment in key industries being divided on sectarian lines. Yet sectarianism initially did not affect the Liverpool Mothers' Welfare Clinic, a SPBCC clinic which was established in 1926.[87] The voluntary Liverpool clinic quietly proceeded with its work, relying primarily on voluntary funds. However, in April 1936 the local Labour Party split over the municipal grant to Liverpool Mothers' Welfare Clinic. It was opposed, amongst others, by David Logan, the local Liverpool MP, a Catholic and father of ten. The campaign for the grant's continuation was successfully led by Labour Party councillor and future MP, Mrs Bessie Braddock. Instead of employing emotive language, she framed her argument in health terms by calling for birth control to save the lives of mothers. Bessie defeated her opponents in Liverpool City Council by 72 votes to 41, so ensuring the continuation of the grant.[88]

This chapter has discussed doctrinal and ideological issues, and the next chapter examines the choices individual birth controllers made with regard to their membership of other organisations.

6 Shifting Ideologies: Birth Controllers, Feminists, the Malthusian League and Eugenics Society

In the period after the Second World War there was a reluctance to examine the connection that feminist and birth control pioneers had with social engineering. Olive Banks in her comprehensive two-volume *Biographical Dictionary of British Feminists* covered many prominent feminists including Mary Stocks, Lady Trudie Denman, Edith How-Martyn, Lella Secor Florence, but excluded mention of eugenics in their individual entries or in the subject index.[1] Yet it will be shown they all had strong links either with the Malthusian League or with the Eugenics Society. Prominent birth control pioneers, such as Dr Alice Vickery and Stella Browne, were connected with the Malthusian League. Such was the attraction of social engineering that even committed feminists such as Mary Stocks and Eleanor Rathbone demonstrated ambivalence in their approach to eugenics. The President of the FPA, Trudie Denman was for four years a fellow and council member of the British Eugenics Society, only resigning in 1943. Eugenics, with its origins in the theories of Charles Darwin, was seen by contemporaries to be in tune with the modern age and in the inter-war years was popular with intellectuals from both the left and the right of the political spectrum, including the literary figures George Bernard Shaw and H.G. Wells.[2]

The pioneering scholarship of Anne Allen, who researched the connections between feminism and eugenics in Germany and Britain, and Angela Wanhall, who examined feminism and eugenics in New Zealand, is to be welcomed as opening up the debate.[3] Ann Curthoys also found this contradiction between feminism and eugenics when she profiled the activities in the early part of the twentieth century of

Australian feminist and eugenicist, Marion Piddington. She explored how it was possible for Marion to retain membership of an organisation that took an anti-feminist stance as it put the value on women as breeders of the future race.[4]

In Britain the importance to the SPBCC of both the Malthusian League and Eugenics Society can be seen in both practical action and attempted ideological persuasion. The case of the health visitor Nurse E.S. Daniels raised important issues with regard to the birth control movement as a whole. Nurse Daniels was a member of the Malthusian League and Eugenics Society and her dismissal by Edmonton District Council in 1922 was an initiating event in the birth control campaign. After her dismissal she was portrayed as a martyr. Dr Charles Drysdale, founding President of the neo-Malthusian New Generation League, used Nurse Daniels to enhance the profile of the birth control issue through the columns of its magazine.[5]

This chapter examines how the feminists and birth controllers framed their arguments to specific audiences and attempted, not always successfully, to forge new policy advocacy coalitions. In 1877 the Malthusian League modified the doctrine of moral restraint advocated by Reverend Thomas Malthus in 1798. The trial of Charles Bradlaugh and Annie Besant over the publication of Charles Knowlton's birth control tract, *The Fruits of Philosophy*, gave impetus to the formation of the Malthusian League. The League changed direction at the start of the twentieth century when the importance of birth control in family limitation was recognised. This allowed Drysdale to distance himself from Malthus' economic theories and instead stress 'family prudence' or birth control as opposed to abstinence.[6] This was a far more positive and welcome message. Significantly the Malthusian League's regular monthly journal, *The Malthusian*, with a winsome cherub on the cover, carried discreet advertisements for contraceptives in the 1920s.

Yet not all contemporary political activists were willing to acknowledge the change in emphasis by the neo-Malthusians, and the organisation continued to attract hostility from some parts of the Labour movement. Jane Lewis suggested many socialists rejected the idea of birth control because it implied the poor were responsible for their own misery.⁷ Socialists believed that what was necessary was a more equitable distribution of wealth. Birth controllers were accused of being anti-socialist, which undeniably some were. As late as 1926 this theme was taken up by Ramsay MacDonald, speaking for the Executive at the Margate Labour Conference in the birth control debate. He raised the spectre of Malthus in a birth control debate: 'Was it a question of health, or might he put it a little bluntly, was it a question of neo-Malthusianism?'⁸ There were also critics of the neo-Malthusians amongst socialists and feminists. Mary Stocks, Vice-President of the National Union of Societies for Equal Citizenship and joint founder of the Manchester and Salford Mothers' Clinic, possessed a first class degree in Economics from the London School of Economics and was highly critical of Malthus. Mary Stocks was also a Fabian and in her 1920 economics text book, *The Industrial State*, argued against Malthus' proposition that the population, if allowed to grow unchecked, must inevitably outgrow the means of subsistence. Although some socialists such as the Fabian George Bernard Shaw supported eugenics, many members of the Malthusian League, such as Drysdale, were virulently anti-socialist.

Relations were initially strained between the neo-Malthusians and feminists. Lucy Bland's research has shown that many of the early suffragists, often single professional women, looked aghast at the birth control movement and regarded it as an abhorrent diversion from their cause.⁹ The fact that the birth control movement involved discussion of sexual relations meant it was not regarded as respectable by many feminists. The veteran suffrage campaigner Mrs Charlotte Despard, at a Women's Freedom League meeting addressed by the Malthusian League, referred to 'those horrible preventative methods' and advocated sexual abstinence.¹⁰ Certainly birth control was perceived as diversionary by feminists anxious to appear respectable.

An important influence on the direction of policy of the Malthusian League was Dr Alice Vickery who advocated practical feminism. Simon Szreter did Vickery a disservice when he dismissively termed her in a footnote as Dr Charles Drysdale's mistress.¹¹ Richard Soloway, like Simon Szreter also devalued Alice Vickery's significance when he described Vickery as a former chemist and midwife. He omitted to state that she had only qualified as a chemist to aid her qualification as a doctor.[12] Indeed Dr Alice Vickery, as shown in my Collective Biography, eventually became a qualified doctor in her own right. Miriam Benn praised her commitment, as it took Alice eleven years to qualify at the London Medical School, including two years' study in France.[13] By 1880 she was one of only five women in England to hold a medical degree.[14] The strength of Alice's Malthusian commitment can be appreciated by her appearance as an expert witness at the Bradlaugh-Besant trial which could have permanently jeopardised her career.[15]

As early as 1873 Dr Alice Vickery held a suffrage meeting in Dover and she translated from the French a number of books advocating women's rights. Though she felt that she was too old to take an active part in the suffrage movement, she supported her daughter-in-law who was a militant suffragette.

Dr Alice Vickery was unusual in that she consistently maintained a well-developed feminist philosophy on the right of mothers to self-determination:

> No set of human beings has the right to deprive others of information conducive to their wellbeing. Poor people, poor women especially, had been deliberately deprived of the power of using their own judgement in regard to what was beneficial to themselves and their offspring.... The women of the poorer class were demanding today that information which had benefitted the better classes. It was not natural that a poor woman should desire to bring into the world one child after another without proper intervals of rest and recuperation.[16]

She framed birth control in terms of the well-being of working-class women. Dr Alice Vickery linked her feminist philosophy with initiating practical action, 'At once organise vigorous Neo-Malthusian propaganda among the poorest women... with the object of freeing them from the servitude of uncontrolled maternity... woman's body belongs to herself for herself.'[17] These sentiments would also have been appropriate in 1970s Britain and the USA.

The women of the Malthusian League progressed from producing pamphlets to providing personal advice. The American birth control pioneer, Margaret Sanger, explained, 'I realised that it [birth control] involved much more than talk, much more than books or pamphlets.'[18] Even before the first birth control clinics were founded in England,

Dr Alice Vickery started outreach work by giving talks to groups of working-class mothers. These groups included local branches of the Women's Co-operative Guild for whom she had a great deal of respect. In 1908 she travelled to dockside Rotherhithe to talk to a large group of a hundred working-class mothers on methods of birth control. She donated funds for the women to purchase contraceptive materials under the direction of Miss Anna Martin, and this group survived into the 1920s. Alice advocated home visits to poor women where a combination of 'gentleness, perception, commonsense and thoroughness' should be used.[19] In 1914 Dr Alice Vickery is again mentioned as giving a talk to the WCG in Tottenham.[20]

Dr Alice Vickery's son, Dr Charles Vickery Drysdale, when he became President, advanced the Malthusian League's feminist credentials. He argued that he did not agree that the interests of the individual (especially of women) must be antagonistic to race.[21] He addressed the Women's Freedom League and drew parallels between the two campaigns: 'It was obvious that emancipation from excessive maternity was as essential as political freedom.' Richard Soloway was surely right to conclude that the neo-Malthusians, as an organisation were exceptional in tying the success of the women's struggle for political emancipation to the rearing of smaller families.[22]

The evidence challenges the view, conveniently held by Marie Stopes and later repeated by Angus McLaren, that the Malthusian League was reluctant to provide birth control information to the general public and preferred to work through the medical profession.[23] Although initially the League only recommended literature, in 1913 it published a free pamphlet, *Hygienic Methods of Family Limitation*, which gave much more explicit birth control instruction. In 1922 the staid Malthusian League rebranded itself as the New Generation and the subtitle changed from 'a crusade against poverty' to 'for rational birth control'. The New Generation also increased its leafleting activities, and proudly proclaimed in 1922 that the Society had given out tens of thousands of leaflets and it had great hopes of the revised *Hygienic Methods of Family Limitation* which contained illustrations of the more popular contraceptive devices.[24]

A dramatic event by the New Generation in 1925 was the motorised drop of over a million leaflets, one of the few examples of gesture politics by women in the 1920s. The leaflet-drop underlined the League's modern approach as women drove from one end of the country to the other distributing literature from their cars. This again had symbolic significance as 'new women' like Winifred Strange from Wolverhampton Mothers' Clinic and Mary Stocks from the MSMC, were themselves car drivers.[25] Their aim was to encourage a mass response, so pressurising the Minister of Health to change government policy and permit doctors at municipal infant and child welfare clinics to give birth control advice. The women deliberately motored through industrial districts such as Birmingham, Derby, Sheffield and Newcastle-upon-Tyne. Tribute was paid to those who assisted their motorised campaign including the Labour Party, ILP and Women's Co-operative Guilds. Amongst those financially supporting the leaflet drop were Dr Alice Vickery and the Hon. Mrs Gilbert Murray from the SPBCC.[26] A further high-profile event was the Malthusian Ball held in 1933 and organised by Mrs Eileen Laski of the SPBCC and Dr Edith Summerskill, and which was attended by aristocrats and intellectuals. Donations included two novels from sympathetic writer Winifred Holtby.

Perhaps the most valuable pioneering action of the neo-Malthusians was on 9 November 1921 when they opened the second birth control clinic in the United Kingdom in Walworth Road, just behind the Elephant and Castle public house.[27] This birth control clinic was an extension of their previous activities. These included Dr Alice Vickery's talks in 1908 and Dr Binnie Dunlop's work in 1914 when he proffered birth control advice to working-class mothers in the East End of London. By 1922 *New Generation* was able to proudly publish photos of the clinic's refurbished exterior and interior.[28] Although relations between Marie Stopes and Margaret Sanger subsequently became fraught, Margaret always remained on cordial terms with Dr Alice Vickery and had encouraged the neo-Malthusians to open their own birth control clinic. Indeed the young Fenella Paton, founder of the SPBCC clinic in Aberdeen, was inspired through working in the East End with the Malthusian League to start her own SPBCC birth control clinic in 1926 in Aberdeen.[29]

Financial necessity forced a closer alliance between the New Generation and the SPBCC. In 1922 the Malthusian League, which had been losing members since the turn of the century, was forced to relinquish the Walworth Centre. The clinic was taken over by a specially formed committee which the following year developed into the SPBCC. The energetic supervisor, Evelyn Fuller, was appointed to run the clinic and she provided a unifying element for the SPBCC, passing on organisational recommendations and research findings to the other SPBCC clinics. However, there was friction between the male doctor, with pronounced eugenic views, the committee and patients. Numbers further increased when Dr Haire was replaced by a female doctor and the clinic became an all female environment.

As well as the structural relationship between the New Generation and the SPBCC there was also an overlapping of members. Besides the Hon. Mrs Gilbert Murray at Walworth Road there were other local committee members of SPBCC clinics who were also members of the New Generation. These included Ella Gordon from Wolverhampton and Edith How-Martyn who in 1929 founded her own international birth control organisation.

Although both Dr Alice Vickery and Stella Browne had ideological differences with the Malthusian League, the League itself was far more sympathetic to feminism and more involved with practical action than has often been believed.

In her perceptive biography Lesley Hall described how the campaigner Stella Browne was one of those experiencing tensions in belonging simultaneously to feminist, socialist organisations as well as the Malthusian League. Stella regarded birth control as widening human freedom and she believed the Malthusian League was the only organisation to have this as its main aim. Unusually for a birth controller she was a single woman and took practical action by working with Dr Binnie Dunlop on outreach birth-control projects.[30] She left the Communist Party in 1923 over the birth control issue, became a Labour Party member and campaigned for birth control through the Workers' Birth Control Group.

Stella became a high-profile supporter of the Malthusian Society. Initially by contributing letters to the *New Generation* but then she submitted articles for publication. She was not a passive member but actively participated in the League. Stella attended the Fifth International Birth Control Conference in 1922 and presented a paper on the 'Feminist aspect of birth control.'[31] In 1923 she lectured in Rhondda, South Wales and aimed at 'synthesising the theory and practice of birth control with Socialist principles, quite independently of the neo-Malthusian axiom about food and population increase'.[32]

Stella Browne went on to join the Eugenics Society although she continued to attack its view that women should bear children and often. She had earlier asserted to the *Freewoman* that 'our right to refuse maternity is an inalienable one.'[33] Stella must have realised by that time that the Eugenics Society was not going to change its principles, but retained her membership as she needed allies with abortion law reform.[34]

Eventually there was a change in the balance of power between the older established Malthusian League and the Eugenics Society (originally the Eugenics Education Society). It was popularly seen that Malthusians emphasised the quantitative nature of the population problem, while eugenicists put it in qualitative terms. However, in 1912 Dr C.V. Drysdale disputed this differentiation and argued the neo-Malthusians were also concerned with quality. He condemned the exhortation for the 'fit' to reproduce bountifully, seeing this as brutal and immoral because of the suffering it would involve for women. Even before the First World War their President had already stated, 'We neo-Malthusians are eugenicists to the core.'[35] After the First World War, Dr Drysdale stated in their magazine *New Generation*, 'I am bound to regard better eugenic selection as more important now than greater restriction of the total birth rate.'[36]

The debate between eugenicists and neo-Malthusians was exemplified by a joint meeting on 19 October 1920 which was chaired by the Eugenics Society President, Major Leonard Darwin.[37] Those who spoke included the redoubtable Dr Alice Vickery who maintained that the nation needed an A1 population and this would be provided by access to birth control. She was of course telling her audience of eugenicists what they wanted to hear. The Leicester Medical Officer of Health, Dr Killick Millard believed that the one form of birth control allowed by the Churches, abstinence, was ineffective and dysgenic because of the willpower involved. He held that welfare workers sympathised with the poor worn out mothers overburdened by maternity. Eventually in 1927 Dr Drysdale declared the work of the Malthusian League complete and successfully proposed the winding up of the organisation.

However, many members of the Malthusian League had joined the Eugenics Society and Dr Charles Drysdale remained a valued member of the Eugenics Society until his death.

Eugenicists were at first wary of the birth control movement which they regarded with suspicion. There is an undoubted irony, as Robert A. Peel, President of the Eugenics Society pointed out, that the birth control movement which now regarded eugenics with disdain was in the 1920s scarcely regarded as respectable.[38] Eugenic ideas were originally greeted with an almost religious fervour, for instance Bernard Shaw wrote in 1904, 'There is now no reasonable excuse for refusing to face the fact that nothing but a eugenic religion can save our civilisation from the fate that has overtaken all previous civilisations.'[39] Richard Soloway correctly regarded eugenics as the result of profound social, political and cultural changes feeding upon a deeply entrenched belief in the primacy of heredity.[40] Eugenicists stressed their scientific methods such as the collection of statistics and experiments, although Pauline Mazumdar argued that contemporaries regarded eugenics as a political rather than a scientific movement and believed it could offer a solution to the problem of pauperism whose specific pathology was feeble mindedness.[41]

The relationship between the eugenicists and birth controllers was complex because, as Richard Cleminson argued, eugenics had a chameleon-like ability to appear in different guises in order to attract supporters from widely different collectivities.[42] Richard Soloway recognised the relationship between eugenicists and birth controllers, stating that the rise of eugenics and birth control movements were parallel developments of the late Edwardian years. Eugenics became a social movement when it connected to a wider public opinion. Although there were differences amongst eugenicists, they all shared the belief that reproduction was not a private decision but should be informed by social considerations.[43]

A central tenet of positive eugenics was the importance of motherhood and it stressed that the 'sacred duties of motherhood should not be shirked'. Eugenic ideas about the quality of 'the race' placed emphasis on the importance of the role of motherhood. In her article, 'Imperialism and motherhood', Anna Davin argued that the loss of life in the carnage of the First World War meant that the authorities critically examined the country's birth rate. 'Good motherhood was an essential component in their ideology of racial health and purity. Thus the solution to a national problem of public health and politics was looked for in terms of individuals, of a particular role – the mother, and a social institution – the family.'[44] She argued that motherhood had to be made to seem desirable by the authorities to counteract the declining birth rate.

Bearing and rearing children was maintained by eugenicists to be the wife's chief mission and her sacred obligation to the Empire and the human race. Historian David Barker correctly stated that motherhood was considered by many eugenicists to be the prime purpose of a woman's existence, 'the body of a woman is the temple of the life to come.' He felt they likened the destiny of woman to that of a queen bee, revered and protected but having no choice as to her destiny.[45]

A matter of concern for Edwardian eugenicists was the belief that there was a growing disinclination on the part of the more intelligent and talented women to marry.[46] This was regarded as a threat because nothing should distract women from their mission – certainly not the dangerous pursuit of a career or the new social roles. Edwardian socialites flippantly referred to males as VGTBW (very good to breed with).[47] While many feminists regarded modern developments and the emergence of 'the new woman' as evidence of progress, eugenicists regarded these factors as a threat to the race. 'Sleek, sexy and modern she neglected domestic duties and child rearing and, as a result, generated concern that women were rejecting the duties of their race.'[48]

There were two eugenic organisations that were particularly influential in the 1920s: the Eugenics Society and the Francis Galton Laboratory for National Eugenics. Angela Wanhalla argued that eugenics was particularly attractive to two groups of women: aristocratic and middle-class women who focused on negative eugenics of family limitation, and professional women who were attracted to the health reforms of eugenics.[49]

The Eugenics Society was founded in 1907 and by 1920 quickly eclipsed its neo-Malthusian predecessor, attracting directly and indirectly thousands of birth control supporters who could never have overcome their aversion to the League's economic philosophy or their suspicion it was a regressive organisation. By 1914 the Eugenics Society claimed to have six hundred and thirty-four members and, besides London, there was strong membership in the provincial towns of Birmingham, Liverpool, Manchester and Oxford.[50] Women formed 47.7% of the membership in Birmingham in 1914. Eugenics gained prestige from the fact that from 1911 to 1928 the society was run by its President, Leonard Darwin, the son of the illustrious Charles Darwin whose principles eugenicists recognised. The reforming eugenicist Dr C.P. Blacker was in 1931 appointed General Secretary of the Eugenics Society. He made it clear that he wanted to take the Society in new directions by abandoning its emphasis on stockbreeding. He stated that he intended to remain as Secretary to the Birth Control Investigative Commission and to continue to co-operate with the SPBCC.[51]

Indeed the Eugenics Society was already turning its attention to the human population and the concepts of positive and negative eugenics were explored. Positive eugenics referred to the encouragement of procreation by the 'fit' to provide at least a replacement rate, and negative eugenics to the discouragement of procreation by those deemed 'unfit'. Eugenicists advocated, for those they termed dysgenic, marriage regulation, birth control, sterilisation and segregation. Organisations such as the Royal Institute of Public Health projected their views onto the birth control clinics, producing headlines in contemporary newspapers such as 'Birth control clinics demand sterilisation of the unfit.'[52] *The Eugenics Review* of April 1923 called for a ban on the marriage of sub-normals, who should not breed. These people should only be able to marry when the woman was over forty-five and past childbearing age. Two types of mother were contrasted by the eugenicists, 'the mother of tomorrow' and the 'moron girl', the latter regarded as threatening to the race.[53] Margaret Sanger succinctly put the case for 'more children from the fit, less from the unfit.'[54]

The vast majority of eugenicists at first deplored the birth control movement as they believed this led to a widening gap between the reproduction of the middle classes and 'the less desirable elements'.[55] In 1922 E.W. MacBride, Vice-Chairman of the Eugenics Society, explained how the Society was reluctant to support birth control as it would 'prejudice the production of sufficient babies by the competent and far-seeing members of the community'.[56] Initially middle-class women were blamed by eugenicists for putting their outside interests before family and duty to the race. This was regarded as dysgenic and led to the eugenicists, according to Mrs Edith Bethune-Baker, being perceived as prejudiced against the women's movement.

Richard Soloway correctly concluded that by 1926 the Eugenics Society had overcome the reservations of Leonard Darwin and decided that in the battle with differential fertility, 'prevention' or negative eugenics was likely to be more effective than positive efforts to increase fertility from the upper classes.[57] It argued that making birth control knowledge readily available would not change upper-class fertility as those women already had that knowledge from private physicians, but it could affect working-class mothers. Therefore eugenicists revised their assessment of birth control.

Doctors were influential in deciding birth control provision and a number were members of the Eugenics Society. Speaking in that year to Rotarians in Aberdeen where there was a birth control clinic, Professor J.A. Thomson, spokesman for the Eugenics Society, pronounced, 'Birth control, wisely and medically regulated, was part of practical eugenics.'[58] Dr Herbert, a county councillor for Denbighshire, who held eugenic views, in 1931 persuaded the council to make birth control provision available to married mothers. He equated poverty with eugenic undesirability stating that 'the disease-ridden are breeding copiously.'[59]

Angela Curthoys perceptively stated that there was a strong link between eugenics and feminism, although she felt this relationship had not always been recognised in the twenty first century.[60] However, this overlap was recognised by contemporaries in the early twentieth century. In 1912 American feminist Doris Stevens wrote in the *Common Cause*. 'It is significant that this new outburst of eugenic energy is coincident with the women's movement.'[61]

By 1913 the substantial female membership of the Eugenics Society included unmarried professional women who had taken part in the suffrage struggle. Pauline Mazumdar convincingly argued that they were attracted to a movement that addressed their concerns as women; 'They were drawn to a movement that dealt with a choice of mate, an enhanced status for motherhood and the bearing of healthy children.'[62] Indeed some eugenicists believed that a better education made women better mothers. Feminist SPBCC member Mrs Bethune-Baker showed an awareness of the difficulties inherent in the eugenic position for women. She criticised the eugenic suggestion that educated middle-class women who pursued their careers instead of raising large families were 'neglecting their duties to the race' and held that these arguments were 'prejudiced against the women's movement'.[63]

Many birth controllers and eugenicists subscribed to the concept of voluntary motherhood rather than the absolute prescription that some classes should not have children. Lesley Hall rightly argued that, far from being in opposition, the common ground of feminists and eugenicists was that of the ideology of motherhood and child welfare. These were central concerns of the two social movements. She maintained that there was a significant difference between telling a woman she must not have children and giving her the knowledge to space them.[64]

Although they did not serve on the council in large numbers, women were valuable members of the Eugenics Education Society just as they had been in the Malthusian League. Widowed at the age of twenty-one and interested in social problems, Mrs Sybil Gotto displayed exceptional organising ability. Inspired by Francis Galton's works, she engineered a meeting with him via a barrister friend of hers, Montague Crackanthorpe. Together they established the Eugenics Education Society with Montague Crackanthorpe as President and Sybil Gotto as General Secretary.[65] She already had contacts and knew how to utilise them to make the Society a success. Sybil quickly built up the Society's membership which included Lady Emily Lutyens, wife of the famous architect. Her achievements were all the more remarkable as at the same time she was heavily involved with National Council for Combating Venereal Disease. As Secretary she linked this to her eugenic work by organising joint projects.[66]

The Eugenics Society was part of a broad social and political complex, so that the same person might join the Eugenics Society, the Moral Education League, the Society for the Study of Inebriety or the National Association for the Care and Protection of the Feeble Minded. The Eugenics Society shared interests, activities and programmes with these older societies. Members included doctors, teachers, social workers and ladies generally concerned about social problems. Besides Sybil Gotto, the National Council for Combating Venereal Disease included in its membership Eugenics Society members such as Leonard Darwin, Dr Mott and Dr Mary Scharlieb.

Another influential female in the Eugenics Education Society was Mrs Cora Hodson. In 1921 she was appointed as secretary with administrative duties and ran an office of female volunteers. In 1928 she was promoted to Education Secretary in recognition of her energetic and efficient management of the society's external relations. Cora was a graduate of Lady Margaret Hall, Oxford and set out to cultivate relationships with Eleanor Rathbone and Eva Hubback, with both women becoming members of the Eugenics Society. One of her main achievements was, with Dr C.P. Blacker, to convince eugenicists that birth control was not dysgenic.[67] It was thus possible for the eugenicists to form an alliance with the birth controllers. However, although both Sybil Gotto and Cora Hodson made an important input into the Eugenics Society the available evidence does not support Anne Allen's assertion that women played a leading role in the Eugenics Society policy formation.[68]

My Collective Biography shows there were a number of birth controllers who were also members of the Eugenics Society. These included Mary Stocks, co-founder of the MSMC, who contributed reviews to the *Eugenics Review*, and Lady Trudie Denman, Chairman of the WI and President of the National Birth Rate Commission.[69] Lella Secor Florence, an American supporter of women's suffrage, was a founder member in 1925 of the Cambridge Women's Welfare Association and was a convinced eugenicist. In her report on the opening of the clinic published in the *Eugenics Review*, Lella referred to the fact that eugenicists would be interested in the scientific study of methods of contraception as the present methods were beyond the grasp of the stupidest and the most undesirable members of society.[70] She continued, 'Among the manual labourers and poorest members of society scientific methods are almost unknown, with the result that the poorest class is increasing at a rate out of all proportion both to its means and to the increase in the rest of the community.'[71] Fellow Cambridge SPBCC founder member Mrs Bethune-Baker was also a member of the Eugenics Society, and Margery Spring Rice, one of the founders of the North Kensington SPBCC, believed that eugenics was 'at the heart of the birth control doctrine'.[72]

Edward Fuller wrote an article for the *Eugenics Review*, emphasising that the clinic had eugenic potential as it was treating women from the nearby mental hospital to 'prevent feeble minded or lunatic offspring'.[73] He stressed the importance to the Eugenics Society of the statistics they were compiling of success rates, and this was later emphasised with regard to the newly formed clinics in Aberdeen, Glasgow and Birmingham who also professed willingness to co-operate with the Society.[74]

The other influential eugenic institution was the Biometric Laboratory and the Eugenics Laboratory at University College, London under the direction of pioneering statistician Professor Karl Pearson. He provided access to higher education in a way that was ordinarily denied to women and so provided career opportunities for able scientific women. By 1916, admittedly war years, half the research staff were women. Alice Lee and Ethel Elderton were two high-profile women who flourished in that institution. Their political views are not known, but they voiced objections to Francis Galton opposing the women's movement and being a member of the Anti-Suffrage Review. Although limited funds meant that they were paid less than a man, they were encouraged to pursue their own lines of enquiry and be credited for them. Both were awarded doctorates for their research. Alice Lee studied skull capacity and intellectual ability and Ethel Elderton wrote a joint paper with Karl Pearson on the relationship between heredity and the environment.

In 1914 Ethel Elderton carried out what was for many years the definitive study of the English birth rate north of the Humber. She started with the fact that the English birth rate had declined since the 1880s and then looked at whether there was deliberate family limitation and if this was so in all sections of the community. The statistically based report focused on the fertility of the working class. As the 1911 Census returns for the upper and middle classes were not yet available, she compiled her own statistics and carried out a series of interviews in that area. She found that, in spite of Charles Bradlaugh's visit, there was no hawking of contraceptive appliances, but the mothers freely admitted taking patent pills and remedies to procure illegal abortions. Ethel Elderton condemned the damage done to the mother's health by these illegal measures and harm to subsequent children. The researcher concluded that the fall in birth rate did not have a physiological cause but was due to artificial restriction of the families. She exhorted fit parents to fulfil their social duty by having children.[75] Ethel believed that while the prudent had small families, bad social conditions resulted in large families. She concluded that unwanted pregnancies produced deficient offspring.

The cases of Alice Lee and Ethel Elderton raise the question of whether these two women could be deemed to be feminist. Undoubtedly they were useful role models showing that women could succeed in science but their detailed political opinions are not known. Neither is it known how much these women were involved in political campaigns such as the suffrage. As the evidence of their political activities is absent, they cannot be regarded as feminist in the manner outlined by Olive Banks. Although, due to their careers, they may well have been role models for young women there is no evidence that they fought for social change for other women. However, they can be seen as an example of the 'new women' who Olive Schreiner described as shaking off their sex parasite role.[76]

Some feminists like Dora Marsden, editor of *Freewoman*, were vigorously opposed to the Eugenics Society. She attacked eugenics as a danger to the community, and accused not the poor but the rich of being unfit and workshy. Dora went on to state that the 'defective' was so 'because [of] the demands [that] the rich wastrel and workshy [had] made upon his forbears'.[77] She was disgusted that eugenicists had supported the Mental Deficiency Bill of 1913 which enabled those certified as feeble minded by two physicians to be detained indefinitely in a mental institution.

Leonard Darwin led the Eugenics Society into a complex net of alliances with Women's Co-operative Guilds, the National Institute of Motherhood, the Association of Infant Welfare Centres, the National Association for the Prevention of Infant Mortality.[78] However, the Eugenics Society itself was approached by organisations and individuals wishing to form alliances, such as Marie Stopes and Eleanor Rathbone, who wanted to enlist its support for their projects. Marie Stopes had written extensively on birth control and as described in Chapter Two was to open the country's first birth control clinic in 1921. Eleanor Rathbone, President of the National Union of Societies for Equal Citizenship, also wanted support for family endowment proposals as outlined in Chapter Three and successfully moved NUSEC in that direction.

Marie Stopes contributed to the meeting with the Eugenics Society on 19 October 1920. She had belonged briefly to the Malthusian League which welcomed the brave outspokenness of *Married Love*. Characteristically she changed her allegiance and became a member of the Eugenics Society in 1912, only five years after it was founded and her writings contained much mainstream eugenic thought. Marie believed that the population problem was not, as the neo-Malthusians believed, that there were too many people, but too many children being born to the poor and not enough to the wealthy.[79] Her writings were completely opposite in style to the didactic neo-Malthusian literature. She told her audience what they wanted to hear and gave permission for them to enjoy sexual satisfaction. Lesley Hall wrote that Marie's vision was not about 'preventative restraint', but a gateway into a new world of healthy, wanted babies and sexual joy.[80]

There is a debate as to what extent Marie Stopes held eugenic views and to what extent these informed her actions. Simon Szreter described her as a 'maverick eugenicist'.[81] Richard Soloway emphasised the strength of Marie Stopes' eugenic views, stating that she was a eugenicist long before she became a birth controller.[82] This assessment is questionable. The birth control clinic she founded with her husband in 1921 was to be part of what she significantly termed the Society for Constructive Birth Control and Racial Progress, and the rubber check diaphragm was termed the Pro-Race Cap. She certainly was consistent in her support for the Eugenics Society and her eugenic sentiments expressed in *Birth Control News*, have a different tone from the elegiac phrases of her books: 'We must breed for quality, not quantity in the human species, or the end is nigh.'[83] Again Marie declared that 'Unless at the same time the influx of low-caste foreigners, especially from Eastern Europe, is checked, they will fill up the gaps and mongrelize our English and Scottish stock.'[84]

Marie Stopes was largely able to assuage the eugenicists' fears that birth control was dysgenic i.e. that the intelligent middle-class women would be deflected from their duty of motherhood while the working class would carry on breeding. The work of her Constructive Birth Control clinic and also the SPBCC demonstrated that not only did working-class mothers desire to control their fertility, but that they were able to understand and persevere with birth control techniques. Marie Stopes and the SPBCC argued that not only were their mothers healthier, but also that their children who were carefully spaced, would survive. This therefore fulfilled the eugenic aims of healthy mothers and an expanding, fit population. Marie was amongst the first people to make the connection between birth control as improving the health of women and birth control as improving the health of the race. She regarded the two states as being not in conflict but complementary. Numerous government reports in the 1920s into maternal mortality found that it was not significantly decreasing but nevertheless refused to make the connection between mothers bearing large numbers of children and the maternal death rate.

However, Marie Stopes was a complex personality and the philosophy behind the organisation of her birth control clinics was not straightforwardly eugenic. In a perceptive contribution to a Galton Institute Conference which reassessed Marie Stopes' work, Deborah Cohen argued there was a problem in assuming her eugenic beliefs were necessarily translated into eugenic action. Deborah Cohen gave a balanced view of Marie's views, arguing that, 'It is evident that Marie Stopes subordinated eugenic and political considerations to a broader concern with helping the poor, often desperate women who visited the facility.'[85] That Marie was a convinced eugenicist was not in doubt, but Deborah Cohen provided a number of instances where Marie departed from the received wisdom of the eugenics movement. Indeed, Marie violated eugenic principles when she decided that all mothers, regardless of income, social class or race, would be treated at her clinics. Deborah Cohen quoted Marie as declaring that, 'Her husband may be a millionaire, but I shall still describe her as a poor woman if she did not know how to control her own motherhood and suffered from that want of knowledge.'[86] Unlike many eugenicists Marie considered it a middle-class woman's right to plan her family and viewed working-class mothers not as 'pawns of the eugenics movement but as people who wanted to change their lives'. Her comments, scribbled into books in her personal library, now held at University of Manchester John Rylands Library, demonstrated a genuine concern for the mothers who wrote to her. The correspondence held in the British Library show her sympathetic, handwritten comments on personal replies to birth control questions. Marie Stopes' eugenic proclamations apparently did not affect her birth control practices.

Marie Stopes held many eugenic views, but the Eugenics Society largely resisted her overtures. On a personal level they believed, probably correctly, that her abrasive personality would antagonise the medical members of Eugenics Society who comprised nearly a quarter of their membership. However, in spite of their fraught relationship, she demonstrated her commitment to the Eugenics Society by leaving them her premises at Whitfield Street, London on her death in 1958.

Eleanor Rathbone's personality was in contrast to that of Marie Stopes as Eleanor was far more politically aware. Her major work, *The Disinherited Family* was published in 1914 and she subsequently outlined her ideas in a paper that she read to the Eugenics Society entitled 'Family endowment and its bearing on the population question' on 12 November 1924. The next year this was deemed important enough to be reproduced along with the ensuing discussion in the *Eugenics Review*.[87] She framed her proposed family endowment policy as being eminently eugenic and pointed to the Separation Allowances paid to wives of soldiers and sailors during the First World War as providing a successful precedent. Her proposed measure would allow the State to take a more proactive role in the provision of maternity support. She believed that the State could guard against racial decay by being able to influence the birth rate without violating the liberties of individual citizens. Family endowment via 'direct provision paid to the mother would raise the standard of life of the poorer wage-earner.' Eleanor held that an orderly and self-respecting living was the best cure for indiscriminate and dysgenic breeding.[88]

Eleanor Rathbone countered the criticisms from her opponents, particularly the eugenicists, who held that family endowment would encourage an increase in the birth rate, particularly amongst those they would deem undesirable, such as alcoholics. Eleanor quoted from the statistics of the 1911 Census, and she believed that by enabling slum dwellers to be housed with decency, their birth rate would decrease. Rather than be dysgenic the proposed family endowment would increase with income, possibly via employers' contribution to the scheme, so encouraging the most valuable sections of society to produce slightly larger families. Conversely, unfit parents, such as alcoholics, would be disqualified from the scheme.

In the tradition of new feminism, Eleanor Rathbone argued for the right of women to control their destinies and be able to take relief from excessive childbearing. She quoted approvingly from Carr-Saunders' comments on the dignity and status of mothers, believing that family endowment would give the mother some degree of self-determination. Family endowment would help even the most oppressed wife and mother by giving some relief from complete dependence and enabling her to protect herself. The granting of family endowment would not lead to an increase in size in the families of lower classes. However, Leonard Darwin, President of the Eugenics Society, opposed Eleanor Rathbone as he still believed that allowances might make low-paid workers even less responsible in the number of children they produced. Throughout the 1920s and 1930s the Society was only prepared to support family allowances if they were graded to give higher earners increased financial benefits. They regarded a flat rate as dysgenic.

It is true that Eleanor Rathbone was concerned with issues such as 'race stock' and used metaphors such as seed-time and harvest. Yet at a number of points in *The Disinherited Family* she denounced the eugenicists for simply seeing the male population as cannon fodder:

> Public opinion in this country oscillates between fear of a declining birth rate and the fear of over population. The motive of the former fear is usually political; those who fear it are either ambitious for the spread of Anglo-Saxon civilisation over the earth or obsessed with the thought of jealous continental neighbours and teeming Oriental millions.[89]

Although there were occasions when Eleanor used eugenicist imagery, for instance when addressing the Eugenics Society, Johanna Alberti correctly drew attention to the importance of context in framing her arguments. 'My sense is that when writing for a non-eugenicist audience in the 1920s, she was at her most confident and hopeful.'[90]

In the inter-war years many members of the Eugenics Society joined the SPBCC and Marie Stopes' SBCRP. Eva Hubback, who had recently joined the Eugenics Education Society, was also a member of the SPBCC as well as NUSEC. By the end of the decade Carr-Saunders was extremely enthusiastic about the potential of the birth control movement, 'I am more and more impressed with the fact that birth control is the greatest thing that has come over our species.'[91] By the mid-1920s the Eugenics Society conceded that birth control could be useful if it could limit the reproduction of the undesirables of society and accepted the research which demonstrated that British birth control clinics were operating eugenically. Eugenicists put forward the argument that birth control provision which could be extended to the dysgenic poor could eradicate the heavy burden threatened by racial degeneration.

A number of members of the Eugenics Society realised the benefits of co-operation with the SPBCC, for instance in research. The birth control statistics they collected from the SPBCC were of particular interest to eugenicists such as Norman Himes and Caroline Hadleigh Robinson.[92] In 1927 a Birth Control Investigation Committee was set up to undertake research in all aspects of birth control, including effectiveness of methods and the social background of those visiting the clinics. The President of the Eugenics Society, successfully urged co-operation with the SPBCC and consequently it awarded generous funding to the Birth Control Investigation Committee. Several Eugenics Society members were represented on the Commission and the Eugenics Society in 1928 gave £200 to the Birth Control Investigation Committee under Sir Humphrey Rolleston. In return the Eugenics Society was able to draw on large scale data from the SPBCC clinics to determine the efficacy of the various birth control materials and methods.

The Eugenics Society saw a greater involvement with the SPBCC as a way of reaching larger numbers of potential members. Subsequently attempts were made by the Eugenics Society to bring about an even closer relationship with the NBCC of which the SPBCC became a part. There was discussion of a merger which was proposed by Blacker, Secretary of the Eugenics Society, and Margaret Pyke, Secretary of the NBCC.[93] It is possible that Margaret Pyke's support of eugenics was tactical rather a wholehearted embrace of eugenic principles.

It is important to ask what the attraction was of the Eugenics Society to the SPBCC. Certainly finance was an important consideration. The SPBCC, though it had a few wealthy donors, was a comparatively poor organisation. On the other hand the Eugenics Society from 1923 benefitted from the philanthropy of an eccentric Australian sheep farmer, Henry

Twichin. On his death the Twichin Bequest transformed the Eugenics Society into a wealthy organisation, as he bequeathed it £70,000.

Martin Pugh argued that, because of its small numbers, the Eugenics Society was more of a hindrance than a help to the SPBCC.[94] However, this ignored the important factor of prestige by association and the SPBCC wanted to acquire respectability. As has been seen, a number of suffragists had condemned birth control as immoral and initially many eugenic supporters were also repelled by the negative image of birth control. In contrast, throughout the 1920s the Eugenics Society was regarded as academically respectable and an 'insider' by universities and research bodies. Grant-making trusts tended to be cautious in allocating funding and so supported established charities which were generally considered to be reputable. This may have been one reason why Professor Carr-Saunders, who published a popular book, *Eugenics*, was invited by the MSMC to be a platform speaker at their inaugural meeting in 1926. Carr-Saunders was described by Richard Soloway as a thoughtful, balanced student of sociology and biology with strong academic credentials.[95] Thus co-operation between the two societies both formally and informally could be regarded as mutually beneficial.

However, although there was close co-operation between the two organisations in the inter-war period there was never a formal alliance. The Eugenics Society had reservations about potentially having to support costly social welfare schemes. Mrs Margery Pyke realised that because of the socialist political affiliations of the grassroots membership of the NBCC, the SPBCC's successor, the proposal was unlikely to have gained its approval. Although the Eugenics Society generously funded birth control research, there was not a formal alliance. The SPBCC clinics were not even prepared to adopt the Eugenics Society's system of case cards, and none of the minutes of the local SPBCC clinics examined for this thesis expressed eugenic sentiments. Liverpool Mothers' Clinic discussed the Eugenics Society letter on case cards and decisively rejected their proposal.[96]

Thus, though there continued to be co-operation between individual members of the two societies, there was no institutional amalgamation. The tensions regarding feminism and birth control seen in the Malthusian League and Eugenics Society can also been seen in the attitudes of the major political parties.

7   Working the Political Parties

In the 1920s the newly enfranchised birth controllers worked for change through the national and local structures of the Labour Party, the WCG and the Women's Liberal Association. (Birth control was never on the political agenda of the Conservative Party although individual members such as Charis Frankenburg were active in the SPBCC.) The tensions Labour women felt on this issue are illustrated by the conflicting attitudes on birth control of two leading Labour women, Dr Marion Phillips and Ellen Wilkinson. The effectiveness of the policy advocacy coalitions in advancing birth control is examined at both the national and local levels.

It would be simplistic to see the birth control controversy in terms of dichotomies between male and female, Labour and Conservative or even in terms of competing religious membership. Indeed Stephen Fielding, in his study of Salford, showed that besides social class there were also identities based on gender, ethnicity, age and occupation.[1] Karen Hunt correctly pointed out that it is all too easy to homogenise Labour women, for example at the 1926 Labour Party Women's Conference working-class Catholic Mrs Simpson opposed the views of former suffragette Miss Quinn who was also a Roman Catholic.[2] Mrs Simpson, a mother of thirteen said she believed many Catholic women did in fact practise birth control. The birth-control campaign may have begun with middle-class feminists, as Pamela Graves claimed, but it was soon embraced by politicised working-class women.[3]

My Collective Biography shows that Labour members were prominent in the birth control campaign. Labour Party teacher Leah

Manning and her friend Ruth Dalton founded the Cambridge birth control clinic and they were joined there by Labour Party activist Helen Pease. Both Leah and Ruth went on to be Labour MPs. As has been seen, Mary Barbour, Glasgow Labour councillor, was active in founding the SPBCC clinic there. The Wolverhampton clinic was started by Labour activists Ella Gordon and Alice Onions and supported by Lady Cynthia Mosley, who was at that time a Labour MP. In Birmingham there was also a strong Labour presence on the clinic's Executive Committee. The Labour Party family of Lawthers was active in establishing the Newcastle-upon-Tyne clinic, and the Collective Biography shows Mrs Lawther contributed to the debate on birth control clinics at the 1927 Labour Party Women's Conference.

It appeared SPBCC members were able to put aside political differences in order to pursue a clearly defined practical aim. As Alderman Nellie Beer of the Manchester Maternity Mortality Committee remarked, 'although we were of different parties we were never at loggerheads'.[4] Charis Frankenburg, an active Conservative, was asked by Brian Harrison how she felt being outnumbered by left-wing members in the SPBCC.[5] Charis had disagreements with the Liberal, Shena Simon in Manchester but these appeared to be personal not political. Another Conservative birth controller was Flora Blumberg of the MSMC. Indeed the MSMC Executive contained Labour Party members, Liberals, Conservatives and the Receptionist was a Communist Party member.

Prominent Liberal women were active in the SPBCC. In Manchester Shena Simon, the Liberal councillor, was married to Ernest Simon, the Liberal MP for Withington. In Aberdeen, the founder of the clinic was Fenella Paton, daughter of John Crombie who was Liberal MP for Kincardine and a Privy Councillor. She was herself President of the Women's Liberal Association.[6] Margery Spring Rice, an active Liberal, was Chairman of the North Kensington's Women's Welfare Centre on its foundation in 1924. As a lay expert she took part in a national committee of enquiry into the health and conditions of working-class wives and subsequently published a book on this subject.[7] The Quaker Elizabeth Cadbury was well known in the Birmingham area for her council work as a Liberal and was a founder member of the birth control clinic. She was profiled on the front page of *Liberal Women's News* in April 1925.

The granting of the franchise to women created new political opportunities and heralded enthusiastic political mobilisation by women in the Labour and Liberal parties. For many women, Conservative Party membership could be an important social activity, but joining the Labour Party was seen as a definite political step. Karen Hunt and June Hannam commented that 'with no formal barriers to their participation at any level in Socialist organisations, they believed they had the opportunity for self-fulfilment as political activists and also a space to pursue women's collective interests as a sex.'[8] There was a surge in Labour's female membership. Only six years after the granting of the partial franchise the 1924 Labour Party Annual Report stated that there were 1,332 Women's Sections. It may have been that the Labour Party's Chief Woman Officer was sometimes over-optimistic in her submissions but nevertheless these figures of female membership represent a considerable achievement.

Party membership included a wide range of social classes. Beatrice Webb commented about the two miners' wives she had staying with her for the 1924 Labour Party Women's Conference, 'They were attractively clothed and their talk was mostly about public affairs, the one emotionally stirred by the Socialist faith and familiar with all its shibboleths; the other shrewd, cautious matter-of-fact in her political expectations.' Beatrice confided in her diary that they all agreed that the Conference, which included a discussion on birth control, was a success.[9]

These political organisations reflected the desire for their own women members to become more involved politically. Pamela Graves drew attention to this mobilisation which surprised even men of their own movement and confounded those who had argued that working-class housewives were not amenable to political organisation.[10] Dr Marion Phillips was also keen to stress, in her other role as editor of *Labour Woman*, the involvement in politics of the newly enfranchised voters. 'Wherever a few come together, whether at their door steps, in social intercourse in their homes, or in the long waiting queues outside shops, the talk necessarily centres more or less consciously upon the political events of our times.'[11] Perhaps this was an over-optimistic view of women's priorities but it did present a positive image of working-class women voters.

Middle-class professional women were also eager to display their socialist beliefs. General practitioner, Dr Mabel May of the Manchester

Rusholme District Labour Party and Manchester and MSMC enthusiastically declared to Manchester's Hulme Women's Co-operative Guild that 'even if she had not been a socialist the environment with which she came into contact would have made her a socialist.'[12] Significantly Mabel May was identified by Declan McHugh as one of the most important two hundred Labour Party members in Manchester in the 1920s.[13]

This increase in the Labour Party's female membership was paralleled by a similar increase in membership in the WCG. The WCG annual reports from 1919 to 1921 reported an influx of twenty thousand new members, mostly married working-class women. Such was the enthusiasm for political action amongst women that there was a considerable overlapping of membership in socialist organisations. About half of the Labour Women were also WCG members. The WCG's first General Secretary, Margaret Llewelyn Davies, claimed that this self-governing organisation could speak with greater authority than any other body for the voteless and voiceless millions of married working women in England. The Co-operative Party tried to encourage its newly enfranchised women members to be politically active and regarded them as making a positive contribution electorally. The Guilds attracted respectable working-class women whose families had grown up.[14]

The Liberal Women's Federation was established before the Labour Party Women's Sections and its membership fluctuated in the 1920s. Nevertheless in 1923 there were 71,040 Liberal women in 788 branches. The minutes of local groups from the Women's Liberal Federation, the largest of the three women's political organisations, also demonstrated a high degree of political commitment to their party. The Secretary of Rochdale Women's Liberal Association stirringly recorded that in 1918:

> With little warning we found ourselves faced with a general election in December. This being the first since the enfranchisement of women it naturally created great interest and stimulated debate such that had never been experienced. I think we may humbly claim that the women rose magnificently to the occasion in organising and speaking at public meetings. We confidently believe that a very favourable impression was made upon the public.[15]

Nevertheless, the numbers involved in these organisations were small compared to the Conservative and Unionist Party whose women's organisation had a membership of over a million by 1928.

Pat Thane has argued that the issue of state-funded birth control clinics was one of the main points of disagreement between Labour Party Women's Sections and the leadership in the 1920s.[16] This friction had its roots in the transition from the Women's Labour League, founded in 1908 as a body 'set up by women for women', to being translated into Women's Sections of the Labour Party.[17] In 1918, a new Labour Party constitution was constructed and the WLL accepted the Labour Party's proposals. It was rather patronisingly decided by the leadership that there should be a measure of positive discrimination because the newly enfranchised women needed to be educated politically. Superficially it appeared that the women had made significant gains, although they already held national conferences and published their own magazine. The women only paid half the male subscription but there was the new appointment of a Chief Woman Officer, the women were given four seats on the NEC, their own Conference, a Women's Advisory Committee and the continuation of their own magazine. Women had the option of joining the women-only sections of their branches or 'mixed branches'. This apparently fulfilled one of the WLL's main aims which was 'to educate themselves on political and social questions by means of meetings, discussion' and no doubt the WLL initially believed that having educated themselves they could actively help shape Labour Party policy on women's issues. They were to be disappointed on the birth control issue.

The Labour Party leadership believed that women had the same opportunity as men of being selected as MPs, councillors and conference delegates and so being involved in policy making. However, Eleanor Barton, Secretary of the WCG and prospective parliamentary candidate, criticised this assumption. 'It is said that there is equality for men and women in the movement. Certainly most of the doors are open. But the seats are full and possession is nine tenths of the law so that in reality is not open and the seats are hard to win.'[18] The grassroots women soon realised that their socio-economic position militated against opportunities for political activism as most women did not work outside the home. They did not belong to the large unions with their bloc votes which dominated the annual conferences. In the 1926 birth control debate, Dorothy Jewson MP stated that it was a pity that there were only about seventy women attending the conference, presumably for the reasons listed above.[19]

The male Labour Party policy makers would have preferred to suppress any discussion of birth control by framing the issue as falling outside traditional politics. It was presented by the leadership as an issue that should not be part of normal political debate as it was a matter for individual conscience. Dorothy Jewson protested at the 1928 Labour Party Women's Conference: 'If this [birth control] was not to be a Party question how was it to be got through Parliament?'[20] The editor of *Liberal Women's News* similarly argued that as birth control had been discussed both in the House of Commons and the House of Lords, it was a political matter and should be discussed at the Liberal Party Women's Conference. The Liberal Party leadership adopted a more relaxed position on birth control.[21]

The leadership attempted to present support for the birth control campaign in an unfavourable way, for instance as exhibiting a lack of faith in a socialist future or as a scandalous sexual issue. Obviously these arguments were not exclusive and could be used in conjunction with one another. The leadership was apparently pursuing an agenda of different priorities concerning economic and social issues. This conflict was evidenced in the long struggle between the Labour Party Annual Conference, which was the central decision-making body of the Labour Party, and the Labour Party Women's Conference, which was held earlier in the year.

There were substantial majorities in favour of the creation of municipal birth control clinics at the Labour Party Women's Conferences. At the 1925 Labour Party Women's Conference in Birmingham a pro-birth control resolution was carried by 876 to 6 votes; and at the 1926 Annual Labour Party Conference a birth control resolution was carried. A pattern emerged that between 1924 and 1927 the Labour Party Women's Conference would pass resolutions in favour of wider access to birth control information, but with the exception of 1926, similar resolutions would subsequently be omitted from debate or defeated at the Labour Party Annual Conferences.

June Hannam and Karen Hunt correctly remarked that 'birth control as an issue was entangled with the fight of women members of the Labour Party to empower their annual conference and to establish an equal role within the party.'[22] It soon appeared that a key weakness of the Labour Party Women's Conference was that, unlike bodies such as the ILP, it could not submit resolutions directly for consideration by the Labour Party. Dorothy Jewson MP said that in 1926 fifty resolutions had been put on the agenda of the Labour Party Women's Conference and birth control had completely dominated the conference but their concerns were ignored at the Labour Party Annual Conferences. In 1927 she asked at the Labour Party Annual Conference why the Women's Conference was still not recognised as an official Labour Party conference and why, unlike trade unions, it was not allowed to put three questions on the agenda. The issue was brushed aside by Arthur Henderson for the Executive.

In 1926 Labour women mobilised behind the birth control issue, which had also been successfully raised at the previous two Labour Party Women's Conferences. The 1926 Women's Party Conference programme listed sixty-seven Labour Party Women's Sections which had submitted resolutions on birth control. The resolution which had the most number of signatories was Number Thirty Nine which stated:

> that in view of the almost unanimous vote of the National Conference of Labour Women in 1924 and 1925 in favour of giving birth control information at Welfare Centres under public control, this Conference deeply deplores the recommendation made by the Executive and passed by the National Conference at Liverpool in 1925. While making no demands that the Labour Party identify itself with birth control propaganda, this Conference calls upon the whole Party to realise the crying need of mothers and to pledge itself to lift the ban on giving scientific information to working mothers who are forced by economic necessity to rely for economic advice on the Maternity Centres.[23]

The forty-three Women's Sections which supported this amendment included Oxford City and Wolverhampton where there were already SPBCC clinics. There was also backing for the resolution from regions where there were no birth control clinics. There was a diverse geographical spread. Bournemouth, Chelsea and Greenwich had Women's Sections in the more affluent South whereas Barrow-in-Furness Joint Council of Women's Sections was in one of those areas most affected by the economic depression. Once again the birth control resolution was passed overwhelmingly.

The birth control advocates went on from the Labour Party Women's Conference to have their most successful Labour Party Conference in the autumn of 1926. Dora Russell presented the campaign in terms which resonated with the men's class struggle and took advantage of the women's support for the strikers. She referred to the 'ancient and honourable Trade Union of mothers'. She wanted the Conference to realise that to women, birth control was as important an issue as the seven-hour day was to the miners. Dora pointed out that although mining was the most dangerous male occupation, there were more fatalities in childbirth per year than in the mining industry.[24]

In spite of the favourable vote, the Labour Party's constitution meant the campaign had to begin all over again at the 1927 Women's Conference. The women who were chosen to lead the debate for the birth controllers were as significant for what they represented as for what they argued. As my Collective Biography shows, Helen Pease was a Labour councillor, a member of the Cambridgeshire District Labour Party as well as founding the SPBCC clinic in Cambridge. She was the daughter of Rt Hon. Sir Josiah Wedgwood who was then a Labour minister. Helen said she wanted to clarify what the last Women's Conference had requested, i.e. all they had wanted was for medical officers of health to give birth control information when requested. They agreed that ideally birth control should not be a political matter, but they were informed that the adverse ruling by the Conservative, Sir Alfred Mond, could only be changed by Parliament. She presented the issue as one of public debate rather than private conscience. Helen believed that 'there were a great many subjects upon which they as members of the Party disagreed, but she had yet to be told that they might not discuss those subjects in Conference for fear of offending the convictions of the Labour members in the House of Commons.'[25]

Similar arguments were rehearsed in the columns of *Labour Woman*. Birth control was presented as a salacious issue which would alienate respectable voters if it were placed on the party programme. This had been a view held by some suffragists, and indeed *Liberal Women's News* contained a letter from the Yorkshire Women's Federation complaining that birth control was not a suitable subject for public discussion.[26] On the other hand Ethel Carroll from Colne had felt driven to write to *Labour Woman* that as regards 'free-love and illegitimacy' any Labour woman who advocates birth control does so, not to help free love but to help overburdened parents.[27] There was also the feeling amongst the Labour leadership that when a socialist government was firmly established, there would be enough resources to feed all families and so to discuss a policy of birth control would be showing a lack of faith.

Many Labour MPs believed that the impact of the birth control issue on the Catholic voters could damage their electoral chances.[28] The redoubtable Miss Quinn, former suffragette and militant Catholic, correctly stated at the 1927 Labour Party Women's Conference that a good many Labour MPs had been returned on Irish Catholic votes. Arthur Henderson, successfully concluding for the Executive at the 1927 Labour Party Women's Conference, made the point about how disastrous it would be for the Party if religious scruples were aroused. He reiterated this theme at their 1928 Conference.

After the 1926 General Strike, even though the Catholic hierarchy was suspicious of the Labour Party, many working-class Catholics continued to identify with the Labour Party as they regarded the Conservative Party as the party of wealth and privilege. It must have seemed to the Labour leadership that there were few obstacles to the party's total annexation of the Catholic working-class vote. Stephen Fielding highlighted the tension of the Catholic electorate over the birth control issue and believed that determined Catholic opposition led to the Labour Party avoiding publicly debating the issue.[29]

Nonetheless not all prominent Labour Party members were opposed to birth control. Henry Brailsford, the editor of the ILP paper *New Leader*, was consistently sympathetic to birth control and believed that the Labour leadership was simply frightened of losing Catholic votes. He argued that principles should take precedence over votes. 'Unless we are to be a mere vote-getting caucus, the honest mass of the Labour Party must over-rule its officials.' A similar view was adopted by Dorothy Jewson MP. 'The officials of the Labour Party, exaggerating a small electoral risk, are deliberately offending the strong, even passionate opinion of the women of the Party who know what misery and degradation is caused by ignorance in this matter.'[30]

The public birth control debate was finally terminated by the leadership with a speech by Arthur Henderson at the 1928 Labour Party Women's Conference. The closure of discussion at both the Labour Party Conference and also the Labour Party Women's Conference provoked widespread frustration and anger. At the of Labour Party Women's Conference in 1929 at Buxton, Mrs Gledhill moved:

> That this Conference feels that women only should take part in the debates at the Business and Public National Conferences of Labour Women and that no men members of the National Executive should be invited to speak and reverse a decision arrived at by women at a previous Conference.[31]

In seconding the resolution Mrs Tait complained that there was no point in having a women's conference at all if they were going to allow people to come in after the Conference had made a decision and say 'it should not be.' Winifred Horrobin remarked that the Conference 'gets more and more like a Mothers' Meeting holding a garden party with the Vicar in attendance, and...it is just about as politically effective in the life of the movement.'[32]

This sense of dissatisfaction with the role of the Labour Party Women's Conference was felt in local Labour Party Women's Advisory Committees. Gorton Women's Section in their minutes of 1 July 1929 was highly critical of that year's Conference. The Secretary said that in her view it 'was purely a demonstration' because resolutions never progressed further than the Conference Hall.[33] The Manchester Women's Advisory Committee also felt the Women's Labour Party Conference did not fulfil any useful purpose unless it could get resolutions onto the agenda of the Labour Party Annual Conference.[34]

The birth control issue posed difficult moral issues which resulted in contradictions and ambiguities on the part of leading Labour women. In particular these can be seen in the attitudes of Marion Phillips and Ellen Wilkinson who both feature in the Collective Biography. They were both single women, in powerful positions in the Labour Party who were in a position to test the party's structures. Ellen Wilkinson was first elected an MP in 1924 and Marion Phillips became an MP in 1929.

Marion Phillips had been active in the WLL, and came to be the most powerful woman in the Labour Party, acquiring multiple positions. She was appointed as Chief Woman Officer, acted as Secretary to the SJC and remained as editor of *Labour Woman*. As Chief Woman Officer she was directly responsible to the NEC rather than the Women's Sections. Her feminism was always subordinated to her socialism. She usually, but not always, placed party loyalty first, arguing a Labour electoral victory would lead to a more just society.[35]

On the surface Marion Phillips' position on birth control was quite clear and was publicly stated in, amongst other publications, *Labour Woman*. As early as 1913, when Editor of the WLL magazine, she published a discussion on the politics of birth control.[36] Eleven years later when the birth control controversy was again aired in *Labour Woman*, she included a letter signed by amongst others Dora Russell, Ruth Dalton and Frida Laski of the SPBCC advancing the argument for birth control clinics.[37] In response Marion Phillips provided a comprehensive whole page editorial, 'Birth control, a plea for careful consideration', which set out her own and her party leadership's position on birth control. The issue was framed by her as a matter of individual conscience rather than a party issue, but in reality the debate was framed by the leadership to avoid offending religious beliefs. Marion declared that:

> There are many thousands of women to whom moral considerations dictate a certain view against even a discussion of this subject. Many of us do not share that view, but we are bound in our loyalty to the common cause of Labour not to force them to separate themselves from us, which is not a political one, but is, in a special sense one of private conviction.[38]

Marion in many ways acted as a gatekeeper on behalf of the male Labour Party leadership. At the 1924 Labour Party Women's Conference she demanded that Dora Russell withdraw her Women's Section's birth control resolution, 'Sex should not be dragged into politics. You will split the Party from top to bottom'.[39] After a confrontation Dora Russell famously concluded that the Labour Party Chief Woman Officer 'existed not so much to support the demands of the women as to keep them in order from the point of view of the male politician'.[40] She has been described as 'a policing agent for the male party leaders who tried to weaken and contain the struggle'.[41]

Yet Marion Phillips appeared to have a strong moral sense and an academic's view that all the evidence should be presented, even if unpalatable. She must have been one the few women with a research doctorate to edit a woman's political paper.[42] Her intellectual honesty can be seen in her reaction to the Rev. Barr's actions. In February 1926 a Private Member's Bill, was introduced into the House of Commons, by the Labour MP, Ernest Thurtle, a member of the WBCG. This challenged the ruling which stopped maternity and child welfare authorities from giving contraceptive advice to married women who required it for health reasons. However, he was opposed by another Labour MP Rev. James Barr, MP for Motherwell.[43] The Bill was lost with 81 votes in favour and 167 against. Of the Labour Party MPs 44 had voted against the Bill and only 27 in favour. Significantly, Marion Phillips did not approach James Barr privately, but publicly berated him in *Labour Woman*. She attacked Rev. Barr for leading the parliamentary opposition to a fellow Labour member's Bill.[44] She argued that he had missed the point as the Bill was not about his private convictions on birth control but rather about removing restrictions to those that needed it. This in fact was the policy of the SPBCC and WBCG which she had earlier criticised.

Marion Phillips was also frustrated by the lack of influence of the SJC of which she was, amongst her many roles, Secretary. The committee of Labour women and of the WCG were chosen by industrial and political organisations of working women, though in practice Labour women set the agenda. In June 1925 the SJC urged the Executive to give approval to the resolutions on birth control presented at the three previous women's conferences. They pointed out that Catholic women themselves were divided over the issue. In December 1926 after the Labour Party's Women's Conference the SJC once again presented to the Executive a report which they thought clarified the position of the conference.[45] The SJC courageously asserted they thought there had been a misunderstanding. The Committee did not ask for an expression of opinion on the matter but only the right of working-class mothers to gain such information from doctors at municipal clinics. However, the SJC's weak structural position was now revealed. The SJC was only an advisory body and the Executive decided to ignore the recommendations of some of the most senior women members of the Party over the birth control issue.

Marion loyally continued to serve but was obviously dissatisfied with the status of the SJC.

Similar ambiguities can be found in the career of Ellen Wilkinson. Karen Hunt and June Hannam adopted a critical view of Ellen Wilkinson's political career and concluded that 'she increasingly compromised her "feminist" views of issues such as birth control, if they affected her Party's electoral success and emphasised class rather than gender loyalties.'[46] Ellen Wilkinson's position was complex and she was certainly aware of the structural difficulties impeding the birth control cause. Although in 1918 women were given four representatives out of the twenty-strong National Executive, these women were voted on not by the Labour Party women but by the Labour Party Annual Conference with its strong male trade union element. She wrote a letter on 3 December 1921 on behalf of the Manchester and Salford Labour Women's Advisory Council which was, circulated to General Secretary, Arthur Henderson and all Women's Sections, and urged that the women NEC members should be directly elected.[47]

Ellen Wilkinson was initially sympathetic to the birth control campaign and when chairing a session at the Labour Party Women's Conference in 1925 she stopped the Catholic Miss Quinn from attacking birth control supporters as being 'filth', 'impure and unchaste' and a 'device against God and humanity'.[48] She said she could not allow Quinn to make any more insulting remarks to delegates. Ellen Wilkinson who had been one of the few Labour MPs to support Thurtle's 1926 Private Member's Bill on birth control and was the only woman MP to vote for it. Dora Russell regarded Wilkinson as a birth control ally and wrote in 2 March 1926, 'Miss Ellen Wilkinson, as all who know her would expect, stood by the women of the party.'[49]

However, Ellen Wilkinson became more circumspect in her utterances on birth control and this was reflected in her political position. She confided to Dora that as a single woman she had to be careful in her pronouncements in case she was accused of immorality. However, this had not stopped her before. Ellen Wilkinson did not just refrain from speaking out on birth control but seconded Arthur Henderson's resolution at the 1928 Labour Party Women's Conference to stop vexatious debates every year on birth control. Ellen now spoke for the Executive and maintained that birth control 'was not an issue on which there were class differences, and thus it should not be part of the Labour Party programme'.[50] This had been Marion Phillips' position but up to this time was not one that Ellen shared. It might be assumed that Dora Russell of the WBCG would have regarded Ellen as a traitor to the birth control cause. However, Ellen appeared to have continued to be on friendly terms with Dora and privately continued to adopt a pro-birth control stance.

Not surprisingly similar structural tensions concerning the birth control issue could be found in the Women's Co-operative Guild. The Co-operative Party was formed in 1917 and entered into electoral alliances with the Labour Party. However, the WCG courageously refused the Labour Party's overtures, and Margaret Llewelyn Davies kept the WCG's autonomy and continued to give support for causes that were not generally popular.[51] Margaret Davies had always fought to preserve the WCG's separate voice on contentious issues such as divorce.[52]

The WCG also had a long tradition of campaigning on maternity issues. In 1915 the members were requested by Margaret Davies to record their thoughts on childbearing, and as a result twenty women volunteered the information that they either used or approved of birth control. These letters were subsequently edited by Margaret and formed the classic work, *Maternity: Letters from Working Women*.[53] Significantly, in the early 1920s the birth control issue was given prominence in *Women's Outlook*, the WCG's popular magazine. There was in 1921 an illustrated double page spread in *Women's Outlook* covering the opening by Marie Stopes of her first birth control clinic in London.[54] In a subsequent issue there followed an interview with Margaret Sanger.[55] However, after 1922 there was no mention of birth control in *Women's Outlook*.

At first, the WCG, as a body, was united in its support for the provision of birth control advice but then splits between national and local policy appeared. In June 1923 a resolution was passed by the Annual Congress in Cardiff supporting the dissemination of birth control information following the dismissal of Nurse Daniels that year. Mrs Johnson (Sale, Manchester) argued 'that in the movement for women's health, the Ministry and the local authorities should recognise the advisability of information in regard to Birth Control being given at all maternity and child welfare centres in the country.'[56] She went on to state that her branch was not for destroying home life, but bettering it. She argued that the health of mothers could be improved by enabling them to have fewer, but healthier children. This resolution was overwhelmingly passed with three votes against. Just one Catholic member, Mrs O'Kane (Eccles) put forward an opposing view. This should have been a turning point in WCG policy, and Gillian Scott emphasised the significance of this resolution: 'The Women's Co-operative Guild thus became the first women's organisation and the first working class organisation formally to support birth control.'[57]

The grassroots membership could have reasonably expected their leadership to carry out their central concern. However, their call for action was studiously ignored by the national leadership. In September 1923 the minutes of the Central Committee showed that they received a letter of objection from Mr Tom Burns, Organising Secretary of the Salford Catholic Federation, who had previously led the Catholic objections to divorce law reform by threatening a Catholic boycott of Co-operative owned stores.[58] Tom Burns was known to hold extreme views on Labour Party policies. Nevertheless, his letter was discussed by the national leadership although it was written by someone who probably was not even a member of the WCG. Mrs Matthews then proposed and Mrs Andrews seconded a resolution that the Central Committee decided 'to let the resolution lie upon the table' and for it not to be made a 'special subject'. Branches wanting speakers were advised to contact their local authority for assistance which was ironic as they were precisely the bodies about whose lack of action the birth controllers were protesting against. The WCG was to await the report of the SJC but there is no record of the issue being discussed again by the Central Committee.

After this there was no national campaign by the WCG or any co-ordinated local campaigns. In 1926 there was one last attempt to change WCG policy when Congress passed a resolution demanding that 'birth control information should be given by fully qualified medical officers at Maternity and Child Welfare Centres, assisted out of public funds, to married women requesting such knowledge.'[59] Once again the leadership of the WCG did not take any action and the resolution was not put before Central Council. No assistance was provided to local guilds as to speakers or guidance in pursuing birth control campaigns as had been done with other special topics such as maternal health.

What is the explanation for the dropping of the birth control campaign by the WCG's leadership? One factor was that the women were aware of the divisive effects of the campaign ten years earlier for divorce law reform, which had been opposed not just by Catholic members but also by the male leadership of the Co-operative Union.[60] Furthermore there were a number of influential women who as well as having leadership roles in the WCG also took their lead from Labour Party policy in looking to class rather than gender issues. A key figure in the birth control issue was Eleanor Barton who succeeded Margaret Llewelyn Davies as WCG Secretary in 1921. Eleanor was a highly experienced WCG member, serving as national President in 1914 and was soon to prove an efficient hard-working member the WCG staff. Eleanor Barton, like Marion Phillips, was politically ambitious. For instance, she attempted to make the case that if she was elected to Parliament as a Labour-Co-operative MP this would be advantageous to the Guild. She proposed to retain her post as General Secretary and suggested that the WCG should buy in extra clerical help. She would have been aware through her contacts of the views of the Labour leadership on birth control.[61]

Another important figure involved in the Central Council's decision-making was Councillor Mrs Caroline Ganley from Battersea.[62] She voiced concerns about the birth control issue in the 1923 debate and made a comment about the glory of motherhood. Caroline was Chair of Battersea Health Committee and Maternal and Child Welfare Committee.[63] She was one of the most influential members of the WCG as she was a member of the SJC, sat on the Labour Party NEC and was eventually the first woman President of the London Co-operative Society. Although unsuccessful as a parliamentary candidate in 1935, she won Battersea South in 1945 as a Co-operative and Labour MP.[64]

Gillian Scott argued that 'in order to fit the requirements of Labourism the Guild not only abandoned its feminist aspirations but also the democratic practices that had sustained it vitality as a broad-based movement.'[65] Key members of the Central Committee, for their own reasons, adopted a subservient position to the Labour Party whose female membership outnumbered the WCG. After 1923, the Guild leadership took no significant initiative on family endowment, birth control, or any other issue of concern to working women that did not have the prior approval of the Labour Party.[66] As an organisation the WCG avoided controversy, although individual members and local guilds continued to support their local SPBCC clinics, and raise questions on the subject at the Labour Party Women's Conferences.[67]

There appeared to be less tension between leadership and the grassroots members in the Liberal Party, whose Lord Buckmaster had successfully introduced a Bill in the House of Lords in 1926. The Liberal Party nationally had lost parliamentary seats to the Labour Party, but nevertheless they were still seeking power. The Liberal women had condemned as a disgrace the failure to reduce the maternal death rate which had not been reduced in twenty years. This led to an interest in birth control policies.[68] Individual Liberal women had supported birth control, but it was not till immediately before their 1927 annual conference that there was an article in the *Liberal Women's News*, 'Birth Control Information and the State', which outlined their position concerning the government's constraints on the giving of birth control advice.[69] A full account of the Conference debate on birth control and its outcome was subsequently carried in the *Liberal Women's News* in which Liberal women were invited to support the campaign.[70]

The Liberal Party structure showed considerable agreement between grassroots and leadership. The Women's National Liberal Federation was an enthusiastic supporter of birth control but it was weakened by the fact that their party was not in power nationally. Although the male leadership of the party did not express any views on this controversial topic, the leadership of the Women's National Liberal Federation did make their views known publicly. Not all Liberal women supported birth control measures and in 1924 Mrs Asquith was reported as speaking out against birth control and extolled the virtues of large families.[71] However, she appeared to be outnumbered. Significantly, Lady Violet Bonham-Carter, daughter of Prime Minister Herbert Asquith and President of the Women's National Liberal Federation (1923 to 1925), signed a letter to *Time and Tide* along with others including Bertrand Russell, Dora

Russell and Gilbert Murray, expressing support for the Buckmaster Bill on birth control which was then being presented to the House of Lords.[72] Lady Bonham-Carter's public support for birth control, given her status and connections, was extremely significant.

The birth control campaign was regarded as an important issue by the Liberal Party. In August 1927 Yorkshire Women's Liberal Federation wrote to the editor of *Liberal Woman* arguing that birth control was a personal matter and should not be made a political issue.[73] The reply was that as birth control had been discussed in both the House of Commons and House of Lords it was considered to be a political question. Indeed Manchester Liberal women fiercely debated the issue in their own meetings.[74] Linda Ward was incorrect in asserting that at the local level the Liberal women failed to fight for the issue of birth control like Labour women, because Liberal women could not identify with working-class women.[75]

At the 1927 Liberal Conference, what was known as the 'Manchester motion' was proposed by Lady Howarth JP and seconded by Mrs Norton Barclay. The Liberal women chosen to introduce the resolution were senior women in the Party. Mrs Barclay was to be Mayoress of Manchester in 1929. She was President of the Women's Liberal Council in the Exchange constituency of Manchester where her husband was MP. Lady Howarth was on the Executive Committee of the Women's National Liberal Federation and sat on the Ways and Means sub-committee.

The debate had considerable coverage in *Liberal Woman* and *Birth Control News*. The resolution asked that:

> The Council of the Women's National Liberal Federation, realizing the harm that is done by the promiscuous and unstructured 'advice' already available on the limitation of families, records its opinion that information should be available to those who ask for it at the centres controlled by the Ministry of Health where the doctors are in possession of the medical history of the mother and know to whom such information should be given, by these means enabling the poorest members of the community to obtain the information to which the wealthier classes already have access.[76]

The resolution was carried with only three dissents, and Lady Barclay said she was glad conference had not shrunk from discussing this controversial subject.

Liberal members in the House of Commons and House of Lords were prepared to take the initiative on the birth control issue. There were not the splits between leadership and grassroots as in the Labour Party and WCG. The problem for the SPBCC was that the Liberal Party, unlike the Labour Party, was not in office alone in the interwar years.

The birth control pioneers, having been blocked on the national political arena, constructed alternative pathways to reach their goals. Marion Phillips had stressed the dangers of potential diversions for her women members, and as early as 1920 moved a resolution which instructed them 'to avoid dissipating their energies in non-party political organisations'.[77] Marion Phillips nearly always gave priority to socialism over feminism. In 1925 a resolution which would have forbidden Labour women to be members of the post-suffrage organisation NUSEC was only narrowly defeated.[78] It has already been noted how WCG members after their 1923 Conference were discouraged from taking action over the birth control issue.

In spite of active discouragement from the national leadership, Labour women and the WCG were active in working for birth control at the local level. A detailed reading of surviving Labour Party Women's Section minute books shows how concerned their members were about the birth control issue. Minute books analysed include: Labour Party Women's Sections at Bilston (Wolverhampton), Gorton, Huddersfield, Hunslett Carr (Leeds), Nelson and Colne, Stockport, Manchester Advisory Committee, West Yorkshire Advisory Council for Labour Women and individual WCGs including Blackley (Manchester), Bramley Carr (Leeds), Oakfield (Liverpool) and Charlton (London). These all make reference to some birth control activity. In the first four months of 1926 Charlton WCG discussed the birth control issue on four occasions.[79] Their agreed action included distributing birth control literature, selling tickets for a birth control meeting and renewing their subscription to a birth control organisation. Hunslett Carr Women's Meeting appeared to discuss issues of both the Labour Party Women's Organisation and the WCG at their meeting of 15 April 1930; 'Mrs Freeth gave a very splendid address on Birth Control and much discussion took place.'[80] The Huddersfield Women's Section discussed the issue three times between

5 January 1927 and 4 May 1927 and entered into correspondence with the Workers' Birth Control Group.[81] York Labour Party Women's Section reported receiving correspondence from the WBCG on 6 May 1924, 17 June 1924 and 1 July 1924. The Section decided the matter should be placed before the local executive as 'we feel they ought to take an interest in this subject'. On 16 July 1923 the Section decided to purchase one dozen copies of Sanger's birth control leaflet.

The minutes of Labour Party Women's Sections illustrated the frustrations of grassroots members such as Ella Gordon, seen in the Collective Biography, who was an Executive member of Bilston Women's Section. On 24 June 1924 Bilston passed a pro-birth control resolution for the 1924 Labour Party Women's Conference. The next year, on 24 June 1925, a further resolution was passed and submitted to the 1925 Labour Party Women's Conference. 'This Conference is of the opinion that it should be permissible for Doctors employed in any medical service for which public funds are provided to give information on Birth Control to married people who desire it.' These typed resolutions were separately inserted into the minute book implying liaison with other organisations.[82] However, these resolutions did not have any impact and in 1925 Ella Gordon, with Labour Party member Alice Onions, went on to start the Wolverhampton Mothers' Centre. While she was busy with her birth control activities her political activity appeared to have abated, but on 15 January 1930 Ella again spoke to Bilston Women's Section on birth control and received their support.

The women's organisations enthusiastically listened to talks on birth control. This was not a passive process for the minutes show the organisations were encouraged to subsequently take positive action. As early as 1921 *Co-operative News* reported that the North Kensington Guild had heard a speaker on birth control and this guild went onto to support the SPBCC clinic when it was established three years later. Dr Mabel May, from Manchester, became actively involved with the MSMC and went to address Manchester Hulme WCG in December 1926. Mary Stocks, MSMC, spoke to Manley Park WCG in 1926 and next year travelled to speak to Nelson WCG.[83] In 1927 she spoke to the Downing Street Manchester WCG and three years later addressed them again. Mary Stocks spoke with the Manchester Gorton Labour Party Women's

Section on 3 March 1930 on the indivisibility of health and economic motives of the women attending the MSMC.[84] Amongst her other speaking engagements Charis Frankenburg addressed the Anson Road branch of the WCG in September 1930.[85]

A pattern emerged of a talk being given on a birth control subject and the secretary of the organisation then following this up with letters to the relevant authorities. Thus Gorton Manchester Labour Party Women's Section listened to a talk from Councillor Mrs Chorlton on 'Should Public Health Authorities Give Birth Control Information?' and responded by writing to key decision makers such as the Minister for Health, Gorton Trades Council, to inform them that:

> The fact that 3,000 women die in childbirth each year, was in the opinion of members sufficient to warrant the necessary information being given. The Secretary was instructed to forward the following resolution to the Minister of Health, to the Public Health Committee and to Gorton Trades Council. 'The Authorities to recognise the desirability of making medical information on Birth Control available to married people who need it.' The resolution was carried unanimous [sic].[86]

Seeking allies can be important for a social movement's survival, particularly when, like SPBCC, it is an outsider. One person whose abrasive personality made it difficult for her to make political allies was Alice Arnold, a Coventry councillor. Alice Arnold's political work on the council suffered because of her increasing isolation.[87] In contrast in Manchester where the Labour women worked closely with Liberal supporters to obtain a municipal birth control clinic, Councillor Annie Lee, a single woman and a member of Beswick WCG, wanted to 'fight to protect her sisters'.[88] In 1929 *Birth Control News* reported that Councillor Annie Lee who was the Labour councillor for Gorton, an 'avowed feminist', had asked 'if he (Alderman Jackson) did not think the committee (Public Health Committee) ought to give instruction in birth control in connection with their clinics?'[89] Alderman Jackson stated that he thought it would be extremely unwise to associate the idea of birth control with the infant welfare centres and clinics. After this negative answer, systematic lobbying of councillors was carried out by Councillors Annie Lee and Shena Simon.

Manchester City Council had a Maternity and Child Welfare Committee with a co-opted member drawn from the WCG and by 1930 the minutes of the Maternity and Child Welfare Sub-Committee reported that they had received resolutions from voluntary bodies including the Rusholme WCG, and Manchester Branches Association for Co-operative Guild Representation on Public Bodies.[90] The local branch of the NCW also sent repeated resolutions to the Maternity and Child Welfare Sub-Committee (Mary Stocks, Charis Frankenburg and Norton Barclay were all on the Executive Committee of the NCW) and these same three women, together with Simon, sat on the Executive Committee of the Manchester and Salford Women Citizens' Association which also wrote to Manchester City Council.

In spite of meeting active discouragement from national leadership, birth controllers from four different organisations joined together to mount *The Conference on the Giving of Information on Birth Control by Local Authorities* which was held on 4 April 1930. Grassroots members had overcome political divisions and refused to let the issue go into abeyance. The timing was significant as it was rumoured that the government was considering a change of policy. Mrs Eva Hubback, from NUSEC, explained how the four sponsoring organisations had co-operated for this conference: NUSEC, Women's National Liberal Federation, the Workers' Birth Control Group and the SPBCC. Of the major political parties only the Liberal women had the backing of their national body, the other women who participated were grassroots activists. Delegates attended from thirty-five public health authorities, sixteen maternal and child welfare organisations, seventeen Labour Party Women's Sections, fifty-five WCGs and a hundred and thirty-two other organisations, amongst them the MSMC. These organisations strongly believed the new Local Government Act meant that Local Authorities had more power. 'What we want to discuss this afternoon is how and where and when Local Authorities should make provision for this information being given.'[91]

Charis Frankenburg from the MSMC, a Conservative, addressed the conference after the nationally known figure of Mrs Harold Laski. Charis framed the work of the MSMC to show that women wanted to space their families without putting a strain on their marriage. She claimed that the research of the MSMC showed that hospitals in the area were not giving birth control advice, as they were led to believe, and she presented case studies to prove it. Charis recorded in her autobiography that she felt satisfied with her speech and was pleased that her father was there in the audience.[92] At the conclusion of this conference a resolution was passed, with only three dissenters, calling upon the Minister of Health and Public Health Authorities to 'recognise the desirability of making medical information available on methods of Birth Control to married women who need it'.[93] A memorandum was accordingly sent to the Minister of Health together with a list of organisations being represented at the conference.

Sheila Rowbotham has referred to the lack of upwardly linear progress in political development and this has been shown to be the case in the birth control campaign. 'It is a mistake of course to expect a political process to be smooth unfolding. People in the very act of breaking out of some form of politics protect their behinds tightly with corners of their old covers.'[94] The period 1918 to 1928 when the full franchise was granted, saw enthusiastic political mobilisation and many women felt that at last they would have a voice. However, as the decade progressed it became clear that the newly created political structures did not give the women the necessary power to place their concerns on the political agenda. The Labour Party in 1929 when they took office could have taken decisive action on the birth control issue but for reasons which emerged in their party conferences, the leadership chose not to do so.

Lesley Hoggart identified the separation of leaders from grassroots supporters as presenting difficult choices.[95] Certainly choosing priorities was difficult for both Ellen Wilkinson and Marion Phillips when they held leadership positions. However, grassroots members created effective alliances at the local level and combined together to mount an influential national conference which provided an agenda for action.

After the successful *Conference on the Giving of Information on Birth Control by Local Authorities* held in 1930, the birth control pioneers must have believed that the end of their campaign was near. However, the next chapter analyses why it took so long to achieve their objectives.

8   The End of the Campaign?

The birth control victories in 1930 turned out to be a mirage, as there were to be over forty more years of campaigning to achieve a comprehensive state system of birth control. Throughout this period there was a difference in tactics by the leadership and the grassroots members who locally adopted a much more confrontational approach. The grassroots members continued to provide birth control services in their voluntary clinics as well as confronting politicians and trying to change public opinion.

The mirage of birth control provision can be seen in the government's policy documents. Three months after the *Conference on the Giving of Information on Birth Control by Local Authorities* Arthur Greenwood, Minister for Health in the Labour government, presented Memorandum 153/MCW to the Cabinet in July 1930 and their approval was gained.[1] At first the SPBCC members must have believed that they had won the victory for a comprehensive state system of accessible birth control clinics. They could then have wound up their organisation, having achieved their main objective. Significantly the Memorandum was shrouded in secrecy until Marie Stopes triumphantly revealed its details in her publications. In September 1930 *Birth Control News* had the banner headline 'Month of Triumph' and so the contents of the Memorandum was made public. The restructured National Birth Control Council, to which SPBCC now belonged, was rebuked by civil servants for sending out its own leaflet to local authorities to clarify the situation. However, it was not until 1931 that Memorandum 153/MCW was printed by the government and circulated.

THE END OF THE CAMPAIGN?

The Memorandum noted in the text 'the acute division of public opinion on this subject'. Arthur Greenwood as a Labour minister would have been aware of the acrimony over the birth control issue at the Labour Party conferences. By issuing advice on birth control clinics as a memorandum, he bypassed Parliament and ensured there was no public debate on this matter. This was a complete volte-face as Greenwood's predecessors, including the Catholic John Wheatley, had maintained that a change in birth control policy had to be voted on by Parliament. The memorandum itself was brief, consisting of only four paragraphs, and was framed so that birth control was treated as a medical issue. 'The Government considers that when there are *medical grounds* for giving advice on contraceptive methods to married women in attendance at the Centres, it may be given, but that such advice should be limited to *cases where further pregnancy would be detrimental to health*.' The italics are in the original and stressed the necessity of health grounds for birth control advice.[2]

However, crucially, the Minister did not compel local authorities to create a network of municipal birth control clinics, which was what the SPBCC had urged. Many local authorities, for reasons of religious principle or exigencies of finance, chose not to take advantage of this permissive legislation. Indeed, even after four years, two hundred and fifty local authorities had taken no action whatever on the subject.[3] There were strict rules about how the municipal birth control clinics should be staffed and where they should operate. Birth control advice on health grounds excluded the cases of economic and social hardship which the SPBCC had identified as being in need of advice. Again the clinics were limited to giving advice to married women who were already mothers. There followed a series of government communications which instead of extending the remit of municipal birth control clinics placed even further restrictions on them. On 14 July 1931 the Minister issued guidance to local authorities in Circular 1208 where it was emphasised that local authorities must not establish separate birth control clinics, and medical officers of health must not be compelled to run such clinics. Health exemptions were being increasingly utilised by local authorities to justify a more liberal policy, and so three years later Neville Chamberlain, the new Minister of Health in the National Government, decided that advice could only be given to married women who were suffering from specific diseases such as diabetes, tuberculosis and heart disease 'where pregnancy would be detrimental to the mother'.[4]

There are a number of explanations for the apparent liberalisation of government policy on birth control. Peter Fryer believed that the pressure for a change in birth control regulation had become irresistible.[5] Audrey Leathard over-optimistically believed that with Memorandum 153/MCW 'the battle had been fought and largely won.'[6] She stressed its importance with the help of her personal contacts. Richard Soloway suggested that the severe economic crisis brought on by the world depression was a factor in bringing about a change in governmental policy. He believed that the government may have been influenced by the fear of an increase in population which would drain public funds.[7]

In her doctoral thesis, Linda Ward, while acknowledging the importance of the campaign of Labour women, questioned the role of outside influences in bringing about Memorandum 153/MCW.[8] She argued that the change in birth control policy was an unintentional consequence of the Local Government Act of 1929 which replaced an individual percentage grant system to local authorities with a block grant. This resulted in a shift in power from the central government to the local authorities which had more discretion over funding decisions. The block grant made it administratively complex for government to apply sanctions to local authorities with regard to their spending on individual items. Linda Ward was probably correct in her analysis, as ramifications of this financial legislation were quickly recognised by Ellen Wilkinson. Ellen was by now close to the Labour leadership and privately wrote to her friend Dora Russell that:

> I have been working very hard on the birth control, and confidentially, I find it doubtful whether the Mond Circular holds good under the New Local Government Act and the position is now that the local authorities can do as they please in this matter. What I want is to get an official statement from the Minister in Parliament, but he is taking some time.[9]

No doubt civil servants also appreciated that sanctions against local authorities were now unenforceable.

The SPBCC soon realised that they had to continue campaigning. Memorandum 153/MCW, rather than being an enabling measure leading to the expansion of municipal birth control facilities was, on the contrary, restrictive. Socialist local authorities had become increasingly confident that after the 1929 Local Government Act they would not be prosecuted for allowing birth control advice to be given at municipal clinics. The situation was that an increasing number of local authorities were providing information on birth control. For instance, Shoreditch had written to the Minister and went ahead to start its own birth control clinic. The Editor of *New Generation* wrote that 'all supporters of birth control will offer particularly heartfelt congratulations and appreciation to the Borough of Shoreditch, and to Mr and Mrs Thurtle.'[10] By specifying that birth control advice could only be permitted on a narrow definition of health grounds the Minister prevented local authorities from applying a wider interpretation of need.

The local context became particularly important. The voluntary birth controllers soon realised the shortcomings of the national policy but they continued to make progress at specific localities. After Memorandum 153/MCW Manchester City Council debated whether to establish a municipal birth control clinic. The issue was framed in health rather than economic terms. Councillor Mostyn referred to childbearing wrecking women's lives. Councillor Edwards argued that the immorality was in forcing unfit women to have children. Councillor Mary Kingsmill Jones, the Chair of the Maternity and Child Welfare Sub-Committee gave her support for birth control on health grounds.[11]

Birmingham was expected to become the first local authority in the country to have a birth control clinic but because of medical politics it was superseded by Manchester. Manchester City Council's decision was described in an unpublished exchange of letters from Mary Stocks of the MSMC to Mrs Margery Pyke of the head office of the NBCC, SPBCC's national successor. The first letter from Mary Stocks was dated 5 February 1931 and updated Margery Pyke on the situation in Manchester:

> You will be glad to hear that yesterday the Birth Control Resolution slid through the Council by a majority of 71 to 18. It is a somewhat limited proposal, the idea being to have municipal Birth Control Clinics under the Health Committee, one for the North and one for the South. These are to be held, not at the Child Welfare Centres, but at the two big hospitals,

formerly Poor Law Institutions. But they are to be gynaecological clinics rather than birth control clinics.

There is a clause which we had some heartbreak over i.e. that patients are only to be received on medical recommendations from doctors, welfare centres and midwives... However it was clear that some urgent cases will be lost through this limitation.[12]

Mary Stocks was concerned about the stigma attached to the Poor Law institutions but she was even more worried that, unlike the MSMC, patients would not have the right of self-referral. This went against her feminist principle that mothers should be able to decide family size. The next day Margery Pyke responded to Mary and was obviously trying to be encouraging. She paid tribute to Manchester's achievements. 'I very much appreciate the idea of you singing the *Nunc Dimittis* on the Cathedral steps with chorus of grateful mothers... The size of the majority was really magnificent. I do not see how it can fail to have a great effect on other places and I think you and Mrs Simon ought to be crowned with bay leaves.'[13] Shena Simon, wife of the local Liberal MP for Withington had been one of the leading campaigning councillors.

In Manchester there was a new collaboration between the voluntary sector and the state sector. The energetic Dr Veitch Clark, Manchester Medical Officer of Health, appointed Dr Olive Gimson of the MSMC to the birth control clinic at Withington Hospital and she was able to combine this appointment with her work at the voluntary clinic. At first there was little information provided by Manchester City Council about the new clinics so it was left to the MSMC to create the publicity. The indefatigable Mary Stocks, when speaking to Gorton Labour Party Women's Section stressed the need for women to make known the City Council's decision to give birth control information.[14]

As has been noted there was no rush by local authorities to provide municipal birth control clinics. Lella Secor Florence described the situation in Birmingham where a resolution for a municipal birth control clinic was eventually passed by the council in 1932, but not implemented by reluctant staff.[15] Indeed by 1931 only thirty-six local authorities had decided to take advantage of the provisions of Memorandum 153/MCW. Pat Thane considered that the abating of agitation for birth control in the 1930s showed that the new birth control regulations must have been flexibly interpreted.[16] However, this may not have been the case, for there was local dissatisfaction with Memorandum 153/MCW. What appeared to have happened was that the voluntary associations, while wishing to pursue the arguments for state provision, continued to run their own clinics. Even after the opening of the two municipal clinics in Manchester the MSMC voluntary clinic still operated. Flora Blumberg explained in 1931 that 'our private Clinic is still necessary for cases not covered by the narrow interpretation liable to be placed on the phrase "medical reasons" – for the unemployed, for example, for the spacing of families, and as a centre for the instruction of doctors and nurses.'[17] Therefore the voluntary birth control movement, far from being redundant, continued to expand its activities.[18]

After the events of 1930 there was a change of direction as the birth control organisations reassessed their priorities. The national SPBCC changed its identity several times in the 1930s. The first change was in 1930 when the five national birth control organisations, including the SPBCC and Marie Stopes' Constructive Birth Control Society decided to work together in one organisation, the NBCC, although each body kept its own identity. The NBCC in its opening report stated that 'it was to form a connecting link between the various organisations working for the Birth Control Movement.'[19] The next year the organisation changed its name to the NBCA as it argued this would allow greater flexibility of membership. Significantly the emphasis changed from vigorous national activity to the more limited objective to 'encourage Local Authorities to take action.'[20] In 1938 the individual societies, including the SPBCC, were dissolved and merged into one body, the Family Planning Association. The name change was politically astute as by then there was popular concern over a supposedly falling birth rate and 'planning' covered the provision of sub-fertility advice. Like many organisations, it is difficult to determine the precise end of the SPBCC, as there appear to be a number of alternative dates which could mark its closure.

There was a pronounced difference in the SPBCC of the 1920s and its later versions in the 1930s. Audrey Leathard harshly argued that this amalgamation of these birth control societies led 'to the views of the cautious and conservative prevailing over those of the more progressive'.[21] Family planning was seen as a practical issue with narrow goals.

The NBCC selected women to run the organisation who were conciliatory and skilled political negotiators. Lady Trudie Denman had already donated money to the Walworth Road Clinic, and in 1929 the Executive Committee members of the North Kensington Birth Control Clinic invited Trudie have lunch with them to discuss her possible involvement with the birth control campaign. Leading birth controllers Eva Hubback and Ruth Dalton had been impressed by Trudie's work at the WI and believed that she could bring valuable qualities to their organisation. However, they realised tact was required as birth control was a sensitive issue with the WI, and they did not wish to compromise Lady Denman who was also President of the WI. Lady Denman resolved the issue of conflict of interest and accepted the Chairmanship of the new NBCC. Trudie Denman was a conciliator but even she could not retain Marie Stopes and her Society for Constructive Birth Control and Racial Progress in the amalgamated organisation. Marie was furious with Trudie who she called 'that Society woman' for not visiting her clinic and for scooping up heaps of people for herself.

Lady Denman's strength lay in strategic thinking, rather than in the 'hands-on' approach of the original founder members. However, she helped to make the organisation respectable. Lady Denman, according to her biographer, personally approached President Sir (later Lord) Horder and many of the thirty-four vice-presidents of the new organisation were there at Trudie Denman's invitation. These included the well-known figures of Professor (later Lord) Julian Huxley, Lady Limerick, John Maynard Keynes, Bertrand Russell and Lady Diana Mosley. Lady Denman's biographer commented that she 'made the fullest use of her reputation and influence and prestige for a movement which initially had enjoyed so little of either'.[22] In addition, distinguished medical men joined the executive committee, and there was a continued emphasis on research into contraception.

The SPBCC had relied on volunteers for administrative work, but now in the NBCA an efficient bureaucracy was created. The SPBCC had been an ad hoc body with no permanent staff or premises. In

THE END OF THE CAMPAIGN?

contrast, the NBCA worked from permanent premises, albeit in a house that Lady Denman owned. Trudie Denman, in a drive for efficiency, appointed Margery Pyke as salaried General Secretary. Margery Pyke was a dedicated, efficient administrator but had no prior knowledge of the birth control movement. In addition to Margery Pyke, there were also appointed four local area organisers. The organisers contacted influential people in their locality who might have an influence on birth control provision there. These included local medical officers of health, councillors, doctors, health visitors, members of maternity and child welfare committees. The NBCA, and its successor the FPA, needed to be seen as non-threatening as it wanted to take advantage of local authority premises and grants. By 1935 the NBCA had a staff of seven and expenditure of £6,000 covering five years work.[23]

The composition of the NBCA Executive also changed. Although the NBCA did contain a representative from the Workers' Birth Control Group and experienced women such as Mary Stocks and Charis Frankenburg, the organisation had lost many of those with practical birth control experience. Socialist Mrs Frida Laski, criticised the new organisation as consisting of 'do-gooders' with little interest in the working class.[24] This view was unjust, but certainly the leading members of the NBCA were drawn from a narrower social spectrum than the SPBCC in the 1920s. The alliances of the committee were with fellow professionals rather than women's groups and socialist organisations. There were no overt attempts to raise the birth control issue at party conferences. The organisation's campaigning became more limited in scope.

This new-found respectability of the birth control movement resulted in different alliances. There were now personal meetings with senior members of the Ministry of Health and discreet ongoing contacts with local authorities. Audrey Leathard, who had conducted interviews with participants active in this period, argued that the NBCA turned away from confrontation and instead sought co-operation and consultation with government officials.[25] For instance, in 1932 Dr Nankivell, Medical Officer of Health for Plymouth, loaned local authority premises at one of his Maternity and Child Welfare Centres for a clinic which was run by the NBCA volunteer birth controllers. Dr Nankivell also gave the help of one of his doctors. Importantly the Ministry of Health did not raise any objections to this innovative arrangement, and so by 1935 another thirteen clinics had been established in joint local authority partnerships which presumably circumvented local opposition as well as saving costs.

There was a marked divergence in birth control activity between the national and grassroots levels. Locally, activity was much more radical than at the centre. The national organisation was policy orientated while the grassroots activities still focused on practical solutions. Although nationally the SPBCC had been replaced with a new organisation, their clinics in areas such as Walworth Road, London, Birmingham and Manchester continued as before. The annual reports showed that many of the birth control clinics retained their original names and ways of operating.[26]

The voluntary clinics were so successful that in many instances they expanded into larger premises or opened new centres. The MSMC moved from Salford to Manchester, and the 1933 Annual Report of the Liverpool Mothers' Welfare Clinic showed that they too were expanding and opening up another clinic. Dilys Dean, a third University of Manchester student placed with the MSMC in 1940, noted the hard work and enthusiasm of the volunteers.[27] Lay workers still interviewed mothers, sold appliances, dealt with administration, and most importantly raised funds from the local community. The Collective Biography shows that volunteers such as Flora Blumberg in Manchester and Ethel Emanuel in Birmingham continued to serve in the clinics at least up to the Second World War.

The clinics survived the hardships of the Second World War when their advice became even more important. Lella Secor Florence painted a dramatic picture of the Birmingham clinic operating in 1940 when volunteers climbed over bombed-out houses to reach the centre. Although when they reached the building they discovered that there was no heating or glass left in the windows they still opened for patients. Remarkably the patients kept their appointments, as they trusted that the clinic would still be open even in these appalling circumstances.[28] A similar commitment was shown in Manchester and Salford where volunteers worked round the blackout restrictions. The volunteers continued to demonstrate enthusiasm and bravery in the face of adversity.

The leadership of the FPA was concerned with moving into the mainstream political arena. The American feminist academic Linda Gordon presented a highly critical view of the birth control movement in the inter-war years in the USA and Britain:

> The timidity of the prosperous women created a spiral away from these working-class women; the less radical and far-reaching their demands, the less attraction they had for the poor; the fewer poor women participated in birth control groups, the less impetus there was for a militant approach.[29]

Indeed Margaret Sanger criticised her American Birth Control League: 'The pioneer days of our initial aggressive activity were to be superseded by a more or less doctrinaire programme of social activity.' She believed that as the movement developed her members had ceased to be militant. Margaret Sanger felt that the birth control organisation had lost its sense of political purpose.[30]

The social movement theorist Sidney Tarrow commented on the forces which lead to the transformation or demise of a social movement, and believed that the ends of protest cycles were never as uniform as their beginnings. He argued that after an initial burst of enthusiasm in a social movement, there was a diffusion of political effort and mobilisation, and members could leave through exhaustion. As movements became better organised they divided into leaders and followers which could result in weariness and disillusionment of the latter. Sidney Tarrow concluded that those on the periphery of the movement, lacking strong motivation, were most likely to defect, while those at the centre would keep their ideological principles and fight on.[31]

Yet the experience of the SPBCC contradicted this part of his theory. It was the grassroots workers who retained their evangelical fervour. In spite of the Head Office policy of persuasion, even by 1939 only eighty-four local authorities had taken any action to establish municipal birth control clinics. In fact two thirds of local authorities had taken no action at all. Action was inhibited by economic recession and then fear of war. The SPBCC workers had to face the classic dilemma of many voluntary organisations: how far should they support, for the good of their clients, a system that they were trying to change? The grassroots workers decided on a policy of expansion and by 1939 the number of voluntary clinics had grown to sixty-six. Thus the local voluntary clinics were to some extent making up for the lack of policy progress by the Head Office.

Although in the post-war era there continued to be some opposition from Catholics, the FPA gradually gained recognition and respectability. In 1955 the Minister of Health, Mr Ian Macleod, visited the FPA and insisted that full publicity be given to this memorable occasion. The visit was made to recognise the Silver Jubilee of the FPA and he publicly praised the work of the Association and Lady Denman. This led to national coverage of the work of the FPA on radio and television which was broadcast without protest. Later, in 1963, the indomitable Margery Pyke (who had boosted Mary Stocks' confidence in the 1930s) was awarded the British Empire Medal and gained official recognition from the establishment.

The FPA's reputation percolated down, and it became respectable at the local level. Elsie Plant, who had originally hosted Marie Stopes in the 1920s, continued to promote family planning in Stockport after the Second World War.[32] At first the clinic had a number of discreetly hidden premises down back alleys, but their clients felt unsafe. However, in the 1950s the situation changed. Elsie maintained that there was less opposition from Catholic councillors. In 1955 the FPA was granted permission to use council premises, and by 1960 the FPA had the use of a brand new building in the heart of the town centre. This was purpose-built for the people of Stockport and birth control had literally come in from the cold.

One of the voluntary birth controllers whose work proved to be hugely influential was the American Lella Secor Florence. She was married to an academic and was heavily involved in the formation of the first SPBCC clinics in Cambridge and then in Birmingham. In 1956 she wrote *Progress Report on Birth Control* in which she evaluated the achievements of the Birmingham birth control clinic and found the difficulties the patients had in using contraception. With her roots in feminism Lella wrote in 1952 that 'we must educate men to realise that women are their equals and have equal rights.'[33]

Lella's main objective was to find a simpler more universal method of contraception for women and to help them persevere with birth control.

THE END OF THE CAMPAIGN?

In 1957 she met Dr Gregory Pincus in the USA where he was already conducting trials for the oral contraceptive pill. In 1960 she invited him to address a meeting at Birmingham Medical Institute. She then worked tirelessly to set up a trial in Birmingham in spite of opposition from Head Office. Instead of the diaphragm that had to be fitted by a doctor and inserted by the woman before sex, here was something that was as easy to take as an aspirin and even easier to use than male condoms. All the women recruited were volunteers and were closely monitored. Birmingham was the only family planning clinic to take part in the trial until a smaller sample was set up in the London area.

From 1970 the oral contraceptive pill was provided free by the FPA. Dr Libby Wilson, an FPA doctor in the 1960s was only slightly exaggerating when she wrote that an efficient oral contraceptive was a historical event equivalent to the discovery of the circulation of the blood.[34] She felt it was an exciting time to be working in family planning. Women now had control over their own bodies.

The tide of popular opinion had turned in favour of birth control measures provided by the State. It was one of key demands of the Women's Liberation Movement in the 1970s. By now this demand was also taken up by a number of mainstream women's organisations including the WIs, which in the inter-war period had been reluctant to commit themselves. In 1972 a resolution was passed at the AGM of the WI urging the government to provide a full and free family planning service now that the value of the contraceptive pill was recognised. This was in line with other liberal social reforms passed by Parliament in the late 1960s. These included Abortion Law Reform in 1967 which widened the grounds on which abortions could be obtained. Abortion had been very much linked to birth control by ordinary women in the inter-war years.

Contraception was now framed as an acceptable topic for discussion, coinciding with the concerns of government with over-population. Sir Keith Joseph, Conservative Secretary of State for Social Services, in a statement that echoed the eugenic thought popular in the 1920s and 1930s, was quoted (or misquoted) as saying that 'a rising proportion of children are being born to mothers least fitted to bring children into the world.' Over-population was raised in Parliament, at party conferences and in the popular press such as the *Daily Mail*. In 1973 there was even a Minister for Population Affairs. All this encouraged the Conservative government to frame the need for the State to provide contraception for those that wanted it. Contraception was framed as being socially responsible rather than encouraging immoral behaviour. There was a debate within the Conservative Party about whether contraception should be provided free by the State. The outcome was that Sir Keith modified his position and on 5 July 1973 the NHS Reorganisation Bill was passed with only a 20p prescription charge for those not exempt, being the charge for contraception.

When the Labour Party was returned to power, Barbara Castle, Secretary of State for Social Services and Health, decided to take Keith Joseph's ruling to its logical conclusion so that free family planning for all would be now provided by the NHS. She called it part of her new social policy and announced in the House of Commons on 28 March 1974 that 'from 1st April 1974, family planning will be open at National Health Service Clinics to all who ask for it, irrespective of age or marital status… We have decided that it would be wrong to impose prescription charges for family planning obtained from NHS Clinics and Hospitals.'[35] This was a victory for the voluntary birth controllers. Even when the NHS was created in 1948 free contraception was not included in its provisions.

Barbara Castle, with her red hair, was nicknamed 'Labour's Red Queen' with echoes of Ellen Wilkinson. She was married to a journalist and like Ellen was childless. Like Ellen she was an MP for a northern constituency and when first elected had a reputation for being on the left of the Labour Party. Given the long history of Labour women campaigning for birth control it was appropriate that it was a Labour woman minister who finally introduced free contraception on the NHS. Although in her constituency in Blackburn there was a strong Catholic element, religious opposition did not appear to have been a factor in making her decision. In her autobiography she accepted the *Daily Mirror's* derision of 'Barbara's Free Love' because she believed that common sense was on her side.[36]

It was ironic that it fell to Barbara Castle to implement the last part of the voluntary birth controllers' strategy because for most of her political career Barbara had regarded women's issues as a backwater.

'I have never had any conscious determination not to take up women's issues. I have just not been particularly interested in them. I have always thought of myself as an MP, not as a woman MP.'[37] In 1968, speaking on the fiftieth anniversary of the granting of the female suffrage, she stated that it was time to move on from thinking of men and women as adversaries.[38] Nevertheless in 1970 she had successfully introduced the Equal Pay Act, of which the equality feminists would have been proud, and promoted the new feminists' demand for affordable birth control. Barbara made the difficult decisions about the balance between socialism and feminism which had so exercised Marion Phillips and Ellen Wilkinson in the 1920s.

In later life when Barbara had left the House of Commons and served as an MEP in the European Parliament, she was far more openly sympathetic to women's issues. She gave the keynote speech at a Women's International Day Celebration at Manchester Polytechnic when she analysed the achievements of British women in the last three decades. Barbara also brought along to the event a French woman Socialist MEP colleague to accompany her. She also turned to study the equal rights feminists and wrote a biography which contrasted the leadership styles of the suffragettes Sylvia and Christabel Pankhurst, daughters of Emmeline Pankhurst.[39]

The structure of birth control provision now changed after government legislation. General practitioners who had been unenthusiastic about performing intimate procedures were now to be paid for providing contraceptive services. The popularity of the contraceptive pill meant internal examinations were largely redundant. The issuing of contraceptive pills could be seen in the same category as the issuing of other medical tablets which were easy to take. Significantly the FPA, who had been providing free services, decided to hand over its network of voluntary clinics to the NHS. The FPA had opened over a thousand clinics, the last one being opened in Thamesmead. Part of this decision was influenced by financial considerations, as in 1972 the FPA income was £4,276 368 and expenditure £4,310, 348. This decision allowed the FPA to concentrate on its educational work.[40]

In the 1970s birth control became part of a medical paradigm. The original birth control clinics were founded by concerned lay women who in turn interviewed and employed doctors. However, this changed when contraception was medicalised. The contraceptive pill and IUD were prescribed by doctors in the medical environment of their surgeries. Women who had felt comfortable going to the railwaymen's cottages in Wolverhampton or the rented terraced houses in Birmingham were now entering an unfamiliar environment. They often felt the surgeries were inaccessible and inconvenient. In Wolverhampton, as in other clinics, the line between the lay workers and patients was blurred because they came from similar social backgrounds. Given the changing situation in the birth control clinics it is not surprising that Alice Onions and Winifred Strange from Wolverhampton used their skills to train as marriage guidance councillors.[41] The FPA had reached the Holy Grail of free universal contraception, but often had to sacrifice emotional support for working-class mothers.

It has been increasingly apparent that this research is about far wider issues than birth control. It has involved the feminist view of society and the right of women to control their bodies, the relationship of women from different classes in a social situation, the relationship and tensions of feminists engaging with emerging social and political movements. Colin Barker rightly commentated on the complexities of social movements with their networks of social groups, and this has been applied to the birth control pioneers.[42] This study traces the complexities of the birth control movement which, besides feminists and socialists, also included neo-Malthusians and eugenicists. This research shows that the SPBCC was by no means completely middle class as there were valuable contributions from working-class women, either as individuals or through organisations such as the Women's Co-operative Guild. Although particularly strong in London, the movement covered the Midlands, North West and Scotland.

Women's history has been defined by its subject matter, whereas feminist history has been as informed by the ideas of feminism and concerned with ideas of gender. However, it is being increasingly acknowledged that these two enterprises have now moved closer together. This research underlines this convergence, as though its subject matter is women's struggle to control their reproduction, it also explores feminist debates concerning the direction of feminism.

THE END OF THE CAMPAIGN?

Dale Spender hypothetically asked in 1984 whether it mattered to know that there was a vigorous and varied women's movement which addressed similar issues and conducted comparable campaigns to that of twenty-first-century women.[43] She answered in the affirmative. Mrs Cooke, who in 1924 asserted that a woman must control her own body, would have agreed.

Appendix
Collective Biography of Birth Control Activists

The basic material was drawn from the annual reports of the SPBCC clinics and supplemented by autobiographies and contemporary correspondence. Oral interviews with the activists have also been utilised. Full biographic references for each activist have been given which also include newspaper reports.

Adams, Mrs was on the foundation committee in 1926 of Wolverhampton Birth Control Clinic.
>Wolverhampton Birth Control Clinic First Annual Report 1926. Dora Russell Archives in International Institute for Social History, Amsterdam, Dora Russell papers. Wolverhampton Women's Welfare Centre.

Agnew, Mrs Howard was a founding member in 1926 of the Manchester, Salford and District Mothers' Clinic and sat on the General Advisory Council.
>Manchester and District Mothers' Clinic Annual Report 1926-1927.

Agnew, Lady was on the Executive Committee of the Oxford Family Welfare Association at its foundation.
>Oxford Family Welfare Association First Annual Report 1926-1927.

Baines, Mrs Cuthbert was a founding member of the Executive Committee of North Kensington Women's Welfare Centre.
>North Kensington Women's Welfare Centre's Annual Report 1925-1926.

Barbour, Mrs Mary, JP (1875-1958) was a member of the Glasgow Women's Welfare Centre.

Many of the founders of the clinics were upper-class women who had gone into higher education, but this was not always the case. Mary Barbour was one of the founders in 1925 of the Glasgow Women's Welfare and Advisory Clinic and was its first Chairman. Her father was a carpet weaver and she became a thread twister and then a carpet printer. In 1896 she married David Barbour who became an engineer in the shipyards and they settled in Govan, Glasgow. She became an active member of Kinning Park Co-operative Guild and joined the ILP. Like Lella Secor Florence in Birmingham, Mary regarded housing issues, the Women's Peace Crusade and women's issues as being interconnected.

Glasgow in this period was highly politicised and in the rent strike of 1915 Mary became politically active in organising them. Later Mary stood as a councillor and was the first Labour woman to be elected to Glasgow City Council. She had a special interest in issues that affected women in their everyday lives such housing conditions, municipal laundries and children's playgrounds. Between 1924 and 1927 Mary served as Glasgow Corporation's first woman Baillie and was appointed as one of Glasgow's first women magistrates. Mary retired from the council in 1931 but retained her active interest in women's issues including the Glasgow Women's Welfare and Advisory Centre. Glasgow Women's Welfare Association gave advice and support to the newly founded Aberdeen SPBCC.
    'Profile of Mary Barbour', *Women's Outlook*, February 1921, p.108.
    Canning, Audrey, 'Mary Barbour.' *The Biographic Dictionary of Scottish Women* (Edinburgh, 2008).

Barrett, Mrs was a founder member of the Mothers' Welfare Clinic, Liverpool and a member of its Council.
    Liverpool Mothers' Welfare Clinic First Annual Report 1926-1927.

Beale, Mrs E.P. was a committee member of Birmingham Women's Welfare Centre in 1927.

Beavan, Miss Jessie was a member of the Liverpool Mothers' Welfare Clinic in 1926 serving on its Executive Committee. She was also an active member of a number of other women's voluntary bodies including being Hon. Secretary of the Liverpool Women's Citizenship Association. She was the sister of Margaret Beavan.
    Liverpool Mothers' Welfare Clinic First Annual Report 1926-1927.
    Cowman, Krista, '*Mrs Brown is a Man and a Brother!*' (Liverpool, 2004).

Beavan, Miss Margaret, JP (1877-1931) attended Liverpool High School and was in the same form as Rev. Maude Royden. She attended Holloway College but did not pursue a degree course. Instead she became involved with voluntary work, in particular the Invalid Children's Aid (ICA) which was connected with the Rathbone family. She was Secretary and an ambitious fund-raiser. This was to lead to the opening in 1914 of the purpose-built Leasowe Hospital for Children. They could be taken from the slums and nursed in a healing environment to overcome diseases such as tuberculosis. In spite of the demands of the war, Margaret managed to achieve in 1918 the purchase of further premises to provide

APPENDIX

convalescent treatment for city children and milk for delicate children. Her next project, Highfield, was opened by King George and Queen Mary and so was renamed the Royal Liverpool Babies Hospital. As well as infant welfare she was also concerned with maternal welfare, although her 'Tired Mothers' scheme was more tactfully renamed the 'Mothers' Holiday Rest'.

Margaret was well aware of the issue of maternal mortality which was not decreasing in line with infant mortality. She then turned the ICA into a national federation so it could campaign on issues such as the 1918 Maternity and Child Welfare Act. Since 1918 she had been a co-opted member of the Liverpool City Council Maternity and Child Welfare Sub-Committee.

She had the support of a number of local women's organisations being a member of the Women's Co-operative Guild and the Women Citizens Association.

After twenty years Margaret widened her interests beyond the voluntary sector. In 1920 she was appointed a Justice of the Peace and successfully stood in the municipal elections for the City Council as a Coalition-Liberal. She was a city councillor at the same time as Eleanor Rathbone. The next election she held her seat as a Conservative candidate. Margaret Beavan became a popular Mayor in 1926 but stood unsuccessfully as the Conservative MP for Everton. She was unprepared for the personal hostility, although her social work had always been an issue in municipal elections. In the 1929 general election she lost to the Labour candidate by 1,600 in a poll of 26,000.

Liverpool councillor, Margaret Simey gave a highly damaging account of Margaret Beavan's career and criticised her both professionally and politically. Margaret Simey served her apprenticeship under Eleanor Rathbone and was the first student on the social science degree pioneered by the University of Liverpool. She believed Margaret Beavan's philosophy of voluntary action was anachronistic in the 1920s and termed her Queen Canute. She accused her of 'sticking plaster' philanthropy, of playing out the voluntary agencies against the statutory ones. As a former Labour councillor, Margaret Simey criticised Margaret Beavan's politics. Ivy Ireland refers to Margaret Beavan being called affectionately 'little mother' whereas Margaret Simey relates that in the general election she was called Maggie Mussolini, being a reference to her official visit as mayor to Italy.

The controversy over the career of Margaret Beavan brings into focus the issues Olive Banks raised as feminism.

Archives: Mersey Record Office Archives.
Profile: *Women's Outlook* (1927) p.268; (1931) p.51.
Liverpool Annual Yearbook 1926.
Ireland, I., *Margaret Beavan of Liverpool. Her Character and Work* (Liverpool, 1938).
Simey, Margaret, *The Disinherited Family* (Liverpool, 1996).
Pedersen, Susan, *Eleanor Rathbone and the Politics of Conscience* (New Haven, 2004).

Bethune-Baker, Mrs Edith, JP (1863–1949) was in 1925 a founding member of the Cambridge Women's Welfare Association and member of its Council. Edith studied Science at Mason College which was to become the University of Birmingham. She devoted much of her life to women's suffrage, travelling great distances to speak. She later became an Executive Committee member of the National Union of Societies for Equal Citizenship resigning over the issue of protective legislation for women. She was chairman of the Cambridge Women Citizens Association, member of NCW and a welfare campaigner, being a member of the Standing Joint Committee of Industrial Women's Organisations. She was one of the first women magistrates to be appointed.

Edith was an enthusiastic eugenicist who argued that concerns over the fall in the birth rate amongst the middle class were 'prejudiced against the woman's movement'.

Edith was married to Rev. Bethune-Baker, Professor of Divinity at Lady Margaret's College, and a Liberal.
Cambridge Women's Welfare Association First Annual Report 1925–1926.
Cambridge Daily News, 1 November 1947, p.7.
Law, Cheryl, *Women. A Modern Political Dictionary* (London, 2000).
Richardson, A., *Love and Eugenics in the late Nineteenth Century* (Oxford, 2008).

Bigland, Dr Phoebe the founding doctor of the Mothers' Welfare Centre in Liverpool, was a member of the Medical Women's Federation. In 1922 she sat on its committee to examine the effects of birth control on 'imperial health and national welfare'. She had heard an inspirational speech by Marie Stopes in Liverpool. However, when appointed as clinic doctor in 1926 she did not visit Marie's Society for Constructive Birth Control and Racial Progress but instead underwent her training at Walworth Road with the SPBCC. She was a member of the Association of Medical Women and in November 1921 attended a committee meeting.

Phoebe had pronounced views on abortion, prostitution and the number of children a mother should bear. She died after just a few years in post. Dr Macaulay believed Phoebe possessed tremendous intellectual and physical courage.

APPENDIX

Liverpool Mothers' Welfare Clinic First Annual Report 1926–1927.
Macaulay, Dr M., *The Story of the Mothers' Welfare Clinic, Liverpool* (privately published, 1952).

Binham, Mrs was on the Executive Committee of the Oxford Family Welfare Association at its foundation.

Oxford Family Welfare Association Annual Report 1926–1927.

Blumberg, Mrs Flora sat on the Executive Committee of the Manchester and Salford Mothers' Clinic at its foundation in 1926. She took over as Chairman from Stocks in 1936 and remained in this position for over forty years. Blumberg made the journey to Geneva in 1931 to present a paper on the MSMC at a conference organised by the American birth control pioneer Margaret Sanger. However, though extremely conscientious she could be impatient of those women who struggled with the MSMC regime. This is evidenced in her follow up of their patients.

Unusually amongst birth controllers, Flora was a Conservative Party activist and stood unsuccessfully as a Conservative councillor for New Cross, Manchester in 1934.

Jewish identity was important to Flora and throughout her life she maintained strong links with Jewish organisations serving as President of the Women's Lodge of B-nai Brith, the international Jewish organisation.

She was a friend of fellow Jewish Conservative MSMC member Charis Frankenburg.

Manchester and District Mothers' Clinic Annual Report 1926–1927.
Manchester and District Mothers' Clinic, 'Only 8 Failures' in 1,212 Cases,' 1931. Wellcome Library A&M: SA/FPA.
Obituary. Manchester Central Reference Library, Archives and local Studies Section.
Sanger, Margaret and Stone, Hannah, *The Practice of Contraception* (Baltimore, 1931).

Boswell, Mrs R. was a founding member of the Executive Committee of North Kensington Women's Welfare Centre.

North Kensington Women's Welfare Centre's Annual Report 1924–1925.

Braddock, Mrs B., JP, MP (1899–1970) supported the Liverpool Mothers' Clinic. Her mother, Mary Bamber was an active socialist campaigner. Bessie was briefly a member of the Communist Party but joined the Labour Party in 1926. She married Jack Braddock who had also joined the Labour Party and was leader of Liverpool City Council in the post-war era. Bessie was elected a councillor for St Ann's ward in 1930 and in 1945 she was returned as MP for Liverpool Exchange.

Her interests included mental health, prison reform and maternal welfare. She was Chair of the Maternity and Child Welfare Sub-Committee from 1934. In April 1936 the local Labour Party split over the municipal grant to Liverpool Mothers' Welfare Clinic. It was opposed in the council by, amongst others, David Logan, the local Liverpool MP and Catholic father of ten. The campaign for the grant's continuation was successfully led by Bessie Braddock who won by 72 votes to 41. In July 1936 she organised a conference in Liverpool on Maternity and Child Welfare.

> Davies, Sam, *Liverpool Labour. Social and Political Influences on the Development of the Labour Party in Liverpool 1900-1939* (Keele, 1996).
> O'Toole, Millie, *Bessie Braddock. A Biography* (London, 1957).

Brooks, Lady, CBE, JP was a founding member of the Birmingham Women's Welfare founding committee but soon resigned.
> Birmingham Women's Welfare Centre First Annual Report 1927-1928.

Browne, Stella (1882-1955). In 1974 when researching *Hidden from History* Sheila Rowbotham recognised the importance of Stella Browne. However, it took until 2011 for Lesley Hall to write a rounded biography of Stella.

Stella, although she never married, had close relationships with men. Her circle of friends included such leading figures as Havelock Ellis, Edward Carpenter, Bertrand and Dora Russell, and the American birth control pioneer, Margaret Sanger. She contributed to *Freewoman* founded by fellow suffragette, Dora Marsden and edited by the writer, Rebecca West.

She was an active member of the Malthusian League and later the Eugenic Society. Although these organisations were hostile to socialism Stella retained her membership of the Labour Party. Stella vigorously campaigned for the Labour Party to adopt birth control clinics as part of its welfare programme. Undeterred by Labour minister John Wheatley's rejection of municipal birth control clinics Stella joined with other Labour Party members in forming the Workers' Birth Control Group which acted as a 'ginger group' within the Labour Party to change their policy.

Lesley Hall's perceptive biography shows how Stella moved from campaigning on the birth control issue, which she believed had been largely resolved in 1931, to that of abortion rights. Birth control, though controversial was not illegal, but abortion was against the law. The birth controllers were attacked in the religious press as 'scarlet women', but the advocates of abortion were even more vilified. It was not a popular cause and Stella, a single woman, was vulnerable to attack. She argued the ability to control fertility was a basic right for women and in 1935 wrote that 'the right to abortion does not depend on crimes which the conventions of romantic tradition deem worse than death'. Stella believed abortion should be available to any woman without red tape or ruinous financial charges for 'our bodies are our own.'

In 1936 Stella Browne took her beliefs to their logical progression and joined other campaigners in founding the Abortion Law Reform Association (ALRA). Stella continued to speak to socialist and women's groups, write on the subject and attempted to make allies of sympathetic MPs and doctors. On 13 October 1937 the ALRA delegation gave evidence to the Inter-departmental Committee on Abortion set up by the government with Norman Birkett QC as Chairman. In her evidence Stella dramatically revealed that she was speaking from personal experience as she had experienced abortion and suffered no ill effects. She did go on to make less emotive points about poverty and abortion.

Stella was undoubtedly a complex character with her moral certitudes. For instance, her gesture politics in the Birkett Committee may well have been counter-productive in influencing their decisions. Dora Russell in a well-known passage in her autobiography expressed the fear that Stella with her 'wisps of hair flowing from her untidy coiffure' and outspoken views on abortion would damage the birth control campaign by frightening supporters.

> Banks, Olive, *Biographical Dictionary of British Feminists*, vol. 1 (Hemel Hempstead, 1985).
> Hall, Lesley A., 'Women, feminism and eugenics' in Peel, R. (ed.) *Essays in the History of Eugenics* (London, 1997) pp.36–51.
> Hall, Lesley A., *The Life and Times of Stella Browne. Feminist and Free Spirit* (London, 2011).
> Rowbotham, Sheila, *A New World for Women. Stella Browne Socialist Feminist* (London, 1977).

Burrows, Lady Doris sat on the Executive Committee of the Manchester and Salford Mothers' Clinic in 1926. She was the Hon. Treasurer, and fellow members of the Committee paid tribute to her financial acumen. Doris lived at Bonis Hall, Cheshire and was a personal friend of both Frankenburg and Stocks. Her husband, Robert was a wealthy colliery owner.

> Manchester and District Mothers' Clinic Annual Report 1926–1927.
> Stocks, Mary D., *My Commonplace Book* (London, 1970).

Cadbury, Mrs Elizabeth, JP, later Dame Cadbury (1858–1951) was married to the Quaker industrialist, George Cadbury, and in 1927 was a founding member of Birmingham Women's Welfare Centre. She donated the considerable amount of £25.00 to help the Centre become established.

She had undertaken social work in the London docklands before her marriage and throughout her life retained a keen interest in the condition of working-class families, especially their housing conditions. This was put into practice in the Cadbury family model, Bourneville Village.

Elizabeth was Hon. Treasurer and then President of the National Union of Women Workers (forerunner of the National Council of Women) in 1906-7. She was a non-militant suffragist and in 1919 was Vice-President of National Union of Societies for Equal Citizenship. She was active in the local National Council of Women from 1896 to her death, and served as President. Elizabeth was the first woman President of the Free Church Council.

She was an active Liberal and was a Birmingham City councillor from 1919 to 1924. In 1923 she stood unsuccessfully as their parliamentary candidate and in 1925 was featured on the front page of *Liberal Women's News*.

Elizabeth was appointed a magistrate in 1926 and received numerous honours including an honorary MA from the University of Birmingham (although she passed the senior Cambridge examination she never entered higher education).

Her humanitarian work with refugees was also recognised by many foreign governments. She was a committed pacifist and pressed for the inclusion of women's issues in the Congress of Versailles. Elizabeth was Convenor of the Peace and Arbitration Standing Committee of the International Council of Women.

> Birmingham Women's Welfare Centre First Annual Report 1927-1928.
> Profile: *Liberal Women's News*, April 1925, pp.1-2. Her profile was presented on the front page.
> *Who's Who in Birmingham*, 1925, 1927.
> Delamont, S., *Oxford Dictionary of National Biography* (Oxford, 2004).
> Law, Cheryl, *Women. A Modern Political Dictionary* (London, 2000).
> Scott, R., *Elizabeth Cadbury 1858-1951* (London, 1955).

Carter, Mrs W.H. was on the foundation committee in 1926 of Wolverhampton Birth Control Centre.

> Wolverhampton Birth Control Clinic First Annual Report 1926. Russell Archive, Box 405, IISH, Amsterdam.

Castle, Barbara, MP, later Baroness Castle of Blackburn (1910-2002). Barbara Betts, her maiden name, lived in Bradford and after a grammar school education attended St Hugh's College, Oxford. She married Ted Castle, a journalist, and entered Parliament as MP for Blackburn in 1945. She followed Aneurin Bevan and supported radical causes popular with the left of the Labour Party. She became Chairman of the Labour Party and obtained Cabinet rank in 1964 as Minister for Overseas Development. This was followed by a post of Minister for Transport in

APPENDIX

1965. She was then appointed as Secretary of State for Employment and Productivity and controversially tried to introduce a prices and incomes policy. This aroused hostility amongst the trade unions and the Labour movement generally. Her last ministerial appointment was as Minister of Health for Health and Social Security.

After a change in Labour Leader, she returned to the back benches but in 1979 was elected to the European Parliament and became Vice-Chairman of the Socialist Group.

> Castle, Barbara, *Fighting All the Way* (London, 1993).
> Castle, Barbara, *Sylvia and Christabel Pankhurst* (London, 1987).
> Castle, Barbara, *The Castle Diaries 1964–1970* (London, 1984).
> Castle, Barbara, *The Castle Diaries 1974–1976* (London, 1980).
> Childs, David, *Britain since 1945. A Political History* (London, 2001 reprint 2010).

Chance, Mrs Janet (1885–1953) served on the Executive Committee of the Walworth Women's Welfare Centre in 1928 and was a socialist and feminist. She and her husband had joined the Malthusian League, though they opposed much of its teaching. Janet campaigned for birth control to be freely available. She campaigned for abortion law reform and in 1936 she helped found the ALRA and became its Chairman. Her husband Clifton, a wealthy Manchester stockbroker, also backed the birth control campaign.

> Chance, Janet, *The Back Street Surgery* (Abortion Law Reform Association, 1947).
> Hall, Lesley A., 'Janet Chance,' *A Biographical Dictionary of Scottish Women* (Edinburgh, 2007).

Cole, Mrs served as a founder member on the Council of Liverpool Mothers' Welfare Clinic.

> Liverpool Mothers' Welfare Clinic First Annual Report 1926–1927.

Collier, Mrs W. was one of those who set up the Oxford Family Welfare Association in 1926 and served as its first Chairman. She was married to Dr Collier, a First World War hero, who also served on the Association's Medical Advisory Committee and was one of the chief instigators of the birth control clinic in Cambridge. When Dr Collier died in 1934 Mrs Collier continued to serve on the Executive Committee.

Mrs Collier appeared to be very much her own person being the only known local councillor on the Executive Committee. As a Liberal she represented South Ward in Oxford from 1925 until well into the 1930s.

> *Kelly's Directory for Oxford* (Oxford, 1926).
> Little, Dr Isabelle, 'Forty years back,' *Family Planning*, 3 November 1966.

Cozens-Hardy, Lady served as a founder member on the Council of Liverpool Mothers' Welfare Clinic.

> Liverpool Mothers' Welfare Clinic First Annual Report 1926–1927.

Crombie, Mrs in 1926 helped her daughter Fenella Paton found the Aberdeen Women's Welfare Centre. She was married to J.W. Crombie, Liberal MP for Kincardine.
<blockquote>Press and Journal, 4 December 1972.</blockquote>

Dale, Mrs was on the foundation committee in 1926 of Wolverhampton Birth Control Centre.
<blockquote>Wolverhampton Birth Control Clinic First Annual Report 1926. Russell Archive, Box 405, IISH, Amsterdam.</blockquote>

Dalton, Mrs Ruth, MP, later Lady Dalton (1890–1966). She was involved with the foundation of the SPBCC birth control clinic in 1921. In 1924 she served on the Executive Committee of the newly formed North Kensington Women's Welfare Centre representing Walworth Road. In this period she also lived part time in Cambridge where her husband Hugh was a Labour Party prospective parliamentary candidate. She was involved with the founding the Cambridge Women's Welfare Association and in 1925 sat on the clinic's General Council. In May 1930 *Birth Control News* reported that she had been to speak to Newcastle Women's Luncheon Club on the value of the provision of birth control clinics for working-class wives.

Ruth was awarded a BSc from the LSE where she met Hugh Dalton, the future Labour Chancellor of the Exchequer. Ruth was always politically active, being elected to the London County Council for Peckham. She eventually became an Alderman of the LCC in 1936. Ruth Dalton had a brief parliamentary career in 1929 when she became a Labour MP for Bishop Auckland in a by-election so her husband could stand in the general election. She served for four months and was offered a seat of her own but she reportedly replied that she preferred her council work, 'There we do things. Here it all seems to be all talk.' Ruth was also a member of Peckham Women's Co-operative Guild.

She was a close friend of Leah Manning.
<blockquote>Profile: Women's Outlook, 1 April 1925, p.13.
Jones, Helen, 'Ruth Dalton,' Oxford Dictionary of National Biography (Oxford, 2004).</blockquote>

David, Mrs Albert in 1931 officially joined the Council of the Liverpool Mothers' Welfare Clinic. However, the clinic's minutes of November 1925 showed that she supported the clinic from its inception but had not wanted her name made public. She felt that it might compromise her husband who was the Anglican Bishop of Liverpool (1923–44). Bishop David continued to assist the clinic discreetly but Mrs David was eventually forced to resign because of religious pressure.

APPENDIX

Macaulay, Dr M., *The Story of the Mothers' Welfare Clinic, Liverpool* (privately printed, 1952).
Woolton, Lady, '"Liverpool": Four Clinics', *Family Planning*, January 1956.
The Liverpudlian, 'Profile of Dr Albert Augustus David', December 1933, p.5.

Davies, Mrs. J. was on the foundation committee in 1926 of Wolverhampton Birth Control Centre.
> Wolverhampton Birth Control Clinic First Annual Report 1926. Russell Archive, Box 405, IISH, Amsterdam.

Denman, Lady Trudie (Gertrude) (1884–1954) took delight in her two children and grandchildren. However, her biographer believed that the tensions in Trudie's marriage meant that she looked for fulfilment in outside interests.

Unlike many prominent feminists Trudie did not have a university education, but rather the conventional one of a girl who attended a finishing school and was presented at Court, but she was exposed to party politics. Her father was a Liberal MP and her mother was for many years on the Executive of the Women's Liberal Federation. One of the issues with which the Liberal Party was concerned was that of the suffrage. The Women's Liberal Federation rejected militant tactics and supported constitutional means to obtain votes for women. It is significant that the Women's Institutes, a non-suffrage organisation, retained the suffrage colours and had as its official anthem 'Jerusalem' which had been sung in celebration of the suffrage victory.

Her friend Gervase Huxley wrote a biography of Trudie Denman shortly after her death. This contains a great deal of factual information but Jane Robinson's pen portrait of Trudie in her history of the Women's Institutes gives a much more rounded picture. As a young woman Trudie was said to love racing round England in her car, dressed in breeches, with a half-smoked cigarette hanging from her mouth.

Trudie's genius was in transforming a quango set up to serve the needs of the government into a federation of self-governing Women's Institutes. In 1916 she had become Chairman of the sub-committee of the Agricultural Organisation Society which in 1917 was transferred to the Board of Agriculture. These had originally been founded in Canada as farm co-operatives. Trudy managed to persuade officials that her organisation should be self-governing and the guilds should not be mixed. In 1918 the National Federation of Women's Institutes was formed and fittingly she was elected Chairman. She held this post until her resignation in 1946 and was extremely powerful.

The SPBCC was very different from the WI as it was concerned with co-ordinating those who had a medical interest in birth control rather than being a mass movement. Trudie had the ability to be a conciliator to rival factions and brought together five birth control organisations into the National Birth Control Council.

In the Second World War, Trudie's organisational skills were once again called upon. The WI were involved in the war effort through initiatives such as evacuation from the inner cities. In 1938 she became involved in plans for the Women's Land Army. She virtually ran her own government department which tried to regulate supply and demand for the Women's Land Army's services. During the war she fought for better pay and conditions of service for the Land Army and to bring comparability with the other women's services.

When discussing Trudie's achievements, Olive Banks provocatively concluded, 'her vision of a powerful organisation (WI), run by women, to serve the needs of women may have more to offer the feminists than an absorption in the issues of party rather than gender.'

> Andrews, Maggie, *The Acceptable Face of Feminism. The Women's Institute as a Social Movement* (London, 1997).
> Banks, Olive, *Biographical Dictionary of British Feminists*, vol.2 (Hemel Hempstead, 1990).
> Denman, Gertrude, *Suggestions for Proceedings at Meetings* (National Federation of Women's Institutes, 1920).
> Huxley, Gervase, *Lady Denman G.B.E.* (London, 1961).
> Robinson, Jane, *A Force to Be Reckoned With. A History of the Women's Institutes* (London, 2011).
> Stott, Mary, *Organisation Woman* (London, 1978).

Dighton Pollock, The Hon. Mrs was a founder member of the North Kensington Women's Welfare Centre in 1924 and served on its Executive Committee. She was the daughter of Lord Buckmaster who successfully raised the issue of birth control in the 1926 debate in the House of Lords.
> North Kensington Women's Welfare Centre's Annual Report 1927–1928.

Elliot-Nish, Mrs in 1928 served as a founder member and Vice-Chairman of the Liverpool Mothers' Welfare Clinic.
> Liverpool Mothers' Welfare Clinic First Annual Report 1926–1927.

Elwell, Mrs was on the foundation committee in 1926 of Wolverhampton Birth Control Centre.
> Wolverhampton Birth Control Clinic First Annual Report 1926. Russell Archive, Box 405, IISH, Amsterdam.

Emanuel, Mrs Ethel was a founder member of Birmingham Women's Welfare Centre, sat on their first Committee and became Chairman from 1932 to 1951. She donated a guinea to the Centre in 1927.

Ethel Emanuel was married to Dr J.G. Emanuel who also actively supported the birth control clinic.

Ethel was active in the Jewish community and a founder member in 1908 of the local National Council of Women. She was Secretary, Treasurer and President of that branch. Ethel was an active member of the NEC in the 1920s, frequently reporting on Birmingham's activities such as the campaigns to get women appointed to public office (NCW Executive Committee Minute 15 February 1928).

> Birmingham Women's Welfare Centre First Annual Report 1927-1928.
> Birmingham Women's Welfare Centre Fifth Annual Report 1931-1932.
> Court, Audrey and Walton, Cynthia, *Birmingham Made a Difference. The Birmingham Women's Welfare Centre 1926-1991* (Birmingham, 2001).

Florence, Mrs Lella Secor (1887-1966) was a committed birth control pioneer whose experience ranged from setting up two SPBCC clinics in the 1920s in Cambridge and Birmingham to pioneering the trial of the oral contraceptive pill in the 1960s.

Lella was American and a peace campaigner in the First World War. In 1917 she married Philip Sargent Florence and came with him to England. She wrote in her diary in October 1917, 'I hadn't realised how radiantly happy one could be as the wife of such a man as Philip.' They had two sons.

In 1921 the family moved to Cambridge where Philip had a lectureship at the university. In 1925 she was a founder member of Cambridge Women's Welfare Association, sat on their first Committee and was Hon. Secretary. Lella, originally an investigative journalist, wrote the influential book *Birth Control on Trial*, published in 1930. This looked at the experiences of the first three hundred women attending the Cambridge clinic and critically evaluated the success of their methods. Lella believed that there was still no satisfactory method of birth control and so aroused the ire of Marie Stopes who would accept no criticism.

Lella's main objective was to find a simpler more universal method of contraception for women and to help them persevere with birth control. In 1957 she met Dr Gregory Pincus in the USA where he was already trialling the oral contraceptive pill. In 1960 she invited him to address a meeting at Birmingham Medical Institute. She then worked tirelessly to set up a trial in Birmingham in spite of opposition from Head Office.

Lella's campaigns were wide ranging and included world disarmament, Labour politics, women's rights, slum clearance and family planning.

Image: National Portrait Gallery, London.
Swarthmore College Peace Archive, PA, USA. Email: wchmiel@swarthmore/edu/Library/ Peace.
Cambridge Women's Welfare Association First Annual Report 1925–1926.
Birmingham Women's Welfare Centre Third Annual Report 1927–1928.
Florence, Barbara M., *Lella Secor. A Diary in Letters 1915–1922* (New York, 1978).
Florence, Lella S., *Birth Control on Trial* (London, 1930).
Florence, Lella S., *Progress Report on Birth Control* (London, 1956).
Court, Audrey and Walton, Cynthia, *Birmingham Made a Difference 1926–1991* (Birmingham, 2001).

Frankenburg, Mrs Charis U. (1892–1985) was co-founder and Honorary Secretary of the Manchester and Salford Mothers' Clinic. After winning a scholarship to St Paul's School, Charis went to Somerville College, Oxford. Her autobiography shows that she had a highly enjoyable time and formed close friendships, such as with Dorothy Sayers. The novelist Vera Brittain recalled Charis being a student with her at Somerville in the period immediately before the First World War and described her as potentially interesting in her *Testament of Youth*. She joined a number of the societies including the debating society and explored the surrounding countryside. She carried on with her Latin which no doubt helped with writing the highly popular books *Latin with Laughter* which Marie Stopes' son Harry Stopes-Roe remembered reading with enthusiasm. Later in 1921 the Frankenburg family watched Charis receive her War degree.

Charis realised the seriousness of the First World War and so wanted to serve in France as a nurse. Her brother was killed in the War. She enrolled on a midwifery course at Clapham Maternity hospital. This could be taken in three months, but she decided to take the longer more in-depth course of six months. The course cost £37.6.0 plus uniform. She used a legacy from her godmother to pay for this. Amongst her fellow students was the feminist Maude Royden (later Rev.) who she rated outstanding as a nurse. Charis became a Certified Midwife with the Clapham Maternity Hospital Midwife Certificate of Honour.

Charis arrived at Chalons-sur-Marne Maternity Hospital in France on 4 October 1915. Her French was good, she had a sound training but nevertheless less the work was hard. She wrote that 'I felt like a marionette on the verge of hysteria.' This was a common experience of volunteer nurses in the First World War and similar frustrations were voiced by Vera Brittain. Charis later said she gained valuable experience and enjoyment. She was awarded the Medaille Commemorative de la Grand Guerre.

APPENDIX

On her return to England, Charis married her Jewish cousin Sydney Frankenburg, a wealthy industrialist. It was a very happy marriage and he was always supportive to her activities both financially and morally. She had four, perfectly spaced, children. It was in this period that she wrote *Commonsense in the Nursery*.

Charis kept up her interest in childbirth and was a member of the local Maternal Mortality Committee. She was involved with the enquiry of a young Jewish mother from alleged hospital negligence. She campaigned for an increased status of midwives, claiming that their record on home births was superior to that of hospitals.

Charis developed her interest in maternal welfare to the birth control campaign. None of the other volunteers in the SPBCC had her professional knowledge. She was an excellent organiser and knew what was required for the MSMC. She organised premises, staff and publicity for the clinic. Naturally as co-founder she sat on its Executive Committee holding the key position of Hon. Secretary. After establishing the Manchester, Salford and District Mothers' Clinic she helped in the formation of other clinics – for instance donating 10/- to the Wolverhampton clinic in its first year and speaking to the newly founded Liverpool clinic. Because of their depth of experience both Mary and Charis were asked to sit on the Co-ordinating Committee of the Society for the Provision of Birth Control Clinic and its successor the National Birth Control Council.

Charis understood the power of women's organisations. She had gone with her mother to listen to the suffragettes and subsequently she became a member of the Salford Women Citizens Association and joined the National Council of Women. Charis networked assiduously. In 1930 she became Chairman of Moss Side Women's Conservative Association. In her seventies Charis continued to give talks which included birth control. She bravely publicly supported the ALRA. She wrote in her 1975 autobiography, 'If the proper precaution of contraceptive instruction has been lacking, must the escape route also be forbidden.'

 Manchester and District Mothers' Clinic Annual Report 1927.
 Ursula Kennedy, daughter, interviewed by Clare Debenham, 2 July 2004.
 Ruth Rapport, cousin, interviewed by Clare Debenham, 12 June 2005.
 Roger F., male relative, interviewed by Clare Debenham 1 October 2003.
 Charis Frankenburg interviewed by Brian Harrison, 12 April 1977 and 22 July 1981. Brian Harrison digital recordings, 8SUF/B/144B and 8SUF/B/194). Women's Library London.
 Frankenburg, Charis U. (nee Barnett) *Commonsense in the Nursery* (London, 1922).

Frankenburg, Charis U., *Latin with Laughter* (London, 1934).
Frankenburg, Charis U., *More Latin with Laughter* (London, 1934).
Frankenburg, Charis U., 'Manchester and Salford Mothers' Clinic', *Family Planning*, 1956, p.6.
Frankenburg, Charis U., *Not Old, Madam, VINTAGE!* (Suffolk, 1975).
Logan, Anne, *Feminism and Criminal Justice. A Historical Perspective* (London, 2008).
Powell, A., *Women in the War Zone. Hospital Services in the First World War* (Stroud, 2009).

Frankenburg, Mrs Frances Ann sat on the General Advisory Council of the Manchester, Salford and District Mothers' Clinic in its launch year of 1926. She was three times Lady Mayoress of Salford and mother-in-law of Charis Frankenburg, the founder of the MSMC.

Fuller, Mrs Evelyn (1895–1938), aka Miss Kitty Evelyn Read, aka Miss Alice Craig, aka Miss Howard. Evelyn trained as a teacher and was appointed Superintendant of Walworth Women's Welfare Centre when it was taken over by the SPBCC. She remained Secretary from 1923–36 and under her leadership the clinic gradually expanded and provided a model for other SPBCC clinics. She was also Secretary of the SPBCC.

In 1926 Evelyn wrote an illustrated booklet for those volunteers considering starting a birth control clinic. She included a diagram of the Walworth Road layout. This was a practical booklet covering the choice of accommodation, sanitary arrangements and hours of opening. She pointed out the opening of the clinic must fit in with school hours and there must be toys for young children. Evelyn also provided a list of recommended equipment as well as an example of a case card. She placed great emphasis on the lay workers being sympathetic, as many of their patients were shy and nervous.

Evelyn travelled to Zurich in 1931 and delivered a paper on the SPBCC to an international symposium on contraception. Although her delivery was hesitant, her paper was well received because it arose out of her experience at Walworth Road. She stressed that the most important thing was to gain the confidence of the patient.

Evelyn continued her work efficiently and conscientiously until 1936 when she complained of overwork and suffered from a nervous breakdown. Voluntary organisations often care more about their clients than their workers and her breakdown split the SPBCC. Evelyn was admitted to an asylum and then certified as insane. The SPBCC believed that they had behaved correctly by paying for Evelyn to stay

APPENDIX

in a private lunatic asylum, from which she had escaped as Miss Alice Craig. There was no suggestion of any cure and she was dismissed from her post with one month's notice. Evelyn was quoted as saying, 'What can I do now with all my savings gone and no job?' The reason she was given for being made redundant was her illness and the organisation's merger with the Family Planning Association. No doubt her bizarre behaviour, bringing unwanted scandal, was also a factor in her dismissal. Friends described Evelyn's job as being her life's work and, being estranged from her brothers and sister, she regarded those at Walworth as her family.

Evelyn efficiently rented a bungalow in Canvey Island under an assumed name of Miss Howard. In April 1938 she tragically took her own life by deliberately placing herself in front of an unlit gas stove. Suicide was then illegal and she tried to remove all identifying marks from her clothes However, eventually she was traced through the label on her glove and as a result the story of her life unravelled. The local paper reported that she was not Evelyn Fuller and she was not married. She was Miss Kitty Evelyn Read aged forty-four.

Mrs Lawther, founding member of the East London Clinic and SPBCC clinic was prevented by the Coroner from giving contentious evidence at the inquest. She indignantly accused the SPBCC Executive Committee of discharging Evelyn in a heartless manner because of her illness. She and others resigned from the SPBCC East London clinic in protest at Evelyn's treatment.

Evelyn had become a Eugenics Society member in 1937 and it was the Eugenics Society that gave her glowing testimonial in their obituary in the *Eugenics Review*. Dr C.P. Blacker wrote without irony in the *Eugenics Review* that 'few people outside the birth control movement knew Mrs Fuller's name; but those within the movement recognised in her one of the really few essential people.' Tactfully her last years were not mentioned.

        Fuller, Evelyn, *On the Management of a Birth Control Clinic* (SPBCC, 1926).
        Fuller, Evelyn, 'A note on the work of the Society for the Provision of Birth Control Clinics, England' in Sanger, Margaret and Stone, Hannah M., *The Practice of Contraception. An International Symposium and Survey* (Baltimore, 1931).
        News of the World, 24 April 1938.
        Southend Pictorial Telegraph, 23 April 1938.
        Eugenics Review, July 1938, vol. 30 (2). pp.125–7.
        Leathard, Audrey, *The Fight for Family Planning* (Basingstoke, 1980).

Gamon, Mrs served as a founder member and Council member of the Liverpool Mothers' Welfare Clinic.
> Liverpool Mothers' Welfare Clinic First Annual Report 1926-1927.

Gilchrist, Dr Marion was listed in 1934 as being an Executive Committee member of the Glasgow Women's Welfare and Advisory Clinic – there are no previous records of the clinic. After a brilliant academic career in Arts subjects she enrolled in the medical faculty of the University of Glasgow and in 1894 was the first woman doctor to qualify. She later specialised in ophthalmic medicine.

While at university Marion developed an interest in politics and was convenor of the Queen Margaret College committee of the Glasgow University Liberal Club. She went on to join the Glasgow and West of Scotland Association for Women's Suffrage but dissatisfied with its progress she left to join the Glasgow branch of the Women's Social and Political Union. She then became involved in medical politics and was one of the first members of the Medical Women's Federation and first woman Chairman of the Glasgow division of the British Medical Association. Marion used her position to advance women's progress in the medical profession.
> Dougall, Rona, 'Marion Gilchrist,' *A Biographical Dictionary of Scottish Women* (Edinburgh, 2007).

Gilson, Mrs Marianne Caroline was in 1927 a founding member of Birmingham Women's Welfare Centre and sat on their first Executive Committee. She held an MA although it not known what university she attended. Marianne was married to Robert Cary Gilson who was headmaster of the Schools of King Edward VI, Birmingham. She donated a guinea in 1927 to the Centre.
> Birmingham Women's Welfare Centre First Annual Report 1927-1928.
> Cornish's Year Book, *Who's Who in Birmingham*, 1927.

Gimson, Dr Olive, MB, ChB was a founding member in 1926 of the Manchester and Salford Mothers' Clinic. Olive had attended the Victoria University of Manchester and qualified as a doctor in 1919, only six years before the founding of the MSMC. Mary Stocks commented, 'Our own young clinic doctor, Olive Gimson, glowed like a kindly light, in the encircling gloom of professional non-cooperation'. It is not known how her working-class mothers regarded her, but certainly patients such as Emily Glencross acknowledged their gratitude. The annual accounts for 1926-7 show the doctor and nurse were paid £207.00 for their services but Dilys Dean reported that in the early years of the MSMC, Olive Gimson generously waived her salary in order to give the voluntary

APPENDIX

clinic more resources. As the MSMC was in a violent area Olive Gimson, a dog breeder, is remembered for taking her two dogs to guard her car.

When Manchester City Council created two new municipal birth control clinics in 1931 Gimson was appointed to the clinic at Withington Hospital. The doctor was able to combine this appointment with her work at the MSMC and continued in the training of medical staff.

> Dilys Dean, unpublished notes written in the 1950s about the clinic's early years and donated to Clare Debenham by her daughter in 2003.
> Nurse Alice Farnworth interviewed by Clare Debenham, 27 February 2003.
> Manchester and District Mothers' Clinic Annual Report 1926–1927.
> General Medical Council Annual Yearbook, 1926.
> Stocks, Mary D., *My Commonplace Book* (London, 1970) p.161.
> Glencross, Evelyn, *For Better or For Worse. Salford Memories 1938–45* (Manchester, 1993), p.8.

Gledhill, Mrs Caroline was in 1927 a founding member of Birmingham Women's Welfare Centre.

> Birmingham Women's Welfare Centre First Annual Report 1927–1928.

Gordon, Mrs Ella was the driving force behind the Wolverhampton Women's Welfare Clinic which opened in 1925 and was the first provincial birth control clinic outside London. Described as comfortably off by Alice Onions, Gordon distributed handbills and held a public meeting on birth control in a local school. Gordon collected birth control literature and loaned Onions a copy of Stopes' *Married Love*. Gordon then invited Onions to help start a birth control clinic and they rented two rooms in a railwayman's home. However, because of the demand they moved to Heath Street and formed a small committee. In the First Annual Report Gordon is shown as Hon. Secretary and Superintendant and donated ten pounds to the Centre. Gordon and Onions subsequently carried out outreach work amongst the miners' wives around Cannock Chase.

Gordon was an active member of the Labour Party and pushed for conference resolutions on birth control. She gave talks on birth control to Bilston Labour Party Women's Section.

> Wolverhampton Birth Control Clinic First Annual Report 1926. Russell Archive, Box 405, IISH, Amsterdam.
> Wolverhampton Archives and Local Studies. Bilston Labour Party Women's Section. M.D.-Lab./2/1/.
> Browne, Stella F.W., *New Generation*, January 1927, p.4.
> *New Generation*, June 1927, p.36.
> Rowley, J.J., 'Reminiscences of Alice Onions'. *West Midlands Studies*, 1983, 16, 30–3.

Hall, Mrs Lawrence served as a founder member and Council member of the Liverpool Mothers' Welfare Clinic.

> Liverpool Mothers' Welfare Clinic First Annual Report 1926–1927.

Harrison, Mrs Herbert served as a founder member and Executive Committee member of the Liverpool Mothers' Welfare Clinic.
    Liverpool Mothers' Welfare Clinic First Annual Report 1926–1927.

Hartree, Mrs Eva, JP was in 1925 a founder member of the Cambridge Women's Welfare Association and was Chairman of their first Committee.

Eva was born in 1873 and attended Girton College, Cambridge University, taking her tripos in 1895. She then married William Hartree. The family moved to Farnham, Surrey where she was Hon. Secretary of the Farnham Suffrage Society and later Hon. Secretary of Guildford Women's Suffrage Society.

After returning to Cambridge in 1919 she was elected a councillor in 1921 and took a particular interest in Public Health, Maternity and Child Welfare. She served on the council for a total of twenty years. In 1924 Eva Hartree was the first woman to be elected Mayor of Cambridge. She was sent a letter of congratulations by the Executive Committee of the National Council of Women, Executive Committee Minute, 6 October 1924.

Eva encouraged women to stand for public office, saying they should not be discouraged because of inexperience or cost. She claimed her election to council had cost £11 and other campaigns had been even cheaper. She was a member of the Cambridge branch of the National Council of Women, and their national President in 1935–7.
    Cambridge Women's Welfare Association First Annual Report 1925–1926.
    Minutes of joint meeting of NCW with WCA, 10 July 1930.
    Cambridge Daily News, 10 October 1947, p.68.

Hescott, Mrs was a founding member in 1926 of the Manchester, Salford and District Mothers' Clinic and served on the Executive Committee. As Secretary of the Manchester Branch of the Women's Co-operative Guild she stood in an official capacity rather than as an individual. However, next year when a new Secretary took over she continued to serve on the Committee.
    Manchester and District Mothers' Clinic Annual Report 1926–1927.
    Manchester and Salford Co-operative Herald, July 1928.

Hicks, Mrs Alice was named in 1927 in a questionnaire returned to Margaret Sanger as the Honorary Superintendent of the Glasgow Women's Welfare and Advisory Clinic. Mrs Hicks was the first Treasurer of the WBCG but she was replaced at her request in 1926 by Mrs Lendon so she could concentrate on propaganda work. Alice Hicks found that when she visited Scotland her research convinced her, contrary to popular opinion, that the miners actively encouraged their wives to seek birth control advice, Workers' Birth Control Group Conference, 2 December 1926.

APPENDIX

She appeared to have been seconded from London to assist the Glasgow clinic and the Executive Committee paid tribute to her dynamism. They reported that Alice in 1927 has also addressed thirty meetings, mainly women's meetings but one or two mixed meetings and several men's meetings. These meetings represented various Trade Unions, the Labour Party, ILP, the Women's Co-operative Guild.

Alice Hicks was middle aged and not in good health but Dora Russell described her as 'wiry, indefatigable, the best type of working class woman'. The two went campaigning together to Motherwell to the constituency of the Rev. James Barr MP, a leading opponent of birth control in the House of Commons They paid their own fares.

> Browne, Stella F.W., *New Generation*, January 1927, p.4.
> Questionnaire on the Glasgow Women's Welfare and Advisory Clinic completed on 11 November 1927 and returned to Margaret Sanger. Margaret Sanger Papers, Box 60, Sophia Smith Collection. Smith College Archives, USA.
> Russell, Dora, *The Tamarisk Tree* (London, 1975 reprint 1989). pp.173-4.

Hislop, Mrs W.A. was a founding member of the Executive Committee of the North Kensington Women's Welfare Centre.
> North Kensington Women's Welfare Centre's Annual Report 1925-1926.

Hobhouse, Catherine was Honorary Secretary and later Chairman of the Liverpool Mothers' Welfare Clinic from the twenty years from the 1930s. Her connections were most useful as her husband, later Lord Hobhouse, was a partner in the shipping firm Albert Holt and Co. Ltd. He was well known for his charitable work and could approach potential supporters confidentially.
> Jones, E.L., 'The establishment of voluntary family planning clinics in Liverpool and Bradford, 1926-1960: a comparative study.' *Social History of Medicine, Advanced Access*, 13 August 2010.

How-Martyn, Mrs Edith (1875-1954) was an early supporter of the Walworth Women's Welfare Centre and was active in the campaign to give working-class mothers birth control information. In 1929 she founded the Birth Control Information Centre and the next year wrote an influential book on the achievements of the birth control campaign. She was also a member of the Malthusian League.

Edith was awarded a degree from the University College, Aberystwyth. She was a member of the Women's Franchise Society and was an early member of the Women's Social and Political Union, being one of the first sent to prison. However, she resented the Pankhurst's autocratic style and left to join the Women's Freedom League.

Edith unsuccessfully stood for Parliament in 1918 as an Independent Feminist candidate but she did succeed in becoming Middlesex County Council's first woman member. She was also a member of the Women's Co-operative Guild.

> How-Martyn, Edith and Breed, Mary, *The Birth Control Movement in England* (London, 1930).
> Law, Cheryl, *Women. A Modern Political Dictionary* (London, 2000).

Hubback, Mrs Eva (1886-1949) was a close friend of Shena Simon, Mary Stocks and Eleanor Rathbone. She had three children like Mary Stocks and the families took holidays together. Eva had been widowed in the First World War. She continued to enjoy travel, theatres and parties.

Eva Hubback attended Newnham College, Cambridge University where she took the economics tripos and was awarded a first class degree. She later taught economics there and Mary Stocks quoted some of her students. She became politically active joining the Fabian Society and in 1917, after becoming widowed, became parliamentary secretary to NUSEC, the suffrage organisation. She worked closely with its President, Eleanor Rathbone in promoting family allowances. Mary Stocks described her as a brilliant political tactician. One her most successful achievement, was the Matrimonial Causes Act of 1923 which gave equal grounds for divorce. Eva Hubback's legislative achievements included the Matrimonial Causes, which gave equal grounds for divorce, and the Guardianship of Infants Act. Other legislation which she promoted included the Widows, Orphans and Old Age Contribution Act of 1925 and the Summary Jurisdiction (Separation and Maintenance) of 1925 which tried to improve the situation of separated women.

Eva believed that many of NUSEC's objectives had been achieved and it should look for a change of direction. She admired the structure of the Women's Institutes and persuaded the organisation to adopt the education objective of a system of women's clubs to be known as Townswomen's Guilds.

She played an important role in the birth control movement and was involved in the publicising Memorandum 153/MCW. She was also instrumental in persuading Lady Trudie Denman of the Women's Institute to become Chairman of the SPBCC and its immediate successor.

Eva was elected a Labour member of London County Council in 1945.

Towards the end of her life she moved away from feminism to population concerns. Olive Banks is critical of Eva Hubback's portrayal of idealised family life which was to be challenged in the 1960s.

> BBC Written Archives, Caversham. Mary Stocks on Eva Hubback, 3 October 1952. Light programme.

APPENDIX

Hubback, Eva M., *The Population of Britain* (West Drayton, 1947).
Banks, Olive, *Biographical Dictionary of British Feminists*, vol. 2: *A Supplement 1900-1945* (Hemel Hempstead, 1990).
Kuzmack, Linda G., *Woman's Cause. The Jewish Movement in England and the U.S.A. 1881-1933* (Ohio, 1990).

Hudson, Mrs served as a founder member and Council member of the Liverpool Mothers' Welfare Clinic.
Liverpool Mothers' Welfare Clinic First Annual Report 1926-1927.

Irvine, Mrs W. Ferguson served as a founder member and Executive Committee member of the Liverpool Mothers' Welfare Clinic.
Liverpool Mothers' Welfare Clinic First Annual Report 1926-1927.

Irwin, Miss Margaret, CBE (1858-1940) was on the Committee in 1934-5 of the Glasgow Women's Welfare and Advisory Council.

Margaret attended classes at St Andrews and Glasgow universities, as well as Glasgow School of Art but was not able to receive a degree.

Margaret became involved in campaigns for working women's rights including becoming Secretary for the Scottish Council for Women's Trades and working for the establishment of a separate Scottish TUC. In the 1920s she wrote numerous reports on sweated trades such as laundry work and tailoring. In her lifetime she was criticised for not being radical enough and being more in sympathy with the Liberal Party than with the newly emerged Labour Party. However, her contribution to the advancement of women workers has now been much more positively reassessed.
Canning, Audrey, 'Margaret Irwin.' *A Biographical Dictionary of Scottish Women* (Edinburgh, 2008).

Keats-Behrend, Mrs served as a founder member of the Liverpool Mothers' Welfare Clinic.
Liverpool Mothers' Welfare Clinic First Annual Report 1926-1927.

Laski, Mrs Eileen (later Mrs Norman Blond) was a founding member of the Manchester, Salford and District Mothers' Clinic. Eileen was the sister of Simon Marks, of Marks and Spencer fame, and her first marriage was to Norman Laski. When Marks and Spencer became a public company in 1926 she became an extremely wealthy woman. After the break-up of her marriage she moved to London but still continued her support for birth control. In 1933 Eileen served on the Executive Committee of the Society for the Provision of Birth Control Clinics. She became friendly with Dr Edith Summerskill, who became the Labour MP for West Fulham, and they organised a Malthusian Ball to raise funds for the birth control movement. Her second marriage, in middle age, was

to Norman Blond. Her step-son had a good relationship with Eileen but described how she could be extremely demanding.
> Manchester and District Mothers' Clinic Annual Report 1926-1927.
> National Birth Control Association. Third Annual Report 1932-1933.
> Margaret Sanger papers. Box 60. File 8. Smith College, MA.
> Blond, Anthony, *Jew Made in England* (London, 2004).
> Bookbinder, P., *Simon Marks* (London, 1993).
> Summerskill, Edith, *A Woman's Memoirs* (London, 1967).

Laski, Mrs Frida was on the Executive Committee of the Walworth Women's Welfare Centre in 1928. She was a socialist-feminist and believed it wrong that working-class mothers should be denied birth control information that had been easily available to middle-class women for the last twenty to thirty years. She spoke on birth control at Hyde Park and like her fellow members was pelted with tomatoes. She was an active member of the Abortion Law Reform Association. In 1953 she was made a fellow of the Eugenics Society.

Frida was married to Professor Harold Laski, the left-wing political scientist at the London School of Economics.
> BBC Written Archives, Caversham. Broadcast, 24 March 1969.
> Handel, Keith and Simms, Madeleine, *Abortion Law Reformed* (London, 1971).
> Banks, Olive, 'Frida Laski', *The Biographical Dictionary of English Feminists*, vol. 2 (Hemel Hempstead, 1990).

Lawder, Mrs Gertrude was the wife of Labour councillor J.C. Lawder who in 1926 together with Captain Leigh and Lord Ivor Spencer Churchill founded the East London Women's Welfare Clinic in Mile End. These two men provided funds for the clinic. Gertrude was anxious for this not to be seen as a male-dominated enterprise and wrote to the local paper purporting to put forward the views of the local women to birth control.
> *East London Advertiser*, 31 July 1926.

Lawther, Mrs Lottie, later Lady Lawther was the daughter of a coal miner. She married Will Lawther, also a miner, in 1914. The couple were childless, so Lottie felt she had the time to concentrate on supporting her husband's political career. He became the MP for Barnard Castle 1929-31 and developed a career in the Mineworkers Federation of Great Britain, becoming President in 1939. He then rose to become President of the National Union of Miners in 1947.

Lottie, a member of Blaydon District Labour Party, spoke at the 1927 Labour Party Conference in favour of birth control. In an articulate speech she stated that she had worked in industry for fifteen years and was an active Trade Unionist. She appealed to the miners

APPENDIX

whom the women had supported in their dispute to now support the women.
>   Labour Party Annual Report 1927.
>   Saville, John, 'Sir William Lawther', *Oxford Dictionary of National Biography* (Oxford, 2004).

Lawther, Mrs Steve was one of the sisters-in-law of Lottie Lawther and was also a miner's wife and member of Blaydon District Labour Party. Steve Lawther was described by the local paper as 'the stormy petrel of the Lawther family' and was imprisoned during the General Strike.

The couple played host to Dora Russell when she visited Durham to speak on behalf of the Workers' Birth Control Group in 1925. 'Their lodging was very simple. Mrs Lawther, pregnant at the time, had to carry coals up several flights of steps.' She represented Chapwell and Durham on the Workers Birth Control Group in 1926. Mrs Lawther stood at the back of the 1927 Labour Party Conference with a baby in her arms during the birth control debate. Mrs Lawther helped start the Newcastle-upon-Tyne Women's Welfare Centre in January 1929 when she hosted experienced birth controllers from the Walworth Road Clinic, London who gave her valuable advice. Mrs Claire Tamplin was one of her guests, 'How she squeezed us all into her little house is a mystery to me.'
>   Russell Archives, International Institute of Social History, Amsterdam, File 404.
>   Russell, Dora, *The Tamarisk Tree* (London, 1975 reprint 1989) p.183.
>   Labour Party Annual Report 1927. p.233.
>   Laski, Frida, *New Generation*, July 1928. p.74.
>   Tamplin, Claire, 'Early days in Newcastle,' *Family Planning*, October 1962.
>   Saville, John, *Dictionary of Labour Biography*, vol. 7.

Lee, Councillor Annie was a Labour councillor for Gorton, Manchester. She never married and was an outspoken feminist. Lee was a member of Beswick WCG and elected a Poor Law Guardian. She first raised the issue of birth control advice being given in Manchester Maternity and Child Welfare clinics and she continued to campaign until the council reversed its decision
>   Profile: *Women's Outlook*, 27 September 1924.

Lennard, Mrs was a founder member of Birmingham Women's Welfare Centre. She was also at that time a local councillor.
>   Birmingham Women's Welfare Centre First Annual Report 1927–1928.

Little, Dr Isabelle was one of the doctors who worked for Oxford Family Welfare Association in its founding year of 1926–7. She waived her fee and the Committee paid tribute to the amount of time she had devoted to treating mothers at the clinic. She also gave talks to local nurses. In her medical officer's report Isabelle commented on the fact that nearly all the

women had unsuccessfully tried some form of contraceptive previously. She felt the clinic's method was successful even though some mothers had difficulty learning its use.
>Oxford Family Welfare Association Annual Report 1926-1927.
>Little, Isabelle, 'Forty Years Back,' *Family Planning*, vol. 15, 1966, issue 3, pp.78-82.

Lloyd, Mrs Margaret was a founder member of the North Kensington Women's Welfare Centre. She was a cousin of Bertrand Russell and used her connections to fund the Centre which included Mrs Pethick Lawrence, Lady Balfour of Burleigh and her friend Mrs Margaret Pollock who was initially Treasurer. Her mother, the Hon. Mrs Rollo Russell, lent money to obtain premises. She wrote that they were 'moved to anger and pity that few uneducated and poor people had access to advice on birth control'. Dora Russell in *The Tamarisk Tree* described Margaret as being devoted to left-wing and women's causes.
>North Kensington Women's Welfare Centre's Annual Report 1925-1926.
>Russell, Dora, *The Tamarisk Tree* (London, 1975 reprint 1989) p.174.

Longson, Mrs was a founding member in 1926 of the Manchester, Salford and District Mothers' Clinic.
>Manchester and District Mothers' Clinic Annual Report 1926-1927.

Macirone, Dr Clara was a founding member in 1927 of Birmingham Women's Welfare Centre and served on its first Committee. Clara, as well as providing strategic advice, took birth control sessions herself. She was described in the Centre's *Annual Report for 1927-1928* as 'having great sympathy with working women'. She also had the political advantage of being medical officer with one of the municipal Ante-Natal Clinics. She donated a guinea to set up the Centre.

Local Birmingham resident Mrs Bacon, in a letter to Marie Stopes of November 1926, described Dr Macirone as 'was wavering, now definitely for, and on our voluntary committee for clinic'. Clara was a member of Handsworth Labour Party and spoke in favour of municipal birth control clinics in the Birth Control debate at the Ninth National Conference of Labour Women in 1928.

She was nominated by Ella Gordon of the Wolverhampton Clinic for the Committee of the Workers' Birth Control Group.
>Birmingham Women's Welfare Centre First Annual Report 1927-1928.
>Conference of Labour Women 1928 Annual Report, p.26.
>Stopes Collection, British Library, Correspondence with Bacon. 4735.

McNair, Mrs Marjorie was a founding member in 1925 of the Cambridge Women's Welfare Association and served on its first Committee. After two unsuccessful attempts she was elected a Cambridge borough councillor in 1928 serving on five committees including Maternity and Child Welfare. She was a member of the NCW and WCA.

Marjorie, the daughter of Sir Clement Bailhache, attended Somerville College, Oxford. She then worked for the LCC in East Islington before moving to Cambridge.
> Cambridge Women's Welfare Association First Annual Report 1925-1926.
> Cambridge Independent Press, 28 November 1930.
> Who's Who in Cambridge (Cambridge, 1936).

Malcolm, Dr Flossie was a founding member in November 1926 of Aberdeen Women's Welfare Centre. She was general practitioner in Kintore.
> Press and Journal, 4 December 1972.

Malleson, Dr Joan qualified in 1926 and, unusually for a female doctor, was married. She subsequently worked at the Walworth Road clinic succeeding Dr Norman Haire. Walworth Road became the headquarters of the SPBCC and specialised in research and training. Joan publicly campaigned for birth control facilities, being a member of the Workers' Birth Control Group. She secretly trained medical students after hours and subsequently became involved in the campaign for abortion law reform.
> Malleson, Dr Joan, The Principles of Contraception. A Handbook for General Practitioners (no publisher given, 1935).

Manning, Mrs Leah, MP, later Dame (1886-1977) was a founder member in 1925 of the Cambridge Women's Welfare Association. She trained as a teacher at Homerton College, Cambridge teaching at New Street School in a poor part of Cambridge and later became head teacher of an experimental Open Air School for malnourished children. She campaigned for free school milk through her position on the Trades Council. In 1930 Leah became President of the National Union of Teachers. Manning was appointed a magistrate and was a prominent member of the Women's Co-operative Guild and National Council of Women.

While at college Leah became friendly with Hugh Dalton and became a lifelong Labour supporter. When he stood as parliamentary candidate for Cambridge his wife, Ruth helped her run the Cambridge Women's Welfare Clinic 'at that time thought not to be very respectable'.

Leah Manning joined the ILP becoming its delegate to the Trades Council and eventually Chairman. In 1931 she was elected Labour MP for East Islington. After the Second World War she was re-elected to Parliament and continued to fight for women's rights, particularly equal pay.

When Leah retired from Parliament she rekindled her enthusiasm for family planning and helped found the FPA clinic in Harlow new town. In 1964 they received permission from Head Office to sell contraceptives to unmarried people and this was later turned into a permissive policy decision for all FPA clinics.

>Cambridge Women's Welfare Association First Annual Report 1925-1926.
>*Women's Outlook*, March 1931.
>Manning, Leah, *A Life for Education* (London, 1970), p.58.
>Banks, Olive, 'Leah Manning', *The Biographical Dictionary of English Feminists*, vol.2 (Hemel Hempstead, 1990).

Marshall, Mrs Rachel was a founder member in 1925 of the Cambridge Women's Welfare Association.

>Cambridge Women's Welfare Association First Annual Report 1925-1926.

Masefield, Mrs Constance was a founder member of the Oxford Family Welfare Association in 1926. She was a graduate of Newnham College and became a senior mistress at Roedean, the prestigious girls' private school. Unusually she became the proprietor of her own girls' school in London. She was an enthusiastic suffrage supporter and influenced the views of her husband, John Masefield, the poet and novelist. He was appointed Poet Laureate in 1930.

>Oxford Family Welfare Association Annual Report 1926-1927.
>Gervais, D., 'John Masefield', *Oxford Dictionary of National Biography* (Oxford).

Marquis, Mrs Maud, later Baroness Maud Woolton was a founding member of the Liverpool Mothers' Welfare Clinic in 1926 and served on the Executive Committee, with her husband as Treasurer. She continued to keep in touch with the clinic, speaking at the clinic's twenty-fifth anniversary dinner and writing the Forward to Dr Macaulay's history of the clinic.

Her husband, Frederick James Marquis, was Treasurer of the clinic. They married in 1912 when he was Warden of the Liverpool University Settlement but Marquis' political views changed. He moved from Fabian Socialism to Conservative.

>Liverpool Mothers' Welfare Clinic First Annual Report 1926-1927.
>Macaulay, Dr Muriel, *The Story of the Mothers' Welfare Clinic, Liverpool*, Foreword by Lady Woolton (1952).
>*The Liverpudlian* 'Profile of F.J. Marquis,' June 1933.

Matthews, Mrs A.D. was a local Birmingham resident. Mrs Bacon described Mrs Matthews' attitude to the proposed birth control clinic in a letter to Marie Stopes of 1 November 1926 as 'Labour, very enthusiastically for.' Mrs Matthews was evidently active in the National Council of Women and Mrs Bacon described how Mrs Matthews had done much to promote the Centre at their meetings.

>Marie C. Stopes Papers, British Library. Correspondence with Bacon. 4735.

APPENDIX

May, Dr Mabel, MB, ChB was a member of the Manchester and Salford Mothers' Clinic in the inter-war years. The General Medical Council's records showed that she graduated as a doctor from the Victoria University of Manchester in 1911. Mabel was a charismatic doctor and Freda Lightfoot's later novel *Favourite Child*, was loosely based on Mabel's career. As well as being on the Executive Committee May occasionally took birth control sessions at the clinic.

Mabel May had strong feminist views. During the First World War she served abroad with her sister, Dr King May Atkinson. At first she worked in Serbia then in 1916 she organised a maternity unit for the relief of refugees in Russia. This was sponsored by the suffrage organisation NUWSS.

Mabel May was the most politically active of the female doctors in the SPBCC. She was well known in Labour and left-wing circles. She was selected by Declan McHugh as being one of the two hundred most active Manchester Labour members in the inter-war years. Mabel was a member of Rusholme District Labour Party and gave talks on birth control to the local Labour parties and Women's Co-operative Guilds. According to the *Manchester and Salford Co-operative Herald* she told Hulme WCG in December 1926, 'Even if she was not a Socialist the environment with which she came into contact in the course of her professional duties would have made her so.'

Her political enthusiasm could sometimes deflect her from professional duties. Mrs Gaddiam described how Mabel was so pleased to meet her husband, an active Communist, that she proceeded to launch into a political discussion leaving him still in agony with his sprained shoulder.

Mrs Gaddiam interviewed by Clare Debenham, 8 March 2005.
Manchester and District Mothers' Clinic Annual Report 1926–1927.
McHugh, D., 'A "mass" party frustrated. The development of the Labour Party in Manchester 1918–1931,' Unpublished PhD 2001, University of Salford.
Lightfoot, Freda, *Favourite Child* (London, 2001).

Melly, Mrs Albert was a founding member and served on the Council of the Liverpool Mothers' Welfare Clinic.

Liverpool Mothers' Welfare Clinic First Annual Report 1926–1927.

Mitchison, Mrs Naomi, later Lady Mitchison (1899–1999), with her husband Dick Mitchison, were founder members in 1924 of the North Kensington Women's Welfare Centre. She was passionate about causes such as birth control and abortion. In 1930 Naomi wrote *Comments on Birth Control* where she argued that without birth control, conditions were unbearable: 'deliberate and unskilled abortion, maternal ill health, terrible infant mortality and incredibly difficult economic and housing conditions to strive against'.

Her mother had been an active suffragist. The family lived in Oxford but although she passed the examination for what is now St Ann's College she never completed the Diploma. In 1916 she married Dick who was later to become a Labour MP and life peer. Naomi also joined the Labour Party, although she was a critical member.

She was a prolific novelist whose work explored the themes of sex and sexuality.

> North Kensington Women's Welfare Centre's Annual Report 1925-1926.
> Mitchison, Naomi, *Comments on Birth Control* (London, 1930).
> Elphinstone, M., *A Biographical Dictionary of Scottish Women* 'Naomi Mitchison.' (Edinburgh, 2007).

Mosley, Lady Cynthia, MP supported the Wolverhampton Birth Control Centre by making a generous donation of £20.00 to support its early work in 1926. In 1931 she was one of the Vice-Presidents of the National Birth Control Council.

Cynthia Mosley was the wealthy daughter of the Conservative peer Lord Curzon and first wife of Sir Oswald Mosley. Cynthia together with her husband changed from Conservative Party to support Labour in 1924. Cynthia was acknowledged as bringing glamour to politics and in 1929 was elected the Labour MP for Stoke-on-Trent. Although Oswald held eugenic views on the value of birth control, Cynthia is not recorded as sharing these. She resigned with her husband from the Labour Party and joined his New Party. Cynthia Mosley did not stand again at Stoke because of ill health – her husband stood in her place. She died of peritonitis in 1933. Fellow MP and birth control campaigner Leah Manning painted a sympathetic portrait of Cynthia in her own autobiography.

> *Labour Woman*, Profile of Cynthia Mosley, 1 July 1927, p.99.
> Wolverhampton Birth Control Clinic First Annual Report 1926.
> Russell Archives, International Institute of Social History, Amsterdam, File 405.
> National Birth Control Council, 1931.

Mott, Mrs Lillian was a founding member of the Liverpool Mother's Welfare Committee and in 1926 was on its Executive Committee. It was she who persuaded Mrs Marquis to become involved with the clinic and serve on its committee. Lillian became Deputy Chair in 1935.

Lillian came from a comparatively poor family and was delighted to win a scholarship to Cheltenham College and eventually a further scholarship to Cheltenham Ladies College. In 1897 she took the London University BSc. Lillian was an outstanding mathematician. She entered Newnham College, Cambridge in 1898 and as her work in Mathematics was so promising she stayed on with a scholarship for a fourth year to carry out research in the Cavendish Laboratories.

Lillian married her tutor, Charles Mott, who later became the distinguished Director of Education for Liverpool. When they moved to Settle she was able to do some University Extension School lecturing but resisted her husband's encouragement to pursue an academic career.

Lillian became involved with the women's suffrage cause lecturing at the Adult School. She admired the courage of the WSPU but did not approve of their methods. However, she was a great supporter of Eleanor Rathbone. When the couple moved to Stafford they played host to six thousand suffrage pilgrims on their march to London. After the family's move to Cheshire she continued to be involved with NUSEC and the Liverpool Women Citizens Association. In November 1929 Lillian seconded Mary Stocks' resolution on birth control at the Annual Conference of the National Council of Women in Manchester.

Lillian was brought up as a Conservative but later moved to the Liberal Party as she felt it was more sympathetic to women's suffrage.

Liverpool Mothers' Welfare Clinic First Annual Report 1926–1927.
Mott, C.F., *Lillian Mary Mott (nee Reynolds) 1879–1952. A Memoir by Her Husband* (Privately printed, 1952).

Murray, The Hon. Mrs Evelyn Graham, OBE was a founding member of the Walworth Women's Welfare Centre and served first as Treasurer and then as Chairman. One of the clinic's first patients described hearing Mrs Murray speak at an open-air meeting when she was pelted with fruit. Evelyn was Vice-President of the New Generation League, representing them at the meeting with John Wheatley, Health Minister, in 1924 and participating in the New Generation women's motorised birth control leaflet drop in 1925.

New Generation, June 1924, pp.63–4.
New Generation, November 1925, p.123.
Murray, Evelyn G. 'Four clinics'. *Family Planning*, January 1956, p.6.

Newton, Mrs was a founding member in 1926 of the Manchester, Salford and District Mothers' Clinic.

Manchester and District Mothers' Clinic Annual Report 1926–1927.

Norburn, Mrs was a founding member in 1926 of the Manchester, Salford and District Mothers' Clinic and sat on the Executive Committee with a fellow member of the Women's Co-operative Guild. Mrs Norburn's branch was the old established Downing Street near the centre of Manchester. The magazine photograph of Mrs Norburn in June 1928 with her fellow Guild members shows a smart, self-assured woman. The

Manchester Guilds, such as Downing Street, were enthusiastic supporters of the MSMC.
>Manchester and District Mothers' Clinic Annual Report 1926-1927.
>*Manchester and Salford Co-operative Herald*, June 1928.

Onions, Mrs Alice was one of the founders of Wolverhampton Women's Welfare Centre in 1925. A mother of three, Alice heard Ella Gordon speak at a meeting and asked so many questions that she was invited by Gordon to start the clinic with her. They located a sympathetic doctor, Cornelia Winter. Onions was in charge of the secretarial work and sterilising equipment. She was shown in the First Annual Report as serving on the committee. They moved to Heath Street and started clinics in the surrounding areas such as Bilston. After the Second World War, Onions trained as a marriage guidance councillor and started a centre in Wolverhampton.

Onions' father, a shop owner, was a great influence on her beliefs. He was an active member of the ILP and supported women's suffrage and was visited amongst others by Keir Hardie and Ramsay MacDonald. As well as being a Labour Party member she was also a member of the Women's Co-operative Guild. One of a family of six, she won a scholarship to train as an Art teacher but she was not allowed to accept it because of lack of finance.

Alice Onions was a friend of Winifred Strange as well as Ella Gordon.
>Wolverhampton Birth Control Clinic First Annual Report 1926.
>Russell Archives, International Institute of Social History, Amsterdam, File 405.
>*Women's Outlook*. Photograph of Alice Onions with her Guild. 12 April 1924.
>Rowley, J.J., 'Reminiscences of Alice Onions', *West Midlands Studies*, 1983, 16, pp.30–3.
>Peace, M., 'Alice Onions – a pioneer,' *Wolverhampton Magazine*, January 1975.
>*Wolverhampton Chronicle*. 'Woman in profile – Alice Onions. A family is a joy that must be planned,' 18 November 1955.

Osler, Mrs Julian was identified in a letter to Marie Stopes of 1 November 1926 by local Birmingham resident Mrs Bacon as supporting the proposed Mothers' Welfare Centre. Mrs Bacon regarded this as significant as Mrs Osler came from a powerful Quaker family who were well respected in Birmingham.
>Marie C. Stopes Papers, British Library Correspondence with Bacon. 4735.

Paget, Mrs was a founding member and served on the Executive Committee of the Liverpool Mothers' Welfare Clinic.
>Liverpool Mothers' Welfare Clinic First Annual Report 1926-1927.

Palmer, Mrs was on the foundation committee in 1926 of Wolverhampton Birth Control Centre.
>Wolverhampton Birth Control Clinic First Annual Report 1926. Russell Archive, Box 405, IISH, Amsterdam.

APPENDIX

Parkes, Mrs A.I. was a founding member of Birmingham Women's Welfare Association.
    Birmingham Women's Welfare Centre First Annual Report 1927–1928.

Paton, Mrs Fenella (1901–49) was the founder in 1926 of the Aberdeen Women's Welfare Centre. Paton had become involved with the birth control movement when she was a young woman living in London and working with disadvantaged women in the East End, probably with the Malthusian League. Although she had only been married three years when she moved to Aberdeen she gathered together her mother and some friends to found a birth control clinic. She did not believe in fundraising and committees and preferred to use her own private income to support the centre. However, this later became a strain on her finances.

Paton entered into a long correspondence with Marie Stopes lasting many years, and Fenella Paton's son remembers Marie coming to stay with them. Fenella rejected Marie's invitation to join her organisation, stressing the importance of the SPBCC and maintaining a Scottish identity, 6 August 1934. Her position later changed with regard to SCBCRP.

Fenella was immersed in Liberal politics as she was the granddaughter of a Liberal Privy Councillor and daughter of a Liberal MP. She herself was President of the Women's Liberal Association of Central Aberdeen.
    Alan Paton (son) interviewed by Clare Debenham, 25 May 2006.
    Debenham, Clare, 'Aberdeen's birth control pioneer.' *Leopard*, October 2007. pp.12–14.
    Horsburgh, F., 'The back-street beginnings of birth control,' *Press and Journal*, 4 December 1972.
    Marie C. Stopes Papers, British Library. Correspondence with Paton. 58617.

Pease, Mrs Helen Bowen, JP was a founding member in 1925, with her husband Michael, of the Cambridge Women's Welfare Association and served on its first Executive Committee. Helen spoke in the debate on birth control at the 1927 Labour Party Conference and reminded members that birth control was linked to female emancipation. She argued that working-class families should have the knowledge to plan their families that was available to the middle class. Helen criticised Marie Stopes' use of statistics in her analysis of the first ten thousand cases of her clinic. Her article was published in the *Eugenics Review*.

Helen was descended from the Wedgwood manufacturers and was the daughter of Colonel the Rt. Hon. Sir Josiah Wedgwood MP (member of the Labour government) and granddaughter of Lord

Justice Bowen. In 1916 Helen took an honours degree in Natural Sciences from Newham College, Cambridge and while a student was Secretary of the Cambridge University Fabian Society. Both she and her husband, a Cambridge University lecturer, were active members of the Labour Party. Before her marriage she became a National Federation of Women Workers organiser in a factory in London's East End. After her marriage she became a councillor in Cambridge. Helen Pease was created a JP in 1924.
> Cambridge Women's Welfare Association First Annual Report 1925–1926.
> *Cambridge Chronicle*, January 1924.
> Labour Party Conference Report 1927.
> *Eugenics Review* XXII (April 1930–January 1931) p.141.

Perry, Mrs Charles was on the foundation committee in 1926 of Wolverhampton Birth Control Centre.
> Wolverhampton Birth Control Clinic First Annual Report 1926. Russell Archive, Box 405, IISH, Amsterdam.

Plant, Mrs Elsie (1890–1982) tried unsuccessfully to start a birth control clinic in Stockport in 1923. Marie Stopes, at her invitation, came to address an audience of over two thousand at the Armoury in that town and encouraged Elsie to start a clinic there. This attempt failed because of opposition from Roman Catholics and lack of support from the local Labour Party. However, Plant persevered after the Second World War and joined the Stockport Family Planning Association as Treasurer. Finally Stockport FPA won a victory in council and were given the use of municipal premises and eventually a purpose-built clinic.

Elsie had been a suffragette. She and her husband William, running a hat block making business, were Labour Party activists organising the Stockport Labour Party Fellowship. Her brother-in-law was the only Labour councillor on Cheshire County.
> Elsie Plant interviewed by Clare Debenham, 10 May 1978.
> *Stockport Express*, 1 November 1923, 8 November 1923.
> Debenham, Clare, 'Mrs Elsie Plant: suffragette, socialist and birth control activist,' *Women's History Review* 19/1 (2010) pp.145–158.

Pollock, the Hon. Mrs Dighton was the daughter of Lord Buckmaster who in 1926 successfully moved a birth control Bill in the House of Lords. In 1924 she was a founder member of the North Kensington Women's Welfare Centre and served on its Committee. She travelled to another SPBCC clinic in Birmingham to give a talk in 1928 at their AGM on birth control in which she drew attention to the fact that the poor who needed it most, were denied birth control knowledge.

APPENDIX

Pollock was a friend of Dora Russell and served on the committee of the Workers' Birth Control Group.
> North Kensington Women's Welfare Centre's Annual Report 1927-1928.
> *Birmingham Post*, 24 April 1928.
> Russell, Dora, *The Tamarisk Tree* (London, 1975 reprint 1989).

Pritchard, Dr Rosemary was the medical officer for the Cambridge Women's Welfare Association from its foundation in 1925. Pritchard was married and at first worked on a voluntary basis. She attended a course of training with her nurse at the SPBCC Walworth Road clinic.
> Cambridge Women's Welfare Association First Annual Report 1925-1926.

Raffle, Mrs was a founding member in 1926 of the Council of the Liverpool Mothers' Welfare Clinic and served on its committee.
> Liverpool Mothers' Welfare Clinic First Annual Report 1926-1927.

Ramsey, Mrs Agnes was a founding member in 1925 of the Cambridge Women's Welfare Association.
> Cambridge Women's Welfare Association First Annual Report 1925-1926.

Rathbone, Miss Eleanor, MP was one of the first women to take advantage of new political opportunities in local and national government. She was a local councillor and in 1929 was elected MP for the Combined English Universities. Although Eleanor Rathbone was a single, childless woman from a privileged background, she saw herself as a representative of the interests of all women, especially married working-class women whose needs she believed were often overlooked. She attacked society's uncaring attitude towards mothers as 'a monstrous injustice and criminal folly.'

The influences on Eleanor were diverse but amongst the most important were those of her father and her long-term companion. In some ways she was a product of her Victorian age and its values. Indeed Eleanor was born in 1872 in the middle of the Victorian age. She was influenced by her father the ship owner William Rathbone. He was a local businessman and Liberal MP for Liverpool He was concerned with Liverpool's poor.

On her return from Somerville College, Oxford University she became involved with social affairs. In her later campaign for Family Endowment, Eleanor drew on her social work experiences in Liverpool during the First World War when she worked for the Soldiers, Sailors, Airmen and Families Association (SSAFA) and came into close contact with working-class mothers. When husbands were away fighting, the women were able to access grants which meant for the first time mothers had control over the household budget.

She argued this view in her book *The Case for Family Endowment* where she explained how people came to support both causes as they both had their roots in the intolerable conditions which working-class mothers endured. Eleanor Rathbone regarded motherhood not as a brief biological event, nor as a service provided for one man, but as a contribution to society as a whole which would absorb women for most of their adult lives. She held that it was vital that the contribution of wives and mothers be recognised by the state. Therefore she wished to reward the mothers' contribution to society by a system of family allowances which would be paid direct to mothers and would be their income to spend on the children as they saw fit. They would have an independent income which they could control. This would end the mothers' economic dependency on the male breadwinner and end what she termed the instinct for male domination. Her arguments were later accepted by William Beveridge who incorporated her ideas into his plan for a welfare state and agreed that the great majority of married women must be regarded as occupied on work which is vital though unpaid, without which the nation could not continue.

Family allowances were far more than a welfare issue for Eleanor. She was horrified to discover after the end of World War Two that the payment arrangements had been changed by the government so that the father drew the allowance. This was presented as a minor administrative matter by male politicians and administrators who argued that it made no difference whether the allowance was paid to husband or wife. However, to Eleanor it was a fundamental point of principle as her whole political philosophy centred round the rights of mothers. Therefore she publicly threatened to vote against the Bill, which she had worked for twenty-five years, unless the original provisions were restored. Eleanor won her central point and in 1945 the Family Allowances Act was passed giving an allowance for all children after the first child with the benefit payable to the mother.

Eleanor Rathbone was a humanitarian who did not restrict herself to British causes. She became actively involved in the campaigns in Europe, Africa and India. The latter involved her in moral difficulties and she was attacked as an outsider. She herself was aware that she was in a difficult position as an Englishwoman who had never lived in India, making judgements about another culture. However, she personally visited India and took up the issue of women's rights and child brides. Other topics in which she publicly spoke included female circumcision in colonial African countries such as Kenya and the forced marriage of Arab girls in Palestine. Anne Logan interestingly disagrees with Susan Cohen and stressed the unity in Rathbone's humanitarian endeavours.

APPENDIX

Her later years were concerned with fighting fascism. Pedersen provides a detailed account of Rathbone's campaigns which all had a humanitarian theme. She was opposed to British non-intervention in the Spanish Civil War and by 1937 the evacuation of Spanish refugees had become her priority. In 1939 with others she hired a ship to run the blockade of Spain and bring threatened Republicans to safety. She bitterly criticised the appeasement of Hitler in the 1938 Munich accord. She fought tirelessly to get the British government to take a stand against Nazi Germany and to rescue those trapped by the regime. She worked with Jewish refugees and became a supporter of Zionism. Susan Cohen has described in detail Eleanor's efforts to save Jews fleeing persecution from Nazi and Fascist Europe. Her efforts earned her the nickname MP for Refugees. In her indomitable manner Eleanor later visited internment camps in Britain, such as the Isle of Man and Huyton Camps where aliens were detained.

Eleanor died exhausted in 1946. Outwardly conventional, many of her arguments were exceedingly radical. Leading academic and feminist writer Olive Banks gave her assessment in the *Biographical Dictionary of British Feminists* that Eleanor was that she was one of the most significant of the post-World War One generation of feminists.

> Alberti, Johanna, *Eleanor Rathbone* (London, 1996).
> Banks, Olive, *Biographical Dictionary of British Feminists*, vol. 1 (Hemel Hempstead, 1985).
> Cohen, Susan, *Rescue the Perishing. Eleanor Rathbone and the Refugees* (London, 2010).
> Harrison, Brian, *Prudent Revolutionaries. Portraits of British Feminists Between the Wars* (Oxford, 1987).
> Logan, Anne, 'Rescue the Perishing,' *Women's History Magazine*, Summer 2011, issue 66, p.44.
> Pedersen, S., *Eleanor Rathbone and the Politics of Conscience* (Yale, 2004).
> Rathbone, Eleanor, *The Disinherited Family* (London, 1924 reprint 1986).
> Stocks, Mary, *Eleanor Rathbone* (London, 1949).

Rea, Mrs Philip was a founding member and Hon. Secretary of the Liverpool Mothers' Welfare Clinic.
> Liverpool Mothers' Welfare Clinic First Annual Report 1926–1927.

Reese, Mrs Miles was on the foundation committee in 1926 of Wolverhampton Birth Control Centre.
> Wolverhampton Birth Control Clinic First Annual Report 1926. Russell Archive, Box 405, IISH, Amsterdam.

Rice, Mrs Margery Spring (1887–1970) helped pioneer the North Kensington Women's Welfare Centre in 1925 and served on the Executive Committee as its first Chairman. She oversaw its work for the next thirty-four years and argued for its expansion in 1932 when the building was doubled in size offering a more comprehensive service. Such was the demand that satellite clinics were established in Hounslow, Edgware and Hayes.

Margery with others, persuaded Lady Denman to become Chairman of the National Birth Control Association which aimed to co-ordinate the work of the five existing birth control organisations and eventually became the Family Planning Association. Margery served on the Executive of the co-ordinating birth control body from 1930 to 1958.

Margery came from a radical feminist background, her aunts being Dame Millicent Fawcett and Elizabeth Garrett Anderson. She took a degree at Girton, Cambridge and after the First World War was the first secretary of the League of Nations Union. She was also Honorary Treasurer of the Women's National Liberal Federation for 1922–7.

In 1933 Margery used material collected by the women's health enquiry commission to form the basis of her book, *Working-Class Wives: Their Health and Conditions*. This work which portrayed widespread poverty and the burden of repeated pregnancies attracted much attention and complemented her practical work on birth control.
: North Kensington Women's Welfare Centre's Annual Report 1927–1928.
: Rice, Margery S., *Working Class Wives. Their Health and Conditions* (Harmondsworth, 1939).
: Dunkely, S., *Oxford Dictionary of National Biography* (Oxford, 1984).

Robertson, Mrs Petica was a founder member of the Cambridge Women's Welfare Association in 1925 and served on its first Committee as Hon. Assistant Treasurer. She was also a Cambridge councillor.
: Cambridge Women's Welfare Association First Annual Report 1925–1926.

Ross, Mrs J.R. was in 1934 the Acting Hon. Secretary of the Glasgow Women's Welfare and Advisory Clinic. She was subsequently confirmed as Hon. Secretary. Mrs Ross was the wife of the Deputy Editor of the *Glasgow Herald* and involved her friends in the running of the clinic.
: Dr Alison Mack interviewed by Clare Debenham, 3 March 2006.

Ryland, Mrs T.H. was in 1927 a founder member of Birmingham Women's Welfare Association and was its first Chairman. Subsequently she became Chairman of the Leamington and South Warwickshire FPA.
: Birmingham Women's Welfare Association First Annual Report 1927.

Sabin, Mrs was in 1927 a founder member of Birmingham Women's Welfare Association and served on its first Committee to which she donated a guinea. Her husband was a local Conservative councillor.
: Birmingham Women's Welfare Association First Annual Report 1927.

APPENDIX

Sandilands, Dr Dorothy was one of the medical officers at Birmingham Women's Welfare Centre in 1927. She was married to a doctor and at that time had a young baby. She worked closely with Dr Clara Macirone and Nurse Fowler.
>Birmingham Women's Welfare First Annual Report 1927-1928.
>Court, Audrey and Cynthia Walton, *Birmingham Made a Difference* (Birmingham, 2001).

Sands, Mrs was a Labour councillor for Smethwick, Birmingham. According to Mrs Bacon, in her correspondence with Marie Stopes, Councillor Sands had already raised the issue of birth control in Birmingham City Council.
>Marie C. Stopes Papers, British Library. Correspondence with Bacon. 4735.

Shufflebotham, Miss Hilda FRCS, later Professor Hilda Lloyd FRCS, later Dame Hilda Rose 1891-1982 was a gynaecological consultant. She did not come from a privileged family, her father being a master grocer. She attended the King Edward VI High School in Birmingham before entering Birmingham University Medical School. She obtained her BSc and qualified with her MB and BCh in 1916. Remarkably for such a young surgeon she had an article published in the *Lancet* in 1917. After house officer posts in London she returned to Birmingham as a resident in obstetrics and gynaecology. Hilda Shufflebotham in 1927 was a founder member of the Birmingham Women's Welfare Centre and sat on its first Committee. Her presence is partly explained by the fact that she was that rarity, a female consultant gynaecologist. Hilda offered to see women presenting at the Centre with unusual gynaecological conditions in her consulting rooms at Birmingham Maternity and Women's Hospital.

Hilda married a fellow member of staff, Bertram Lloyd in 1930 who in 1932 became Professor of Forensic Medicine in 1932. Hilda carried on being a committee member after her marriage. Her biographer pointed out that she was well aware of the problems of poverty and abortions faced by working-class mothers in Birmingham. Unusually for a SPBCC committee member, though not for a female doctor, she never had any children herself. As Dame Hilda Lloyd she served for three years as President of Birmingham Family Planning Association.

Hilda had a most distinguished career achieving many 'firsts' for women doctors. She became one of the first woman consultants in the Birmingham Maternity and Women's Hospital, the first woman professor in Birmingham Medical School, the first woman president of the Royal College of Obstetricians and Gynaecologists (RCOG), the first woman president of any of the four Royal Colleges. Many commentators remarked on her remarkable tact in steering changes through these organisations. Rightly she has been honoured by a splendid portrait at the RCOG. Professor Ellis described her as a slim, fair and graceful woman with outstanding talents.

Hilda died aged ninety and had been widowed twice. Throughout her life Hilda actively supported the Medical Women's Federation and declared their presentation to her 'the greatest pleasure of her professional life' (*British Medical Journal*, 10 November 1951). When she died in 1982 she left that women's organisation the substantial amount of £820,250 in her will. V.E. Chancellor summed up her outstanding career in medicine as a 'successful struggle to reverse the disadvantages under which women have suffered'.

> Birmingham Women's Welfare First Annual Report 1927-1928.
> *British Journal of Obstetrics and Gynaecology* 58/6 (December 1951) pp.1039-41.
> Court, Audrey, and Walton, Cynthia, *Birmingham Made a Difference. The Birmingham Women's Welfare Centre 1926-1991* (Birmingham, 2001).
> Ellis, H., 'Dame Hilda Lloyd: first President of the Royal College of Obstetricians and Gynaecologists.' *Journal of Perioptive Practice*, June 2009.
> Shufflebotham, H.N., 'The case of the ruptured uterus with unruptured membrane', *Lancet* 190/4911 (1917) p.571.

Simon, Mrs Shena, later Lady Simon (1883–1972) was a close friend of Mary Stocks of the Manchester and Salford and District Mothers' Clinic. Her Christian name was Shena not Sheena as cited in Hooper's biography of Stocks. Shena Simon read Economics at Newnham College, Cambridge and later studied at the London School of Economics. She became an active secretary of a committee of National Union of Women Workers concerned with safeguarding women's rights under Lloyd George's insurance Bill. She was involved in the women's suffrage campaign and in the 1920s helped to found Manchester and Salford Women Citizens Association. In 1924 she was elected as a Liberal councillor to Manchester City Council and championed feminist causes such as the fight against the marriage bar for women teachers.

In 1930 Simon was able to persuade Manchester City Council to be the first local authority to pioneer municipal birth control clinics. Mrs Pyke wrote from Head Office to congratulate Mary Stocks, 'The size of the majority was really magnificent. I do not see how it can fail to have a great effect on other places and I think you and Mrs Simon ought to be crowned with bay leaves.' The Manchester Chief Medical Officer of Health drew heavily on the experience of MSMC in creating the two new clinics.

APPENDIX

Shena was introduced to her husband, the industrialist Ernest Simon MP, by fellow Newnham student Eva Hubback. Mary Stocks was also friendly with the Simons and wrote Ernest's biography. Sheila, Mary and Eva were also active in the birth control movement. Ernest also took a keen interest in birth control and raised the subject in the House of Commons on a number of occasions. Ernest and Shena also promoted municipal housing and in particular the development of the Wythenshawe estate on the outskirts of Manchester.

> Papers of Lady Simon of Wythenshawe held at Women's Library GB0106 7/SDS.
> Stocks, Mary D., *Ernest Simon of Manchester* (Manchester, 1963).
> Banks, Olive, 'Shena Simon,' *The Biographical Dictionary of English Feminists*, vol. 2 (Hemel Hempstead, 1990).
> Martin, Jane and Goodman, Joyce, *Women and Education 1800–1980. Educational Change and Personal Identity* (Basingstoke, 2004).

Sinton, Dr was instrumental in setting up the Newcastle-upon-Tyne Women's Welfare Centre. Claire Tamplin explained how no other doctor in Newcastle was prepared to commit to this work. Claire said it was impossible to speak too highly of Dr Sinton's untiring efforts which she felt made the clinic such a success.

> Tamplin, Claire, 'Early days in Newcastle,' *Family Planning*, 1962, p.61.

Smalley, Mrs was a founding member in 1926 of the Manchester, Salford and District Mothers' Clinic.

> Manchester and District Mothers' Clinic Annual Report 1926–1927.

Sprigge, Lady Ethel was a founding member of the North Kensington Women's Welfare Centre in 1924 and a member in 1928 of the Executive Committee of the Walworth Women's Welfare Centre. Many in the medical profession were hostile to birth control so it was significant that she was married to Sir Squire Sprigge, a distinguished doctor who edited *The Lancet* medical journal. In 1931 Ethel joined the Eugenics Society.

> North Kensington Women's Welfare Centre's Annual Report 1927–1928.
> Robinson, Caroline H., *Seventy Birth Control Clinics* (New York, 1930).

Stocks, Mrs Mary JP, later Baroness (1891–1975) and Charis Frankenburg founded the Manchester and Salford Mothers' Clinic.

She attended London School of Economics and was awarded a first class honours degree. She married another academic, John Stocks. At a time when women often gave up a career on marriage, Mary Stocks carried on teaching economics in a variety of different settings: LSE, King's College for Women, London, and Eva Hubback's economics students at Newnham, Oxford. She was especially interested in adult education and taught a number of classes for the Workers' Educational Association. She was later to write a history of the organisation.

Feminism remained important to her throughout her life. As a sixteen-year-old she joined the National Union of Women's Suffrage Societies taking an active part in their campaign for the franchise. Mrs Fawcett was eventually god-mother to her first child. Mary played an influential part in the NUWSS's successor the National Union of Societies for Equal Citizenship. In the debate over 'new feminism' she supported the policies of its Chairman Eleanor Rathbone who had succeeded Mrs Fawcett. This allowed NUSEC to support the birth control campaign. She was joint editor of the *Woman's Leader*, the journal of NUSEC and in 1925 wrote on behalf of NUSEC, *Family Limitation and Women's Organisations*. Mary was also a member of the National Council of Women and the Women Citizens Association and actively campaigned for birth control in all these organisations.

The Stocks family moved from Oxford to Manchester when her husband John was appointed a professor in philosophy at the University of Manchester. Initially it was Charis Frankenburg who wrote to Marie Stopes asking if she could put her in touch with anyone locally who was interested in the birth control issue. Marie gave her the name of Mary Stocks who she recognised as being an old school friend from St Paul's Girls School.

The two women worked together to found the Manchester, Salford and District Mothers' Clinic in 1926. Mary was its first Chairman and retained the post until 1936 when her husband was appointed Vice-Chancellor of Liverpool University. Mary was also a committee member of the Society for the Provision of Birth Control Clinics and its successor the National Council for Birth Control Clinic. She was also a close friend of Ernest and Shena Simon from Manchester who also became involved with the birth control campaign. Mary was one of the few people to maintain an enduring friendship with Marie Stopes.

The Stocks family moved away from Manchester in 1937 when John was elected Vice-Chancellor of Liverpool University. Tragically he died before Mary could enter the cultural and political life of Liverpool. Instead she became Principal of Westfield College in Hampstead. She guided this residential college of one hundred and fifty women through the war years, leaving in 1951. Her experience in Westfield meant that she was an ideal member of the McNair Committee which in 1944 made recommendations changing the structure of teacher training and stated that women should not have to relinquish a teaching career on marriage.

When she retired she increased the commitment to public service that had started before the war by serving on various governmental committees.

APPENDIX

'I am what was described in the House of Lords as 'statutory woman' – the kind of woman they always put on a committee when someone says you must have a woman on the committee. I started on persistent offenders many years ago. I did unemployment insurance, broadcasting, foreign information services, training of midwives, training of teachers, women in the services, recruitment of dentists, and university grants – I could think of a few more. As a result I've achieved a rather superficial knowledge of many things, so that I can talk superficially on almost any question – except Scottish finance.' This self-deprecatory analysis ignores her capacity for hard work and the ability to get to the crux of the matter.

Mary's ability to communicate made her a popular as a broadcaster in the 1960s. I can remember her being a popular contributor to *Any Questions, Woman's Hour* and a host of topical programmes. The early morning *Thought for the Day* was broadcast when I was on my way to school. She came across as intelligent warm and witty.

Mary stood twice unsuccessfully for Parliament, the second time for Eleanor Rathbone's old seat. However, when life peerages were introduced by Harold Wilson her name was in the New Year's Honours List of 1966. No doubt her service as a 'statutory woman' was recognised, but also her popularity as a broadcaster. She sat as a Labour Peer but resigned from the Party partly because she believed Harold Wilson had let Barbara Castle down over the introduction of a prices and incomes policy.

Olive Banks in her entry for May Stocks in her *Biographical Dictionary of Feminists* argued that Mary's main contribution to feminism occurred in the 1920s. Olive Banks argued Mary's success in breaking into the male establishment and that of her birth control campaign, led her to underestimate how far feminism still had to go.

However, transcripts of her contributions to both *Any Questions* and *Woman's Hour* show an awareness of contemporary issues and a continuing commitment to new feminist ideas. As a doctor's daughter she never lost her commitment to women's reproductive rights, and in fact was prepared to go further than in the 1920s. Then abortion was such a controversial subject that the birth controllers took care to distance their organisation from it. Yet in July 1967 when the young David Steel introduced his Private Member's Bill on the Medical Termination of Pregnancy she did not hesitate to support it. Mary was seventy-six years old and the Bill was radical, as it aimed to legalise abortion, with safeguards up to the twelfth week of pregnancy. In the House of Lords, Mary spoke in the debate saying abortion was the counsel of despair. She drew on forty years of experience of working with women who had unwanted pregnancies. She cited the many cases of illegal abortion by desperate women. She tabled an amendment striking out the need for one consultant recommending an abortion to come from the NHS. As there were only 750 relevant NHS consultants in the whole of the country, this stipulation would cause needless delays. Her amendment was passed 113 votes to 79 with the Archbishop of Canterbury amongst her supporters.

Mary ordered all her papers to be destroyed on her death and so we lack her perceptive insights into her relationship with her husband and children. From existing photographs we can see in her later years she enjoyed the company of her children, grandchildren and white cat but we have no direct comments from her.

> Manchester and District Mothers' Clinic Annual Report 1926-1927.
> Hon. Ann Patterson (Mary's daughter) interviewed by Clare Debenham, 4 December 2004.
> Stocks, Mary D. and Bakewell, Joan, 1 February 1968. 'The Suffragettes,' *Late Night Line Up*. BBC2. BBC Archives.
> Mary Stocks interviewed by Brian Harrison, 21 April 1974. Brian Harrison digital recording, 8SUF/B/00, Women's Library London.
> BBC Written Archives, Caversham, files relating to Mary Stocks, various periods 1950-66.
> Board of Education, Teachers and Youth Leaders. Report of the Committee appointed by the President of the Board of Education to consider the Supply, Recruitment and Training of Teachers and Youth Leaders (London, 1944).
> Banks, Olive, *The Biographical Dictionary of British Feminists*, vol. 1 (Hemel Hempstead, 1985).
> Hooper, Barbara, *Mary Stocks 1891-1975. An Uncommonplace Life* (London, 1996).
> Stocks, Mary D., *My Commonplace Book* (London, 1970).
> Stocks, Mary D., *Still More Commonplace* (London, 1973).

Stopes, Dr Marie (1880-1958) was a suffrage supporter, a brilliant academic and a pioneer in the birth control movement.

After a rather unconventional early education Marie was sent to North London Collegiate School where she started to display an aptitude for science. She then enrolled in University College, London rather than a single-sex college. At the end of her first year she won the gold medal for botany and was second in her class for zoology. She proceeded to take two courses at the same time by registering as an external student at Birkbeck College. She therefore obtained a first class pass in botany and geology.

As a result of her outstanding results Marie was awarded a scholarship to study abroad for a year. As a child she had enjoyed hunting for fossils with her father and decided to pursue a career in paleobotany, the study of plant remains in a geological context. She selected the Botanic Institute of the University of Munich. Her specialism was the fertilisation of cycades, an order of plants that existed between two hundred and one hundred thousand years ago. She was awarded her PhD at Munich and later travelled to Japan.

While at Munich she learned of a vacancy in the Science Faculty at the University of Manchester and she became the first woman science lecturer to be appointed. In 1909 her academic contribution was recognised when she had a new post created for her in fossil biology. She was awarded a further doctoral degree, London DSc becoming one of the youngest people in the country to hold this degree. While a lecturer at the university she met Captain Scott in 1904 and unsuccessfully tried to persuade him to take her on his expedition to the South Pole so she could collect samples, but he did collect them for her. However, she did not find Manchester congenial and moved to London where she was elected as a fellow of University College, London which enabled her to use their laboratory and its facilities.

Many of Marie's actions were in line with those of equality feminists. She insisted on retaining her maiden name on marriage, always being known by her title as Dr Marie Stopes. Like her mother Charlotte Carmichael Stopes, she showed interest in social questions and in particular the rights of women and the suffrage. However, although she was undoubtedly later influenced by WSPU gesture politics Marie was not particularly militant, preferring formal means of protest. She advocated Tax Resistance to the consternation of her male friends such as Aylmer Maude. In a letter to the *The Times*, 6 April 1914 she protested about London County Council's ban on married women practicing medicine.

Marie employed her research skills in obtaining the annulment her first marriage. Although she had relationships with men such as the eminent Japanese Professor Kuyiro Fujii she was still unmarried in her thirties. She married fellow scientist Reginald Ruggles Gates but the marriage was not a success. Marie could not afford an expensive and protracted divorce, so took the unusual step in applying to have it annulled. In this she was successful. Her second marriage to Humphrey Verdon Roe was initially much happier. He financed the publication of *Married Love*.

She distilled her research into sexual relationships into her most influential book which was titled, without a hint of irony, *Married Love*. The rationale for her books was that 'in my own marriage I paid such a terrible price for ignorance that I feel knowledge gained at such a cost should be placed at the service of humanity.' This became a best seller and led to other books on marriage and contraception.

Her work moved from the literary to the practical. She founded the Society for Constructive Birth Control and Racial Progress, published *Birth Control News* to disseminate knowledge and in 1921 founded the first birth control clinic in the United Kingdom in London's East End.

Marie wanted to have children. However, she was to be denied a large family. At thirty-eight, her first baby was still-born. Her only other child, Harry Stopes-Roe was born in 1924 when she was forty-three. She tried having a succession of boys as companions for Harry but found them all unsatisfactory.

By 1931 Marie, along with other leading birth controllers, assumed government action had meant the birth control battle was won. She therefore began to turn to writing and literature. She had a successful film, *Maisie's Marriage*, but then turned less successfully to poetry and novels. Her friends such as Mary Stocks tried to offer constructive criticism on her novels but her poems never received critical acclaim. She particularly cultivated Lord Alfred Douglas. She knew many of the leading literary figures of the day including T.S. Elliot, Virginia Woolf and Thomas Hardy. She was close to Aylmer Maude and Keith Bryant who both wrote biographies of her. She sent her poems to all major figures and Adolf Hitler in the 1930s was just one recipient. Typically when Marie died she left a large sum of money to the Royal Society of Literature, of which she was a member, for the establishment of the Marie C. Stopes Memorial lecture.

Marie was not able to co-operate with others. Unsurprisingly in 1933 she resigned from the National Birth Control Council, splitting her Society for Constructive Birth Control and Racial Progress from it. The NBCC continued to expand while, as Greta Jones has pointed out, Marie ran into the same organisational difficulties with her clinic in Belfast. She left her clinic's premises to the Eugenics Society so that the Family Planning Association would not acquire it. Marie's relations with her own family deteriorated. She disagreed with her son's choice of wife. Marie became estranged from Humphrey as he became older.

It is easy to identify Marie's faults. However, Mary Stocks reflected that although Marie could not manage her own relationships she had enriched the lives of thousands of others.

> Interview with Harry Stopes-Roe (son of Marie Stopes), Mary Stopes-Roe (daughter-in-law), and Cathy Stopes-Roe (grand-daughter) by Clare Debenham on 17.6. 2005.

APPENDIX

BBC Written Archives, Caversham. Marie Stopes File 1. 1931-62.

Walker, Caroline, 'Making birth control respectable: the Society for Constructive Birth Control and Racial Progress and the American Birth Control League in comparative perspective, 1921-1938', PhD thesis, University of Bristol.

Banks, Olive, *Biographical Dictionary of British Feminists*, vol. 1 (Hemel Hempstead, 1985).

Box, Muriel, *The Trial of Marie Stopes*. Preface by Mary Stocks (New York, 1967).

Cohen, Deborah, 'Marie Stopes and the mothers' clinic', in Peel, R.A. (ed.) *Marie Stopes and the English Birth Control Movement* (London: Galton Institute, 1997), pp.77-94.

Eaton, Peter and Warnick, Marilyn, *Marie Stopes. A Checklist of her Writings* (London, 1977).

Gelsthorpe, D., 'Marie Stopes the paleobotanist, Manchester and her adventures in Japan', *The Geological Curator*, 2007, 8(8) pp.375-80.

Hall, Ruth, *Marie Stopes. A Biography* (1977, London).

Jones, G., 'Marie Stopes in Ireland: The Mother's Clinic in Belfast, 1936-1947', *Social History of Medicine* 5 (1992) pp.257-77.

McKibbin, R., Introduction to the reprint of *Married Love* (Oxford, 2004).

Rose, J., *Marie Stopes and the Sexual Revolution* (London, 1992).

Stopes-Roe, H.V. and Scott I., *Marie Stopes and Birth Control* (London, 1974).

Taylor, Laurie, 'The unfinished sexual revolution', *Journal Biosocial Science* 3 (1971) pp.473-92.

Strange, Mrs Winifred was one of the founder members of the Wolverhampton Women's Welfare Centre in 1925. She joined Ella Gordon and Alice Onions in a small committee of wives of business and professional people.

A pioneer, Winifred was the first woman to drive a car in Wolverhampton and had an active social life before marrying her husband Ernest, a doctor. In the First World War, Winifred qualified as a nurse and physiotherapist. Winifred helped set up the clinic in Wolverhampton and the First Annual Report showed her as Chairman. Winifred went on to found clinics in the surrounding villages. She travelled the Midlands with Onions giving talks on birth control. In 1936 Winifred was shown in the Eugenic Society records as being on its Executive Committee.

After the Second World War, Winifred became involved with Alice Onions in the marriage guidance movement. They trained as counsellors and started the first Marriage Guidance Clinic in Wolverhampton. Winifred was also twice President of the local National Council of Women.

Wolverhampton Birth Control Clinic First Annual Report 1926.

Russell Archives, International Institute of Social History, Amsterdam, File 405.

Maxfield, D., 'Pioneering spirit,' *Wolverhampton Magazine*, May 1970, p.26.

Sutton-Timmis, Mrs Annie was a founder member of the Liverpool Mothers' Welfare Centre and in 1926-7 served on its Executive Committee. In 1928 she succeeded Mrs R.D. Holt as Chairman. In 1890 Annie had married Mr Sutton-Timmis who was a local businessman and philanthropist.

He was Chair of the Council's School Committee. In 1909 she was Hon. Secretary of the Liverpool Ladies Club in Slater Street which was one of a number of radical clubs for women in pre-suffrage times.
> Liverpool Mothers' Welfare Clinic First Annual Report 1926–1927.
> Crawford, Elizabeth, *The Women's Suffrage Movement. A Reference Guide* (London, 2000), p.124.

Symonds, Mrs H.H. was a founding member and served on the Executive Committee Council of the Liverpool Mothers' Welfare Clinic.
> Liverpool Mothers' Welfare Clinic First Annual Report 1926–1927.

Tamplin, Mrs Claire was one of the founder members in 1924 of the North Kensington Women's Welfare Centre. Her position in the First Annual Report is given as Secretary but she was obviously more like a pioneering Chief Executive: 'Mrs Tamplin has had her hands very full, not only with regular secretarial work, but also with propaganda work with poor women of the neighbourhood. She takes two sessions a week at the Clinic, with some members of the Committee.' The next Annual Report again commended Mrs Tamplin: 'Much of the success of the Centre has been due to Mrs Tamplin's keen and energetic work.' By 1927 the Annual Report records that Claire had changed her role to that of Outside Organiser and had successfully addressed a number of meetings on birth control. It was reported in *Birth Control News* in March 1931 that she addressed the Women's Liberal Association in Hendon on maternal mortality and its relation to birth control.

In 1928 she travelled with a group of committed London birth controllers led by Mrs Laski to Newcastle-upon-Tyne with the aim of starting a birth control clinic. Claire Tamplin lodged with Mrs Steve Lawther. Claire stayed behind on her own in order to find a sympathetic doctor and nurse, recruit volunteers, locate premises and publicise the clinic. 'I was told not to be disappointed if only two or three came but thirty-four came. It was worth every minute of the hard work put into getting it started' (*Family Planning*, 1962, p.61).

Unusually for senior birth controllers Mrs Tamplin was an Anglo-Catholic and an active member of the Mothers' Union. She also spoke on behalf of the Eugenics Society.
> Laski, Frida, *New Generation*, July 1928, p.74.
> Tamplin, Claire, 'Early days in Newcastle,' *Family Planning*, October 1962, p.61.
> Ward, Linda, 'The Right to Choose: A Study of Women's Fight for Birth Control Provisions,' PhD thesis, University of Bristol, 1981, p.103.

Taunton, Mrs R.C. was a founding member in 1927 of Birmingham Women's Welfare Centre.
> Birmingham Women's Welfare Centre First Annual Report 1927–1928.

APPENDIX

Teale, Miss Norah was on the founding committee of the Manchester and Salford Mothers' Clinic in 1926. She was one of nine children and was born in Manchester in 1877. Her father was a safety lamp maker with sufficient funds to afford paid help in the family. Norah was the Superintendent of a voluntary welfare organisation which had branches in Collyhurst and Openshaw. Norah joined the Manchester and Salford Women Citizens' Association in 1917, because of her deep-seated interest in the welfare of children. Her expertise was valued and she was elected to the Association's Central Committee in 1924. Norah continued her visits and talking to branches until 1927 when, although still a Central Committee member, she curtailed her branch work. It is likely that she knew several members of the MSWCA through her membership of the Manchester, Salford and District National Council of Women. She would have known Frankenburg, Stocks and Simon through these organisations through both MSWCA and NCW.

>Manchester and District Mothers' Clinic Annual Report 1926–1927.
>Smith, J., 'The Manchester and Salford Women Citizens' Association: a study of women's citizenship 1913–1948', PhD thesis, Manchester Metropolitan University, 2007.

Thorndike, Miss Sybil (later Dame), married name Mrs Lewis Casson sat on the General Advisory Council of the Manchester Salford and District Mothers' Clinic in its first year, 1926. Already a well-known actor, she lent prestige to the clinic.

Sybil was a member of the Women's Social and Political Union and addressed suffrage meetings in Manchester. However, her theatrical management did not approve of her suffragette activity.

She was an active Socialist and with her husband assisted Labour leaders in the 1926 General Strike. On 25 May 1926 Thorndike issued a letter on behalf of the Women's Committee for the Relief of Miners' Wives and Children. Professionally she was one of the most famous actors of her generation.

>Interview with Sybil Thorndike by Brian Harrison, 2 December 1975, Women's Library, 8SUF/B/063.
>Thorndike, Russell, *Sybil Thorndike* (London, 1929).

Tompkins, Mrs was on the foundation committee in 1926 of Wolverhampton Birth Control Centre.

>Wolverhampton Birth Control Clinic First Annual Report 1926. Russell Archive, Box 405, IISH, Amsterdam.

Trotman, Mrs was on the Executive Committee of the Oxford Family Welfare Association at its foundation.

>Oxford Family Welfare Association Annual Report 1926–1927.

Vernon, Mrs was on the Executive Committee of the Oxford Family Welfare Association at its foundation.
Oxford Family Welfare Association Annual Report 1926–1927.

Vickery, Dr Alice Drysdale (1844–1929) sometimes known as Dr Vickery Drysdale. In 1921 she and her husband financially supported the foundation of the Walworth Road Mothers' Clinic which eventually became the first SPBCC clinic.

Vickery came from a skilled working-class background. She eventually enrolled at the Ladies Medical College and was encouraged to pursue a career in medicine by Dr Charles Drysdale, the tutor who was to become her partner and father of two children.

It took her eleven years to qualify as a doctor at the London Medical School including two years study in France. In 1880 she was only one of five women in England to hold a medical degree. She jeopardised her chance of qualification by giving evidence as an expert witness at the Bradlaugh-Besant trial. Alice became an active member of the Malthusian League and promoted women's interests within it by writing literature aimed at a female audience. Miriam Benn praised Alice Vickery's tenacity as it took her eleven years to qualify at the London Medical School, including two years study in France. By 1880 she was only one of five women in England to hold a medical degree.

As early as 1873 Alice Vickery held a suffrage meeting in Dover and she translated a number of books from the French advocating women's rights. Though she felt that she was too old to take an active part in the suffrage movement, she supported her daughter-in-law who was a militant suffragette.

The women of the Malthusian League progressed from producing pamphlets to providing personal advice. Even before the first birth control clinics were founded in England, Dr Alice Vickery started outreach work by giving talks to groups of working-class mothers. In 1908 she travelled to dockside Rotherhithe to talk to a large group of a hundred working-class mothers on methods of birth control. These groups included local branches of the Women's Co-operative Guild for whom she had a great deal of respect. In 1914 Alice Vickery is again mentioned as giving a talk to the WCG in Tottenham. She donated funds for the women to purchase contraceptive materials under the direction of Miss Anna Martin and this group survived into the 1920s. Alice advocated home visits to poor women where a combination of 'gentleness, perception, commonsense and thoroughness' should be used.

APPENDIX

Later Alice gave practical advice on birth control to groups of the Women's Co-operative Guild. Alice befriended Margaret Sanger on her visit to England.

    Benn, J. Miriam, *Predicaments of Love* (London, 1992).
    Bland, Lucy, *Banishing the Beast* (London, 1995).
    Ledbetter, R., *A History of the Malthusian League* (Ohio, 1976).

Walton, Mrs was a founding member in 1926 of the Manchester, Salford and District Mothers' Clinic and sat on the General Advisory Council.

    Manchester and District Mothers' Clinic Annual Report 1926–1927.

Waterhouse, Mrs was on the Executive Committee of the Oxford Family Welfare Association at its foundation.

    Oxford Family Welfare Association Annual Report 1926–1927.

Watkins, Mrs Shilston was a founder member and served on the Council of the Liverpool Mothers' Welfare Clinic.

    Liverpool Mothers' Welfare Clinic First Annual Report 1926–1927.

Wharton, Mrs Marjorie acted as Hon. Secretary to the Birmingham Women's Welfare Centre at its start.

    Birmingham Women's Welfare Centre First Annual Report 1927–1928.

Wilkinson, Ellen, MA, MP (1891–1947) became an iconic figure. Appropriately because of her political views, and mass of red hair she was known as 'Red Ellen'. She suffered from ill health all her life, in particular from asthma and bronchitis, and was small in stature being just under five foot. She was petite with a striking presence, although she lacked dress sense. Ellen had close relationships with men but never married. She was supportive to a wide range of friends including birth controller Dora Russell.

Her roots were from a working-class background. She came from a Manchester family and was born in Coral Street, Ardwick near the centre of Manchester. Her father was a cotton operative turned insurance clerk and her mother a dressmaker. Like a number of bright working-class girls she bettered herself by winning scholarships. At the age of eleven she was awarded her first scholarship to Ardwick Higher Grade School and this was followed at the age of fifteen by a bursary to study at Manchester Day Training College to become a pupil-teacher. She taught at Oswald Road School for half a week, studying at college for the rest.

However, she soon realised that she did not want a career as a teacher and one of her finest achievements was to win the Jones scholarship to the University of Manchester which was a nationwide scholarship. 'At University I began to live life to the full, as I had always dreamed of living it…books unlimited, lots of friends, interesting lectures, stimulus of teamwork.' The records show she participated fully in student life of the university, being joint secretary of the University of Manchester Fabian Society, the Fabian Women's Group University Socialist Federation. She was briefly engaged to another political activist, Walter Newbold, who became a Communist Party MP. A photograph of university activists *The Scribes* shows Ellen confidently perched on a desk, just in front of Henry Newbold. In the group there were just two women against ten men. Although academically gifted she did not have the academic single-mindedness to be awarded a first class honours degree. She gained an upper second class degree and the next year was awarded an MA.

While at university she was involved with feminism as well as socialism. Ellen became involved in the suffrage struggle. In 1912 she became a member of the Manchester Society for Women's Suffrage. She soon obtained a position as the Manchester organiser for the National Union of Women's Suffrage Societies. She spoke at outdoor meetings as well as running recruitment drives and raising funds. Her sympathies were always going to be with equal rights feminists rather than the new feminists. This ability to organise stood her in good stead politically, as in 1915 she was employed by the national woman organiser of Amalgamated Union of Co-operative Employees.

Ellen's political career took off when in 1923 she was elected as Councillor for Gorton ward, being sponsored by the Gorton Trades and Labour Council but this bought a political dilemma. As a student she had been a high-profile member of the Communist Party, and was active in the Co-operative and trade union movement. In November 1923 she had spoken at a British Communist Party rally to mark the sixth anniversary of the Russian Revolution. When dual membership was proscribed by the Labour Party, she made the decision to leave the Communist Party.

In 1924, aged thirty-three years old, Ellen was returned as Labour MP for Middlesborough East, a northern constituency, which she held until the electoral disaster of 1931. She tried to balance support for women's issues with the socialist concerns of her constituents. At that time only women over thirty could vote and she was one of only four women MPs. In her maiden speech she deplored the lack of franchise for women under thirty and the limitations on women's unemployment benefit. Controversially she attacked the ruling which denied benefits to cleaners and laundresses. She used her position to campaign for the extension of the franchise and to support the General Strike and the subsequent Miners' Strike. In the second Labour administration she worked for Susan Lawrence MP who was parliamentary secretary to the Minister for Health, so gaining valuable experience. She was a conscientious MP with a flair for publicity to highlight the problems of her constituents. She endured the long train journeys from London to the North so that she could carry out her constituency surgeries.

In this period she often worked with the National Union of Societies for Equal Suffrage on equality feminist issues such as pensions and British citizenship for women who had married aliens. She nearly succeeded in removing the marriage bar and implementing equal pay in the Civil Service, but the Prime Minister blocked it. She also tried to introduce welfare reforms such as grants for children's clothing.

However, on two issues Ellen moved away from new feminist principles. The first is the birth control issue. Her biographer Betty Verdon wrote that 'It seems extraordinary that Ellen was not active in the controversy over birth control.' However, Ellen was involved in the birth control debate albeit changing sides. The second issue on which Ellen altered her position was that of family allowances. Initially an active supporter of Eleanor Rathbone, by 1938 she had changed her mind. She held that as a result of family alliances employers would deny men wage increases.

In 1935 she was returned to another northern working-class constituency Jarrow, a town with one of the worst unemployment figures in Britain. The dire economic situation and the increasing likelihood of war dominated the political agenda. In 1936 she helped organise a march of two hundred unemployed workers from Jarrow to London – one of the Hunger Marches. In 1939 she wrote *Jarrow, the Town that was Murdered* to highlight apparent indifference to unemployment. 'Bad housing, overcrowding, underfeeding, low-wages for any work that is going, household incomes cut to the limit by public assistance, or Means Test or whatever is the cutting machine of the time…these mean disease and premature death.'

During the Second World War coalition she served as parliamentary secretary to Herbert Morrison, Home Secretary and Minister of Home Security. Her chief responsibilities were air-raid shelters, introducing domestic Morrison shelters, and later fire-watching services. She spent many nights in air-raid shelters and became an expert on the subject. In the 1920s she had formed relationships with male colleagues and became close to Morrison in the 1930s when he was deeply unhappy in his marriage.

After Labour's victory in 1945 she became Minister for Education, the first woman to hold this post and so had a seat in the Cabinet. Clement Attlee was aware of Herbert and Ellen's scheming but believed he could contain them in the Cabinet. Ellen's achievements as Minister for Education have been heavily criticised. It is claimed that Ellen was too ill for the post and too inexperienced. She has been portrayed as an ineffectual minister who had not considered the educational system. Yet she had grown up in the schools of Manchester, worked as a pupil-teacher, and her 1938 essay shows a determination to allow future generations to have the advantages that were denied to her.

This critical evaluation of Ellen ignores her difficulties in post-war Britain. There were bombed-out buildings, fuel shortages and the war had led to shortages of trained teachers. Just to make the system work, and repair this damage, was a major achievement. In addition she kept faith with Butler's Education Act of 1944 which stated that children should be educated according to age, ability and aptitude, though she believed it would take a generation to implement it. Nevertheless, in the 1946 School Milk Act she did persuade the government to give free school milk to school children and expanded the school meals service. Ellen raised the school leaving age from fifteen to sixteen – though this was delayed. She wanted children to benefit from education whatever their parental wealth. She reduced the number of direct grant schools and instituted university scholarships which provided funding for higher education. She developed the tripartite school system and recognised the value of schools devoted to technical education. Ellen welcomed experiments with comprehensive education in rural areas.

Increasingly suffering from asthma, her death was caused by an accidental overdose of barbiturates on 6 February 1947.

>Banks, Olive, *Biographical Dictionary of British Feminists*, vol. 1 (Hemel Hempstead, 1985).
>Bartley, P., 'Women's History Month: Red Ellen. Ellen Wilkinson, 1891–1947', 7 March 2011. http://womenshistorynetwork.org.blog/.
>Harrison, Brian, *Prudent Revolutionaries* (Oxford, 1987).
>Vernon, Betty D., *Ellen Wilkinson* (London, 1982).
>Wilkinson, Ellen, *Clash* (London, 1929 reprint 1989).
>Wilkinson, Ellen, in Oxford, M. (ed.) *Myself When Young. Reminiscences from Sylvia Pankhurst, Maude Royden, Ellen Wilkinson and others* (London, 1938).
>Wilkinson, Ellen, *The Town That Was Murdered* (London, 1939).

Williamson, Mrs Winifred was a founder member of the Oxford Family Welfare Association in 1926 and held a number of offices. Originally Assistant Secretary, she served as Chairman (1942–56) and Treasurer (1966–76). In 1927 she and her husband purchased the property in Jericho so giving the Association stability in its premises. This was convenient for working-class mothers and, unlike their last location, could be advertised.

>Little, Dr Isabelle, 'Forty years back,' *Family Planning*, 3 October 1966, p.76.

APPENDIX

Willoughby, Lady Muriel was a member of the Executive Committee of the Walworth Women's Welfare Centre in 1928. She was described by Dowse and Peel as being one of a number of high-profile aristocratic women who served on the voluntary birth control committees in the 1930s.
> Dowse, R.E. and Peel, J., 'The politics of birth control', *Political Studies* 13/2 (June 1965).

Winter, Dr Cornelia joined the Wolverhampton Welfare Centre at its foundation in 1925. The New Generation League paid tribute to her in 1927 stating that she 'had risked her practice and career when she stared her birth control work in Wolverhampton'.
> Wolverhampton Birth Control Clinic First Annual Report 1926.
> Browne, F.W. Stella, *New Generation*, January 1927, p.4.
> Rowley, J.J., 'Reminiscences of Alice Onions.' *West Midlands Studies*, 1983, 16, pp.30-3.

Wise, Mrs E.F. was a founding member of the Executive Committee of the North Kensington Women's Welfare Centre.
> North Kensington Women's Welfare Centre's Annual Report 1925-1926.

Wright, Dr Helena (1887-1982) joined the North Kensington Women's Welfare Centre in 1927 in its third year. On her return from China she renewed her acquaintance with Marie Stopes but found her autocratic and unwilling to take medical advice. In contrast she found the atmosphere at the Walworth Road SPBCC clinic more open and when she visited South Kensington she found a similar atmosphere. She also met Mrs Margery Spring Rice and this was the start of a productive working relationship. She was offered a position by Mrs Spring Rice and accepted on condition that she could reorganise the clinic. In 1930 Helena addressed the bishops on birth control on the eve of the Lambeth Conference.

She was also a member of the Eugenics Society.
> Wright, Dr Helena, *The Sex Factor in Marriage* (London, 1930).
> Wright, Dr Helena, 'Fifty years of family planning,' *Family Planning*, January 1972, p.75.

Wrong, Mrs was on the Executive Committee of the Oxford Family Welfare Association at its foundation.
> Oxford Family Welfare Association Annual Report 1926-1927.

Notes

Chapter 1

1. Contemporary feminist magazines such as *Spare Rib* give a feel for the 1970s and there are also influential books such as Mitchell, Juliet, *Woman's Estate* (Middlesex, 1971). There is a comprehensive guide to feminist sources of this period at www.london.met.ac.uk/genesis/sources/archives/women/women home.cfm.
2. Crawford, Elizabeth, *The Women's Suffrage Movement in England and Wales* (London, 2006).
3. Eustance, Clare, Ryan, Joan, Ugolini, Laura (eds), *A Suffrage Reader* (Leicester, 2000).
4. Purvis, June, *Emmeline Pankhurst. A Biography* (London, 2002); Liddington, Jill, *Rebel Girls. Their Fight for the Vote* (London, 2006).
5. Cowman, Krista, *'Mrs Brown is a Man and a Brother!'* (Liverpool, 2004); Crawford, Elizabeth, *The Women's Suffrage Movement in Britain and Ireland* (London, 2006).
6. O'Neil, William, *The Woman Movement* (London, 1969) p.93.
7. Kent, Susan Kingsley, *Sex and Suffrage in Britain* (London, 1990) p.232.
8. Spender, Dale, *There's Always Been a Women's Movement This Century* (London, 1983) p.1.
9. Law, Cheryl, *Suffrage and Power. The Women's Movement 1918-1928* (London, 1997) p.225; Logan, Anne, *Feminism and Criminal Justice. A Historical Perspective* (London, 2008) pp.2-4.
10. Law, *Suffrage and Power*, p.2.
11. Sarvassy, Wendy, 'Beyond the difference versus equality debate: post-suffrage feminism, difference and a quest.' *Signs* 17 (1992) pp.329-62.
12. Law, *Suffrage and Power*.
13. Williams, Gaynor, 'Women in public life in Liverpool between the wars'. PhD thesis, University of Liverpool, 2000.
14. Spender, *There's Always Been a Women's Movement* (London, 1983) p.2.
15. Alberti, Johanna, *Beyond Suffrage* (Basingstoke, 1989).

16 Banks, Olive, *Biographical Dictionary of British Feminists* (Hemel Hempstead, 1985) p.1.
17 Alberti, *Beyond Suffrage*; Logan, *Feminism and Criminal Justice*; Law, *Suffrage and Power*, p.2.
18 Hollis, Patricia, *Ladies Elect* (Oxford, 1987) p.viii.
19 Jones, Helen, 'Ruth Dalton' in *Oxford Dictionary of National Biography* (Oxford, 2004).
20 Rowbotham, Shelia, *Hidden from History. Three Hundred Years of Oppression* (London, 1974).
21 Rowbotham, Sheila, *Dreamers of a New Day. Women Who Invented the Twentieth Century* (London, 2010) p.240.
22 Koopmans, Ruud, 'Protest in time and space: the evolution of waves of contention' in Snow, David A., Soule, Sarah and Kreisi, Hanspieter, *The Blackwell Companion to Social Movements* (Oxford, 2007) pp.19-46; Charles, Nicki, *Feminism, the State and Social Policy* (Basingstoke, 2001) pp.74-93.
23 Bolt, Christine, *The Women's Movements in the United States and Britain* (Hemel Hempstead, 1993) pp.267-82.
24 Thane, Pat, 'What difference did the vote make? Women in public and private life in Britain since 1918.' *Historical Research* 76 (2003), pp.268-85.
25 Titmuss, Richard, 'Essays on the Welfare State.' 1976 quoted in Lewis, Jane, *The Politics of Motherhood* (London, 1980) p.196.
26 Walker, Caroline E., 'Making birth control respectable: the Society for Constructive Birth Control and Racial Progress and the American Birth Control League in comparative perspective, 1921-1938.' PhD thesis, University of Bristol, 2007.
27 Harrison, Brian, *Prudent Revolutionaries* (Oxford, 1987) p.1.
28 Ward, Linda, 'The right to choose. A study of women's fight for birth control provisions.' PhD thesis, University of Bristol, 1981.
29 Fisher, Kate and Szreter, Simon, *Sex Before the Sexual Revolution. Intimate Life in England 1918-1963* (Cambridge, 2010); Fisher, Kate and Dale P., 'Contrasting municipal responses to the provision of birth control services in Halifax and Exeter before 1948.' *Social History of Medicine* 23/3 (2010), pp.567-85; Fisher, Kate, *Birth Control, Sex and Marriage in Britain 1918-1960* (Oxford, 2006); Fisher, Kate, 'Contrasting cultures of contraception: birth control clinics and the working classes between the wars' in Tansey, T. (ed.) *Remedies and Healing Cultures in Britain and the Netherlands in the Twentieth Century* (Amsterdam, 2002) pp.141-57.
30 Snow, D.A., 'Framing processes, ideology and discursive fields' in Snow, Soule and Kriesi, *The Blackwell Companion to Social Movement* (Oxford, 2007) pp.380-412. He drew on Irving Goffman's *Frame Analysis* (New York, 1974).
31 Gordon, Linda, *Woman's Body, Woman's Rights* (London, 1977), Meyer, Jimmy, *Any Friend of the Movement. Networking for Birth Control* (Ohio, 2004).

32 Colin Barker, 'Crises and turning point in revolutionary development' in Barker, Colin and Tyldesley, Mike, *Alternative Futures and Popular Protest* (Manchester, 2006) p.1.
33 Stocks, Mary, 'Pioneers of birth control in the 1920s.' BBC Radio *Yesterdays Witness* series, 1969.
34 Stott, Mary, *Organisation Woman* (London, 1978) p.36.
35 Becker, Howard, *Outsiders* (Illinois, 1963).
36 Sabatier, Paul, *Policy Change and Learning. An Advocacy Coalition Approach* (Colorado, 1993).
37 McAdam, Doug, 'Conceptual origins, current problems, future directions' in McAdam, Doug, McCarthy, John and Zald, Mayer N. (eds), *Comparative Perspectives on Social Movements* (Cambridge, 1996).
38 Tilly, Charles, *As Sociology Meets History* (New York, 1981).
39 Russell papers. Draft copy of *The Tamarisk Tree*. IHSS Amsterdam Files, 446, 448.
40 Melucci, Alberto, *Nomads of the Present* (Philadelphia, 1989).
41 Stott, *Organisation Woman*.
42 Ibid., p.6.
43 Graves, Pamela, *Labour Women. Women in British Working Class Politics 1918–1935* (Cambridge, 1994) p.83.
44 Hunt, Karen, 'Making politics in local communities. Labour women in inter-war Manchester' in Worley, M. (ed), *Labour's Grass Roots* (Aldershot, 2005) pp.79–101.
45 Crawford, *The Women's Suffrage Movement in England and Wales*.
46 Cowman, '*Mrs Brown is a Man and a Brother!*', p.5.
47 Hunt, Karen and Hannam, June, 'Socialist women, birth control and sexual politics in Britain' in Pasteur, P., Neidarcher, S. and Messner, M., *ITH-Tagungsberichte 37. Sexualität, Unterschichtenmilieus und Arbeiter Innenbewegung* (Leipzig, 2002) p.177–87.
48 Marks, Lara, *Model Mothers* (Oxford, 1994) pp.266–70.
49 Smith, J., 'Labour tradition in Glasgow and Liverpool.' *History Workshop* 17 (1984), pp.32–55; Davies, A., *Leisure, Gender and Poverty. Working Class Culture in Salford and Manchester 1900–1939* (Milton Keynes, 1992).
50 Frankenburg, Charis, *Not Old, Madam, VINTAGE!* (Suffolk, 1975); Stocks, Mary, *My Commonplace Book* (London, 1970).
51 British Library, Marie C. Stopes Papers, 21 May 1926. British Library Department of Manuscripts BL. Add. 585989-58642.
52 Mary Stocks to Mrs Pyke, 5 February 1931, Wellcome Library SA/FPA/A11/26.
53 Mitchell, Hannah, *The Hard Way Up*. Forward by Sheila Rowbotham (London, 1968 reprint 1977).
54 Marie Stopes' Library is contained in the John Rylands University of Manchester Library, Deansgate.

55 Ward, L., University of Bristol, 1981.
56 The British Library, Marie C. Stopes Correspondence.
57 *East London Advertiser,* 4 November 1926.
58 *Stockport Express,* 1 November 1923; 8 November 1923.
59 *Oxford Times* advertisement for the birth control clinic was reinstated on 30 November 1926.
60 *Eccles and Patricroft Journal,* 19 February 1926, p.3.
61 *Birth Control News,* 18 May 1930.
62 *Catholic Federalist,* 1 May 1926.
63 *Liberal Women's News,* April 1927.
64 Passerini, Luisa, *Fascism in Popular Memory. The Cultural Experience of the Turin Working Class* (Cambridge, 1984 translated 1987).
65 Alberti, *Beyond Suffrage;* Stanley, Liz, 'Feminism and Friendship.' *Studies in Sexual Politics* 8 (1986), pp.10-46.

Chapter 2

1 Rowbotham, Sheila, *A Century of Women* (London, 1999) pp.119-46; Pugh, Martin, *We Danced All Night. A Social History of Britain Between the Wars* (London, 2008); McKibbin, Ross, Introduction to the reprint of Marie Stopes, *Married Love* (Oxford, 2004).
2 *Sunday Chronicle,* 15 November 1926.
3 Glencross, Evelyn, *For Better or For Worse* (Manchester, 1993) p.8.
4 *Western Mail,* 30 May 1930.
5 Blaazer, D., *The Popular Front and the Progressive Tradition* (Cambridge, 1982).
6 Skidelsky, Robert, *Politicians and the Slump* (London, 1967 reprint 1994).
7 Stocks, Mary, *Still More Commonplace* (London, 1973) p.21.
8 Stopes, *Married Love,* p.xiv.
9 Ibid., p.23.
10 Ibid., p.93.
11 Ibid., p.69.
12 Ibid., p.49.
13 Ibid., pp.99-121.
14 Glendinning, Victoria, *Vita. The Life of V. Sackville West* (London, 1983) p.99.
15 McKibbin, Ross, Introduction to *Married Love* (Oxford, 2004) p.xlvi.
16 Soloway, Richard, *Birth Control and the Population Question* (North Carolina, 1982) pp.211-12.
17 Roberts, Robert, *The Classic Slum* (London, 1971 reprint 1990) p.232.
18 BBC Written Archives, Caversham. Marie Stopes File 1. 1931-62, 1949 interview.

19 Hall, Ruth, *Marie Stopes. A Biography* (London, 1984) p.1.
20 Graves, Pamela, *Labour Women* (Cambridge, 1994) p.84.
21 Elsie Plant interviewed by Clare Debenham, 10 May 1978.
22 O'Toole, Millie, *Bessie Braddock. A Biography* (London, 1957) p.49.
23 Briant, Keith, *Marie Stopes* (London, 1962) p.96.
24 Elsie Plant interview 10 May 1978.
25 Elsie Plant interview 10 May 1978.
26 Taylor, Laurie, 'The unfinished sexual revolution.' *Journal Biosocial Science* 3 (1971), pp.473–92.
27 Rathbone, Eleanor, *The Disinherited Family* (Bristol, 1924 reprint 1986) p.379.
28 Evans, Barbara, *Freedom to Choose* (London, 1984) p.144.
29 Cohen, Deborah, 'Marie Stopes and the mothers clinic' in Peel, Robert (ed.), *Marie Stopes and the English Birth Control Movement* (London, 1997) pp.77–94.
30 Frankenburg, Charis, *Not Old, Madam, VINTAGE!* (Suffolk, 1975).
31 Ibid., pp.87–91.
32 Douglas, Margie, 'Women, God and birth control: the first hospital birth control clinic, Abertillery, 1925.' *Llafur* 6 (1995), pp.110–22.
33 Elsie Plant interviewed by Clare Debenham, 10 May 1978.
34 Stopes-Roe, Harry and Scott, Ian, *Marie Stopes and Birth Control* (London, 1974).
35 Interview of Mrs C. by Clare Debenham, 2 July 1978.
36 Walker, Caroline E., 'Making birth control respectable: the Society for Constructive Birth Control and Racial Progress and the American Birth Control League in comparative perspective, 1921-1938.' PhD thesis, University of Bristol, 2007.
37 *British Medical Journal*, 1922.
38 How-Martyn, Edith and Breed, Mary, *The Birth Control Movement in England* (London, 1930) p.25.
39 *New Generation*, 1 August 1922.
40 Rose, June, *Marie Stopes and the Sexual Revolution* (London, 1992) p.160.
41 Margaret Sanger papers, Box 61, Sophia Smith College, USA.
42 Kreisi, Hans in Snow, Soule and Kreisi (eds) *The Blackwell Companion to Social Movements* (Oxford, 2007) p.80.
43 Graves, *Labour Women*, p.84.
44 Scott, Gillian, *Feminism and the Politics of the Working Women* (London, 1998) p.169.
45 Fryer, Peter, *The Birth Controllers* (London, 1965) p.168; Leathard, Audrey, *The Fight for Family Planning* (Basingstoke, 1980) p.28.
46 Russell, Dora, *The Tamarisk Tree* (London, 1975 reprint 1989) p.161.
47 Ibid., p.174.
48 Ibid., p.169.

49 Workers' Birth Control Group, Membership Form, 1924.
50 Hoggart, Lesley, *Feminist Campaigns for Birth Control and Abortion Rights in Britain* (Lampeter, 2003) pp.79–130.
51 House of Lords Debates, 1926, vol.63, pp.997–1003.
52 Stocks, Mary, *My Commonplace Book* (London, 1970) p.233.

Chapter 3

1 Pedersen, Susan, *Eleanor Rathbone and the Politics of Conscience* (Yale, 2004), p.161.
2 Eoff, Shirley M., *Viscountess Rhondda* (Ohio, 1991) p.98.
3 Ann Patterson (nee Stocks) interview by Clare Debenham, 4 December 2004.
4 Banks, Olive, *Faces of Feminism* (Oxford, 1981); Harrison, Brian, *Prudent Revolutionaries* (Oxford, 1987).
5 *Time and Tide*, 1932.
6 Bryson, Valerie, *Feminist Political Theory* (London, 2003) p.52.
7 Tulloch, G., *Mill and Sexual Equality* (Harvester, 1989) p.99.
8 *Time and Tide*, 9 February 1923.
9 Alberti, Johanna, *Beyond Suffrage* (Basingstoke, 1989) p.164.
10 *Yorkshire Evening Post*, 26 July 1926, later reprinted *Time and Tide* 6 (August 1926).
11 Stocks, Mary, 'The new feminism.' *The Woman's Leader*, 25 February 1927.
12 Banks, Olive, *The Politics of British Feminism in the Twentieth Century* (Lampeter, 1993) p.14.
13 Alberti, *Beyond Suffrage*, p.3.
14 Eleanor Rathbone quoted by Alberti, Johanna, *Eleanor Rathbone* (London, 1996) p.167.
15 Royden, Maude, *The Making of Women* (London, 1917) p.29.
16 National Union of Societies for Equal Citizenship, *Milestones* (Liverpool, 1929).
17 *Woman's Leader*, 13 March 1925.
18 NUSEC, Presidential address of 11 March 1925 in *Milestones* (Liverpool, 1929).
19 *Time and Tide*, 1 November 1926.
20 NUSEC, Minutes, 1923.
21 *Woman's Leader*, 4 April 1923.
22 Pedersen, *Eleanor Rathbone and the Politics of Conscience*, p.194.
23 Lewis, Jane, 'Beyond suffrage. English feminism in the 1920s.' *Maryland Historian* 6 (1975) p.12; *The Politics of Motherhood* (London, 1980) p.197.
24 NUSEC, Minutes, 1923.
25 Stocks, Mary, *My Commonplace Book* (London, 1970) p.163.

NOTES TO PAGES 41-45

26 Stocks, Mary, 'The new feminism.' *Woman's Leader*, 25 February 1927.
27 Stocks, Mary, *Family Limitation and Women's Organisations* (NUSEC, 1925) p.1.
28 *Woman's Leader*, 1 January 1926.
29 Rathbone, Eleanor, 1927 Presidential address in *Milestones* (Liverpool 1929) p.10.
30 Rathbone, Eleanor, *Ethics and Economics of Family Endowment* (London, 1927) p.10.
31 Pedersen, *Eleanor Rathbone and the Politics of Conscience*, p.187.
32 Pugh, Martin, *We Danced All Night. A Social History of Britain Between the Wars* (London, 2008) p.188.
33 *Manchester Guardian*, 24 April 1926.
34 Holtby, Winifred, *South Riding* (London, 1936 reprint 1967) p.199.
35 Holtby, Winifred, *Women and a Changing Civilisation* (Chicago, 1935 reprint 1978) p.67.
36 *Birth Control News*, February 1931, p.151.
37 Martin Pugh, *Women and the Women's Movement in Britain* (London, 2000) p.248.
38 *Daily News*, 5 March 1921.
39 National Council of Women, Executive Committee Minutes, March 1931, London Metropolitan Archives.
40 Board of Education, Teachers and Youth Leaders (London, 1944) p.26.
41 *Woman's Citizen*, 1 December 1927.
42 Oram, Alison, *Women Teachers and Feminist Politics* (Manchester, 1996) p.10.
43 Lewis, Jane, 'Beyond suffrage', *Maryland Historian*.
44 Manchester and Salford Mothers' Clinic, Annual Report 1926.
45 Little, Isabelle, 'Forty years back.' *Family Planning*, 3 November 1966.
46 *Birmingham Post*, 24 April 1928.
47 Loudon, Irvine, 'Maternal mortality, 1880-1950: some regional and international comparisons.' *Society for the History of Medicine*, 1988, pp.183-201.
48 Pankhurst, Sylvia, *Save the Mothers. A Plea for Measures to Prevent the Annual Loss of About 3,000 Child-Bearing Mothers and 20,000 Infant Lives in England and Wales and a Similar Grievous Wasteage in Other Countries* (London, 1930).
49 Davin, Anna, 'Imperialism and motherhood.' *History Workshop Journal* 5/1 (1977), pp.9-65.
50 Stockport Medical Officer of Health, Annual Report for 1926.
51 Lewis, Jane, 'In search of real equality: women between the wars' in Frank Gloversmith (ed.) *Class, Culture and Social Change* (Brighton, 1980) p.224.
52 Campbell, Janet, *Maternal Mortality. Reports on Public Health and Medical Subjects*, no 25, London Ministry of Health, 1924.; *Protection of Motherhood. Reports on Public Health and Medical Subjects*, no 27 (London, 1927).

53 Russell, Dora, *The Tamarisk Tree* (London, 1975 reprint 1989) p.188.
54 Davies, Sam, *Liverpool Labour* (Keele, 1996) p.177.
55 Emanuel, Judith, 'The politics of maternity in Manchester 1919-1939.' MSc thesis, University of Manchester, 1982.
56 Nellie Beer, interview by Manchester Studies, Tape 933.
57 Stocks, Mary, *Still More Commonplace* (London, 1973) p.160.
58 Frankenburg, Charis, *Not Old, Madam, VINTAGE!* (Suffolk, 1975) p.134.
59 Stocks, *My Commonplace Book*, pp.72-6.
60 Ibid., p.77.
61 Thorndike, Russell, *Sybil Thorndike* (London, 1929) p.213.
62 Pugh, *Women and the Women's Movement in Britain*, pp.252-63.
63 Presidential Address in *Milestones* (Liverpool, 1929) p.3.
64 Stocks, Mary D., *Eleanor Rathbone. A Biography* (London, 1949) p.113.
65 Beaumont, C., 'Citizens not feminists.' *Women's History Review* 9/2 (2000) pp.411-29.
66 Pugh, *We Danced All Night*, p.191.
67 Huxley, Gervase, *Lady Denman* (London, 1961) p.101.
68 Pugh, *Women and the Women's Movement in Britain*, p.68.
69 Stott, Mary, *Organisation Woman* (London, 1978), p.18.
70 Howes, J. 'No party, no sect, no politics.' PhD thesis, Anglia Polytechnic, 2003.
71 National Council of Women, London Metropolitan Archives, Acc/3613.
72 National Council of Women, 2005.
73 Court, Audrey and Walton, Cynthia, *Birmingham Made a Difference* (Birmingham, 2001) p.22.
74 NCW Executive Minutes, 31 October 1923, London Metropolitan Archives Acc/3616.
75 *Woman's Leader,* 25 November 1929.
76 *Birth Control News*, November 1929.
77 *Manchester and Salford Woman's Citizen*, 28 November 1929, p.7.
78 *Woman's Leader*, 25 November 1929.
79 Ward, L., 'The Right to Choose.' PhD thesis, University of Bristol, 1981.
80 Smith, Joanne, PhD, Manchester Metropolitan University, 2007, p.63.
81 I am indebted to Joanne Smith, Manchester Metropolitan University, for this information.
82 Martin, Jane and Goodman, Joyce, *Women and Education* (Basingstoke, 2004) p.141.
83 Stocks, Mary, 'The Greengate clinic.' *Manchester Guardian*, 26 November 1962.
84 Glencross, Evelyn, *For Better or For Worse* (Manchester, 1993).
85 *Birth Control News*, January 1929.
86 Manchester City Council Maternity and Child Welfare Sub-Committee, Minutes, 5 August 1930.

Chapter 4

1. McAdam, Douglas et al., *Comparative Perspectives on Social Movements* (Cambridge, 1996) pp.3–4; Edwards and McCarthy, 'Resources and social movements' in Snow, D. et al., *The Blackwell Companion to Social Movements* (Oxford, 2007) p.116.
2. McLaren, Angus, *A History of Contraception* (Oxford, 1990) p.227
3. Fisher, Kate, *Birth Control, Sex and Marriage in Britain* (Oxford, 2006).
4. Fisher, Kate, 'Contrasting cultures' in Tansey, *Remedies and Healing Cultures in Britain* (Amsterdam, 2002) p.155.
5. Mitchell, Juliet, *Woman's Estate* (Middlesex, 1977); Liddington, Jill, *Rebel Girls* (London, 2006); Cowman, Krista, *Women of the Right Spirit* (Manchester, 2007).
6. Logan, Anne, *Feminism and Criminal Justice* (London, 2008) p.6.
7. Cowman, Krista, *Women* (2007) p.12.
8. Dowse, R.E. and Peel, John 'The politics of birth control.' *Political Studies* 13/2 (June 1965).
9. Bookbinder, P., *Simon Marks* (London, 1993).
10. Hon. Ann Patterson, Mary Stocks' daughter, interviewed by Clare Debenham, 4 December 2004.
11. *Catholic Herald* (13.2.1926); (2.3.1926); (19.6.1926).
12. The following were married to doctors: Mrs Collier, Oxford; Mrs Edith Emanuel, Birmingham; Mrs Winifred Strange, Wolverhampton; Lady Sprigge. Lady Sprigge's husband was editor of the medical journal *The Lancet*.
13. SPBCC members Eva Hartree and Margery Spring Rice attended Girton, Cambridge while Constance Masefield, Lillian Mott and Helen Pease attended Newnham College, Cambridge. Leah Manning obtained her teaching qualification from Homerton Teacher Training College, Cambridge. Two SPBCC members attended Oxford University. Eleanor Rathbone read Philosophy at Somerville College and Charis Frankenburg also attended Somerville.
14. Vera Brittain's comments on Charis Frankenburg (1940) p.206. Frankenburg's criticism of Brittain are recorded in the Brian Harrison interviews, 12 April 1977, Women's Library.
15. Stocks, Mary, *My Commonplace Book* (London, 1970) p.8.
16. Mott, C.F., *Lillian Mary Mott* (1952).
17. Logan, *Feminism and Criminal Justice*, p.1.
18. By 1930 there were still only two hundred women magistrates in Britain compared to twenty-three thousand men. Harrison, Brian, *Prudent Revolutionaries* (Oxford, 1987) p.303.
19. Ann Patterson, interviewed by Clare Debenham on 4.12.2004.

20 McAdam, Douglas, 'The recruitment to high risk'. *American Journal of Sociology* 92 (1986) pp.64–90.
21 Cowman, Krista, *Women of the Right Spirit. Paid Organisers of the Women's Social and Political Union, 1904–1914* (Manchester, 2007) p.60.
22 Frankenburg, Charis, *Not Old, Madam, VINTAGE!* (Suffolk, 1975) p.134.
23 British Library Department of Manuscripts. Marie C. Stopes Papers: BL.Add.MSS.5859-58642.
24 *Stockport Express* (1.11.1923).
25 David Paton interviewed by Clare Debenham, 22 May 2007.
26 Pedersen, Susan, *Eleanor Rathbone* (Yale, 2004) p.184; Stocks, Mary, *Eleanor Rathbone* (London, 1949).
27 'The back-street beginnings of birth control.' *Press and Journal*, 4 November 1972.
28 Relative of Charis Frankenburg, interviewed by Clare Debenham, 1 November 2003.
29 Robinson, Caroline, *Seventy Birth Control Clinics* (New York, 1930) p.20.
30 Lightfoot, Freda, *The Favourite Child* (London, 2001) p.103. Lightfoot interviewed Frankenburg's relatives as well as consulting written records.
31 Brian Harrison interview with Frankenburg, 12 April 1977. Women's Library 8SU/B144b.
32 Elsie Plant interviewed by Clare Debenham, 10 May 1978.
33 The *Stockport Express* reported the meeting (1 November 1923 and 8 November 1923) and carried prominent advertisements for it in the previous weeks.
34 Debenham, Clare, 'Mrs Elsie Plant: suffragette, socialist and birth control activist.' *Women's History Review*, 2010, pp.145–58.
35 'Profile of Mary Barbour.' *Women's Outlook*, February 1921, p.108.
36 Rowley, 'Reminiscences of Alice Onions.' *West Midland Studies* 16 (1983) pp.30–3.
37 In the convention of the times she was referred to by her husband's Christian name, not her own.
38 Tamplin, C., 'Early days in Newcastle.' *Family Planning*, October 1962.
39 Interview with Mrs Bessie Wild by Manchester Studies Tape 932.
40 Interview with Mrs Elsie Wild by Manchester Studies Tape 756.
41 Barbara Blaszak, *The Matriarchs of England* (Connecticut, 2000) pointed out that at the turn of the twentieth century even a single female school teacher would have found it hard to afford the WCG subscription.
42 Mary Williams interviewed by Manchester Studies, Tape 73.
43 *Liverpool Mothers' Clinic Minutes* 1926 (no month).
44 *Manchester and Salford Mothers' Clinic Annual Report 1926–1927.*
45 *Manchester and Salford Mothers' Clinic Annual Report 1927–1928.*
46 *Manchester and Salford Co-operative Herald*, October 1930, p.120.
47 *East London Advertiser*, 31 July 1926, 11 September 1926.

48 Douglas, Margie, 'Women, God and birth control.' *Llafur* 6/4 (1995) pp.110-22.
49 Stott, Mary, *Organisation Woman* (London, 1978) p.2.
50 *SPBCC Annual Report 1925-1926*. Very little survives about this clinic.
51 Frankenburg, *Not Old, Madam, VINTAGE!*, pp.134-40.
52 *Manchester and Salford Mothers' Clinic First Annual Report 1926-1927*.
53 Ibid.
54 *Birmingham Women's Welfare Centre Annual Report 1927-1928*.
55 Ibid.
56 Glencross, Evelyn, *For Better or For Worse* (Manchester, 1993).
57 Ibid., p.8.
58 *Liverpool Echo*, 31 March 1926.
59 *Liverpool Mothers' Clinic Minutes*, April 1926.
60 Fuller, Evelyn (1931), 'On the Management of a birth control centre'. Wellcome Trust SA/FPA/SR248/2.
61 Glasgow Mothers' Clinic reply to Margaret Sanger's questionnaire 1927. Smith College archives.
62 Bradshaw, Muriel, *Spaghetti Junction Doctor* (Devon, 1995) p.25.
63 *Wolverhampton Chronicle*, 18 November 1955, 'Woman in Profile, Alice Onions.'
64 Stocks, Mary, *My Commonplace*, p.160.
65 Esther Dean is Dilys Dean's daughter and her mother worked at the MSMC. Interview by Clare Debenham 11 April 2004.
66 Stopes, Marie, *Contraception* (London, 1924) contains a detailed photograph of her clinic in chapter fourteen.
67 *Star*, 9 July 1921.
68 Frankenburg, Charis (1930), *Report on the Conference on the Giving of Birth Control*. Information.
69 Rolph, C.H. (ed.), *The Human Sum* (London, 1957) p.57.
70 Fisher, Kate, 'An oral history of birth control practice. A study of Oxford and South Wales.' DPhil, Oxford, 1997.
71 Fisher, *Birth Control, Sex and Marriage in Britain 1918-1960*.
72 Szreter, Simon and Fisher, Kate, *Sex Before the Sexual Revolution* (Cambridge, 2010).
73 There were similar self-referrals in interviews conducted by Manchester Studies in the 1970s.
74 Florence, Lella Secor, *Birth Control on Trial* (London, 1930) p.49.
75 Glencross, *For Better or For Worse*, p.8.
76 Tebbutt, Melanie, *Women's Talk?* (Aldershot, 1995) p.49.
77 *Liverpool Women's Welfare Association Annual Report 1928-1929* p.4.
78 Interview with Mrs Florence Travis by Clare Debenham, 8 February 1978.
79 *Family Planning*, January 1956.

80 Ibid.
81 *Wolverhampton Chronicle*, 18 November 1955.
82 *Manchester Guardian*, 16 April 1926.
83 *East London Advertiser*, 26 June 1926 and 11 November 1926.
84 Stocks, *My Commonplace Book*.
85 *North Kensington Women's Welfare Annual Report 1925–1926*.
86 *Oxford Times*, 4 November 1926–30 November 1926.
87 *Eccles and Patricroft Journal*, 19 February 1926.
88 Interview with Sister Beatrice Sandys by Clare Debenham, 28 March 2003.
89 *North Kensington Women's Welfare Association Minutes*, 15.11.1927. It is not recorded whether they were able to carry out their poster campaign.
90 Mitchison, Naomi, *Comments on Birth Control* (London, 1930) pp.5–32.
91 *North Kensington Women's Welfare Annual Report 1927–1928*, p.2.
92 Topic Collection Family Planning (1944–9) TC.3/1A. Mass Observation Archives at the University of Sussex.
93 Ferch, J., *Birth Control* (London, 1926) p.12.
94 Fisher, *Birth Control, Sex and Marriage in Britain*, p.239.
95 Dr L. Fairfield (1920), LC 135, pp.420–8. In 1922 Fairfield converted to Catholicism and completely changed her views on birth control.
96 *Cambridge Women's Welfare Annual Report 1927*, p.3.
97 Himes, Norman, 'British birth control clinics.' *Eugenics Review*, 1928, p.158.
98 Fisher, *Birth Control, Sex and Marriage in Britain*, p.77.
99 Elsie Plant interviewed by Clare Debenham 10 May 1978.
100 Florence, *Birth Control on Trial*.
101 *Birth Control News*, December 1933.
102 Aunt Polly was interviewed by Clare Debenham on 30 June 1979. She had left school at eleven and worked as a weaver earning £2.00 a week in the inter-war period in Glossop. She had been married twice.
103 Interview with Mrs Florence Travis from Liverpool by Clare Debenham, 8 February 1978.
104 *Birth Control News*, June 1931.
105 Brookes, Barbara, *Abortion in England* (London, 1988); Jones, Emma, 'Abortion in England.' PhD thesis, Royal Holloway College, 2007.
106 *MSMC Annual Report 1926–1927*, p.5.
107 Interview with Ann Patterson by Clare Debenham, 4 December 2004.
108 It was not until 1803 that new legislation made early abortion illegal (43 Geo.IIIc.58) though there was still the distinction between early and late abortion. Subsequent legislation such as the 1861 Act confirmed that abortion at any stage was a crime and the procurer liable to life imprisonment even if the procurer was the pregnant woman herself. Leeson, Judith and Gray, Judith, *Women and Medicine* (London, 1970) p.110.

109 Interview with Aunt Polly by Clare Debenham, 30 June 1979.
110 Ibid.
111 Fuller, E., 'Eugenic aspects of the Walworth Women's Welfare Centre,' *Eugenics Review* 15 (April 1923–January 1924) p.599.
112 Brookes, *Abortion in England*, p.38.
113 Ibid., p.8.
114 Knight, Patricia, 'Abortion in Victorian and Edwardian England.' *History Workshop*, 1977.
115 Fisher, *Birth Control, Sex and Marriage in Britain*; Jones, 'Abortion in England.' Jones convincingly argued that gender, marital status and locality also shaped abortion experiences as well as social class.
116 Interview with Elsie Plant, 10 May 1978.
117 Marks, Lara, *Model Mothers* (Oxford, 1994) p.246.
118 *Birmingham Women's Welfare Centre Annual Report 1927-1929*. p.4.
119 Himes, N.E. and V., 'Birth control for the British working classes: a study of the first thousand cases to visit a British birth control clinic,' *Hospital Social Service* 19 (1929) p.162. They reported that in a run of 600 cases at the MSMC, 477 women 79.6% were advised to use the dutch pessary. This compared to 41% of patients in Liverpool being given this advice.
120 *Family Planning* 3/5 (1955).
121 Florence, *Birth Control on Trial*.
122 How-Martyn, *The Birth Control Movement* (London, 1932) p.132.
123 Robinson, *Seventy Birth Control Clinics*.
124 Norman Himes, 'British birth control clinics,' p.157.
125 *Liverpool Mothers' Clinic Minutes*, 1 November 1927; *MSMC Annual Report 1927-1928*.
126 ibid.
127 *MSMC Annual Report 1926-1927*; Stocks (1971) p.162.
128 Himes, 'British birth control clinics,' p.161.
129 *North Kensington Women's Welfare Annual Report 1925-1926*.
130 *Evidence to the Inter-Departmental Committee on Abortion* (MH71 23).
131 *Birmingham Women's Welfare Annual Report 1928-1929*.
132 *Liverpool Women's Welfare Clinic Minutes*, 18 November 1927.
133 Glencross, *For Better or For Worse*, p.8.
134 *MSMC First Annual Report 1926-1927*, p.7
135 *MSMC Second Annual Report 1927-1928*.
136 *MSMC First Annual Report 1926-1927*, p.7.
137 Robinson, *Seventy Birth Control Clinics*, p.61.
138 Florence, *Birth Control on Trial*, p.13.
139 *Birmingham Women's Welfare Association Annual Report 1927-1928*, p.7.
140 *Birmingham Women's Welfare Association Annual Report 1928-1929*, p.8.
141 *Cambridge Women's Welfare Association Annual Report 1925-1926*, p.6.

142 *North Kensington Women's Welfare Association Annual Report 1926-1926*, p.3.
143 Ibid. p.11.
144 Brookes, J. (2009), 'Presentation on Lady Sanitary Inspectors.' Women and History Conference; Cowman, Krista, *'Mrs Brown is a Man and Brother!'* (Liverpool, 2004) p.20.
145 Logan, Anne, 'Lady bountiful or community activist?' *Women's History Magazine* 62 (2010) pp.11-18.
146 Fisher, Kate, 'Contrasting cultures of contraception: birth control clinics and the working classes between the wars' in Tansey, T. (ed.) *Remedies and Healing Cultures in Britain and the Netherlands in the Twentieth Century* (Amsterdam, 2002).
147 Walker, C., 'Therapeutic contraception. Marie Stopes, voluntary birth control clinics and public health in Britain.' PhD thesis.
148 Evans, Barbara, *Freedom to Choose* (London, 1984) p.136.
149 *Family Planning*, January 1956.
150 MSMC (1931) *Only Eight Failures.*
151 Ibid., p.3.
152 Quoted Fuller, Evelyn, 'On the Management of a birth control centre,' p.22.
153 Marks, *Model Mothers*, p.255.
154 Dale, P. and Fisher, Kate, 'Contrasting municipal responses to the provision of birth control services in Halifax and Exeter before 1948.' *Social History of Medicine* 23/3 (2010) p.579.
155 Stopes, Marie, *Contraception* (London, 1924) p.382.
156 Frankenburg, *Report on the Conference on the Giving of Birth Control.*
157 Ibid.
158 Florence, *Birth Control on Trial*, p.25.
159 Norman Himes, 'British birth control clinics,' p.583.
160 *Liverpool Mothers' Clinic Minutes,* June 1933.
161 Cohen, Deborah, 'Marie Stopes and the mothers' clinic' in Peel, R.A., *Marie Stopes and the English Birth Control Movement* (London, 1997) p.84.
162 *North Kensington Women's Welfare Centre First Annual Report 1924-1925*, p.2.
163 Fuller, 'On the Management of a birth control centre,' p.4.
164 *Manchester and Salford Woman Citizen*, 28 November 1929, p.9.
165 Mary Williams interviewed by Manchester Studies, Tape 73.
166 Ursula Kennedy interviewed 2 July 2004 by Clare Debenham.
167 Glencross, *For Better or For Worse*, p.8; *Family Planning*, January 1956, p.10.
168 Macaulay, Dr Muriel, *The Story of the Mothers' Welfare Clinic* (Liverpool, 1952) p.6.

169 *Wolverhampton Chronicle*, 18 November 1925, p.14.
170 Davin, Anna, 'Imperialism and motherhood.' *History Workshop Journal* 5/1 (1978) pp.9–65.
171 *Family Planning*, January 1956.
172 Ibid, p.8.
173 Jagger, A.M., 'Love and knowledge: emotion in feminist epistemology.' *Inquiry* 32/2 (1989) pp.151–76.
174 Anna Davin, 'Imperialism and motherhood.' *History Workshop Journal*, pp.9–65.
175 *North Kensington Women's Welfare Annual Report 1925–1926*.
176 *Manchester Guardian*, 16 April 1926.
177 Fisher (2002) p.141.

Chapter 5

1 Stocks, Mary, 'The story of family planning' in Rolph, C.H., *The Human Sum* (London, 1957) pp.43–62.
2 *Manchester Guardian*, 9 April 1924.
3 Stopes-Roe, Harry and Scott, I., *Marie Stopes and Birth Control* (London, 1974) p.66. The book in question was Marie Stopes' *Roman Catholic Methods of Birth Control*.
4 Hall, Ruth, *Marie Stopes* (London, 1977).
5 Box, Muriel, *The Trial of Marie Stopes* (New York, 1967); Rose, June, *Marie Stopes and the Sexual Revolution* (London, 1992).
6 Campbell, Flann, 'Birth control and the Christian Churches.' *Population Studies* 14/2 (November 1960).
7 *Birth Control News*, edited by Marie Stopes, reproduced the article published in *The Universe*, February 1931, p.145.
8 *Catholic Herald*, 18 May 1929.
9 Quoted Richard Soloway, *Birth Control and the Population Question in England* (North Carolina, 1982) p.99.
10 *Sunday Express*, 16 November 1921.
11 Dawson, Bernard, *Love, Marriage, Birth Control* (London, 1921).
12 Ibid., Forward.
13 Ibid., p.21. This phrase resonates with the arguments of Marie Stopes.
14 Peel, John, 'Contraception and the medical profession.' *Population Studies* 18/2 (1964), pp.133–45.
15 Stocks, Mary, *My Commonplace Book* (London, 1970) p.156.
16 Campbell, Flann, 'Birth control.' *Population Studies*, November 1960, p.136.
17 LC152,321, Lambeth Palace Archives.
18 Evans, Barbara, *Freedom to Choose* (London, 1984) p.141.
19 Lambeth Conference (1930) *Encyclical Letter*, pp.43–4.

20 *Birmingham Mothers' Clinic Annual Report 1930.*
21 LC 135,400. Correspondence with the Mothers' Union 1919–1920, Lambeth Palace Library.
22 Letter to Mrs Boustead, President of the Mothers' Union, from Archbishop Temple, 10 November 1930. Archbishop Temple papers, vol. 35, no 49.
23 The minutes of the Liverpool Mothers' Welfare Clinic, November 1925, showed Mrs David wished to become involved with the clinic but did not wish this to be publicised.
24 *The Liverpudlian*, 'Profile of Dr Albert Augustus David.' December 1933, p.5.
25 *Jewish Chronicle*, May 1926.
26 Kuzmack, Linda, *Woman's Cause. The Jewish Movement in England and the USA 1891–1933* (Ohio, 1990) p.161.
27 Interview with Ursula Kennedy by Clare Debenham, 2 July 2004.
28 *Family Planning*, November 1962, p.61.
29 Kuzmack, *Woman's Cause*, p.184.
30 Flora Blumberg Obituary, Manchester Local Studies Archives, no date.
31 Summerskill, Edith, *A Woman's World* (London, 1967) p.52.
32 Marks, Lara, *Model Mothers* (Oxford, 1994); Marks, Lara, *Metropolitan Maternity* (Amsterdam, 1996).
33 Marks, *Metropolitan Maternity*, p.171.
34 Marks, *Model Mothers*, p.268.
35 Dr Mary Scharlieb, 1920, LC135,464.
36 *The Practitioner*, 1923.
37 Dr Florence Barrett, 1920, LC135,143.
38 Himes, Norman, *Medical History of Contraception* (Baltimore, 1936 reprint 1970) p.330.
39 *Family Planning*, 3 October 1966, p.78.
40 *Birth Control Times*, December 1930, p.117.
41 Fairfield, Dr Letitia, 1920, LC135,420-428. On her conversion to Catholicism she reversed her views on birth control.
42 Letter from Dr Newsholme to Dame Janet Campbell, 5 March 1928, PRO856/106.
43 *Birmingham Post*, 24 January 1931.
44 *Post and Journal*, 20 December 1926.
45 Sister Beatrice Sandys interviewed by Clare Debenham, 28 March 2003.
46 North Kensington Women's Welfare, Minutes, 14 September 1924.
47 Browne, Stella, *New Generation*, January 1927, p.4.
48 Macaulay, Dr M., *The Story of the Mothers' Welfare Clinic, Liverpool.* Privately published, 1952.
49 *Manchester and Salford Co-operative Herald*, December 1926.
50 Unpublished memoirs of Dilys Dean written in the 1950s and loaned by her daughter.

51 Welcome Contemporary Medical Archive, Wolverhampton, SA/FPAA4/A18.
52 *North Kensington Women's Welfare Centre Annual Report 1927-1928*, p.6
53 Fenella Paton to Marie Stopes, 12 July 1934. Marie C. Stopes Papers: BL.Add.MSS58617.
54 *MSMC Annual Report 1928-1929*, p.4.
55 Frankenburg, Charis, *Not Old, Madam, VINTAGE!* (Suffolk, 1975), p.136.
56 Horsburgh, F., 'The beginnings of birth control.' *Press and Journal*, 4 November 1972.
57 Douglas, Margie, 'Women, God and birth control.' *Llafur* 6 (1995), pp.110-22.
58 Nurse Daniels' business card was given to the American birth control pioneer Margaret Sanger and is in the Margaret Sanger Research Bureau, Box 8, File 2, Smith College, USA.
59 Wright, Dr Helena, 'Fifty years of family planning.' *Family Planning*, January 1972, p.75.
60 Evans, Barbara, *Freedom to Choose* (London, 1984) p.133.
61 The academic panel included Professor Julian Huxley and Professor Carr-Saunders. The panel of lay members included Mary Stocks, Lella Sargent Florence and Margaret Spring Rice.
62 Sanger, Margaret, *The Practice of Contraception. International Symposium* (Baltimore, 1931).
63 Manchester and District Mothers' Clinic, 'Only 8 failures in 1,212 cases'. Wellcome Library A&M:SA/FPA,1931.
64 Florence, Lella Secor, *Birth Control on Trial* (London, 1930).
65 Henry, John, 'Labour and the Proletarian city.' PhD Manchester Metropolitan University, 2005.
66 Hutt, A., *The Condition of the Working Class in Britain* (London, 1934).
67 *Stockport Medical Officer of Health Annual Report 1926*.
68 *Salford Medical Officer of Health Annual Report 1930*, pp.50-5.
69 Elsie Plant interviewed by Clare Debenham, 10 May 1978.
70 Smith, J., 'Labour tradition in Glasgow and Liverpool.' *History Workshop* 17 (1984) pp.32-55.
71 Father David Lannon interviewed by Clare Debenham at Salford Diocesan Archives, 5 May 2005.
72 Article by Bishop Henshaw, reproduced in the *Manchester Guardian*, 22 March 1926 from the *Catholic Federalist*.
73 *Evening Chronicle*, 10 April 1926.
74 *Salford Reporter*, 18 July 1925.
75 *Catholic Herald*, 18 July 1925.
76 *Manchester Guardian*, 23 March 1926.
77 Hon. Ann Patterson, Mary Stocks' daughter, interviewed by Clare Debenham, 4 December 2004.

78 Letter written by Mary Stocks to Nancy Astor, 25 March 1926. General correspondence Nancy, Lady Astor Collection, University of Reading ArchiveMS1416/1/1/.
79 Letter written by Mary Stocks to Nancy Astor, 30 March 1926, University of Reading.
80 Frankenburg, *Not Old, Madam, VINTAGE!*, p.137.
81 Bishop Henshaw, Lenten Pastoral Newsletter, 1937.
82 Frankenberg, Charis, *Family Planning*, January 1956.
83 *Birmingham Post*, 24 April 1928.
84 Fielding, Stephen, 'The Irish Catholics in Manchester and Salford.' PhD thesis, University of Warwick, 1988.
85 Henry, 'Labour and the Proletarian city,' p.274. In 1926 Salford Municipal elections Labour won seven of the fifteen seats contested, five of which were in wards with Catholic parishes.
86 Frankenburg, *Not Old, Madam, VINTAGE!*, pp.134–40; Stocks, *My Commonplace Book*, pp.148–64.
87 Smith, J., 'Labour tradition.' *History Workshop*, 1984.
88 *Liverpool Mothers' Welfare Clinic Annual Report 1936*. Liverpool City Archives, Acc.5429.

Chapter 6

1 Banks, Olive, *The Biographical Dictionary of English Feminists*, vol.1 (Hemel Hempstead, 1985) p.190.
2 Perry, Michael W. (ed.) *Eugenics and Other Evils by G.K. Chesterton* (Seattle, 2000) p.6, p.8.
3 Allen, Anne, 'Feminism and eugenics in Britain and Germany.' *German Studies Review* 36 (2000) p.483; Wanhalla, Angela, 'To better the breed of men: women in eugenics in New Zealand 1900-1935.' *Women's History Review* 16/2 (2007), pp.163–82.
4 Curthoys, Ann, 'Eugenics, feminism and birth control: the case of Marion Piddington.' *Hecate* 15/1 (1989), pp.73–89.
5 *New Generation*, January 1923, pp.8–9.
6 The term 'neo-Malthusian' was suggested by Dr Samuel Van Houten, a former prime minister of Holland to indicate a lessened emphasis on moral restraint.
7 Lewis, Jane, *The Politics of Motherhood* (London, 1980) p.199.
8 Annual Report of the 1926 Labour Party Conference.
9 Bland, Lucy, *Banishing the Beast* (London, 1995) p.191.
10 *The Malthusian*, 15 March 1916, p.12.
11 Szreter, Simon, *Fertility, Class and Gender in Britain* (Cambridge, 1996) p.308.

12 Soloway, Richard, *Demography and Degeneration: Eugenics and the Declining Birthrate in Twentieth Century Britain* (North Carolina, 1995).
13 Benn, Miriam, *Predicaments of Love* (London, 1992) p.141. Alice Vickery started her medical training aged twenty-five and eventually completed it when aged thirty-six.
14 Bland, *Banishing the Beast*, p.207.
15 Fryer, Peter, *The Birth Controllers* (London, 1965) pp.178–92.
16 *Eugenics Review* 12 (April 1920–January 1921) p.297.
17 *The Malthusian*, August 1914, p.94.
18 McCann, Carol, *Birth Control Politics in the United States, 1916–1945* (Ithaca, 1994) p.159.
19 Benn, *Predicaments of Love*, p.188.
20 Rowbotham, Sheila, *A New World for Women* (London, 1977) p.23.
21 Drysdale, Charles Vickery, *Neo-Malthusians and Eugenics* (privately printed, 1912) pp.10–11.
22 Soloway, *Demography and Degeneration*, p.134.
23 McLaren, Angus, *Birth Control in Nineteenth Century England* (London, 1978) p.112.
24 *New Generation*, June 1922.
25 Winifred Strange was the first woman motorist in Wolverhampton and attracted attention as she drove her father's car. Maxfield, D., 'Pioneering spirit.' *Wolverhampton Magazine,* May 1970, p.26.
26 *New Generation*, November 1925, p.123.
27 *The Malthusian*, 15 January 1921, p.60.
28 *New Generation*, June 1922.
29 Horsburgh, F., 'The back-street beginnings of birth control.' *Press and Journal*, 4 December 1972.
30 Rowbotham, *A New World for Women*, p.12.
31 Browne, Stella, 'The feminist aspect of birth control' in Pierpoint, R., *Report of the Fifth International and neo-Malthusian Birth Control Conference* (London, 1922); Hall, Lesley, *The Life and Times of Stella Browne* (London, 2011).
32 *New Generation*, November 1922, p.3.
33 Jones, Greta, 'Women and eugenics in Britain.' *Annals of Science* 52/5 (1995), p.491, quoted from the *Freewoman*, 1 August 1912.
34 Jones, 'Women and eugenics in Britain,' p.500.
35 *Eugenics Review*, December 1909.
36 *New Generation*, July 1928.
37 *Eugenics Review* 12 (April 1920–January 1921) pp.292–9.
38 Peel, Robert A., *Marie Stopes and the English Birth Control Movement* (London, 1996).
39 Perry, Michael (ed.) *Eugenics and Other Evils* (Seattle, 1998) p.xv–1.
40 Soloway, *Demography and Degeneration*, 1995, p.xxii.

41 Mazumdar, Pauline, *Eugenics, Human Genetics and Human Failings* (London, 1992).
42 Cleminson, Richard, *Anarchism, Science and Sex* (Oxford, 2000) p.9.
43 Soloway, *Demography and Degeneration*, p.86.
44 Davin, Ann, 'Imperialism and motherhood.' *History Workshop Journal* 5/1 (1978) pp.8–65.
45 Barker, David, 'Fostering a eugenic consciousness.' Unpublished paper, University of Salford, 1980.
46 Ibid., p.94.
47 Ruth Hall's *Dear Dr Stopes* (London, 1978) noted this practice. I suspect this was rather facetious.
48 Kline, W., *Building a Better Race* (Berkeley, 1968) p.7.
49 Wanhalla, Angela, 'To better the breed of men: women in eugenics in New Zealand, 1900–1935.' *Women's History Review* 16/2 (2007).
50 Brown, I., 'Who were the Eugenicists?' *History of Education* 17/4 (1988) p.305.
51 Blacker, Dr C.P., 28 September 1930. Eugenic Society papers, EUG/C1.2) Wellcome Library. This is a closed collection accessed via the Eugenic Society.
52 *Manchester Evening News*, 15 May 1931, p.1.
53 Kline, *Building a Better Race*, p.7.
54 Paul, D.B., *Controlling Human Heredity* (New Jersey, 1995) p.20.
55 Hall, Lesley in Bland, *Banishing the Beast*, p.137.
56 Paul, *Controlling Human Heredity*, p.120.
57 Soloway, *Demography and Degeneration*, p.640.
58 *Press and Journal*, 19 November 1926.
59 Grier, J., 'Eugenics and birth control contraceptive provision in North Wales.' *Social History of Medicine* 11/3 (1998) p.453.
60 Curthoys, 'Eugenics, feminism and birth control,' p.73.
61 Allen, 'Feminism and eugenics in Britain and Germany.'
62 Mazumdar, *Eugenics, Human Genetics and Human Failings*, p.9.
63 Richardson, A., *Love and Eugenics in the late Nineteenth Century* (Oxford, 2008) p.7.
64 Hall, Lesley, 'Marie Stopes and her correspondents' in Peel, Robert A., (ed.), *Marie Stopes and the English Birth Control Movement* (London, 1996) pp.48–9.
65 Kevles, Daniel, *In the Name of Genetics* (London, 1985) p.323.
66 Mazumdar, *Eugenics, Human Genetics and Human Failings*, p.9.
67 Allen, 'Feminism and eugenics in Britain and Germany,' p.495.
68 Ibid., pp.480, 482.
69 Mary Stocks reviewed Naomi Mitchison's *Comments on Birth Control* in *Eugenics Review* 22 (April 1930–January 1931), p.143.
70 *Eugenics Review* 17 (1925–6), p.195.

71 *Cambridge Women's Welfare Annual Report 1926–1927.*
72 Richardson, *Love and Eugenics in the late Nineteenth Century*, p.7.
73 Fuller, Edward, 'Eugenic aspects of the Walworth Women's Welfare Centre.' *Eugenics Review* 15 (1923–4) pp.597–9.
74 *Eugenics Review* 18 (April 1926–January 1927) p.350.
75 Elderton, Ethel, 'Report on the English Birth Rate. Part 1. England North of the Humber.' *Eugenics Laboratory Memoirs* (London, 1914) p.238.
76 Love, R., 'Alice in eugenics land: feminism and eugenics in the careers of Alice Lee and Ethel Elderton.' *Annals of Science* 36 (1978) pp.145–58.
77 *Freewoman*, 12 July 1912, pp.181–2.
78 *Eugenics Review*, July 1917, p.112.
79 Soloway, *Demography and Degeneration*, p.55.
80 Hall, 'Marie Stopes and her correspondents,' p.40.
81 Szreter, *Fertility, Class and Gender in Britain*, p.156.
82 Soloway, *Demography and Degeneration*, p.182.
83 *Birth Control News*, August 1922.
84 *Birth Control News*, November 1922.
85 Cohen, Deborah, 'Marie Stopes and the mothers' clinic' in Robert A., (ed.), *Marie Stopes and the English Birth Control Movement* (London, 1997) p.79.
86 Ibid., p.81.
87 *Eugenics Review* 16 (April 1925–January 1926), pp.270–86.
88 Rathbone, Eleanor, *The Disinherited Family* (London, 1924 reprint 1986) p.321.
89 Ibid., p.107.
90 Alberti, Johanna, *Eleanor Rathbone* (London, 1996) p.138.
91 Carr-Saunders to Blacker, 10 June 1932, Wellcome Archives, Eug/C 56.
92 Himes, Norman and Vera, 'Birth control for the British working classes.' *Hospital Social Service* 19 (1929) pp.578–617.
93 Soloway, *Demography and Degeneration*, p.211.
94 Pugh, Martin, *We Danced All Night* (London, 2008) p.150.
95 Soloway, *Demography and Degeneration*.
96 *Mothers' Welfare Clinic, Liverpool*, Minutes 18 September 1926.

Chapter 7

1 Fielding, Stephen, 'The Irish Catholics of Manchester and Salford.' PhD thesis, University of Warwick, 1988, p.x.
2 Hunt, Karen, 'Making politics in the local communities' in Worley, M., *Labour's Grass Roots* (Aldershot, 2005) p.79.
3 Graves, Pamela and Gruber, H., *Women and Socialism* (Oxford, 1998) p.195.

NOTES TO PAGES 132-140

4 Interview with Alderman Nellie Beer, Manchester Studies Tape Collection, 774.
5 Charis Frankenburg interviewed by Brian Harrison, 8SUF/B/194, Women's Library.
6 *Press and Journal*, 4 December 1972.
7 Spring Rice, M., *Working Class Wives* (Harmondsworth, 1939).
8 Hunt, Karen and Hannam, June, *Socialist Women* (London, 2002).
9 Mackenzie, J. (ed.), *The Diary of Beatrice Webb*, vol.4 (London, 1983) p.26. Beatrice Webb made it clear that she regarded herself as coming from a different social class to her visitors and regarded herself as being their teacher.
10 Graves, Pamela, *Labour Women* (Cambridge, 1994) p.1.
11 Phillips, Marion, *Women and the Labour Party* (London, 1918) p.9.
12 *Manchester and Salford Co-operative Herald*, December 1926.
13 McHugh, Declan, 'A mass party frustrated.' PhD thesis, University of Salford, 2001, p.354.
14 Blaszak, Barbara, *The Matriarchs of England's Co-operative Movement* (Connecticut, 2000).
15 *Rochdale Women's Liberal Association Annual Report 1918*, Touchstone, Rochdale Archives, Ref.3/2/2.
16 Thane, Pat, 'Women in the British welfare state' in Koven, S. and Michel, S., *Mothers of a New World* (London, 1993) p.363.
17 MacDonald, J. Ramsay, *Margaret Ethel MacDonald* (London, 1924). Preface.
18 *Women's Co-operative Guild Annual Report 1919 to 1920*.
19 *Labour Party Annual Conference Report 1926*, p.204.
20 Pugh, Martin, *Women and the Women's Movement* (London, 2000) p.189.
21 *Liberal Women's News*, August 1927.
22 Hunt and Hannam, *Socialist Women*, p.169.
23 National Conference of Labour Women Programme 1926, p.6. West Yorkshire Archive Service Ref: WYL 853/84.
24 Russell, Dora, *The Tamarisk Tree* (London, 1989) p.202.
25 Labour Women's Conference Report 1927.
26 *Liberal Women's News*, August 1927.
27 *Labour Woman*, May 1924.
28 Interview with Mrs Elsie Plant by Clare Debenham, 10 May 1978.
29 Fielding, 'The Irish Catholics of Manchester and Salford,' p.172.
30 *New Leader*, 20 August 1925.
31 Labour Party Women's Conference Report 1929.
32 *New Leader*, 7 September 1928.
33 Manchester Archives and Local Studies, Ref: 450.
34 Manchester Archives and Local Studies, Ref: 449/1. Minutes of Women's Advisory Council, September 1930.

35 Goronwy-Roberts, M., *A Woman of Vision* (Wrexham, 2000) pp.131–41.
36 *Labour Woman*, October 1918, p.88; *Labour Woman*, December 1913, p.115.
37 *Labour Woman*, May 1924, p.9; *Labour Woman*, May 1924, p.34.
38 *Labour Woman*, March 1924.
39 Russell, *The Tamarisk Tree*, p.172.
40 Ibid., p.172.
41 Graves, *Labour Women*, p.86.
42 Marion Phillips was awarded her doctorate from the London School of Economics in 1909. Her thesis examined Governor Macquarie and focused on colonial autocracy.
43 *Hansard*, February 1926, vol.151, col.851.
44 *Labour Woman*, March 1926.
45 *Labour Party Women's Annual Report*, 1926, p.68.
46 Hunt and Hannam, *Socialist Women*, p.44.
47 West Yorkshire Archive Service: WYL853/83.
48 1925 Labour Party Women's Conference Report.
49 Dora Russell Archive IHSS, file 104.
50 1928 Labour Party Women's Conference Report.
51 Pugh, *Women and the Women's Movement*, p.102.
52 Graves, *Labour Women*, pp.22–3.
53 Llewelyn Davies, Margaret, *Maternity. Letters from Working Women* (London, 1915 reprint 1978).
54 *Women's Outlook*, October 1921, pp.320–1.
55 *Women's Outlook*, July 1922.
56 *Co-operative News*, 6 June 1923, p.13.
57 Scott, Gillian, *Feminism and the Politics of Working Women* (London, 1998) p.170.
58 WCG Central Committee Minutes, Agenda item 12 November 1923, WCG Archives University of Hull.
59 *Women's Co-operative Guild Annual Report*, 1927. WCG Archives University of Hull.
60 Scott, *Feminism and the Politics of Working Women*, pp.127–50.
61 Eleanor Barton stood unsuccessfully as a parliamentary candidate at Birmingham Kings Barton in 1922 and 1923. She failed to be adopted by any other constituency.
62 I am indebted to Mervyn Wilson, Principal and Chief Executive of the Co-operative College for drawing my attention to the significance of Mrs Ganley.
63 Profile of Caroline Ganley in *Women's Outlook*, October 1920, p.218; *Women's Outlook*, March 1931, p.289.
64 Ganley, Caroline, unpublished papers. Bishopsgate Institute. Ref: Box Caroline Ganley1/1/.
65 Scott, *Feminism and the Politics of Working Women*, p.6.

66 Scott, *Feminism and the Politics of Working Women*, p.172.
67 The determined Rose Adair, WCG, did manage to raise a question on birth control at the 1923 Labour Party Women's Conference.
68 *Liberal Policy for Women*, 1929, pp.14–15.
69 *Liberal Women's News*, April 1927.
70 *Liberal Women's News*, May 1927.
71 *Liverpool Daily Courier*, 17 October 1924.
72 *Time and Tide*, 30 April 1926.
73 *Liberal Woman*, August 1927.
74 Manchester Liberal Central Committee Minutes, 20 November 1926. Manchester Archives and Local Studies. Ref: 283/8/1/1.
75 Ward, Linda, 'The right to choose.' PhD thesis, University of Bristol, 1981, p.76.
76 Full coverage of the debate was in *Liberal Women's News*, May 1927. In preparation for the debate there was an article on 'Birth control information and the state' in the April edition of *Liberal Women's News*.
77 Goronwy-Roberts, *A Woman of Vision*, pp.77–104.
78 Labour Party Conference Report 1925, p.295.
79 Charlton WCG Minutes. 6 January 1926, 20 January 1926, 14 April 1926. Bishopsgate Institute Ref: WCG/8/17/1.
80 Hunslett Carr Women's Meeting Minutes, 15 May 1930. Ref: LP87.
81 Huddersfield Labour Party Archives. Ref: HELP/22.
82 Bilston Labour Party Women's Section Minutes 1921–31. Wolverhampton Archives and Local Studies, Ref: BD/PP/6/3/3.
83 Manley Park WCG Minutes, 2 December 1926; Nelson WCG Minutes, 4 March 1927.
84 *Manchester and Salford Co-operative Herald*, June 1927 reported Mary Stocks as giving a talk to Downing Street WCG on birth control. *Manchester and Salford Co-operative Herald*, January 1930, announced that she had given a further talk to Downing Street WCG.
85 Anson Road WCG Minutes, 1930.
86 Gorton Labour Party Women's Section Minutes, 3 March 1931.
87 Hunt, C.J., 'Alice Arnold of Coventry.' PhD thesis, University of Coventry, 2003.
88 *Women's Outlook*, 27 September 1924, p.456.
89 *Birth Control News*, January 1929.
90 Manchester City Council Minutes of the Maternity and Child Welfare Sub-Committee, 1930.
91 Report of the Conference on the Giving of Birth Control Information by Local Authorities, 4 April 1930.
92 Frankenburg, Charis, *Not Old, Madam, VINTAGE!* (Suffolk, 1975) p.140.
93 Report of the Conference on the Giving of Birth Control Information by Local Authorities, 4 April 1930.

94 Rowbotham, Sheila, *Hidden from History* (London, 1974) p.35.
95 Hoggart, Lesley, *Feminist Campaigns for Birth Control* (Lampeter, 2003) p.104.

Chapter 8

1 *Birth Control News* 8/6 (September 1930) p.72; *Birth Control News* 8/9 (January 1931), p.115.
2 Memorandum MCW/153, Ministry of Health.
3 Leathard, Audrey, *The Fight for Family Panning* (Basingstoke, 1980) p.53.
4 Circular 1408, Ministry of Health. Neville Chamberlain's political task was made easier by the final report in 1932 of the Committee on Maternal Mortality, which recommended that women suffering from diseases such as tuberculosis should not become pregnant and contraceptive methods should be made available to them.
5 Fryer, Peter, *The Birth Controllers* (London, 1965) p.291.
6 Leathard, *The Fight for Family Panning*, pp.43 and 217.
7 Soloway, Richard, *Birth Control and the Population Question* (North Carolina, 1982) pp.304–18.
8 Ward, Linda, 'The right to choose.' PhD thesis, University of Bristol, 1981, p.331.
9 Dora Russell Papers, Box 406, IISH, Amsterdam.
10 *New Generation*, August 1930. Ernest Thurtle was the local MP and his wife Dorothy a local councillor. Both were prominent birth control activists.
11 *Birth Control News*, March 1931, p.165.
12 Unpublished letter, Wellcome Library for the History and Understanding of Medicine (SA/FPA/A11/26).
13 Unpublished letter from Mrs Pyke, Secretary of the National Birth Control Council to Mary Stocks, 6 February 1931. Wellcome Library for the History and Understanding of Medicine (SA/FPA/A11/26).
14 Gorton Labour Party Women's Section Minutes, 3 March 1931.
15 Florence, Lella Secor, *Progress Report on Birth Control* (London, 1956) p.26.
16 Thane, Pat, 'Visions of gender' in Bock, G. and Thane, P., *Maternity and Gender Politics* (London, 1991) p.137.
17 Blumberg, Flora, 'Only 8 Failures in 1,212 cases, Manchester and Salford Mothers' Clinic,' 1931, p.225.
18 Leathard, *The Fight for Family Panning*, p.53.
19 Margaret Sanger Papers, Box 60, File 1, Smith College, MA.
20 NBCC, 'Aims', no date.

21 Leathard, *The Fight for Family Panning*, p.216.
22 Huxley, Gervase, *Lady Denman* (London, 1961) p.102.
23 Leathard, *The Fight for Family Panning*, p.53.
24 Frida Laski interviewed by Audrey Leathard, 12 November 1973.
25 Leathard, *The Fight for Family Panning*, p.51.
26 Court, Audrey and Walton, Cynthia, *Birmingham Made a Difference* (Birmingham, 2001) pp.11–17.
27 Dilys Dean was studying for a Social Science degree at the University of Manchester and undertook a placement at the MSMC. She subsequently sat on its Executive.
28 Florence, *Progress Report on Birth Control*, p.20.
29 Gordon, Linda, *Woman's Body, Woman's Rights* (London, 1977) p.300.
30 Margaret Sanger Papers, Box 60, File 1, Smith College, MA.
31 Tarrow, Sidney, 'The political structuring of social movements,' in McAdam, Douglas, McCarthy, John D. and Zald, Mayer N. (eds), *Comparative Perspectives on Social Movements* (Cambridge, 2005) pp.41–61.
32 Debenham, Clare, 'Mrs Elsie Plant: suffragette, socialist, birth control activist.' *Women's History Review* 19/1 (2010) pp.145–58.
33 Birmingham City Archives, 24 April 1952; Florence, Barbara Moench, *Lella Secor Florence* (New York, 1978).
34 Wilson, Dr Libby, *Sex on the Rates* (Argyll, 2004) p.79.
35 Quoted in Leathard, *The Fight for Family Panning*, p.201.
36 Castle, Barbara, *Fighting All the Way* (London, 1993) p.478.
37 Quoted in Pugh, Martin, *Speak for Britain* (London, 2010) p.312.
38 Castle, Barbara, *The Castle Diaries 1964–1970* (London, 1984).
39 Castle, Barbara, *Sylvia and Christabel Pankhurst* (London, 1987).
40 Leathard, *The Fight for Family Panning*, p.161.
41 Rowley, J.J., 'Reminiscences of Alice Onions,' *West Midland Studies* 16 (1983), pp.30–3.
42 Barker, Colin, 'Crises and turning point in revolutionary development' in Barker, Colin and Tyldesley, Mike, *Alternative Futures and Popular Protest* (Manchester, 2006) p.1.
43 Spender, Dale, *There's Always Been a Women's Movement This Century* (London, 1983).

Bibliography

Unpublished theses

Beaumont, Caitriona. 'Women and Citizenship: A Study of Non-Feminist Women's Societies and the Women's Movement in England, 1928-1950.' PhD thesis, Warwick University, 1996.

Broadley, Maurice. 'The Episcopate of Thomas Henshaw, Bishop of Salford 1925-38.' MPhil thesis, University of Manchester, 1998.

Bruley, Sue. 'Socialism and Feminism in the Communist Party of Great Britain, 1920-1939.' PhD thesis, London School of Economics, 1980.

Doherty, Jenny 'The Birth Control Campaign within the Labour Party 1924-1934.' MA thesis, Manchester Metropolitan University, 1997.

Emanuel, Judith. 'The Politics of Maternity in Manchester 1919-1939. A Study from within a Continuing Campaign.' MSc thesis, University of Manchester, 1982.

Fielding, Stephen. 'The Irish Catholics of Manchester and Salford: Aspects of their Religious History 1890-1939.' PhD thesis, University of Warwick, 1988.

Fisher, Kate. 'An Oral History of Birth Control Practice, c.1925-1950: A Study of Oxford and South Wales.' DPhil thesis, University of Oxford, 1997.

Henry, John F. 'Labour and the Proletarian City: A Study of Politics in Salford 1919-1932.' PhD thesis, Manchester Metropolitan University, 2005.

Howes, J. '"No party, no sect, no politics." The National Council of Women and the National Citizens' Association with particular reference to Cambridge and Manchester in the inter war years.' PhD thesis, Anglia Polytechnic, 2003.

Hunt, C.J. 'Alice Arnold of Coventry: Trade Unionism and Municipal Politics 1919-1939.' PhD thesis, University of Coventry, 2003.

Hunt, Karen. 'Equivocal Feminists. The Social Democratic Federation and the Women Question. 1884-1911.' PhD thesis, University of Manchester, 1988.

Innes, Sue. 'Love and Work: Feminism, Family and Ideas of Equality and Citizenship.' PhD thesis, University of Edinburgh, 1998.

Jones, E.L. 'Abortion in England 1861-1967.' PhD thesis, Royal Holloway College, University of London, 2007.

Kenner, C. 'The Politics of Married Working Class Women's Care.' MPhil thesis, University of Sussex, 1975.

Maini, G.K. 'The Role of Women on Manchester City Council 1907–1945.' M.Phil thesis, University of Manchester, 1991.

McHugh, D. 'A "Mass" Party frustrated? The Development of the Labour Party in Manchester, 1918–1931.' PhD thesis, University of Salford, 2001.

Smith, J. 'The Manchester and Salford Women Citizens' Association: A study of women's citizenship 1913–1948.' PhD thesis, Manchester Metropolitan University, 2007.

Walker, Caroline E. 'Making birth control respectable: the Society for Constructive Birth Control and Racial Progress and the American Birth Control League in comparative perspective, 1921–1938.' PhD thesis, University of Bristol, 2007.

Walker, Linda. 'The Women's Movement in England in the late nineteenth and early twentieth century.' PhD thesis, University of Manchester, 1984.

Ward, Linda. 'The Right to Choose: A Study of Women's Fight for Birth Control Provisions.' PhD thesis, University of Bristol, 1981.

Williams, G.D. 'Women in Public Life in Liverpool between the Wars.' PhD thesis, University of Liverpool, 2000.

Unpublished papers

Barker, David, 'Fostering a eugenic consciousness; the eugenic programme.' University of Salford, 1980.

Dean, Dilys. 'Memoirs concerning the birth control clinic in Manchester and Salford from its foundation.' 1961.

Debenham, Clare. 'The origins and development of the birth control movement in Manchester and Salford 1917–1934: a case study in pressure group politics.' 2006.

Government and official reports published in the 1920s to 1940s

National publications

Birkett, Sir N. *Report of the Inter-Departmental Committee on Abortion.* London: Ministry of Health, Home Office. HMSO, 1937.

Campbell, Janet M. *Notes on the Arrangements for Teaching Obstetrics and Gynaecology in Medical Schools,* no 15 (London, 1923).

— *The Training of Midwives. Reports on Public Health and Medical Subjects,* no 21. London: Ministry of Health, 1923.

— *Maternal Mortality. Reports on Public Health and Medical Subjects,* no 25. London: Ministry of Health, 1924.

BIBLIOGRAPHY

— *The Protection of Motherhood. Reports on Public Health and Medical Subjects,* no 27. London: Ministry of Health, 1927.
Lewis-Fanning, E. *Family Limitation and its Influence on Fertility during the Past Fifty Years,* vol. 1. London: HMSO, 1949.
MacNalty, Arthur S. *Report on the Investigation into Maternal Mortality.* London: HMSO, 1937.
Ministry of Health. *Circular 1208 Birth Control.* London: Ministry of Health, 1931.
Ministry of Health. *Memo 153/ M.C.W. Birth Control.* London: Ministry of Health, 1930.
Ministry of Health. Society for Birth Control Clinics. Correspondence. MH 61/10, 1931.
Parliamentary Debates, Proceedings of the House of Commons 1922–1931, vol. 157–255.
Parliamentary Debates, Proceedings of the House of Lords 1926, vol. 63, 108.
Russell, Dr V. *Evidence to Inter-Departmental Committee on Abortion, Representing Joint Council Midwifery, 'Fifty Cases of Abortion in Kensington.'* MH71 23. London: HMSO.

Local publications

Manchester City Council Minutes 1925–1935.
Manchester City Council Minutes of Maternity and Child Welfare Sub-Committee 1925–1935.
Manchester City Council Minutes of the Public Health Sub-Committee 1925–1935.
Manchester City Council Municipal Year Book 1925–1935.
Ministry of Health, Barrow-in-Furness C.B. Correspondence re: birth control clinics. MH52/221.
Ministry of Health, Birmingham Correspondence re: birth control clinics. MH52/230.
Ministry of Health, Manchester C.B. Correspondence re: birth control clinics. MH52/325.

Reports of birth control debates and conferences

National Council of Women. *Report on the Conference Held in Manchester 14–18 October 1926.* Privately Published, 1926.
Pierpoint, R. *Report of the Fifth International neo-Malthusian and Birth Control Congress.* Privately published, 1922.
Public Health Authorities. *Report of the Conference on the Giving of Information on Birth Control by Public Health Authorities on 4 April 1930, Central Hall, Westminster.* London: Birth Control Information Centre.

Sanger, Margaret. *The Practice of Contraception. An International Survey and Symposium held in Zurich in September 1930*. Baltimore: Williams and Wilkie, 1931.

Society for Constructive Birth Control. *Speeches and Impressions on Constructive Birth Control, Report of the Meeting Held on July 1921 in Queen's Hall, London*, London: Society for Constructive Birth Control, 1921.

Stone, Hannah (ed.) *Society for the Provision of Birth Control Clinics and Public Services. Birth Control and the Public Services Conference on 5 June 1935*.

Archives and manuscript collections

Bishopsgate Institute, London Archives of Caroline Ganley (GANLEY 1916-66). Minutes of Women's Co-operative Guilds (WCG/8).

British Library, London: Marie C. Stopes Papers (BL.Add.MSS.5859-58642).

British Library Newspaper Collection, Archive of local papers of the 1920s and 1930s including *East London Advertiser*.

British Library of Political and Economic Science, London. Birth control ephemera, Collis collection (GB 097 COLL MISC0435).

International Institute of Social History, Amsterdam, Dora Russell Papers.

John Rylands University of Manchester Library. Marie Stopes and the Birth Control Collection (JRUL Deansgate). University of Manchester Museum: Marie Stopes' paleobotany collection.

Lambeth Palace Archives, London. Archbishop Temple Papers, vol. 35.

London Metropolitan Archives: Birth control clinics at general hospitals (LCC/PH/HOSP/01/027). Papers of National Council of Women (ACC/3613).

Manchester Archive and Local Studies: Manchester Labour Party Women (MALS M449). Manchester Liberal Party Women (MALS M283/8/1/1).

Mass Observation Archive, University of Sussex: Family Planning, 1944-9 (TC3).

National Co-operative Archive, Manchester: Archive material relating to individual WCGs and a nearly complete set of *Women's Outlook*.

National Museum of Labour History, Manchester. Archives of Women's Labour League; Labour Party Chief Women's Officer, Ellen Wilkinson.

Salford Catholic Diocesan Archive, Papers of Bishop Henshaw.

Sophia Smith Collection, Smith College, USA, Margaret Sanger Papers.

University of Hull, Women's Co-operative Guild (GB0050 DCW/161/56-57).

University of Reading, Archive of Viscountess Nancy Astor Papers (MS1416/1/1).

Wellcome Library for the History and Understanding of Medicine, London: Archives of Family Planning Association (A&M: SA/FPA). Eugenic Society Archive (closed collection).

Women's Library, London Metropolitan University, Printed collection pamphlet collection (PC/06).

BIBLIOGRAPHY

Working Class Movement Library, Salford (WCML), Minute book of Nelson Labour Party Women's Section (ORG/NECOLP/1/5/ and other unclassified minute books.

Reports from the Society for the Provision of Birth Control Clinics

Birmingham Women's Welfare Centre Annual Reports 1927–1928, 1928–1929, 1929–1930, 1930–1931, 1931–1932, 1932–1933, 1933–1934. Birmingham City Archives.
Cambridge Women's Welfare Association Annual Report, 1926–1927. Cambridge City Archives.
Cambridge Women's Welfare Association Prospectus. Cambridge City Archives.
Glasgow Women's Welfare and Advisory Clinic – Reply to Margaret Sanger 1927. Margaret Sanger Papers, Smith College, Sophia Smith Collection, USA.
Glasgow Women's Welfare Advisory Clinic Annual Report 1934–1935, Mitchell Library, Glasgow Caledonian University.
Glasgow Women's Welfare Advisory Clinic Annual Report, 1934–35. Margaret Sanger Papers, Smith College, Sophia Smith Collection, USA.
Liverpool Mothers' Welfare Clinic, Annual Reports, 1926–1927, 1927–1928, 1928–1929, 1930–1931, 1932–1933, 1936. Liverpool City Archives (Acc.5429).
Manchester and District Mothers' Clinic Annual Reports, 1926–1927, 1927–1928, 1928–1929, 1929–1930. Manchester Local Studies; Wellcome Library A&M: SA/ FPA.
Manchester and District Mothers' Clinic (1931) 'Only 8 Failures in 1,212 Cases,' 1931. Wellcome Library A&M: SA/FPA.
Manchester, Salford and District Family Planning Clinic, Non-Persistent Patient 1954–1955. Wellcome Library A&M: SA/FPA.
Oxford Family Welfare Association, Annual Reports, 1926–1927. Wellcome Library A&M: SA/FPA.
North Kensington Women's Welfare Centre Annual Reports, 1924–1925, 1925–1926, 1926–1927, 1927–1928, 1928–1929. Wellcome Library A&M: SA/FPA.
Society for the Provision of Birth Control Clinics Annual Reports 1924–1925, 1925–1926, 1928–1929, 1933–1934. Wellcome Library for the History and Understanding of Medicine, A&M: SA/FPA.
Walworth Women's Welfare Centre Annual Reports, 1924, 1928–9, 1933. Wellcome Library A&M/SA/FPA.
Wolverhampton Women's Welfare Centre Annual Report, 1925–1926. Wolverhampton Archives and Local Studies.
Workers Birth Control Group Objectives (1927) International Institute for Social History, Amsterdam.

Reports of political parties and women's organisations
National

Labour Party Report on the Twenty Fifth Annual Conference, Liverpool, 1925. London: Labour Party.
Labour Party Report on the Twenty Sixth Annual Conference Margate, 1926. London: Labour Party.
Labour Party Report on the Twenty Seventh Annual Conference Blackpool, 1927. London: Labour Party.
Labour Women. Report on the Annual Conferences 1923-1925 Labour Woman, London: Labour Party.
Labour Women. Report on the Seventh Annual Conference, Birmingham, 1926. London: Labour Party.
Labour Women. Report on the Eighth Annual Conference, Huddersfield, 1927. London: Labour Party.
Labour Women. Report on the Ninth Annual Conference, Portsmouth, 1928. London: Labour Party.
Labour Women. Report on the Tenth Annual Conference, London, 1929. London: Labour Party.
Labour Women, Report on the Eleventh Annual Conference, London, 1930. London: Labour Party.
Liberal Women, Annual Conference Reports 1925-1935, London.
Trade Union Congress (1920-1932) Annual Conference Reports 1920-1932. Museum of Labour History, Manchester.
Women's Co-operative Guild (1925-35) Annual Conference Reports. University of Hull GB0050 DCW/161/56-57.

Local

Bilston Labour Party Women's Section Minutes 1921-1931. Wolverhampton Archives and Local Studies, BD/PP/6/1/3/3.
Brightside and Neepsend Women's Liberal Association Minutes 1924-1932. Sheffield Archives, MD7227/1.
Cambridge and County Women's Liberal Association Minutes 1913-1931. Cambridgeshire Archives and Local Studies, 507/Q1-4.
Charlton WCG Minutes 1921-1931. Bishopsgate Institute, London. WCG/8/17/1.
Chinley, Bugsworth and Brownside Women's Liberal Association Minutes 1926-1931. Stockport Local Archives, D1562/1.
Earlsfield WCG Minutes 1925-1927. Bishopsgate Institute, WCG/8/33/1.
East Dorset Union of Women's Liberal Associations Minutes 1925-1931. University of Bristol DM1193/1/2.
Gorton Labour Party Women's Section Minutes 1929-1934. Manchester Archive and Local Studies M450.

BIBLIOGRAPHY

High Wycombe WCG Minutes 1921-1926, Bishopsgate Institute, WCG/8/47/2.
Huddersfield Labour Party Women's Section Minutes 1927. Huddersfield University Library, HLP1/22.
Kettering WCG Minutes 1923-1925, 1925-1927. Bishopsgate Institute, WCG/8/56/10, WCG/8/56/11.
Manchester Labour Party Women's Advisory Council Minutes 1928-1935. Manchester Archives and Local Studies, MALS M449.
Manchester Liberal Women's Central Council Minutes 1924-1935. Manchester Archives and Local Studies, MALS M283/8/1/1.
Manley Park, Manchester, WCG Minutes 1926-1927. Working Class Movement Library, Salford, Box Z, 13/12.
Nelson and Colne Labour Party Women's Section Minutes 1927-1931. WCML Box Z.
New Mills WCG Minutes 1920-1929. WCML, Box Z13/11.
Norbury WCG Minutes 1923-1925. Bishopsgate Institute, WCG/8/68/1.
Oakfield WCG Minutes 1920-1929. WCM, Box Z13/10.
Pirbright WCG Minutes 1925-1928. Bishopsgate Institute, WCG/8/74/1.
Porthmadog Women's Liberal Association Minutes 1928, Gwynedd Archives, XM10976/3/2/1.
Ramsgate WCG Minutes 1921-1924, 1924-1928, Bishopsgate Institute, WCG/8/77/7,WCG/8/77/8.
Rochdale Women's Liberal Association Minutes 1917-1926 s, Touchstone Rochdale Archives Ref: 3/2/2.
Stockport Labour Party Women's Section and Trades Council Minutes 1927. Stockport Local Heritage Library, B/NN/2/6.
Women's Liberal Federation Annual Reports 1927-1935, University of Bristol DM/193/4/1.
York Labour Party Women's Section Minutes 1920-5, 1927-33. York City Archives, Ac.196.31.

Relevant newspapers and periodicals, 1921-35

Birmingham Post
Birth Control News
Birth Control Review
British Medical Journal
Cambridge Daily News
Catholic Herald
Co-operative News, Woman's Corner
City Reporter, Salford
Daily Dispatch
Daily Herald

East London Advertiser
Eugenics Review
Evening Chronicle
Family Planning
Illustrated London News
Jewish Chronicle
Labour Leader
Labour Woman
Liberal Women's News
Manchester Evening News
Manchester Guardian
Manchester and Salford Co-operative Herald
New Generation
Northern Voice
One Vote
Press and Journal, Aberdeen
Stockport Chronicle
Sunday Sun
The Lancet
The Practitioner
The Times
Woman's Citizen
Woman's Citizen, Manchester
Woman's Leader
Women's Outlook
Woman's Own

Collections of interviews

Interviews by Clare Debenham: Florence Travis, 8.2.1978; Elsie Plant, 10.5.1978; Mrs Critchlow, 2.7.1978; Mrs Burke, 1.6.1979; Aunt Polly, 30.6.1979; Sister Beatrice Sandys, 28.3.2003; Joan Dennison, 25.05.2003; Roger F., 1.10.2003; Nurse Alice Farnworth, 27.2.2003; Mrs Margaret Gaddiam, 8.3.2005; Esther Dean, 1.4.2004; Ursula Kennedy, nee Frankenburg, 2.7.2004; Ann Patterson nee Stocks, 4.12.2004; Ruth Rapport, cousin of Charis, 12.6.2005; Harry Stopes-Roe, son; Mary Stopes-Roe, daughter-in-law; Cathy Stopes-Roe, grand-daughter, 17.6.2005; Father David Lannon, 5.5.2005; Dr Alison Mack, 3.3.2006; Alan Paton, 25.05.2006; Dr Muriel Bradshaw, 14.6.2006; Cynthia Walton, 20.7.2006.

Professor Brian Harrison interviewed birth controllers including Mary Stocks and Charis Frankenburg in the 1980s. The Women's Library, London holds the newly digitalised tapes of interviews in the Brian Harrison Collection.

BIBLIOGRAPHY

Academics from Manchester Studies Unit at Manchester Polytechnic in the 1980s interviewed politically active women in the inter-war years including Mrs Elsie Plant, Mrs Bessie Wild, Mrs Mary Williams, Alderman Nellie Beer Stalybridge Library, Cheshire hold transcripts of interviews.

Professor Elizabeth Roberts and associates carried out interviews in the 1970s with old women about their family lives. North West Regional Studies, University of Central Lancashire holds transcripts of these interviews.

Books and articles

Adams, M.B. (ed.), *The Wellborn Science* (Oxford, 1990).
Alberti, Johanna, *Beyond Suffrage. Feminists in War and Peace 1918-1928* (Basingstoke, 1989).
— 'Elizabeth Haldane as a women's suffrage survivor in the 1920s and 1930s'. *Women's Studies International Forum*, 1990, vol.13, pp.117-25.
— 'Keeping the candle burning: some British feminists between two wars' in Dale, C. and Nolan, M., *Suffrage and Beyond* (New York, 1994) pp.295-312.
— 'The turn of the tide: sexuality and politics, 1928-31.' *Women's History Review* 3/2 (1994) pp.169-90.
— *Eleanor Rathbone* (London, 1996).
Aldred, Gary, *No Traitor's Gate* (Glasgow, 1963).
Allen, Ann T., 'German radical feminism and eugenics.' *German Studies Review* 10/1 (1988), pp.31-56.
— 'Feminism and eugenics in Britain and Germany: a comparative perspective.' *German Studies Review* 36 (2000) pp.477-505.
Anderson, Michael, *Family Structure in Nineteenth Century Lancashire* (Cambridge, 1971).
— 'Fertility decline in Scotland, England, Wales and Ireland.' *Population Studies*, 1998.
Andrews, Maggie, *The Acceptable Face of Feminism. The Women's Institute as a Social Movement* (London, 1997).
Atholl, Katherine, Duchess of, *Women and Politics* (London, 1931).
Banks, Joseph A., *Prosperity and Parenthood – A Study of Family Planning among the Victorian Middle Classes* (London, 1954).
— *The Sociology of Social Movements* (London, 1972).
— *Victorian Values. Secularism and the Size of Families* (London, 1981).
Banks, Joseph A. and Banks, Olive, *Feminism and Family Planning in Victorian England* (Liverpool, 1965).
Banks, Olive, *Faces of Feminism* (Oxford, 1981).
— *The Biographical Dictionary of British Feminists*, vol.1: *1800-1930* (Hemel Hempstead, 1985).

— *Becoming a Feminist. The Social Origins of 'First Wave' Feminism* (Georgia, 1986).
— *The Biographical Dictionary of British Feminists*, vol. 2: *A Supplement 1900-1945* (Hemel Hempstead, 1990).
— *The Politics of British Feminism in the Twentieth Century* (Lampeter, 1993).
— 'Some reflections on gender, sociology and women's history.' *Women's History Review* 8/3 (1999).
Barker, Diane and Allen, Sheila, *Sexual Divisions and Society. Process and Change* (London, 1976).
Barnett (married name Frankenburg) Charis U., *Commonsense in the Nursery* (London, 1922).
Barrow, M., *Women 1870-1928. A Guide to Printed and Archival Sources* (New York, 1981).
Beaumont, Caitriona, 'Citizens not feminists: the boundary negotiated between citizenship and feminism by mainstream women's organisations, 1929-39.' *Women's History Review* 9/2 (2000), pp.411-29.
Beddoe, Deidre, *Women's History* (London, 1983).
Bedford, J., 'Margaret Ashton: Manchester's First Lady.' *Manchester Regional History Review* 3 (1998) pp.3-17.
Benn, J. Miriam, *Predicaments of Love* (London, 1992).
Berry, Paul and Bishop, Alan, *Testament of a Generation* (London, 1985).
Besant, Annie, *The Law of Population. Its Consequences and Its Bearing upon Human Conduct and Morals* (London, 1897).
Bishops of Scotland, *A Grave Moral Evil* (Oxford, 1928).
Blacker, Charles P., *Birth Control of the State* (London, 1926).
Bland, Lucy, *Banishing the Beast. English Feminism and Sexual Morality, 1885-1914* (London, 1995).
Blaszak, Barbara, *The Matriarchs of England's Co-operative Movement. A Study in Gender Politics and Female Leadership* (Connecticut, 2000).
de Blecourt, Willem, 'Cultures of abortion in the Hague in the early twentieth century' in Elder, F., Hall, L. and Hekma, G. (ed.) *Sexual Cultures in Europe - Themes in Sexuality* (Manchester, 1999) pp.195-212.
Blond, Anthony, *Jew Made in England* (London, 2004).
Blumberg, Flora, 'The Manchester and Salford and District Mothers' Clinic' in Sanger and Stone, H. (ed.) *The Practice of Contraception. International Symposium* (Baltimore, 1931).
Bolt, Christine, *The Women's Movements in the United States and Britain from the 1790s to the 1920s* (Hemel Hempstead, 1993).
Bolton, C.A., *Salford Diocese and its Catholic Priests* (Manchester, 1950).
Bondfield, Margaret, *A Life's Work* (London, 1948).
Bookbinder, Philip, *Simon Marks. Retail Revolutionary* (London, George Weidenfeld & Nicolson, 1993).

BIBLIOGRAPHY

Bourke, Janna, *Working Class Cultures in Britain 1890-1960. Gender, Class Ethnicity* (London, 1994).

Box, Muriel, *The Trial of Marie Stopes*. Preface by Mary Stocks (New York, 1967).

Bradshaw, Dr Muriel, *Spaghetti Junction Doctor* (Devon: private publication, 1995).

Branca, Patricia, *Silent Sisterhood. Middle Class Women in the Victorian Home* (London, 1975 reprint 1977).

— *Women in Europe since 1750* (London, 1978).

Branson, Noreen, *Britain in the Nineteen Twenties* (London, 1975).

Branson, Noreen and Heinemann, M., *Britain in the Nineteen Thirties* (London, 1971).

Breitenbach, Esther and Thane, Pat (ed.), *Women and Citizenship in Britain and Ireland in the Twentieth Century* (London, 2010).

Briant, Keith, *Marie Stopes* (London, 1962).

Bristol Women's Studies Group, *Half the Sky* (London, 1979).

British Medical Journal, 'Report of Meeting on Abortion in Liverpool.' 3 April 1937.

Brooke, Pamela, *Women at Westminster*, Preface by Mary Stocks (London, 1967).

Brookes, Barbara, 'Women and reproduction, 1860-1919' in Lewis, J. (ed.) *Labour and Love. Women's Experience of Home and Family, 1850-1940* (Oxford, 1986), pp.149-74.

— *Abortion in England 1900-1967* (London, 1988).

— *Feminist Perspectives on the Body* (London, 1999).

Brooks, J., *Presentation on Lady Sanitary Inspectors to the Women and History Annual Conference* (Oxford, 2009).

Brown, I., 'Who were the Eugenicists? A study of an early twentieth century pressure group.' *History of Education* 17/4 (1988), pp.295-307.

Browne, F.W. Stella, *Abortion* (London, 1935).

Bryson, Valerie, *Feminist Debates. Issues of Theory and Political Practice* (London, 1999).

— *Feminist Political Theory* (London, 2003).

Caine, Barbara, *English Feminism 1780-1980* (Oxford, 1994).

— 'Feminist biography and feminist history.' *Women's History Review* 3/2 (1994) pp.247-59.

Campbell, Flann, 'Birth control and Christian churches.' *Population Studies* 14/2 (1960), pp.131-41.

Canning, Audrey, *The Biographic Dictionary of Scottish Women* (Edinburgh, 2008).

Carr-Saunders, Alexander M., *Eugenics* (London, 1926).

Carr-Saunders, Alexander M. and Jones, D.C., *A Survey of the Social Structure of England and Wales* (Oxford, 1927).

Cartwright, Ann, *How Many Children?* (London, 1977).
Castle, Barbara, *Sylvia and Christabel Pankhurst* (London, 1987).
— *Fighting All the Way* (London, 1993).
Charles, Edith, *The Practice of Birth Control* (London, 1932).
— *The Twilight of Parenthood* (London, 1934).
Charles, Nicki, *Feminism, the State and Social Policy* (Basingstoke, 2000).
Chesser, Dr Eustace, *Love without Fear* (London, 1940).
Chesterton, Gilbert Keith, *Eugenics and Other Evils*. Forward and extra material by Michael Parry (Seattle, 1922 reprint 2000).
Chinn, Carl, *They Worked All Their Lives. Women of the Urban Poor in England, 1880-1939* (Manchester, 1988).
Cohen, Deborah A., 'Private lives in public spaces: Marie Stopes, the Mothers' Clinic and contraception.' *History Workshop*, 1993, no 35, pp.95-116.
— 'Marie Stopes and the mothers' clinic' in Peel, R.A. (ed.) *Marie Stopes and the English Birth Control Movement* (Galton Institute, 1997) pp.77-94.
Cohen, Susan, *Rescue the Perishing. Eleanor Rathbone and the Refugees* (London, 2010).
Cook, Hera, *The Long Sexual Revolution. English Women Sex and Contraception, 1800-1975* (Oxford, 2004).
Cooke, R.G., 'An analysis of 350 cases of abortion.' *British Medical Journal*, 14 April 1938.
Cott, Nancy F., *The Grounding of Modern Feminism* (New England, 1987).
— 'Comment on Karen Offen's "Defining Feminism: A Comparative Historical Approach"', *Signs: Journal of Women in Culture and Society* 15/1 (1999), pp.203-5.
Court, Audrey and Walton, Cynthia, *Birmingham Made a Difference. The Birmingham Women's Welfare Centre 1926-1991* (Birmingham, 2001).
Cowman, Krista, *'Mrs. Brown is a Man and a Brother!'* (Liverpool, 2004).
— *Women of the Right Spirit. Paid Organisers of the Women's Social and Political Union, 1904-1914* (Manchester, 2007).
Crawford, Elizabeth, *The Women's Suffrage Movement: A Reference Guide* (London, 1999).
— *The Women's Suffrage Movement in England and Wales* (London, 2006).
Curthoys, Ann, 'Eugenics, feminism and birth control: the case of Marion Piddington.' *Hecate* 15/1 (1989) pp.73-89.
Daily Telegraph. 'Prosecutions for illegal abortions.' 22 July 1933.
Dale, P. and Fisher, Kate, 'Contrasting municipal responses to the provision of birth control services in Halifax and Exeter before 1948.' *Social History of Medicine* 23/3 (2010), pp.567-85.
Daley, Caroline and Nolan, Melanie, *Suffrage and Beyond. International Feminist Perspectives* (New York, 1994).
Daniels, E.S., *The Children of Desire. A Book on the Practical Knowledge of Family Limitation* (London, 1925).

Davey, Clare, 'Birth control in Britain during the inter-war years.' *Journal of Family History* 13/3 (1988), pp.329-45.
Davidoff, Leonore, Doolittle, Megan, Fink, Janet and Holden, Katherine, *Worlds Between. Historical Perspectives on Gender and Class* (London, 1995).
Davies, Andrew, *Leisure, Gender and Poverty. Working Class Culture in Salford and Manchester 1900-1939* (Milton Keynes, 1992).
Davies, Andrew and Fielding, A., *Workers Worlds, Cultures and Communities in Manchester and Salford 1990-1939* (Manchester, 1992).
Davies, Margaret L. (ed.), *Maternity - Letters from Working Women. Collected by the Women's Co-operative Guild* (London, 1915 reprint 1978).
— (ed.), *Life As We Have Known It* (London, 1931 reprint 1977). The 1931 edition has an introduction by Virginia Woolf and in addition the reprint has a preface by Anna Davin.
Davies, Sam, *Liverpool Labour. Social and Political Influences on the Development of the Labour Party in Liverpool 1900-1939* (Keele, 1996).
Davin, Anna, 'Imperialism and motherhood.' *History Workshop Journal* 5/1 (1978), pp.9-65.
— *Women, Race and Class* (London, 1982).
Davis, M., *Sylvia Pankhurst. A Life in Radical Politics* (London, 1999).
Dawson, Lord Bernard, *Love, Marriage, Birth Control* (London, 1921).
Debenham, Clare, 'Mrs Elsie Plant: suffragette, socialist and birth control activist.' *Women's History Review* 19/1 (2010), pp.145-58.
Delmar, Rosalind, 'What is feminism?' in Mitchell, J. and Oakley, A. (eds) *What is Feminism?* (Oxford, 1986).
Dickens, Emma, *Immaculate Contraception. The Extraordinary Story of Birth Control* (London, 2000).
Doughan, David, *Birth Control – The Equal Knowledge Campaign 1922-1931* (London, Fawcett Papers, 1981).
Douglas, Margie, 'Women, God and birth control: the first hospital birth control clinic, Abertillery, 1925.' *Llafur* 6 (1995) pp.110-22.
Dowse, R.E. and Peel, John, 'The politics of birth control.' *Political Studies* 13/2 (1965), pp.178-97.
Doyal, L. and Elston, M., 'Women, health and medicine' in Beeching, V. and Whitelegg, E. (eds) *Women in Britain Today* (Milton Keynes, 1986).
Draper, Elizabeth, *Birth Control in the Modern World* (Harmondsworth, 1965).
Drysdale, Charles Vickery, *Neo-Malthusianism and Eugenics* (privately printed 1912).
— *The Small Family System* (London, 1913).
Dyhouse, Carol, *Feminism and the Family in England 1880-1939* (Oxford, 1989).
— 'Glamour.' *HerStoria* 5 (2010), pp.9-12.
Eaton, Peter and Warnick, Marilyn, *Marie Stopes. A Checklist of her Writings* (London, 1977).

Edwards, B. and McCarthy, J.D., 'Resources and social movements' in Snow, D., Soule, S. and Kreisi, H., *The Blackwell Companion to Social Movements* (Oxford, 2007) pp.116-52.

Elam, M. de L., *Ellen Wilkinson. Stateswoman and Cabinet Minister, 1891-1947* (Manchester, 1991).

Elderton, Ethel M., Report on the English Birth Rate, Part 1: England North of the Humber. *Eugenics Laboratory Memoirs 19 and 20* (London, 1914).

Elderton, Ethel M. and Pearson, Karl, *The Relative Strength of Nature and Nurture* (Cambridge, 1915).

Eoff, Shirley, *Viscountess Rhondda. Equalitarian Feminist* (Ohio, 1991).

Evans, Barbara, *Freedom to Choose. The Life and Work of Dr Helena Wright* (London, 1984).

Evans, Brendan, Labourn, Keith, Lancaster, John and Haigh, Brian (eds), *Sons and Daughters of Labour* (Huddersfield, 2007).

Eyles, Leonora, *Women's Problems of Today* (London, 1926).

Ferch, J., *Birth Control* (London, 1926).

Ferree, M.M. and Mueller, C.M., 'Feminism and the women's movement' in Snow, D., Soule, S. and Kreisi, H., *The Blackwell Companion to Social Movements* (Oxford, 2004), pp.576-607.

Ferris, Paul, *The Nameless. Abortion in Britain Today* (Harmondsworth, 1966 reprint 1977).

Fielding, Michael, *Parenthood: Design or Accident. A Manual for Birth-Control.* Preface by H.G. Wells (Woking, 1947).

Finch, Janet, '"It's great to have someone to talk to." The ethics and politics of interviewing women' in Bell, C. and Roberts, H. (eds) *Social Researching. Politics, Problems, Practice* (London, 1984).

Fisher, Kate, '"Clearing up misconceptions": the campaign to set up birth control clinics in South Wales between the wars.' *Welsh Review* 18/1 (1998) pp.103-29.

— 'Women's experiences of abortion before the 1967 Act' in Lee, E. (ed.) *Abortion Law and Politics Today* (London, 1998) pp.27-42.

— '"Didn't stop to think. I just knew I didn't want another one": the culture of abortion in interwar South Wales' in Eder, F., Hall, L.A. and Hekma, G. (eds) *Sexual Cultures in Europe - Themes in Sexuality* (Manchester, 1999) pp.213-32.

— 'The delivery of birth control advice in South Wales between the Wars' in Bornat, J., Perks, R., Thompson, P., Walmsley, J. and Wilkinson, R. (eds) *Oral History Health and Welfare* (London, 2000).

— '"She was quite satisfied with the arrangements I made": gender and the conjugal dynamics of contraceptive use.' *Past and Present*, 2000, no 169, pp.161-93.

— 'Uncertain aims and tacit negotiation: birth control practices in Britain 1925-1950.' *Population and Development Review* 26/2 (2000) pp.295-307.

BIBLIOGRAPHY

— 'Contrasting cultures of contraception: birth control clinics and the working classes between the wars' in Tansey, T. (ed.) *Remedies and Healing Cultures in Britain and the Netherlands in the Twentieth Century* (Amsterdam, 2002) pp.141–57.

— *Birth Control, Sex and Marriage in Britain 1918-1960* (Oxford, 2006).

Fisher, Kate and Dale, P., 'Contrasting municipal responses to the provision of birth control services in Halifax and Exeter before 1948.' *Social History of Medicine* 23/3 (2010), pp.567–85.

Fisher, Kate and Szreter, Simon, *Sex Before the Sexual Revolution. Intimate Life in England 1918-1963* (Cambridge, 2010).

Fletcher, Sheila, *Maude Royden. A Life* (Oxford, 1989).

Florence, Barbara M., *Lella Secor. A Diary in Letters 1915-1922* (New York, 1978).

Florence, Lella S., *Birth Control on Trial* (London, 1930).

— Lella S., *Progress Report on Birth Control* (London, 1956).

Forster, Margaret, *Significant Sisters. The Grassroots of Active Feminism 1839-1939* (Middlesex, 1984 reprint 2004).

Fuller, Evelyn, 'Eugenic aspects of the Walworth Women's Welfare Centre,' *Eugenics Review* 15 (April 1923–January 1924).

Frankenburg, Charis U. (published under maiden name of Barnett), *Commonsense in the Nursery* (London, 1922).

— 'Maternity and Child Welfare.' *Woman's Leader*, 27 June 1928.

— *Latin with Laughter* (London, 1932).

— 'Manchester and Salford Mothers' Clinic – Four clinics.' *Family Planning*, 1956, p.6.

— *Not Old, Madam, VINTAGE!* (Suffolk, 1975).

Fryer, Peter, *The Birth Controllers* (London, 1965).

— *British Birth Control Ephemera 1870-1945*. Introduction by David Glass (Leicester, 1969).

Gaffin, J. and Thoms, D., *Caring and Sharing. The Centenary History of the Co-operative Women's Guild* (Manchester, 1983).

Gallagher, W.M., *A Text book of Sex Education* (London, 1919).

Galton, David, *Eugenics* (London, 2002).

Garcia, J., Kilpatrick and Richards, R. (eds), *The Politics of Maternity Care Services for Childbearing Women in Twentieth Century Britain* (Oxford, 1990).

Gates, Reginald R., *Hereditary and Eugenics* (London, 1923).

Georges, W., *Contraceptive Methods and Appliances* (London, 1932).

Giles, Judy, 'Playing hard to get: working-class women, sexuality and respectability in Britain, 1918–40.' *Women's History Review* 1/2 (1992).

— *Women, Identity and Private Life in Britain 1900-1950* (Basingstoke, 1995).

Gittins, Diane, 'Married life and birth control between wars.' *Oral History* 3/2 (1975) pp.50–70.

— 'Women's work. Family size between the wars.' *Oral History* 5/2 (1977) pp.84–100.

BIRTH CONTROL AND THE RIGHTS OF WOMEN

— *Fair Sex – Family Size and Structure 1900–1939* (London, 1982).
— *The Family in Question* (Basingstoke, 1985).
— 'Marital status, work and kinship 1850–1930' in Lewis, J. (ed.) *Labour and Love. Women's Experience of Home and Family, 1850–1940* (Oxford, 1986) pp.249–67.
Glass, David V. (ed.), *Introduction to Malthus* (London, 1953).
Glass, David V. and Blacker, C.P., *Population and Fertility* (London, 1939).
Glass, David. and Revelle, R. (eds), *Population and Social Change* (London, 1972).
Glencross, Evelyn, *For Better or For Worse* (Manchester, 1993).
Glendinning, Victoria, *Vita. The Life of V. Sackville West* (London, 1983).
Glick, Diane, *The National Council of Women. The First One Hundred Years* (privately published, 1995).
Gluck, Sherna B. and Patai, Daphne, *The Feminist Practice of Oral History* (London, 1991).
Gordon, Linda, *Woman's Body, Woman's Rights. A Social History of Birth Control in America* (London, 1977).
— *The Moral Property of Women. A History of Birth Control Politics in America* (Illinois, 2002).
Gordon, P. and Doughan, David, *Dictionary of Woman's Organisations* (Woburn, 2001).
Gorham, Deborah, 'Have we rounded seraglio point? Vera Brittain and interwar feminism' in Smith, H.L. (ed.) *British Feminism in the Twentieth Century* (Lampeter, 1990) pp.84–103.
— *Vera Brittain. A Feminist Life* (Oxford, 1996).
Goronwy-Roberts, Marian, *A Woman of Vision. A Life of Marion Phillips, MP* (Wrexham, 2000).
Grant, L., *The First Sixty Years 1895–1955. The National Council of Women* (privately published, 1955).
Graves, Pamela, *Labour Women. Women in British Working Class Politics 1918–1939* (Cambridge, 1994).
Graves, Pamela and Gruber, H., *Women and Socialism/Socialism and Women* (Oxford, 1998).
Greenwood, Victoria and Young, Jock, *Abortion in Demand* (London, 1976).
Greenwood, Walter, *Love on the Dole* (Harmondsworth, 1933 reprint 1976).
Greer, Germaine, *Sex and Destiny. The Politics of Human Fertility* (London, 1984).
Grier, J., 'Eugenics and birth control contraceptive provision in North Wales 1918–1939.' *Social History of Medicine* 11/3 (1998) pp.443–58.
Griffith, Edward F., 'Birth control; the midwives responsibility.' *Nursing Times*, 28 November 1933.
— *Modern Marriage and Birth Control* (London, 1937).
Guardian, 'One in three. Overview and case studies of women who had experienced abortions.' 12 November 2002.

BIBLIOGRAPHY

Gupta, J.K., Mires, G. and Khan, K.S., *Obstetrics and Gynaecology* (London, 2001).

Hadley, J., *Abortion. Between Freedom and Necessity* (London, 1997).

Haire, Norman, *Hygienic Methods of Family Limitation* (London, 1922).

— *Hymen or The Future of Marriage* (London, 1928).

— *Some More Medical Views on Birth Control* (London, 1928).

— *Birth-Control Methods – Contraception, Abortion, Sterilisation*. Forward by Aldous Huxley (London, 1936).

Hall, Lesley A., 'Archives of birth control in Britain.' *Journal of Society of Archivists* 16/2 (1995).

— 'Marie Stopes and her correspondents: personalising population decline in an era of demographic change' in Peel, R.A. (ed.) *Marie Stopes and the English Birth Control Movement* (Galton Institute, 1997) pp.27-48.

— *Sex, Gender and Social Change in Britain since 1880* (Basingstoke, 2000).

— '"What a lot there is still to do" – Stella Browne' in Eustance, C., Ryan, J. and Ugolini, L. (eds) *A Suffrage Reader* (Leicester, 2000) pp.190-205.

— '"A suitable job for a woman." Women doctors and birth control to the inception of the N.H.S.' in Hardy, A. and Conrad, L. (eds) *Women and Modern Medicine* (Amsterdam, 2001) pp.127-47.

— 'Women and friendship.' Paper given to Centre for Women's Studies, University of York. Lesley Hall Web Page, access 7 July 2009, www.lesleyahall.net.

— *The Life and Times of Stella Browne. Feminist and Free Spirit* (London, 2011).

Hall, Ruth, *Marie Stopes. A Biography* (London, 1977).

— (ed.), *Dear Dr Stopes. Sex in the 1920s* (London, 1978).

Hamer, E., 'Keeping their fingers on the pulse: lesbian doctors in Britain, 1890-1950' in Eder, F.X., Hall, L.A. and Hekma, G., *Sexual Cultures in Europe* (Manchester, 1999) pp.139-58.

Hamilton, Margaret A., *Margaret Bondfield* (no place of publication given, 1924).

— *Remembering My Good Friends* (London, 1945).

Harris, J., *Private Lives, Public Spirit. A Social History of Britain 1870-1914* (Oxford, 1993).

Harrison, Brian, *Prudent Revolutionaries. Portrait of British Feminists Between the Wars* (Oxford, 1987).

— 'Class and gender in modern British labour history.' *Past and Present* 124 (1989) pp.121-58.

— 'Women and health' in Purvis, J. (ed.) *Women's History of Britain 1850-1945* (London, 2002) pp.157-92.

Henry, John F., 'Salford Labour: a party in waiting 1919-1932'. *Manchester Region History Review* 14 (2000) pp.47-59.

— 'Coquetting with Socialism: Salford Labour Party and the Roman Catholic dimension 1918-1932'. *North West Catholic History Society Journal* 35 (2008) pp.13-39.

Himes, Norman E., 'British birth control clinics. Some results and eugenic aspects of their work.' *Eugenics Review*, 1928, pp.157-65.
— 'Contraceptive methods: the types recommended by nine British birth control journals.' *Boston: New England Journal of Medicine*, 1 May 1930, 222, pp.866-73.
— *A Guide to Birth Control Literature* (London, 1931).
— *Medical History of Contraception* (Baltimore, 1936 reprint 1970).
Himes, Norman E. and Vera, 'Birth control for the British working classes: a study of the first thousand cases to visit a British birth control clinic,' *Hospital Social Service* 19 (1929) pp.578-617.
Himmelweit, S., *Abortion. Individual Choice and Social Control* (London, 1980).
Hodson, C.B.S., *Human Sterilisation Today* (London, 1934).
Hoggart, Lesley, *Feminist Campaigns for Birth Control and Abortion Rights in Britain* (Lampeter, 2003).
Holdsworth, Angela, *Out of the Dolls House* (London, 1988).
Hollis, Patricia, *Ladies Elect. Women in English Local Government 1865-1914* (Oxford, 1987).
Holtby, Winifred, *Women, and a Changing Civilisation* (Chicago, 1935 reprint 1978).
— *South Riding* (London, 1936 reprint 1967).
Holton, Sandra S., *Feminism and Democracy. Women's Suffrage and Reform Politics in Britain 1900-1918* (Cambridge, 1986).
— '"In sorrowful wrath." Suffrage militancy and the romantic feminism of Emmeline Pankhurst' in Smith, H.L. (ed.) *British Feminism in the Twentieth Century* (Lampeter, 1990) pp.7-24.
— 'The suffragist and the average woman.' *Women's History Review*, 1992, no 1, pp.9-24.
Hooper, Ruth, *Mary Stocks. An Uncommonplace Life* (London, 1996).
Hornibrook, E., *Practical Birth Control* (London, 1931).
Horobin, G. (ed.), *Experience with Abortion. A Case Study of North-East Scotland* (Cambridge, 1973).
Houlton, B., *Democracy and Structural Change. Co-operative Women's Guild Centenary. 1883-1938* (Manchester, 1983).
How-Martyn, Edith and Breed, Mary, *The Birth Control Movement in England* (London, 1930).
Hubback, Eva M., *The Population of Britain* (West Drayton, 1947).
Humm, M., *The Dictionary of Feminist Theory* (Hemel Hempstead, 1989).
— *Feminisms. A Reader* (Brighton, 1992).
Hunt, Karen, *Equivocal Feminists* (Cambridge, 1996).
— 'Why Manchester? Why the Pankhursts? Why 1903? Reflections on the centenary of the Women's Social and Political Union.' *Manchester Region History Review* 17 (2004) pp.2-9.

— 'Making politics in local communities: Labour women in inter-war Manchester' in Worley, M. (ed.), *Labours Grass Roots. Essays on the Activities of Local Labour Parties and Members* (Aldershot, 2005), pp.79–101.

Hunt, Karen and Hannam, June, 'Socialist women, birth control and sexual politics in Britain in the 1920s.' in Pasteur, P., Neideracher, S. and Mesner, M., *ITH-Tagungsberichte 37. Sexualitat, Unterschichtenmilieus und ArbeiterInnenbewegung* (Leipzig, 2002) pp.177–87.

— *Socialist Women, Britain 1880s to 1920s* (London, 2002).

Hutchley, Prof. Julian, *Birth Control and Public Health London* (London, 1932).

Hutt, A., *The Condition of the Working Class in Britain* (London, 1934).

Huxley, Gervaise, *Lady Denman. G.B.E.* (London, 1961).

Institute of Ideas, *Abortion – Whose Right?* (London, 2002).

Jackson, M., *The Real Facts of Life. Feminism and the Politics of Sexuality c.1850–1940* (London, 1994).

Jacobs, E., '"Travelling Fellows": women Social Scientists and their political narratives in inter-war Britain.' *Women's History Magazine* 50 (2005), pp.14–24.

Jagger, A.M., *Feminist Politics and Human Nature* (Brighton, 1983).

— 'Love and knowledge: emotion in feminist epistemology.' *Inquiry* 32/2 (1989), pp.151–76.

Jarvis, David, 'Mrs Maggs and Betty: the Conservative appeal to women voters in the nineteen twenties.' *Twentieth Century British History* 5/2 (1994), pp.129–52.

Jeffreys, Sheila, *Anticlimax* (London, 1990).

Jeffs, M., 'Margaret Llewelyn Davies 1861–1944: co-operator and social reformer.' *North West Labour History* 19 (1994/5).

Jeger, Lena, 'The politics of family planning.' *Political Quarterly* 13 (1962) pp.48–58.

Jenkins, Alice, *Law for the Rich – The Case for Reform* (London, 1960).

Joachim, J., 'Framing issues and seizing opportunities: the UN, NGOs and women's rights.' *International Studies Quarterly* 47 (2003) pp.247–74.

Johns, Angela V., *Evelyn Sharpe. Rebel Woman* (Manchester: Manchester University Press, 2009).

— 'Evelyn Sharpe.' *HerStoria* 5 (2010) pp.28–32.

Jones, Emma L., 'The establishment of voluntary family planning clinics in Liverpool and Bradford, 1926–1960: a comparative study'. *Social History of Medicine Advanced*, accessed online, 13 August 2010.

Jones, Greta, 'Eugenic and social policy between the wars.' *The Historical Journal* 25/3 (1982) pp.717–28.

— 'Marie Stopes in Ireland: the Mother's Clinic in Belfast, 1936–1947'. *Social History of Medicine* 5 (1992) pp.257–77.

— 'Women and eugenics in Britain: the case of Mary Scharlieb, Elizabeth Soane Chesser and Stella Browne.' *Annals of Science* 52/5 (1995), pp.481–502.

Jones, Helen, *Women in British Public Life, 1914-50. Gender, Power and Social Policy* (London, 2000).
— 'Ruth Dalton.' *Oxford Dictionary of National Biography* (Oxford, 2004).
Kean, H. 'Searching for the past in present defeat: the construction of historical and political identity in British feminism in the nineteen twenties and nineteen thirties.' *Women's Historical Review* 3/1 (1994), pp.57-79.
Kennard, J.E., *Vera Brittain and Winifred Holtby* (New Hampshire, 1989).
Kent, Susan K., 'Gender reconstruction after the First World War' in Smith, H.L. (ed.) *British Feminism in the Twentieth Century* (Lampeter, 1990).
— *Sex and Suffrage in Britain* (London, 1990).
— *Aftershocks. Politics and Trauma in Britain 1918-1931* (London, 2009).
Keown, J., *Abortion, Doctors and the Law. Some Aspects of the Legal Regulation of Abortion in England from 1803 to 1982* (Cambridge, 1988).
Kevles, Daniel J., *In the Name of Genetics* (London, 1985).
Kingston, B., "Yours very truly, Marion Phillips.' *Society for the Study of Labour History*. Australia, 1975.
Knight, Pamela. 'Abortion in Victorian and Edwardian England.' *History Workshop* 4 (Autumn 1977), pp.57-69.
Kohler, M.S., *Marie Stopes and Birth Control. Catalogue of the Books from the Library of the Society for Constructive Birth Control* (Dorking, 1989).
Koopmans, R., 'Protest in time and space: the evolution of waves of contention' in Snow, D., Soule, S. and Kreisi, H. (eds) *The Blackwell Companion to Social Movements* (Oxford, 2007) pp.19-46.
Kopp, M., *Birth Control in Practice* (New York, 1934).
Koven, Seth and Michel, Sonya, *Mothers of a New World* (London, 1993).
Kuzmack, Linda Gordon, *Woman's Cause. The Jewish Movement in England and USA 1881-1933* (Ohio, 1990).
Lafitte, F., 'The users of birth control clinics.' *Population Studies* 16/1 (1962) pp.12-30.
Lancet, 'Female remedies in Bethnall Green.' 20 June 1935.
— 'Slippery elm case documented.' 12 November 1935.
Land, H., 'Eleanor Rathbone and the economy of the family' in Smith, H.L. (ed.) *British Feminism in the Twentieth Century* (Lampeter, 1990).
Langer, Wendy L., 'The origins of birth control in nineteenth century England.' *Journal of Interdisciplinary History*, 1975, 5, pp.669-86.
Langford, C.M., 'Birth control practices in Great Britain: a review of the evidence from cross-sectional surveys.' *Population Studies* 45 (1991), supplement, pp.49-68.
Law, Cheryl, *Suffrage and Power. The Women's Movement 1918-1928* (London, 1997).
Leathard, Audrey, *The Fight for Family Planning The Development of Family Planning Services in Britain 1921-1974* (Basingstoke, 1980).
Ledbetter, Rosanna, *A History of the Malthusian League* (Ohio, 1976).

BIBLIOGRAPHY

Leonard, Dianne and Speakman, M.A. (eds), *The Changing Experience of Women. Unit 9. The Family: Daughters, Wives and Mothers* (Milton Keynes, 1983).

Leunbach, Dr J.H., *Birth Control, Abortion and Sterilisation* (London, 1930).

Lewis, Jane, 'Beyond suffrage: English Feminism in the 1920s.' *Maryland Historian* 6 (1975), pp.1-17.

— 'The ideology and politics of birth control in inter-war England.' *Women's Studies International Quarterly* 2 (1979) pp.33-48.

— *The Politics of Motherhood* (London, 1980).

— 'In search of real equality: women between the wars' in Gloversmith, Frank (ed.) *Class, Culture and Social Change* (Brighton, 1980) pp.208-339.

— *Women in England 1870-1950* (Sussex, 1984).

— *Labour and Love. Women's Experiences of Home and the Family* (Oxford, 1986).

— 'Mothers and maternity policies in the twentieth century' in Garcia, J., Kilpatrick, R., Richards, M. (eds) *The Politics of Maternity Care* (Oxford, 1990) pp.16-27.

— 'Models of equality for women: the case of state support for children in twentieth century Britain' in Bock, G. and Thane, P., *Maternity and Gender Politics. Women and the Rise of the Welfare State, 1880-1950* (London, 1991) pp.73-9.

Liddington, Jill, *The Life and Times of a Respectable Rebel, Selina Cooper 1864-1946* (London, 1984).

— *Rebel Girls. Their Fight for the Vote* (London, 2006).

Liddington, Jill and Norris, Jill, *One Hand Tied Behind Us - The Rise of the Women's Suffrage Movement* (London, 1978).

Lightfoot, Freda, *The Favourite Child* (London, 2001).

Logan, Anne, 'In search of Equal Citizenship: the campaign for women magistrates in England and Wales, 1910-1939.' *Women's History Review* 16/4 (2007) pp.501-15.

— *Feminism and Criminal Justice. A Historical Perspective* (London, 2008).

— 'Lady bountiful or community activist?' *Women's History Magazine* 62 (2010), pp.11-18.

Loudon, Irving, 'Maternal mortality: 1880-1950. Some regional and international comparisons.' *Society for the Social History of Medicine*, 1988, pp.183-228.

Love, R., 'Alice in eugenics land: feminism and eugenics in the careers of Alice Lee and Ethel Elderton.' *Annals of Science* 36 (1978) pp.145-58.

Lovecy, Jill, 'Framing claims for women: from "Old" to "New" Labour' in Annersley, C., Gains, F., Rummery, K. (eds) *Women and New Labour* (Bristol, 2006) pp.63-92.

Lovenduski, J. and Randall, V. *Contemporary Feminist Politics* (Oxford, 1993).

McAdam, D., McCarthy, J. and Zald, M.N. (eds), *Comparative Perspectives on Social Movements* (Cambridge, 1996).

Macaulay, Dr Muriel, *The Story of the Mothers' Welfare Clinic, Liverpool 1926-1951.* Forward by Lady Wooton (Liverpool, privately printed, 1952).

McCann, Carol R., *Birth Control Politics in the United States, 1916-1945* (Ithaca, 1994).

McCann, F.J., 'Medico-legal problems in general practice. criminal abortion.' *Practitioner,* 1934, pp.321-33.

McCleary, G.F., *The Maternity and Child Welfare Movement* (London, 1935).

McCrindle, J. and Rowbotham, Sheila, *Dutiful Daughters. Women Talk About Their Lives* (London, 1977).

MacDonald, James Ramsay, *Margaret Ethel MacDonald* (London, 1924).

McHugh, D., 'Labour, the Liberals and the Progressive Alliance in Manchester 1900-14.' *Northern History* 39/1 (2002), pp.15-23.

McIntosh, Tania, 'An abortion city. Maternal mortality, abortion and birth control in Sheffield, 1920-40.' *Medical History* 44 (2000) pp.75-96.

Mackenzie, J. (ed.), T*he Diary of Beatrice Webb,* vol.4 (London, 1983).

McKibbin, Ross, *The Ideologies of Class. Social Relations in Britain 1898-1950* (Oxford, 1990).

— Introduction to the reprint of Marie Stopes' *Married Love* (Oxford, 2004).

McLaren, Angus, 'Women's work and the regulation of family size – The question of abortion in the nineteenth century.' *History Workshop* 4 (1977) pp.70-81.

— *Birth Control in Nineteenth Century England* (London, 1978).

— *A History of Contraception from Antiquity to the Present Day* (Oxford, 1990).

Malleson, J., 'Criminal abortion – suggestion for lessening its incidence.' *Lancet,* 11 February 1939.

Manchester Evening Chronicle, 'Judge favours birth control.' 30 November 1931.

Manchester Guardian, 'Professor Laski's plea for birth control.' 24 November 1931.

Manchester Women's History Group, *Resources for Women's History in Greater Manchester* (Manchester, 1993).

Marchant, J., *The Control of Parenthood* (London, 1920).

Marks, Lara V., *Model Mothers. Jewish Mothers and Maternity Provision in East London 1870-1939* (Oxford, 1994).

— *Metropolitan Maternity. Maternity and Infant Welfare Services in Twentieth Century London* (Amsterdam, 1996).

— *Sexual Chemistry. A History of the Contraceptive Pill* (Yale, 2001).

Martin, Jane, 'Beyond suffrage: feminism, education and the politics of class.' *British Journal of the Sociology of Education* 29/4 (2008), pp.411-23.

Martin, Jane and Goodman, Joyce, *Women and Education, 1800-1980* (Basingstoke, 2004).

Mass Observation, *Britain and her Birth Rate* (London, 1945).

Mayer, A., *Women in Britain 1900-2000* (London, 2002).

BIBLIOGRAPHY

Mazumdar, Pauline, *Eugenics, Human Genetics and Human Failings* (London, 1992).

Medawar, Jean and Pyke, David, *Family Planning* (Middlesex, 1971).

Melling, A., 'Wicked women form Wigan and other tales: licentious leisure and social control in Wigan and St. Helens 1914–1930.' *North West Labour History* 24 (2000).

Melling, J., *Rent Strikes. Peoples Struggles for Housing in West Scotland, 1890–1916* (Edinburgh, 1983).

Meyer, Jimmy Elaine Wilkinson, *Any Friend of the Movement. Networking for Birth Control 1920–1940* (Ohio, 2004).

Mitchell, Hannah, *The Hard Way Up*. Forward by Rowbotham Sheila (London, 1968 reprint 1977).

Mitchell, Juliet, *Woman's Estate* (Middlesex, 1971).

Mitchell, Juliet and Oakley, Ann (eds), *The Rights and Wrongs of Women* (Middlesex, 1979).

— (eds), *What is Feminism?* (Oxford, 1986).

Mitchison, Naomi, *Comments on Birth Control* (London, 1930).

Mohr, J.C., *Abortion in America The Origins and Evolution of National Policy, 1800–1900* (Oxford, 1978).

Morley, S., *Sybil Thorndike. A Life in the Theatre* (London, 1977).

Morrison, Blake, *Things My Mother Never Told Me* (London, 2002).

Mott, C.F., *Lillian Mary Mott (nee Reynolds) 1879–1952. A Memoir by Her Husband* (Liverpool: Privately printed, 1952).

Mure, Mrs, 'Walworth,' *Family Planning*, 1956, p.10.

National Council of Women. *Brief History of National Council of Women* (privately published, 2005).

Newson, John and Elizabeth, *Patterns of Infant Care in an Urban Community* (Middlesex, 1963).

Oakley, Anne, 'Interviewing women' in Roberts, H. (ed.) *Doing Feminist Research* (London, 1981).

— *The Captured Womb. A History of the Medical Care of Pregnant Women* (Oxford, 1984 reprint 1986).

Okim, S.M. and Mansbridge, J. (eds), *Feminism*, vols 1 and 2 (Aldershot, 1994).

Offen, Karen, 'Defining feminism. A comparative historical approach.' *Signs* 14/1 (1988), pp.119–57.

— Karen, 'Reply to Cott.' *Signs* 15/1 (1989), pp.206–9.

— Karen, *Globalizing Feminisms 1789–1945* (London, 2010).

Oman, Elsie, *Salford Stepping Stones* (Manchester, 1984).

O'Neil, William, *The Woman Movement. Feminism in the United States and England* (London: George Allen and Unwin, 1969).

Oram, Alison, *Women Teachers and Feminist Politics 1900–1939* (Manchester, 1996).

Orwell, George, *The Road to Wigan Pier* (Middlesex, 1937 reprint 1989).
O'Toole, Millie, *Bessie Braddock. A Biography* (London, 1957).
Oxford, Margot, Duchess (ed.), *Myself When Young. Reminiscences from Sylvia Pankhurst, Maude Royden, Ellen Wilkinson and Others* (London, 1937).
Pankhurst, E. Sylvia, *Save the Mothers. A Plea for Measures to Prevent the Annual Loss of About 3,000 Child-Bearing Mothers and 20,000 Infant Lives in England and Wales and a Similar Grievous Wastage in Other Countries* (London, 1930).
Pedersen, Susan, *Eleanor Rathbone and the Politics of Conscience* (Yale, 2004).
Peel, John, 'The manufacture and retailing of contraception in England.' *Population Studies* 17 (1963) pp.113-65.
— 'Contraception and the medical profession.' *Population Studies* 18/2 (1964) pp.133-45.
Peel, Robert A. (ed.), *Marie Stopes and the English Birth Control Movement* (Galton Institute, 1996).
— (ed.) *Essays in the History of Eugenics* (Galton Institute, 1997).
Pember Reeves, Maude, *Round About A Pound A Week*. New introduction by Sally Alexander (London, 1913 reprint 1979).
Pfeffer, Naomi, *The Stork and the Syringe. A Political History of Reproductive Medicine* (Bristol, 1993).
Phelps, A., *Children by Desire* (London, 1930).
Phillips, Marion, *Women and the Labour Party* (London, 1918).
— 'Birth control: a plea for careful consideration.' *Labour Woman*, 1 March 1924.
Pickstone, John V., *The Quest for Public Health in Manchester* (University of Manchester, 2010).
Pierce, Rachel and Rowntree, Griselda, 'Birth control in Britain, Part I.' *Population Studies* 15 (1961), pp.3-31.
— 'Birth control in Britain, Part II: contraceptive methods used by couples married in the last thirty years.' *Population Studies* 15 (1961) pp.121-59.
Pierpoint, Raymond, *Report of the Fifth International Neo-Malthusian and Birth Control Conference* (London, 1922).
Porter, Roy and Hall, Lesley A., *The Facts of Life. The Creation of Sexual Knowledge in Britain, 1650-1950* (Yale, 1995).
Potts, M. and Diggory, P., *Abortion* (Cambridge, 1977).
Pugh, Martin, 'Domesticity and the decline of feminism 1930-50' in Smith, H.L. (ed.) *British Feminism in the Twentieth Century* (Lampeter, 1990) pp.144-66.
— 'The impact of women's enfranchisement in Britain' in Dale, C. and Nolan, M., *Suffrage and Beyond* (New York, 1994) pp.313-30.
— *Women and the Women's Movement in Britain* (London, 2000).
Purvis, June, 'Using primary sources when researching women's history from a feminist perspective.' *Women's History Review* 5 (1992), pp.259-80.

BIBLIOGRAPHY

— *Women's History. 1850-1945* (London, 2000).
— 'Olive Banks, 1923-2006 – an appreciation.' *Women's History Review* 29/4 (2006), pp.363-8.
Rathbone, Eleanor, *The Disinherited Family* (London, 1924 reprint 1986).
— *Milestones* (Liverpool, 1929).
Reid, A., 'Neonatal mortality and still births in early twentieth century Derbyshire.' *Population Studies* 55/3 (2001).
Reynolds, Jack and Laybourn, Keith, *Labour Heartland. The History of the Labour Party in West Yorkshire* (Bradford, 1997).
Rhodes, M., 'The contribution of professional training to becoming a midwife' in Bornat, J., Perks, R., Thompson, P., Walmsley, J. (eds), *Oral History, Health and Welfare* (London, 2000) pp.119-38.
Rhondda, Viscountess, *This Was My World* (Basingstoke, 1933).
Rice, Margery Spring, *Working Class Wives. Their Health and Conditions* (Harmondsworth, 1939).
— 'North Kensington clinic – Four clinics.' *Family Planning*, 1956, p.6.
Richardson, Angelique, *Love and Eugenics in the late Nineteenth Century* (Oxford, 2008).
Riddle, John M., *Eve's Herbs. A History of Abortion and Contraception in the West* (Harvard, 1997).
Roberts, Elizabeth, *A Woman's Place. An Oral History of Working Class Women, 1890-1940* (Oxford, 1984).
— 'Women's strategies, 1870-1940' in Lewis, J. (ed.) *Labour and Love* (Oxford, 1986) pp.223-48.
— *Women's Work 1840-1940* (Basingstoke, 1988).
— *Women and Families. An Oral History 1940-1970* (Oxford, 1995).
Robinson, Caroline H., *Seventy Birth Control Clinics* (New York, 1930 reprint 1972).
Robinson, J., *A Force to Be Reckoned With. A History of the Women's Institutes* (London, 2011).
Robinson, W.J., *Practical Prevenception* (New York, 1929).
Rolph, C.H. (ed.), *The Human Sum* (London, 1957).
Rose, Rev. C.P.G., *The Christian Case for Birth Control* (publisher unknown).
Rose, June, *Marie Stopes and the Sexual Revolution* (London, 1992).
Rose, Lionel, *The Massacre of the Innocents* (London, 1986).
Rose, Sonia O., *What is Gender History?* (Cambridge, 2010).
Rover, Constance, *Love, Morals and the Feminists* (London, 1970).
Rowan, C., 'Women in the Labour Party 1906-1920.' *Feminist Review* 1 (1982), pp.74-91.
Rowbotham, Sheila, *Woman's Consciousness, Man's World* (London, 1973).
— *Hidden from History. Three Hundred Years of Oppression* (London, 1974).
— *A New World for Women. Stella Browne Socialist Feminist* (London, 1977).

— 'The Woman's movement and organising for Socialism' in Rowbotham, S., Segal, S., Wainwright, H., *Beyond the Fragments. Feminism and the Making of Socialism* (London, 1979) pp.121–56.
— *A Century of Women* (London, 1999).
— *Dreamers of a New Day. Women Who Invented the Twentieth Century* (London, 2010).
Rowntree, Griselda and Pierce, Rachel M., 'Birth control in Britain.' *Population Studies*, 1961, 15, p.128.
Royden, A. Maude, *The Making of Women* (London, 1917).
— *Sex and Commonsense* (London, 1921).
— Maude, in Ferch, J., *Birth Control* (London, 1932).
Ruhl, K., 'The influence of women in the British Labour Party in the 1920s.' Giessener Electonische Bibliothek (GEB), April 2004.
Russell, Dora, *The Tamarisk Tree. My Quest for Liberty and Love* (London, 1975 reprint 1989).
Russell, Dr Valerie and Malleson, Joan, 'The problem of abortion.' *Journal of Public Health*, 1938.
Sabatier, Paul, *Policy Change and Learning. An Advocacy Coalition Approach* (Colorado, 1993).
Sanger, Margaret, *Family Limitation* (London, 1920).
— *The Practice of Contraception. International Symposium in Zurich* (Baltimore, 1931).
— *My Fight for Birth Control* (London, 1932).
Sangster, J., 'Telling our stories: feminist debates and the use of oral history.' *Women's History Review* 3/1 (1994), pp.5–28.
Sarvassy, Wendy, 'Beyond the difference versus equality debate: post-suffrage feminism, difference and a quest.' *Signs* 17 (1992), pp.329–62.
Sauer, R., 'Infanticide and abortion in nineteenth century England.' *Population Studies*, 1978, pp.81–93.
Scott, Gillian, *Feminism and the Politics of Working Women. The Women's Co-operative Guild 1880's to the Second World War* (London, 1998).
Scott, J.W., *Feminism and History* (Oxford, 1996).
Seal, Vivienne, *Whose Choice? Working Class Women and the Control of Fertility* (London, 1990).
Seccombe, Wally, 'Starting to stop. Working class fertility in decline in Britain.' *Past and Present*, 1990, pp.151–88.
Seyd, P. and Whitely, R., *New Labour's Grassroots. The Transformation of Labour Party Membership* (London, 2002).
Shaw, George Bernard, *The Intelligent Woman's Guide to Socialism, Capitalism, Sovietism and Fascism* (London, 1928 reprint 1949).
Shaw, Marion, *A Clear Stream. A Life of Winifred Holtby* (London, 1999).
Simey, Margaret, *Eleanor Rathbone 1872-1946. A Centenary Tribute* (Liverpool, 1974).

— *The Disinherited Family* (Liverpool, 1996).

Simms, Madeleine, 'Parliament and birth control in the 1920s.' *Journal of the Royal College of General Practitioners* 28 (1978), pp.83–8.

— *Abortion in Britain. Before the Abortion Act* (Birth Control Trust, 1981).

Simms, Madeleine, 'Gynaecologists, contraception and abortion. Birkett to Lane.' *World Medicine*, 23 October 1974, pp.49–60.

— 'Midwives and abortion in the 1930s.' *Midwife and Health Visitor* 10 (1974) pp.114–16.

— Marie Stopes Memorial Lecture. 'The compulsory pregnancy lobby – then and now.' *Journal of Royal College of General Practitioners* 25 (1975) pp.709–19.

Simon, Ernest D., *How to Abolish the Slums* (London, 1929).

Slater, Elliot and Moya Woodside, M., *Patterns of Marriage. A Study of Marital Relations in the Working Class* (London, 1951).

Sloan, D.G., 'The extent of contraceptive use and the social paradigm of modern demography.' *Sociology* 17 (1983) pp.380–7.

Smith, Howard L. (ed.), *British Feminism in the Twentieth Century* (Lampeter, 1990).

Smith, J., 'Labour tradition in Glasgow and Liverpool.' *History Workshop* 17 (1984) pp.32–55.

Smyth, J.J., *Labour in Glasgow 1896–1936. Socialism, Suffrage, Sectarianism* (Edinburgh, 2000).

Snow, D., Soule, S. and Kreisi, H. (eds), *The Blackwell Companion to Social Movement* (Oxford, 2007).

Soloway, Richard A., *Birth Control and the Population Question in England, 1877–1930* (North Carolina, 1982).

— *Demography and Degeneration: Eugenics and the Declining Birthrate in Twentieth Century Britain* (North Carolina, 1995).

— 'The perfect contraceptive, eugenics and birth control in Britain and America in the inter war years.' *Journal of Contemporary History* 30/2 (1995) pp.634–7.

Spender, Dale, *There's Always Been a Women's Movement This Century* (London, 1983).

— *Time and Tide Wait for No Man* (London, 1984).

Stanley, Liz, 'British feminist histories: an editorial introduction.' *Women's Studies International Forum*, 1990.

— *The Auto/Biographical I. The Theory and Practice of Feminist Auto/Biography* (Manchester, 1992).

— *Sex Surveyed 1949–1994. From Mass-Observation's 'Little Kinsey' to the National Survey and Hite Reports* (London, 1995).

Stepan, N.L., *The Hour of Eugenics* (Ithaca, 1991).

Stocks, Mary D., *Family Limitation and Women's Organisations* (National Union of Societies for Equal Citizenship, 1925).

— *The Case for Family Endowment* (London, Labour Publishing Company, 1927).

- 'The new feminism.' *Woman's Leader*, 25 February 1927.
- 'The Gospel of Dr Marie Stopes.' *Woman's Leader*, 14 December 1928.
- *Eleanor Rathbone. A Biography* (London, 1949).
- *Eleanor Rathbone Memorial Lecture* (Liverpool, 1953).
- 'The story of family planning' in Rolph, C.H., *The Human Sum* (London, 1957) pp.43–62.
- 'The Greengate Clinic.' *Manchester Guardian*, 26 November 1962.
- *Family Planning – Memorial Supplement*, 1966.
- Preface to Box, M. *The Trial of Marie Stopes* (New York, 1967).
- *My Commonplace Book* (London, 1970).
- *Still More Commonplace* (London, 1973).

Stopes, Marie C., *Married Love. A New Contribution to the Solution of Sexual Difficulties* (London, 1918).
- *Wise Parenthood. A Sequel to Married Love. A Book for Married People* (London, 1918).
- *A Letter to Working Mothers On How to Have Healthy Children and Avoid Weakening Pregnancies* (Mothers' Clinic for Constructive Birth Control, 1919).
- *Radiant Motherhood. A Book for Those Who Are Creating the Future* (London: Putnam, 1920).
- *Contraception. Its Theory, History and Practice* (London, 1924).
- *The First Five Thousand. Being the first Report of the First Birth Control Clinic in the British Empire* (Mothers' Clinic for Constructive Birth Control, 1925).
- *The Human Body and its Functions* (London, 1926).
- *Enduring Passion* (London, 1928).
- *Preliminary Notes on Various Aspects of the Control of Contraception. Based on Analysed Data of Ten Thousand Cases* (Constructive Birth Control Bulletin, no 1, 1930).
- *Marriage in My Time* (London, 1935).
- *Equipping a Birth Control Clinic* (Constructive Birth Control Bulletin no 3, no date).

Stopes-Roe, Harry V. and Scott, I., *Marie Stopes and Birth Control* (London, 1974).

Stott, Mary, *Organisation Woman. The Story of the National Union of Townswomen's Guilds* (London, 1978).

Strachey, Ray, *The Cause. A Short History of the Women's Movement* (London, 1928 reprint 1978).

Summerfield, Penny, *Reconstructing Women's War-time Lives. Discourses and Subjectivity in Oral History of the Second World War* (Manchester, 1998).

Summerskill, Edith, *A Woman's World. Her Memoirs* (London, 1967).

Sykes, N., *Nancy, The Life of Lady Astor* (London, 1972).

Szreter, Simon, *Fertility, Class and Gender in Britain 1860–1940* (Cambridge, 1996).

BIBLIOGRAPHY

— 'Falling fertilities and changing sexualities in Europe since circa 1850: a comparative survey of national demographic patterns' in Elder, F., Hall, L.A. and Hekma, G. (eds) *Sexual Cultures in Europe* (Manchester, 1999) pp.159-94.

Szreter, Simon and Fisher, Kate, *Sex Before the Sexual Revolution. Intimate Life in England 1918-1963* (Cambridge, 2010).

Tamplin, Claire, 'Early days in Newcastle.' *Family Planning*, October 1962, p.61.

Tanner, Dennis, Thane, Pat and Tiratsoo, N., *Labour's First Century. A Centenary History of the Labour Party* (Cambridge, 2000).

Taylor, Barbara, *Eve and the New Jerusalem* (London, 1983).

— *Mary Wollstonecraft and the Feminist Imagination* (Cambridge, 2003).

Tebbutt, Melanie, *Women's Talk? A Social History of 'Gossip' in Working Neighbourhood, 1880-1960* (Aldershot, 1995).

Thane, Pat, 'The women of the British Labour Party and Feminism 1906-1945' in Smith, H.L. (ed.), *British Feminism in the Twentieth Century* (Lampeter, 1990) pp.124-43.

— 'Visions of gender in the making of the British welfare state: the case of women in the British Labour Party and social policy, 1906-1945' in Bock, G. and Thane, P., *Maternity and Gender Politics. Women and the Rise of the Welfare State, 1880-1950* (London, 1991) pp.93-118.

— 'What difference did the vote make? Women in public and private life in Britain since 1918.' *Historical Research* 76 (2003), pp.268-85.

— 'Women in the British Welfare State' in Koven, S. and Michel, S., *Mothers of a New World. Maternalist Politics and the Origins of the Welfare State* (London, 1993) pp.343-77.

— 'Women and political participation in England, 1918-1970' in Breitenbach, Esther, and Thane, Pat, *Women and Citizenship in Britain* (London, 2010) pp.11-28.

Thomson, Paul, *Voices of the Past* (Oxford, 1988).

Thorndike, Russell, *Sybil Thorndike* (London, 1929).

Thurtle, Dorothy, *Abortion - Right or Wrong. Forward by Norman Birkett* (London, 1940).

Tilly, Charles, *Historical Studies of Changing Fertility* (Princeton, 1978).

— *As Sociology Meets History* (New York, 1981).

— 'Why birth rates fell: a review of essay on Simon Szreter's "Fertility Class and Gender in Britain, 1860-1940"', *Population and Development Review* 22 (1996) pp.557-62.

Tilly, Louise, 'Women, work and citizenship.' *International Labor and Working Class History* 52 (1997), pp.1-26.

Vallance, Elizabeth, *Women in the House* (London, 1979).

Vernon, Betty, *Ellen Wilkinson* (London, 1982).

Wanhalla, Angela, 'To better the breed of men: women in eugenics in New Zealand, 1900-1935.' *Women's History Review* 16/2 (2007), pp.163-82.

Ward, L., 'The Right to Choose.' PhD thesis, University of Bristol, 1981.

Webb, C., *The Woman with a Basket. History of the Women's Co-op Guild 1883–1927* (Manchester, 1927).
Weeks, Jeffrey, *Sex, Politics and Society. The Regulation of Sexuality Since 1800* (London, 1989 2nd edition).
Weinar, G., 'Olive Banks and the collective biography of British feminism.' *British Journal of Sociology of Education* 29/4 (2008) pp.403–10.
Wilkinson, Ellen, *Clash* (London, 1929 reprint 1989).
— *Myself When Young. Reminiscences from Sylvia Pankhurst, Maude Royden, Ellen Wilkinson and others* (London, 1938).
— *The Town that was Murdered. The Life Story of Jarrow* (London, 1939).
Williams, Shirley, *Climbing the Bookshelves* (London, 2010).
Wilson, Libby, *Sex on the Rates. Memoirs of a Family Planning Doctor* (Argyll, 2004).
Wood, Clive and Suitters, Beryl (eds), *The Fight for Acceptance. A History of Contraception* (London, 1970).
Wood, I.S., 'Hope deferred. Labour in Scotland in the 1920s' in Donnachie, I., Harvie, C. and Wood, I.S., *Labour Politics in Scotland 1888–1988* (Edinburgh, 1989).
Woods, R., 'Working class fertility in decline. Debate with Secombe.' *Past and Present* 134 (1992) pp.200–11.
Woolf, Virginia, *A Room of One's Own* (London, 1928 reprint 2004).
Woolton, Lady M., '"Liverpool": Four Clinics', *Family Planning*, 1956, p.6.
Workman, J., 'Wading through the mire: an historiographical study of the British women's movement between the wars.' *University of Sussex Journal of Contemporary History* 2 (2001) pp.1–12.
Worley, Matthew, *Labour's Grassroots. Essays on the Activity of Local Labour Politics* (Aldershot, 2002).
Woycke, James, *Birth Control in Germany 1871–1933* (London, 1988).
Wright, Dr Helena, *The Sex Factor in Marriage* (London, 1930).
— *Birth Control. Advice on Family Spacing and Healthy Sex Life* (London, 1935).
Zweiniger-Bargielowska, Ina (ed.), *Women in Twentieth-Century Britain* (Harlow, 2001).

Radio, television programmes and tape collections

Woman's Hour, Radio 4 (16 July 2011). Clare Debenham in discussion with Jennie Murray on the early birth control pioneers.
Women's Hour, Radio 4 (13 April 2006 repeated 8 May 2007). Discussion commemorating the opening of the Manchester and Salford Mothers' Clinic in 1926.
Fifty Years of the Family Planning Association (1982). Discussion. Tape held at North West Sound Archive.

BIBLIOGRAPHY

Labours of Eve, BBC 2 (9 June 1997). Copy in Women's Library, London.
Out of the Doll's House, BBC2 (1988). Copy in Women's Library, London.
Pioneers of Birth Control in the 1920s. Yesterdays Witness Series (BBC Radio 4, 1969) Discussion including Mary Stocks, Charis Frankenburg and Dr Olive Gimson.
Ref: NP6084W TR1 Held in British Sound Archives. London.
The Secret Life of Marie Stopes, Channel 4 (1995). Copy in Women's Library, London.

Index

Local birth control activists have their details given in the Appendix. The Appendix also provides further biographical information on national activists.

Abertillery birth control clinic 28, 65, 101
abortion 70, 72–4, 78, 165
Alberti, Johanna 4, 16, 128
Astor, Lady Nancy, MP 48, 106

Balfour of Burleigh, Lord 33
Banks, Olive 4, 35, 109, 124, 273
Barbour, Mary 5, 62–3, 64, 105, 132
Barton, Eleanor 135, 146
Braddock, Bessie, MP 22, 45, 108
Brailsford, Henry 14, 18, 139
Brittain, Vera 17, 43, 58
Broad, F.A, MP 30–1
Browne, Stella 31, 109, 115, 116
Buckmaster, Lord 33, 51, 147

Carr-Saunders, Professor 128, 130
Castle, Barbara, MP 16, 166–7
Catholics 14, 89, 90, 104, 131, 164
  Burns, Tom (Salford) 105, 145
  Catholic Women's League 52
  Catholic Young Men's Guild 104
  Henshaw, Thomas, Bishop of Salford 105
  Quinn, Miss 131, 139, 143
  Wheatley, John, MP 31, 103, 155

Church of England 89–92
  Dawson, Lord 91
  Mothers' Union 52, 93, 97
  Circular 1208 155
Communist Party activists 62, 63
Conference on Giving of Information on Birth Control Information 153–4
contraceptive methods
  abstinence 71
  coitus interruptus 71–2
  female appliance methods 25, 75, 80, 103
  male appliance methods 72
  oral contraceptive pill 165
Cooke, Mrs M.B. vi, 3, 7, 18, 169
Cowman, Krista 11, 57, 60
Crawford, Elizabeth 11

Dalton, Ruth 5, 48, 58, 132, 141, 160
Daniels, Nurse E. 10, 30–1, 33, 101, 110, 144
Denman, Lady Trudy 49–50, 109, 122, 160, 164
Drysdale, Dr Charles Vickery 110–13, 116, 117

Elderton, Ethel 123–4
eugenics 111, 165, 168
   Eugenics Society 10, 76, 109, 116–30

family endowment 38, 41
Family Planning Association 159, 161, 163–5, 167, 168
feminist debates 36–41
Fisher, Kate 4, 7, 27, 56, 68, 71, 76–7, 83–4, 88
Florence, Lella Secor 58, 68, 72, 75, 81, 84, 103, 109, 122, 158, 162, 164
Frankenburg, Charis 9, 12, 27–8, 46, 53, 58, 59, 60, 61, 65, 73, 74, 85, 86, 87, 89, 96, 102, 105, 106, 132, 151, 152

Hall, Lesley 115, 121, 125
Holtby, Winifred 37, 42, 58, 114
How-Martyn, Edith 5, 29, 47, 58, 75, 109, 115
Hubback, Eva 4, 35, 48, 92, 94, 122, 128, 152, 160
Hunt, Karen 12, 131, 133, 143

Jewish activists 94–95
Jewson, Dorothy, MP 32, 136, 137, 139

Labour Party 14, 103, 131–5, 144, 149, 166
   Labour Party Women's Sections 11, 133, 137, 149–51
Liberal Party 131–6, 147–9
Logan, Anne 4, 57, 82

Macadam, Elizabeth 35
McLaren, Angus 56, 57, 113

Malthusian League 109–14, 115, 116–17, 125, 168
   Hygenic Methods of Family Limitation 113
   motorised leafleting 113
   New Generation 113
Manning, Leah, MP 48, 132
Marks, Lara 12, 84
Marsden, Dora 124
maternal mortality 42, 45, 79
   Manchester Maternal Mortality Committee 132
medical profession 95–6
Memorandum 153/MCW 14, 154–6, 158–9
Mond, Sir Alfred 18, 29

National Birth Control Council 130, 154, 157, 159
National Council of Women 50–1, 55, 60
National Union of Societies for Equal Citizenship 14, 34, 36–8, 39, 40, 48, 53, 55, 124, 149

Onions, Alice 15, 63, 64, 66, 70, 86, 87, 132, 168

Phillips, Dr Marion, MP 14, 16, 131, 133, 140–4, 149, 153

Rathbone, Eleanor, MP 4–5, 10, 15, 17, 19, 28, 29, 34, 38–41, 42, 46, 48–9, 55, 59–60, 109, 122, 124, 127–8
Rhondda, Viscountess Margaret Haigh 36, 37
Roe, Humphrey Verdon 22–3, 31
Rowbotham, Sheila 6, 17, 153
Royden, Rev. Maude 4, 18, 28, 29, 38, 43

INDEX

Russell, Dora 10, 31, 32, 45, 63, 138, 141, 143, 144, 147–8, 156

Sackville West, Vita 20
Sandys, Sister Beatrice 15, 70, 97–8
Sanger, Margaret 94, 112, 114, 119, 144, 150, 163
social movement theory 8–9
  mobilising structures 10
  outsider groups 9
Society for Constructive Birth Control and Racial Progress 23, 24, 40, 81, 83, 159
  Holloway Road 67
  Marlborough Street, London 24
  mobile clinics 28
Society for the Provision of Birth Control Clinics 4, 7–8, 10, 15, 24, 40, 76, 77, 79, 80, 100, 102, 129–30, 155, 159, 163
  Aberdeen 25, 61, 66
  Birmingham 25, 66, 74, 82, 103, 107, 108, 162
  Cambridge 5, 25, 48, 69, 82
  East London 25, 65
  Glasgow 25, 62, 64
  Liverpool 25, 66, 84, 96, 108
  Manchester and Salford 25, 27, 44, 61, 64, 66–7, 85, 101, 107, 162
  Newcastle-upon-Tyne 25, 63, 69, 72
  North Kensington 25, 48, 57, 66, 69, 78, 82–7, 101
  Oxford 25, 44, 66, 96
  Walworth Road Women's Welfare Centre, London 24–5, 48, 57, 66, 69, 73, 74, 85, 101, 162
  Wolverhampton 25, 66, 70, 86
Spender, Dale 3, 4, 169

Stocks, Mary 4, 9, 12, 14, 19, 27, 33, 35, 39, 40, 43, 50, 54, 58, 59–60, 67, 73, 85, 87, 89, 91–2, 106, 109, 124–7, 157–8
Stopes, Marie 7, 12–15, 17, 28, 30, 55, 60, 87, 89, 101, 113, 114, 124, 125–7, 154
  Contraception: Its Theory and Practice 22, 84
  Letter to Working Mothers 21
  Married Love 19–21, 125
  Radiant Motherhood 22
Stott, Mary 4, 11, 65
suffrage
  former suffragists 47
  National Union of Women's Suffrage Societies 2
  suffrage legislation 2, 17–19
  Women's Social and Political Union 2, 11

Thane, Pat 7, 48, 135, 158–9
Thurtle, Ernest and Dorothy 33, 142, 143, 157

Vickery, Dr Alice 109–16

Ward, Linda 7, 13, 52, 148, 156
Webb, Beatrice 133
Wells, H.G. 31, 109
Wilkinson, Ellen, MP 29, 131, 140, 143, 153, 156, 166
Williams, Shirley, MP 21
Women Citizens Association 50, 52
  Manchester and Salford Women Citizens Association 53, 60
Women's Co-operative Guild 10, 14, 16, 32, 63–4, 88, 131–47, 168
Women's Liberation 1, 6, 165
Workers' Birth Control Group 32, 161